Social Issues, Justice and Status Series

SOCIAL DEVELOPMENT

Social Issues, Justice and Status Series

Risk and Social Welfare
Jason L. Powell and Azrini Wahidin (Editors)
2009. ISBN: 978-1-60741-691-3

Handbook on Social Change
Brooke H. Stroud and Scott E. Corbin (Editors)
2009. ISBN: 978-1-60741-222-9

Social Development
Lynda R. Elling (Editors)
2009. ISBN: 978-1-60741-612-8

Social Issues, Justice and Status Series

SOCIAL DEVELOPMENT

LYNDA R. ELLING
EDITOR

Nova Science Publishers, Inc.
New York

Copyright © 2009 by Nova Science Publishers, Inc.

All rights reserved. No part of this book may be reproduced, stored in a retrieval system or transmitted in any form or by any means: electronic, electrostatic, magnetic, tape, mechanical photocopying, recording or otherwise without the written permission of the Publisher.

For permission to use material from this book please contact us:
Telephone 631-231-7269; Fax 631-231-8175
Web Site: http://www.novapublishers.com

NOTICE TO THE READER

The Publisher has taken reasonable care in the preparation of this book, but makes no expressed or implied warranty of any kind and assumes no responsibility for any errors or omissions. No liability is assumed for incidental or consequential damages in connection with or arising out of information contained in this book. The Publisher shall not be liable for any special, consequential, or exemplary damages resulting, in whole or in part, from the readers' use of, or reliance upon, this material. Any parts of this book based on government reports are so indicated and copyright is claimed for those parts to the extent applicable to compilations of such works.

Independent verification should be sought for any data, advice or recommendations contained in this book. In addition, no responsibility is assumed by the publisher for any injury and/or damage to persons or property arising from any methods, products, instructions, ideas or otherwise contained in this publication.

This publication is designed to provide accurate and authoritative information with regard to the subject matter covered herein. It is sold with the clear understanding that the Publisher is not engaged in rendering legal or any other professional services. If legal or any other expert assistance is required, the services of a competent person should be sought. FROM A DECLARATION OF PARTICIPANTS JOINTLY ADOPTED BY A COMMITTEE OF THE AMERICAN BAR ASSOCIATION AND A COMMITTEE OF PUBLISHERS.

LIBRARY OF CONGRESS CATALOGING-IN-PUBLICATION DATA

Elling, Lynda R.
  Social development / Lynda R. Elling.
      p. cm.
  Includes index.
  ISBN 978-1-60741-612-8 (hardcover)
  1. Socialization. 2. Social planning. I. Title.
  HM686.E45 2009
  303.3'2--dc22

                                                                    2009018835

Published by Nova Science Publishers, Inc. ✛ *New York*

CONTENTS

Preface		**vii**
Chapter 1	Reflective Positioning: The Impact of Conversations in the Social and Cultural Environment of Midwifery Practice Settings on Professional Learning for Students *Diane Phillips*	**1**
Chapter 2	Development of Northern Irish Catholic and Palestinian Muslim National Identities and the Role of Common Histories *Stephen Vertigans*	**51**
Chapter 3	Biosphere Reserves as Learning Sites of Sustainable Development (A Case Study of the Czech Republic) *Drahomíra Kušová, Jan Těšitel and Michael Bartoš*	**87**
Chapter 4	Social Development Needs Better Politics *Paul E. Smith*	**125**
Chapter 5	Water Policy Reforms in Brazil: The Contradiction between Economic Approaches and Socionatural Needs *Antonio A. R. Ioris*	**133**
Chapter 6	The Microcluster Value Chain Analysis *Josep Capó-Vicedo*	**149**
Chapter 7	New European Policy toward Chronically Ill Employees *Helen Kopnina and Joke Haafkens*	**165**
Chapter 8	Social Capital, Entrepreneurial Capital and Economic Growth *Inmaculada Carrasco and M. Soledad Castaño*	**185**
Chapter 9	How General Managers Influence Organizational Social Capital: The Need of New Theoretical Perspectives *David Pastoriza*	**201**
Chapter 10	How Does Personality Develop over the Life-Course: Results of the Brno Longitudinal Study on Life-Span Development *Marek Blatný, Martin Jelínek and Terezie Osecká*	**213**

Chapter 11	Disruption of Social Development in Children with Autism Spectrum Disorders *Gianluca Esposito and Sergiu P. Paşca*	**247**
Chapter 12	Children's Social Interactions in Cultural Context *Rachel Lechcier-Kimel, Janet Chung, Celia Hsiao and Xinyin Chen*	**259**
Chapter 13	"Why Should I Behave in this Way?" Rule Discrimination within the School Context Related to Children's Bullying *Simona C. S. Caravita, Sarah Miragoli and Paola Di Blasio*	**269**
Chapter 14	Everyday Theorizing and the Construction of Knowledge *Sherrie Bade*	**291**
Chapter 15	On Snips and Snails: Perceptions of the Origins of Gender Differences *Jessica W. Giles, Christa G. Ice and Talia C. Gursky*	**295**
Index		**317**

PREFACE

Social development can be summarily described as the process of organizing human energies and activities at higher levels to achieve greater results. Development increases the utilization of human potential. This new book contains important research in the field of social development, both of children and of societies.

Chapter 1 - Literature reviews on the topic of reflection and reflective practice encompassed midwifery, nursing, medicine, allied health, education and professional education. This investigation also included socio-psychological theories by leading authors such as Benner (nursing), Schön (professional education) and positioning theory by Harré and others. Positioning is a psycho-sociological ontology in which individuals metaphorically position themselves within three entities: people, institutions, and societies, where conversations are constructed and make an impact upon the social world. The social and cultural structures and interactions developed in Archer's morphogenesis were examined in terms of the impact of possible encounters and the transformational effects of learning experiences in practice settings. These bodies of work provided the theoretical framework for the author's research of students' experiences in midwifery education for postgraduate students from which selected excerpts with three participating students and their supervising midwives are presented. These excerpts are related to reflective practices and the professional conversations conducted between students and midwives. It was found that reflective positioning applied in midwifery education by students can serve as an analytical tool in explaining social and cultural elements of clinical placements to influence and transform their learning. The potency of conversations that occur in everyday moment-to-moment interactions do contribute to students' induction in professional midwifery practice and their identity formation as a midwife.

Chapter 2 - In this paper, comparative analysis of the processes behind the social development of Catholic and Muslim nationalist identities in Northern Ireland and the Palestinian territories respectively is undertaken. This is designed to try to enhance levels of understanding about the maintenance and duration of nationalist conflicts and ultimately the likelihood of resolution. Particular attention is placed on the social processes that recreate and reinforce 'common histories' and religio-nationalist identities. Important commonalities are identified including the role of historical memories, religious institutions, education, family members and peers in transmitting messages and images about the 'other' and physical divides that collectively contribute to geographical and social demarcation.

Chapter 3 - Established under the UNESCO's Man and the Biosphere (MAB) Programme, biosphere reserves represent protected areas intended to demonstrate well balanced relationship between a high level of nature protection and an appropriate local development, as articulated in the Seville Strategy and reinforced by the Madrid Declaration. According to their definition, biosphere reserves are to simultaneously fulfill four functions – conservation of biological diversity, ecological education, research and promotion of sustainable forms of socioeconomic activities. They can be theoretically considered learning sites of sustainable development. The chapter contributes primarily to the discussion on social part of the relationship between nature protection and socioeconomic development, namely on quality of life of local population living in protected areas, problems of social acceptance of biodiversity conservation measures and institutional arrangements applied when biosphere reserve concept is aimed to be practically implemented. Comparative analysis was conducted in three selected Czech biosphere reserves in order to challenge a cliché on nature protection and socioeconomic development to be a priori in contradiction as well as the belief in state nature protection being the exclusive leader in the process of the concept of biosphere reserve implementation. Triangulation approach was applied as a fundamental frame for empirical data acquisition and analysis, combining spatial analysis of data describing socioeconomic parameters of particular municipalities, semi-standardized interviews with key personalities, extensive questionnaire survey addressing general public, content analysis of regional periodicals and case study analysis focused on success and failure factors in the process of a concrete project implementation. The research results suggest that biosphere reserves did not differ in quality of life of their inhabitants compared with surrounding areas. In some cases, the existence of biosphere reserve was even seen as a comparative advantage – certificate of high quality nature as a base for local tourism development. In the Czech legislative environment, biosphere reserves are institutionally associated with administration of protected landscape areas. Such an institutional arrangement enables executing of state nature protection, providing public with ecological education, and guaranteeing research on a satisfactory level. There are problems, however, in supporting of sustainable forms of development. Goal oriented network, projects driven, of engaged stakeholders is suggested as a more efficient organizational form in this respect. Evidence of a still ongoing process of learning by interacting, aimed at using biosphere reserve as a trade mark of some kind, indicates that the biosphere reserves could as well in practical terms be considered learning sites of sustainable development. The chapter intends to contribute to the debate on ideas of the UN Decade on Education for Sustainable Development 2005-2014.

Chapter 4 - Social development is a public good and therefore likely to depend at least partly on the performance of government. However, liberal democracies have basic structures that appear to make them act with some irresponsibility and ignorance. This challenges us to replace or alter these structures or introduce new institutions to counter their effects. The latter approach may be the most feasible as its initiation may not require the assistance of the existing political establishment. Research into institutional design is still in its infancy, which points to a need for experimentation, so a new institution is proposed for trial. The structural dysfunction noted above indicates that this could be a forum based on an opinion poll designed to cultivate deliberative public participation in democratic government. Two of the many elements of this design are that the poll is run regularly, say at the same time each year, and it repeats the same questions in each poll. This institution could be initiated without official support and may then develop a public demand that compels politicians to make it a permanent part of democratic government. This should improve the delivery of public goods, thereby fostering social development.

Chapter 5 - In the last two decades, water use and conservation have been the object of an intense process of institutional reforms, which have helped to introduce new approaches to the assessment of problems and the formulation of solutions. According to the international doctrine, the responses to water management problems should normally include a combination of regulatory requirements and market-based incentives. Nonetheless, despite improvements in some areas and changes in discourse, there are growing evidences that mainstream approaches have largely failed to deal with the degradation of water systems and promote different bases of water use. The Brazilian experience is a case in point, where a new regulatory framework was recently implemented, but it is restricted to calls for environmental governance, integrated measures and, crucially, the recognition of the economic value of water. Related adjustments in the provision of public services have facilitated the involvement of private companies in water supply and in hydroelectricity generation, without enough consideration of environmental and social demands. Making use of empirical and secondary data, this paper argues that the new regulatory framework have so far failed to prevent the multiplication of environmental impacts and the maintenance of social inequalities in the water sector. The overall conclusion is that effective alternatives to water problems will require a more organised reaction from water user and local communities, together broader political and economic reforms.

Chapter 6 - This paper tries to study the particular workings of clusters, proposing a tool that helps with the empowerment and development of inter-organisational networks that might exist in them. It is a new tool for territorial strategic analysis focused in clustering policy based on the innovation; the microcluster value chain analysis.

Territorial competitiveness should be looked for by starting from the generation of external economies, from strategic decisions taken by those responsible for the interrelated networks, and from the identification and the empowerment of the key relationships among the agent leaders. These are the objectives that the tool proposed will try to resolve.

To achieve this, the most important thing will be to know how to locate and to diffuse the necessary knowledge to be able to identify the opportunities or key success factors that can motivate the creation of concrete inter-organisational networks in the heart of a microcluster.

Chapter 7 - This article provides an overview of current policies related to the chronically ill employees in the Netherlands. Different levels of policy are discussed: those formulated at the European, Dutch and organizational levels. A significantg percentage of Dutch employees suffer from longstanding diseases (classified by International Classification of Diseases - ICD), others experience impairments at work (classified by International Classification of Functioning, Disability and Health - ICF). Current policies in the European Union and in The Netherlands increasingly encourage participation of those who are impaired or disabled based on definitions of ICD and ICF formulated by World Health organization (WHO).

Recently, there has been a significant change in the Dutch policy concerning employment of chronically ill, impared or disabled people. Before 2007, employers were responsible for the management of sickness absence in order to prevent any claims for disability benefits. The new Dutch Working Conditions Act reflects the need of the government to reduce the administrative burdens on companies and eliminate superfluous rules to give companies more scope for introducing individual arrangements. According to the European Agency for Safety and Health at Work, working conditions regulations have been made simpler and easier to implement. The working conditions policy within companies became more flexible, dividing responsibility for safety, health and reintegration between both employers' and employees'. The switch to less detailed rules and more scope for individual arrangements ties in with absence and reintegration policy. In this article, we examine some of the implications of this shift.

Chapter 8 - Under the framework of endogenous economic growth theory, this chapter is focused on entrepreneurial capital and its effects on economic growth. More concretely, we have centred our attention on the interactions between some proxy variables of social capital and one indicator of entrepreneurial capital.

After the two sections devoted to the literature review summary where concepts coming from economics, sociology and psychology are taken in, the empirical section of this chapter confirms firstly the positive relationship between entrepreneurial capital and economic growth. After that, we have proved that the more social capital reserve, the more entrepreneurial capital endowment. Besides that, the better institutions functioning is and the more social structure adequacy, the more social capital and entrepreneurial capital endowment. This positive connection between the social capital indicators and the entrepreneurial capital indicator, allow us to conclude that they promote economic growth not only because these variables create social capital, but also because they encourage entrepreneurial capital.

Statistical information about 28 countries collected in 2005 has been used. A GEM data set on entrepreneurial activity has been related to data from the United Nations Development Programme (UNDP), Transparency International and the Heritage Foundation. Some graphical results on the tendency among the different variables relationships are presented.

Chapter 9 - The incapacity of theories like Transaction Cost Economics or Agency Theory to explain how management may influence social capital should induce scholars to advance in new conceptual developments that allow a better understanding of the managerial processes that allow social capital to flourish. This paper revisits and reconsiders whether the classic management functions that portrait the executive as a strategist, resource allocator, and structure and systems designer, are really contributing to the creation of social capital in the firm. The aim of the paper is not to propose specific mechanisms of managerial influence, but to reflect on the necessity of new theoretical perspectives that profound on the general management roles that truly lead to social capital creation.

Chapter 10 - The chapter gives an overview of the main results of the Brno Longitudinal Study on Life-span Development. This builds upon the longitudinal study of children carried in the Institute of Psychology at Brno, Czech Republic, in the sixties and seventies. The paper starts with information about the original project and how we have searched for participants and built on current sample from the original cohort. A great deal of attention is paid also to methodology which combines quantitative and qualitative approaches.

Results from five studies concerning personality development are presented. First of them deals with the prediction of adult personality from behaviors observed in the nursling and toddler stages, the second with stability and developmental trends of intelligence in childhood and adolescence, the third with stability and change of personality in adolescence, the fourth with longitudinal stability of personality traits and self-concept between adolescence and middle adulthood, and the fifth with subjective perception of personal change in life-long perspective.

Chapter 11 - During the last few decades, a number of studies have emphasized that children who exhibit signs of developmental delay often display abnormal trajectories in their social development. Among these conditions, Autism Spectrum Disorders (ASD) stand as a special case. ASD is a complex neuropsychiatric group of disorders that affects the brain's typical development of social and communication skills to varying degrees. Common features of ASD include impairment in social interaction, communication (both verbal and nonverbal), information processing, and patterns of behavior that are restricted and repetitive. One of the signature aspects of ASD points to the social-skills deficit. Most children with ASD have tremendous difficulty engaging in everyday social interaction and seem unable to form emotional bonds with others. Research has suggested that, although children with ASD are attached to their caregivers, their expressions of attachment are unusual and difficult to interpret. Furthermore, children with ASD have difficulty in understanding unspoken social cues, which are fundamental for social interaction (e.g. a smile or a grimace). Children with ASD also have difficulties with regulating their emotions and lack the ability to attribute mental states to themselves and others, making them unable to comprehend or predict other people's responses to their own actions. The aim of this article is to review several watershed studies that have investigated the disruption of social development in ASD, and to close with a presentation of current knowledge about the underlying neurobiology of social abnormalities that characterize this spectrum of disorders.

Chapter 12 - Over the past 20 years increased attention has been given to the study of cultural influence on socialization, social interactions and relationships, and individual socioemotional and cognitive development (Chen & French, 2008; Cole, Tamang, & Shrestha, 2006; Edwards, 2000). Findings from a variety of research projects have indicated that culture plays a vital role in determining the experiences of children with different characteristics. Social interactions serve as a major context that mediates the links between cultural forces and individual development.

Culture is often defined as a system of shared beliefs, values, and customs that people within a group, community, or society endorse and use to guide their social interactions and to cope with their world (Ji, Peng, & Nisbett, 2000). The cultural system is transmitted and develops from generation to generation through learning as well as continuous construction and innovation (Best & Ruther, 1994). Cultural norms and values provide guidelines for understanding and interpreting social behaviors and thus influence the manifestations of the behaviors (Chen, Wang, & DeSouza, 2006). Cultural norms and values play a role in child development largely through children's interaction with their environment (Greenfield, Suzuki & Rothstein-Fisch, 2006). Culture not only shapes and organizes the environments in which children's social interactions occur, but also affects the ways in which children interact with others.

Chapter 13 - Social domain model states that by interacting with the social contexts, children organize their moral knowledge in distinct domains, mainly related to (1) moral obligations, aimed at granting persons' well-being and rights and non-dependent on social expectations, (2) social-conventional rules, aimed at preserving the social orders and dependent on authorities' dictates [Turiel, 1983], and (3) personal choices. A more social-conventional perception of moral obligations may express a less mature morality, and make easier rule breaking actions, such as aggressive behavior.

This chapter aims to explore the relationships between morality and aggressive behaviors, in particular bullying. First, research and theorizations on morality and social behaviors are presented, mainly focusing on the social domain model of morality. Then, bullying is analyzed as a group-phenomenon in which children participate in different ways, that is as bullies, victims, defenders of the victimized peer(s), and bystanders. The associations between moral processes, bullying behavior and the other forms of participation in bullying situations are discussed.

A study is described, investigating children's perceptions of moral and social-conventional rules, related to roles of involvement in bullying episodes. 129 children (aged 7–10 years), and 182 early adolescents (aged 11–15 years) filled in the Participant Role Questionnaire, assessing forms of participation in bullying, and a self-report measure, assessing the discrimination of moral and social-conventional rules in the school context. Children perceive moral and social-conventional rules as distinct kinds of obligations. Bullies do attribute more characteristics of the social-conventional domain to all the rules, and in adolescence judge the breaking of social-conventional rules more acceptable than peers, especially defenders, do. The age-level (mid-childhood vs. early adolescence) has some moderation effects. Practical implications for the anti-bullying intervention are discussed.

Chapter 14 - In modern societies non-academic citizens are rarely recognized for their ability to construct knowledge. Engagement with theory that contributes to knowledge development is considered the mandate of professionals or those who are situated within academic circles. It is apparent to many individuals, including academics, that through day-to-day decision making the average person, although not associated with traditional research bodies, actively theorizes and constructs knowledge. A general acknowledgement of these abilities encourages collaboration among all citizens and prevents the unhealthy marginalization of a large segment of the population. As well, theory development and knowledge construction become demystified and result in communities of learning, collaboration and civility.

Chapter 15 - The present study examines children's tendency to engage in stereotyping and essentialist reasoning about gender-related preferences. Across 2 studies, 132 3-8-year-olds engaged in individual interviews where they were asked to make predictions about hypothetical 5-year-olds' toy, color, and occupation preferences, and then asked to make a series of inferences about the nature and causal origins of those preferences. Several patterns of results emerged. There was a curvilinear relationship between the tendency to suggest gender stereotypical preferences and participant age, with stereotype-consistent responses peaking at age 5 and then declining afterwards. Children's tendency to engage in essentialist reasoning showed a similar age-related pattern. In addition, although children provided more stereotype-consistent responses when reasoning about boys than girls, they showed an increased tendency to essentialize the preferences of girls. These results contribute to growing evidence that although essentialist reasoning is accessible in a wide range of domains, it is differentially instantiated across contexts.

In: Social Development
Editor: Lynda R. Elling

ISBN: 978-1-60741-612-8
© 2009 Nova Science Publishers, Inc.

Chapter 1

REFLECTIVE POSITIONING: THE IMPACT OF CONVERSATIONS IN THE SOCIAL AND CULTURAL ENVIRONMENT OF MIDWIFERY PRACTICE SETTINGS ON PROFESSIONAL LEARNING FOR STUDENTS

Diane Phillips[*]

Deakin University; Faculty of Health, Medicine,
Nursing and Behavioural Sciences; School of Nursing;
221 Burwood Highway; BURWOOD VICTORIA; AUSTRALIA; 3125

ABSTRACT

Literature reviews on the topic of reflection and reflective practice encompassed midwifery, nursing, medicine, allied health, education and professional education. This investigation also included socio-psychological theories by leading authors such as Benner (nursing), Schön (professional education) and positioning theory by Harré and others. Positioning is a psycho-sociological ontology in which individuals metaphorically position themselves within three entities: people, institutions, and societies, where conversations are constructed and make an impact upon the social world. The social and cultural structures and interactions developed in Archer's morphogenesis were examined in terms of the impact of possible encounters and the transformational effects of learning experiences in practice settings. These bodies of work provided the theoretical framework for the author's research of students' experiences in midwifery education for postgraduate students from which selected excerpts with three participating students and their supervising midwives are presented. These excerpts are related to reflective practices and the professional conversations conducted between students and midwives. It was found that reflective positioning applied in midwifery education by students can serve as an analytical tool in explaining social and cultural elements of clinical placements to influence and transform their learning. The potency of conversations that

---

[*] Email: diane.phillips@deakin.edu.au; Telephone: 61 3 9244 6119; Fax: 61 3 9244 6159

occur in everyday moment-to-moment interactions do contribute to students' induction in professional midwifery practice and their identity formation as a midwife.

INTRODUCTION

This chapter presents a literature review of midwifery, nursing, medicine, allied health, education and professional education, including socio-psychological theories. The work by Benner (nursing) and Schön (professional education) were central to this investigation of reflective practices and in relationship with the work by Harré and others who promote positioning. The social and cultural structures and interactions developed in Archer's morphogenesis were examined in terms of the impact of possible encounters and the transformational effects of learning experiences in practice settings. These bodies of work provided the theoretical framework for Phillips in her doctoral research of students' experiences of their professional learning in midwifery education, specifically related to the Graduate Diploma of Midwifery, Melbourne, Australia. This research was undertaken using a case study approach for qualitative research design over an academic year and conducted as a series of interviews with ten participating students and their supervising midwives over the course of an academic year to learn about their experiences. The excerpts of three students and their supervising midwives are presented pertaining to each of the student's experiences in midwifery practice settings and their conversations with their respective supervising midwives related to the delivery of care.

The connection between reflective practice and positioning was made on the basis of the author's experience as a midwife and understanding of the professional conversations that midwives typically engage in. The conversations that were of particular interest were those conducted between both midwives and students midwives in practice settings and where students were and continue to supported in a supervised model of learning. This model is referred to as 'preceptorship' throughout this chapter and midwives providing support of students are called 'preceptor/midwives'. As a consequence of this arrangement or similar models of student support, midwives have and continue to influence student professional learning through the moment-to-moment interactions of conversations related to everyday midwifery practices. The impact of midwives upon students is through induction to professional practice and as role models in practice settings. Midwives therefore, influence each student in their professional identity formation as a future midwifery practitioner. In this process of induction into professional practice each student employs a variety of strategies, whether consciously or unconsciously, to position themselves to achieve the best possible learning opportunities and where reflective practice is encouraged.

MIDWIFERY EDUCATION

There are three pathways in midwifery education in the state of Victoria, Australia. They include first, a postgraduate course, the Graduate Diploma of Midwifery available only to registered nurses and described as a 'pre-masters' course; second a Bachelor of Midwifery (undergraduate) and; finally the combined undergraduate degree course, Bachelor of Nursing/Bachelor of Midwifery. All three pathways are subject to each graduate submitting an application for endorsement as a midwife by the legislating authority, the Nurses Board of Victoria (NBV).

The NBV influences the design of course curricula through mandating the prescribed number of practice hours and minimum experiences the student of midwifery is compelled to achieve. When each student successfully completes both course and mandated practice requirements, an application for endorsement as a midwife can then be made by graduates to the NBV. The Graduate Diploma of Midwifery is generally considered by nurses as a pathway to a second career, where established nursing knowledge and skills are enhanced and where the focus of care is shifted to the predominance of healthy childbearing women. Professional induction into this second career is critical so students learn best practice in the delivery of care for childbearing women and their families.

In Australia 'reflection' has been promoted in clinical teaching for both nursing and midwifery education, since the 1990s to link teaching of theory and practices (Taylor, 2006). The national authority, the Australian Nursing and Midwifery Council promotes reflection in midwifery education as it is understood to facilitate induction into professional practice, promote professional development, and appraisal of practice (ANMC Australian Nursing and Midwifery Council, 2006).

LITERATURE REVIEW

Reflection in its application for professional education has had wide rhetorical use over many years by a number of notable authors from a variety of disciplines. For example, Schön (1983, 1988, 1991) (adult education and management); Mezirow (1991, 1994, 1996, 1998), (adult education); Boud, Keogh and Walker (1985) (adult education) and Shulman (1987, 1998) (teacher education); Benner (1984); and Benner, Tanner and Chesla (1996) (nursing education), are some of the prominent figures who have characterized in reflective practice by drawing heavily on Deweyian pragmatism and, more recently, on the critical social theory of Friere and Habermas.

Benner's characterization (Benner et al., 1996; Benner, 1984) is of particular relevance for both nursing and midwifery education. Her model comprising of five developmental levels or stages of reflective competence (novice, advanced beginner, competent, proficient, and expert levels), has contributed significantly to competency based frameworks for curricula of nursing and midwifery.

A specific purpose of the promotion of reflection within midwifery education has been to uphold active adult learning, not only from the theoretical context but also from clinical placements and learning experiences. The purpose of reflection, succinctly presented by Taylor (1998, p. 134) is for all learners in practice (nurses and midwives) "… to reflect on their practice worlds …" whereupon individuals can create meanings from clinical experiences to support their professional knowledge.

In summary, reflective practice has been held to:

- Bridge the gap between theory and practice with the expectation that it leads to articulation and development of knowledge embedded within practice (Smith, 1998; Davis, 1998; Kuiper & Pesut, 2004).

- Encourage the practitioner to not only acquire knowledge but also generate a cycle of learning that is similar to the action research process (Rolfe, 1998).
- Support the practitioner in the examination of her/his decisions and the application knowledge acquired within practice (Heath, 1998).
- Develop skills such as self-awareness, description, critical analysis, synthesis, evaluation (Heath, 1998; Thompson & Rebeschi 1999; Yost, Sentner & Forlenza-Bailey, 2000), or transformative learning (Mezirow, 1991).
- Afford insights through professional conversations with the preceptor/midwife. Guided reflection is typically conducted within problem-based or situated learning environments and strongly advocated by Schön (1988, 1991); Mezirow (1991); Benner (1984); and Benner et al. (1996).
- Promote learning, that health care providers practice with moral integrity and professional commitment to maintain standards of safe practice (Ferrell, 1998; Lumby, 1998; Gustafsson & Fagerberg, 2004).
- Create records that can be referred to at a later stage to appraise and reinforce learning, (Taylor, 2000, 2006).

PSYCHOLOGICAL AND SOCIAL MEANINGS

In the literature related to education, nursing, and midwifery, there is an assumption that there is a universal meaning and significance in reflection as a cognitive activity. The development of practical reasoning at this intersection of individual purposes and social action is fundamental in this literature review.

A variety of viewpoints have placed emphasis on reflection as a social or political act, as opposed to it being a psychological act. Dewey (1933) considered reflection and thinking to be interdependent activities. In drawing on Dewey, Schön (1983, 1988) described reflection as the process of executive or higher order 'thinking on their feet' in performing a specific task through 'reflection-in-action' and 'reflection-on-action'. The pedagogical model promoted by Shulman (1987), also after Dewey, spoke of appraising advanced reasoning that encompasses comprehension, transformation (preparation, representation, selection, and adaptation), instruction, evaluation, reflection, and new comprehensions. Shulman (1987) described reflection as "... what a teacher does when he or she looks back at the teaching and learning [of practical content] that has occurred, and reconstructs, reenacts, and/or recaptures the events, the emotions, and the accomplishments" (p. 18). He was principally concerned with reflection as a tool for psychological analysis of the teacher's pedagogical knowledge content. Mezirow (1991, 1994, 1996), in drawing on critical social theory, described reflection as a transformational process whereby each learner develops opinions based on previous experiences to create new meaning from new experiences. Reflection here plays a key role in the transformation of personal social meaning(s), a process that is grounded in the transformation theory (Mezirow 1998) based upon values, moral issues, and feelings.

Types of Reflective Thinking and Learning

It is presumed that individuals who are capable of thinking are also capable of reflection on experience and learning from these experiences. As a complex phenomenon, superficial practices can be opposed to deep practices in reflection. Superficial learning is also referred to as the 'surface approach' by which individuals tend to memorize information, usually for the purpose of examinations. Conversely, individuals employing the 'deep approach' are making a conscious decision to explore and understand a problem, and arrive at a solution (Boud, Keogh & Walker, 1985). The deep approach is, therefore, a deliberate act of reflection and, as presented by Boud et al is described as a solitary and private exercise.

Wellington and Austin (1996) identified five orientations of reflective practice in a useful taxonomy based on the distinction between the immediate demands of a task (from no immediate reflection) to transformation, in which reflective narratives become more deliberate and meaningful. Figure 1 provides a diagrammatical representation of the five orientations of reflective practice, all of which are typically adopted in the everyday conversations of students and midwives.

Gonzalez Rodriguez and Sjostrom (1998) argue that the promotion of a variety of reflective practice activities for adult learners is essential because there are diverse intellectual levels, as well as the need to recognize and acknowledge past experiences. Critical social thinking is considered to be fundamental for professional practice where demands in health care services are dynamic and challenging (Thompson & Rebeschi, 1999).

In other taxonomies, Kemmis (1985) and Hatton and Smith (1995) related reflection to meeting social need through action as teachers and learners. They drew upon the trichotomy of 'technical, practical and emancipatory' needs explained by Habermas (1976). Problem solving of the 'technical kind' is the most prevalent type and is typically observed amongst new graduates in professional practice. A second type, practical deliberation, refers to appraisal of a situation and subsequent decision-making, and the third, speculative thought, occurs when emphasis is placed upon transformative critical reflection.

Along with 'critical reflection' there is reference to 'transformational reflection', terms that are implied to have a shared meaning. Both are applied by Kemmis (1985) in the promotion of learning from social actions. The terms reflection and critical reflection are often used interchangeably in the literature, but Hatton and Smith (1995) found instances of the latter to be relatively rare compared to the descriptive reflective accounts in student teacher journals. Hatton and Smith (1995) defined critical reflection as "… involving reason giving for decisions or events which takes account of the broader historical, social, and/or political contexts" (p. 41).

For Mezirow (1991), critical self-reflection occurs when an individual has conducted an assessment of problems and reassessed their personal meaning and perspective.

> When the object of critical reflection is an assumption or presupposition, a different order of abstraction is introduced, with major potential for effecting a change in one's established frame of reference. Assumptions upon which these habits of mind and related points of view are predicated may be epistemological, logical, ethical, psychological, ideological, social, cultural, economic, political, ecological, scientific, spiritual, or pertain to other aspects of experience.

> (Mezirow, 1998, p. 186)

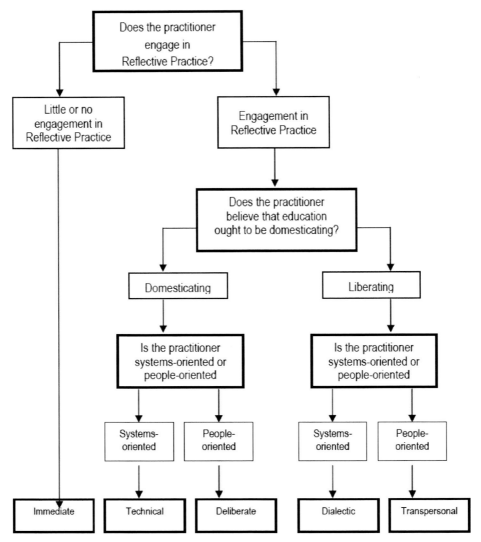

Adapted from "Orientations to reflective practice" by B. Wellington and P. Austin, 1996, *Educational Research, 38*, (3), p. 312.

Figure 1. Orientations to reflective practice.

Lumby (1998) also postulated that the space between critical reflection and re-visioning leads to transformation "… when one views the old with new eyes, seeing possibilities not previously imagined." (p. 95). Personal transformation has been the desired explicit or implicit outcome in the professional development literature. This process is undertaken in a variety of settings in universities or workplaces, for example, through students' journals, group activities, 'debriefing' sessions or the conversational sharing of stories or narratives. Through these diverse settings and methods of learning leads to the exploration of theories related to 'tacit knowledge'.

EDUCATING TACIT KNOWLEDGE

The concept of tacit knowledge was introduced by Polanyi (1958) who argued that it "… exceeds the powers of articulation …" (p. 92). This is understood to mean, for example, that previous learning and perceptions are influential factors on one's actions, even though the individual concerned may be at a loss to explain such actions. Further, skills developed in this manner may be lost altogether if they are not continued to be related to action (Schön, 1983, 1988; Boud, Keogh & Walker, 1985; Kemmis, 1985).

Schön (1988, 1991) applied the term 'technical rationality' to refer to an implicit problem-solving ability that arises from the influence of positivist epistemology in those professions aligned with science or applied science, such as medicine. It is understood that such professionals have an existing body of technical knowledge and expertise, the exactness of which defines their profession. Schön described this as tacit knowledge, problem solving using implicit knowledge rather than explicit knowledge, which he saw as important components of technical rationality.

Fawns (1984) described a cycle of reflection incorporating self-analysis (planning, transacting and reviewing) applied to teacher education, stimulated by conversations related to professional praxis. This cycle encompassed three elements of Polanyi's (1958) personal knowledge; theoretical and disciplinary knowing through 'skilful-tacit knowing'; 'common sense or value knowing'; and 'skilful knowing'. These forms of knowledge, the 'what, why and how', are found in the dialogical cycle of reflective practice in problem-solving for professional learning. Butler (1992) was concerned with the uncovering of the self by the process of reflection that, he argued, must take place prior to the formulation of action that leads to the Schön processes. Butler's analysis of this improved insight into personal and professional domains awareness is theoretically supported in using Gadamerian hermeneutics (Silverman, 1991).

Johns (1998), a nurse academic, described professional intuition as the manifestation of tacit knowledge — "a knowing that is deeply embodied but unable to be expressed in rational ways" (p. 3). Taylor (2000), Johns (1998) and Rolfe (1998) observed that a nurse with twenty years experience should not be assumed to be an expert practitioner and their professional intuition is developed from experiential knowledge, but not necessarily from simple exposure to situations. Heath (1998) argued that qualified nurses perform at different levels related to their understanding of formal theory and exposure to diverse experiences that contribute to reflective decision-making processes. Clearly not all experiences in practice are diverse, and not all activities would require reflective analysis by the practitioner.

The term, practical knowledge' is embedded in social sciences and it is articulated in discursive acts and actions. Giddens (1979) equates practical knowledge with Polanyi's tacit knowledge. It was Giddens who characterized practical knowledge as containing internalized rules, resources, and beliefs that guide social interactions without conscious attention to those rules and beliefs.

The social setting for professional praxis in reflection was described by Boud and Feletti (1991) as 'problem-based learning', where they saw it as an approach to structuring the curriculum that "involves confronting students with problems from practice which provide a stimulus for learning" (p. 21). To develop professional competence, it is expected that students require more than knowledge in subjects relating to their future profession. While critical reflective practice is understood to be essential for effective problem-based learning, the psychological process of learning and the 'problem' itself is often not theorized. Self-directed learning, communication skills, critical reasoning, logical and analytical approaches to problems, reasoned decision-making and self-evaluation are required for problem-based learning, but do not constitute it. Although there is not a clear definition of these skills within the context of nursing or midwifery education, professional problem-solving is established, for example, in Benner's phenomenological stages. The highest level of reflection is embodied knowledge that is equated to Dewey's executive intelligence (Benner, 1984; Benner et al., 1996).

Yost et al. (2000), for example, described reflection as a problem-solving process in which an experienced individual attempts to make sense of a challenging situation. The individual concerned identifies areas of practice requiring scrutiny, determines goals for improved practice and undertakes actions to achieve the identified goals. The aim of problem-based learning is to modify and enhance professional practice through the progression of problem-solving, resulting in the reconstruction of knowledge.

With reflective practice, confusion may emerge with problem-based learning related to the terminology associated with different applications in curriculum planning. Ross (1991) found these meanings in the literature. They include: (a) 'problem-oriented' curricula, where problems are used as selection criteria for contents and method; (b) 'problem-based' curricula, where students work on problems as part of the course; and (c) 'problem-solving' curricula, where students are given specific training or development experiences for solving problems. The word 'specific' in this context was a relative term.

REFLECTION AND PROFESSIONAL DIALOGUE

While the work by Schön, Shulman and Benner are primarily concerned with the codification of social, psychological, and technical knowledge of professionals, Van Manen (1994), Sockett (1993) and others have placed emphasis upon the ethical dimensions of decision-making of professionals. Professionals observed to make decisions often do not attempt to articulate explicitly the rationale for their actions. According to Schön (1983, 1988), this is often tacit, embodied in a particular context such as previous experiences in conversations that equate with reflection. This suggests that Schön's reflective practice is not an individual construction, but rather a social-professional dialogue in which logical and moral knowledge can be achieved through a process of undefined inductive acts in particular social settings. The mentor role in social constructions of professional identity is acknowledged, but also undeveloped in the professional induction of a neophyte.

Greenwood (1998), an Australian nurse academic, made a related observation when she criticized Schön's model because it does not acknowledge the 'reflection-before-action' or the preparation process that usually occurs before an action is undertaken in social settings. However, dialogue between a mentor and a student may occur in preparation for action that may be indistinguishable from reflection on action.

Watson (1998) and Heath (1998) argued for guided reflection in its application to the Benner model whereby novices require rules from supervisors, while advanced beginners require guidance in an individualized process designed to provide genuine opportunities for dialogue between the supervisor and the learner concerned. Kemmis (1985) and Knights (1985) however, stated that reflection simply does not occur unless another person is involved. They argued that reflection is primarily a social event, but did not locate this in practice.

Magnussen Ironside (1999) observed that supervisors share experiences with learners through dialogue. Situations are created for thinking that is typically 'reflective' and 'reflexive' with new possibilities opened to the learner. While the differences between reflective and reflexive are not developed, the outcomes include dealing with clinical problems that also embody understanding of ethical concerns related to patient care. Yost et al. (2000) and Hatton and Smith (1995) identified the necessity for multiple dialogues whereby reflective abilities could be enhanced, for example, by seminar instruction (group reflection), critical thinking dyads (supervisor and the learner together), peer collaboration, and structured verbal guidance.

Fitzgerald and Chapman (2000) drew attention to aspects of the Schön model that placed emphasis upon skill development in specific social contexts of practice to promote competence in order to assist the new graduate to meet standards of professional work. This application of situated reflective practice could be considered to be in opposition to a holistic reflective approach in practice. Shulman (1998) explained reflective practice as a mechanism for learning from experience and the development of new theories and critical thinking that is situated and transforming. Learners may be provided with the opportunity to discuss their thinking and establish connections between course activities and practice that could illuminate their knowledge and skill development as a cycle of learning. Benner et al. (1996) and Benner (1984) presented the argument that the practitioner who is more skilled has advanced understanding of situations within practice and is able to provide appropriate and effective nursing care. Rich and Parker (1995) argued that claiming the apparent benefits of reflection enables the learner to 'uncover knowledge' in specific clinical situations and assists with the delivery of care using knowledge gained from previous experiences. It could be said that knowledge is not only uncovered, but rather it is only gained from explicit and implicit workplace conversations. Professional practice is, therefore, developed through a process of situated learning; the basis for professional development of which, even the experienced practitioner, may be unaware (Benner, 1984; Benner et al., 1996). This type of reflective practice education is proclaimed to produce a 'connoisseurship' (authentic knowledge of a craft), which Polanyi (1958) coined as 'ineffable', yet for Eisner (1979) it is a paradigm of professional culture.

METHODS TO PROMOTE REFLECTION

Methods to promote reflection include written and dialogical activities and have been considered separately.

Written Reflection

A variety of labels have been applied to individual written reflective narratives within the educational context, for example, journals, diaries, record books, portfolios, verbatims, sociological diaries, dossiers and logs (Walker, 1985; Rich & Parker, 1995).

Story telling is a powerful technique for nurses and midwives who have a "… rich oral tradition …" (Taylor, 1998, p. 139). As Australian nurse academic, Koch (1998) puts it:

> People live stories, and in their telling of them reaffirm them, modify them, and create new ones. Constructions of experience are always on the move. Stories, when well crafted, are spurs to the imagination and through our imagination participation in the created worlds, empathic forms of understanding are advanced.
>
> Stories can make nursing practice visible. Stories can make us proud practitioners. Stories can show where we as health care professionals have gone wrong. Story telling can be therapeutic. Stories can inform social policy. Stories can facilitate change in organizations.
>
> (Koch, 1998, p. 1183)

Koch (1998) presented a plea for the person in research in the health care system that is increasingly being dominated by the rhetoric, technology, and market forces. Walker (1985) claimed that both oral and written narratives allow individuals to express themselves in their unique manner and identify development, leading to a sense of empowerment on the basis of a growing body of self-awareness as a result of reflection. This was supported by Lumby (1998) in a statement that the "… written word can be a powerful and simultaneous act of knowing and doing, leading to a transformed and collective wisdom" (p. 94). Lukinsky (1990) also claimed that the written word assisted the individual in the identification of concerns without the responsibility for information exchanged in the course of conversations with others. However, Fitzgerald and Chapman (2000) observed that rhetoric or written reflection has the potential to produce, "… obstruction to radical learning and [be] out of tune with emancipatory pedagogy" (p. 12).

Writing about experiences is generally considered, in both midwifery and nursing education, as a mechanism to promote learning by a process of critical analysis and evaluation (Paterson, 1995). The word 'experiences' is applied to incorporate other terminology such as 'clinical incidents' or 'clinical events'. Regardless of the nomenclature applied to writing in portfolios, journals, dossiers or clinical logs, the fundamental key to writing is the process of problem-solving that links to self-awareness related to the individual's professional practice (Walker, 1985). A clinical incident could be a situation in which a student felt concern about components of care or issues that emerged following the delivery of care. It may be about the student's own perception of care and their participation in it or the participation of other health care providers. It was believed that writing a short description of an incident would assist students in the critical analysis process and would impact upon practice development (Brown & Sorrell, 1993).

In an article about reflective writing, Bolton (1999) described the power of journal writing for medical practitioners in the following quotation, which could also be applied to the midwifery practitioner.

Writing is different from talking or thinking: It can have a far deeper reflective and educative function. Writing enables the writer to express and clarify experiences, thoughts, and ideas that are problematic, troublesome, hard to grasp, or hard to share with another. Writing also enables writers to discover and explore issues, memories, feelings, thoughts they hadn't acknowledged.

Why does writing have this power? Writing stays on the page unchanged, so it can be worked on the next day or year, and then extended. Unlike thinking and talking, written thoughts and ideas can be organized and clarified at this later stage.

(Bolton, 1999, p. 243)

Reflective journals may assist in the clarification and extension of individual thoughts, thereby providing the teacher/supervisor with insight into the learner's professional development (Collier, 1999) and in particular decision-making processes (Bolton, 1999). In this sense, it is to be a professional journal rather than a personal diary. Koch (1998) argued that the aim of the journal writing should be to keep an account of daily activities that may help practitioners address some disturbing or troublesome practice-based issues, developed upon analytical skills rather than just description of events. Lumby (1998) and Hatton and Smith (1995) acknowledged that writing in 'professional journals' developed upon descriptive accounts rarely moves learners to critical reflection. Yost et al. (2000) suggested strategies that could reduce the application of a lower form of reflection to include encouragement to utilize questions such as: (a) what do I mean? (describing); (b) what does it mean? (informing); (c) how did I come to this? (confronting); and (d) how might I do things differently? (reconstructing). Other specific instructions could be presented to the learner as guidelines, to promote critical reflection, such as the time, place, actions and feelings involved. Brookfield (1990), Smith (1998), and Taylor (1998, 2000) suggested different strategies such as dialogical practices to promote critical reflection. Phillips and Morrow (2008) promote the application of reflective practice in midwifery education using online modalities, rather than hand written journals. This is designed to encourage students to use their 'private space' as an ongoing journal and available to lecturers on a continued basis rather than at the completion of the semester. This access by lecturers is advantageous for students in that there is early identification of potential issues, rather than later.

Dialogical Reflection

Dialogical reflection, often conducted with for example midwives in their function as a 'preceptor' (to guide and influence students during their placements in maternity practice settings) and described by Lumby (1998, p. 101), "... offers a stepping back from the actions or events ..." and is often conducted within a social context with mentors or preceptors. Taylor (1998) stated that "coaching in reflective processes also encourages co-operative communication between the instructor and participants" (p. 139). Reflection of this type is assumed to be a form of dialogue with one's self as well as others, with examination of possible reasons that cause concern in practice (Hatton & Smith, 1995). The aim of dialogue is to allow learners to 'externalize' thinking skills and develop a clearly thought out point of view (Yost et al., 2000). Within this context, support from for example, a preceptor can play a key role in the process of guided reflection for nursing education and practice. Johns and

McCormack (1998) found that "reflection-on-experience provides the supervisor with a rich feedback of practitioner performance and effectiveness, although this information depends on the extent of the practitioner's disclosure" (p. 64).

Although it is not theorized in this literature review, participation in conversations related to institutional practice is held to be a potent mechanism amongst peers and colleagues. Lumby (1998) acknowledged that the benefits are conditional because the participating individual should know "… how to make sense of the stories without destroying their meaning …" (p. 100). Lumby suggested that the individual should be encouraged in discussion in educational programs to reflect upon the narrative, and to question the key aspects within the narrative. The stated assumption is that it will promote meaningful learning outcomes, specific to the individual concerned.

Hatton and Smith (1995) found that either written or dialogical reflections are sometimes rejected by some students and supervisors simply as an academic pursuit that can be perceived to be a diversion from the development of technical skills. In addition, Hatton and Smith observed in practice that the lack of time, opportunity, and adverse reactions of peers often severely hindered or inhibited effective personal dialogical reflection. They noted 'critical friends' often responded adversely to expressive feelings and issues related to best practice, which may also inhibit discussion and damage self-engagement. The place of reflective practice in education programs and research often appears to lack integrity, cohesion and human authority. A research framework, with attention to the person and the context without at any time losing focus on each entity is required. Benner's iconic development of the phenomenological stages for reflective practice in nursing education provides an excellent foundation, (Benner, 1984; Benner et al., 1996) but even this requires elaboration of a discursive model of transformational action.

BENNER'S STAGES OF REFLECTIVE PRACTICE FOR PROFESSIONAL COMPETENCE

Benner's (1984) model is based upon the narratives of nurses and refers to the actual on-the-job behaviours of experienced nurses who were considered to be experts by their peers and supervisors. Developed on the basis of narrative descriptions from newly qualified and expert nurses to capture both clinical and ethical judgments, Benner (1984) developed five stages of practice according to the Dreyfus model of skill acquisition (Benner et al., 1996; Dreyfus & Dreyfus with Athanasiou, 1986). The five stages of practice served as a guide for nurse administrators in the allocation of workloads for nurses and for nurse educators to support situational learning rather than "task analysis, competency lists and applications of abstract scientific concepts thought to be related to nursing" (Benner, 1984, p. vi). Benner's groundbreaking phenomenological research on nurses, their experiences, and their comprehensions, provoked many questions pertaining to the complexities of practical knowledge and professionalism.

Merleau-Ponty observed that all knowledge occurs through perception of the world in which the person "… is not a pure thinker but a body-subject, and that any act of reflection is based on that pre-personal, anonymous consciousness which is incarnate subjectivity" (Langer, 1989, p. xv). Skills, therefore, are acquired by dealing with situations and they in turn determine individual responses in dealing with situations. The model of skill acquisition developed by Hubert and Stuart Dreyfus, placed the phenomenology of skill acquisition in relation to how the world is transformed as skills are acquired is grounded in Merleau-Ponty's existential phenomenology (Dreyfus & Dreyfus in association with Athanasiou, 1986). Figure 2 provides a summary of the characteristics for each of the five stages of the Dreyfus model of skill acquisition.

This model of skill acquisition later, adapted by Benner (1984) for professional nursing practice, is also grounded in Merleau-Ponty's existential phenomenology (Benner, 1984; Benner et al., 1996).

Stages	Summary of each stage
Novice	"The novice learns to recognize various objective facts and features relevant to the skill and acquires rules for determining actions based upon those facts and features" (p. 21). It is further stated that elements of a situation can be treated as relevant and objectively since these elements are "context free" and where rules can be applied regardless of what else is happening. The beginner is like a computer in following a program.
Advanced beginner	With the advanced beginner, "performance improves to a marginally acceptable level only after the novice has considerable experience in coping with real situations' (p. 21). As a consequence of prior experiences the advanced beginner learns to recognize new elements "situational" to distinguish them from context free elements.
Competence	As a result of more experiences "… a competent performer with a goal in mind sees a situation as a set of facts. The importance of the facts may depend on the presence of other facts" (p. 24). This means that the competent at this stage no longer follows rules and seeks new rules and reasoning procedures to decide upon a plan or perspective. These rules do not come as easily as the rules given to beginners in texts and lectures. Competent performers must decide for themselves in each situation what they plan to choose without being sure that it will be appropriate action for a particular situation.
Proficiency	The proficient performer becomes deeply involved in tasks while intuitively organizing and understanding tasks. The performer's theory of the skill, as represented by rules and principles, will gradually be replaced by situational discriminations accompanied by associated responses. The proficient performer, after seeing the goal and the important features of a situation, must still decide what to do.
Expertise	The expert usually knows what to do due to a repertoire of situational discriminations to achieve goals. The expert is distinguished from the proficient performer through their ability to make more subtle and refined discriminations in the world of skillful activity, where the expert has learned to identify those situations that require action from those demanding another. The expert reduces situations into subclasses, each of which shares the same action. This allows the immediate intuitive situational response that is characteristic of expertise.

Adapted from *Mind over Machine: The Power of Human Intuition and Expertise in the Era of the Computer* (pp. 16-51), by H.L. Dreyfus and S.E. Dreyfus with T. Athanasiou, 1986, New York: The Free Press.

Figure 2. Dreyfus' model of skill acquisition

Further research was conducted by Benner over a period of six years and involved 130 hospital nurses to address questions that emerged from the initial research. This subsequent research was an interpretive study of nursing practice in critical care units conducted between 1988 and 1994. Benner et al. (1996) claimed the findings enhanced awareness of "… distinctions between engagement with a problem or situation and the requisite nursing skills of involvement, knowing how close or distant to be with patients and families in critical times of threat and recovery …" (p. xiii). According to Benner et al. these can be learned over time and experientially. Benner et al. argued that clinical judgment is a technical-rational process of professional practice that incorporates the identification by the nurse of what is good and right (requiring moral judgment), and is reliant upon extensive practical knowledge (intuition and tacit judgment), and is referenced to the nurse's emotional responses related to the practice issues. The five stages of professional development that Benner (1984) described include novice, advanced beginner, competence, proficient and expert. The stages are briefly characterized in figure 3.

Stages	Summary of each stage
Novice	The rule-governed behaviour typical of the novice is extremely limited and inflexible since they do not have any experiences of a situation and refer to rules to guide them in practice. "Beginners have had no experience of the situations in which they are expected to perform" (Benner, 1984, p. 21).
Advanced beginner	This level is typical of newly graduated nurses who manage to cope with common situations, to note the recurring meaningful situational components that are referred to as "aspects of the situation" (Benner, 1984, p. 22) in the Dreyfus model. In an explanation of the term 'aspects', Benner (1984) stated Aspects, in contrast to the measurable, context-free attributes or the procedural lists of things to do that are learned and used by the beginner; require prior experience in actual situations for recognition. Aspects include overall, global characteristics that can be identified only through prior experience. For example, assessing the patient's readiness to learn depends on experience with previous patients with similar teaching-learning needs. (p. 22)
Competent	The competent level is typified by the practitioner who has been in practice in the same setting for a period of time, for example, as stated by Benner for two to three years and "when the nurse begins to see his or her actions in terms of long-range goals or plans of which he or she is consciously aware" (Benner, 1984, p. 25-26).
Proficient	The proficient practitioner "… perceives situations as a whole rather than in terms of aspects and performance is guided by maxims [long term goals]. Perception is a key word here" (Benner, 1984, p. 27).
Expert	An expert practitioner, "… no longer relies on an analytic principle (rule, guideline, maxim) to connect her or his understanding of the situation to an appropriate action" (Benner, 1984, p. 31). Expert nurses possess an enormous background of experience, as well as an intuitive grasp of each situation and the ability to focus on the accurate region of the problem (Benner, 1984, p. 38).

Adapted from *From Novice to Expert: Excellence and Power in Clinical Nursing Practice* (pp. 21-38), by P. Benner, 1984, Menlo Park, California: Addison-Wesley Publishing Company.

Figure 3. Benner model of skill acquisition.

However, there has been no elaboration by Benner (1984) or by Benner et al. (1996) of the psychosocial ontology relating to personal 'meaning making' that professionals engage in for their learning and the translation of experiences into transformational action.

Benner's model does not help to understand or research the dynamic interface between personal intention and social reality. For instance, where some practitioners have had many years experience but are not considered by their peers as experts, while others who have only a few years experience may be considered to be experts. In this respect, Benner's model is a static model rather than dynamic.

Figure 4 provides a schematic cycle of the personal and professional identity formation individuals engage in, beginning in the public realm and proceeding through the interactions represented between the 'public' and 'private' domains for reflective practice (van Langenhove & Harré, 1994). Principal elements within such interactions include, for example, private or personal reflection occurring within the individual, such as private thoughts. Public reflection is embedded within professional conversations with peers (singly or within a group), midwives or the midwife/preceptor, and occurs within the 'collective'. These underpinning principles have drawn upon Vygotskian theories (Hanfmann & Vakar, 1962) where public (external) and private (internal) language may impact upon actions that individuals may take following discussion with others (public) or thinking (private) through a problem. Harré (1983) observed that "in the private-public dimension: language is understood as a common instrument of representation" (p. 45). Individuals as agents interpret and respond to the world in a subjective and social manner that is appropriate for them. Harré (1983) also argued that "... an individual's linguistic capacities and knowledge of conventions ensures the presence of the many through the persistence of collective conventions and interpretations of what can be thought and planned" (p. 42).

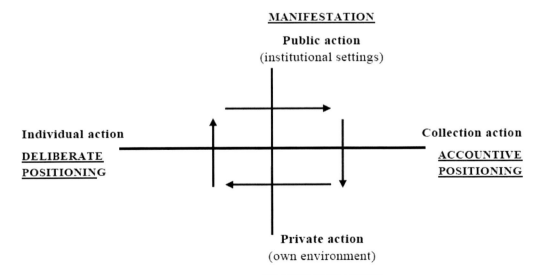

Adapted from "Cultural stereotypes and positioning theory", by L. van Langenhove and R. Harré, 1994, *Journal for the Theory of Social Behaviour, 24*, (4), p. 365.

Figure 4. Social psychological dimensions in reflective practice.

A TRANSFORMATIONAL MODEL OF SOCIAL ACTION IN AGENCY AND STRUCTURES

In recent years, attempts have been made to articulate the agency of the learner within the culture of professional education. More precisely, professional agency is the intentional causal intervention in the practice world where reflexive monitoring of such interventions is undertaken by both learners (students) and their supervisors (midwives/preceptors). Students should be viewed as active agents in their learning culture in assuming responsibility for their psychosocial determinations within the cultural world of professional practice.

A purpose of Phillips's doctoral research was to explore the theoretical platform for clinical and research in midwifery education to facilitate understanding of transformational behaviours. Social theorists of critical realist schools, such as the transformative model of social action, have sought to explicate the relationships between structures of agency in developing a transformational model of social action (Bhaskar, 1978; Giddens, 1979; Archer, 1988). They argued that the social structures function of our everyday actions results in the unconscious reproduction of culture.

Social and cultural organizations are, according to Archer (1995), analytically separate and once this is done "… it becomes possible to assert that discursive struggles are socially organized and that social struggles are culturally conditioned" (p. 324). An agent is an individual who possesses properties as agents to facilitate social identity.

In reference to agency, Bhaskar (1978) observed "… we are aware of ourselves as causal agents in a world of causal agents; and that unless we were so aware we could not act intentionally, or come to know ourselves as causal agents at all" (p. 215). This is understood to mean that agents coexist through awareness of each other's intended actions. Archer (1995) pointed out that each individual is an 'agent' prior to becoming an 'actor' because the properties of an agent are acquired through collective memberships such as gender groups, indigenous, middle or working class groups, which are a system of social stratification. This entity, as described by Archer (1995) as agency, is an efficient mediating mechanism of elaboration of self-identity. Harré and van Langenhove (1999a) observed

> There are kinds of identity which we attribute to people, and that we refer to by the use of the word 'self'. There is the self of personal identity, which is experienced as the continuity of one's point of view in the world of objects in space and time. This is usually coupled with one's sense of personal agency, in that one takes oneself as acting from that very same point.

(Harré and van Langenhove, 1999a, p. 7)

Archer (1995) said structures referred to relational properties that include friendships and commitment, as well as the laws of society and forms of censorship, whereas Bhaskar (1978) stated that structures in a metaphorical sense "… place conditions on the inner workings of the world" (p. 110). Archer referred to structure and agency as being located in social theory, while traditional theorists, such as Bhaskar, considered these entities to be quite distinct and irreducible to individuals and their interactions. This has been taken from an assumption of stratified ontology. Harré (1976) stated that social structures are immanent in conversations, while Archer (1995) advocated the interrelationship of cultural layers in stratified ontology.

Morphogenesis and Transformation Theories

As a process, morphogenesis refers to a complex interaction that results in change in a social system, structure or state, with the end product termed elaboration (any form of elaboration is concerned with culture, agency and structure) (Archer, 1988). Such actions are ceaseless and imperative to a stable continuation or further elaboration. When morphogenesis occurs, the subsequent interaction will be different to the earlier action because it has been conditioned by the elaborated consequences of that prior action. The morphogenetic perspective is concerned with structure and agency. It is not only dualistic but sequential as well because it encompasses three-part cycles that include structural conditioning, social interaction, and structural elaboration. Time is incorporated as a theoretical variable rather than as a medium in which events take place. The critical factor that makes the morphogenetic perspective unique is the notion that culture and agency operate over different time periods (Archer, 1988).

Figure 5 provides a summary of Archer's morphogenesis of ontological strata from which new structural configurations emerge, as depicted in (a), and new cultural configurations in (b). Ontologically, this process is time dependent for the uniqueness of both structural and cultural transformations that each agent must pass through. The morphogenesis of agency in midwifery education requires a different ontological movement, as shown in (c), because agents act on the basis of their structural and cultural conditions and resources, as well as changes that may occur within group configurations. Such changes can lead to discursive or structural ramifications.

In this background to social theory, three intrinsic characteristics exist. Firstly, social sciences are inseparable from human components because of human activities; secondly, society is transformable in that there is no preferred state; and finally, individuals are not immutable as social agents as they are transformed by their social actions (Archer, 1995). It is from this backdrop that a 'Transformational Model of Social Action' (TMSA) is applied in this research. The individual narratives of the student participants in this research present in their dialogical accounts the transformation of their personal professional identity.

Each individual brings into situated learning his/her interpretations, new meanings of the social world in which he/she has entered, developed on the basis of social interaction. Each individual arrives at conclusions about his/her and 'other' moral agency or purposes within everyday conversations in, for example, areas of midwifery practice such as birthing rooms, in education. The compelling relationship of reflection within the realms of a social ontology is introduced as positioning theory, a tool for exploring reflective and social constructions in discursive practices.

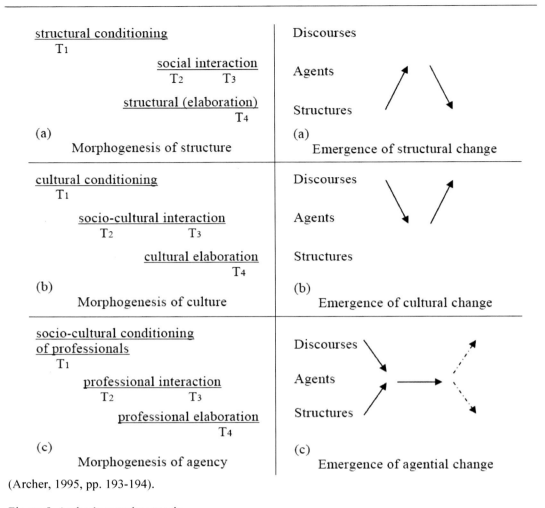

(Archer, 1995, pp. 193-194).

Figure 5. Archer's morphogenesis.

POSITIONING AND SOCIAL EPISODES

Positioning theory is a recent development that initially emerged from the work of Hollway (van Langenhove & Harré, 1999a), who examined positions and gender differentiation, with underpinning theories from social constructionist psychology including Wittgenstein and Vygotsky, (Howie & Peters, 1996; Gillett & Harré, 1994; Davies & Harré, 1990). The relationship of positioning theory to midwifery education and practice is presented in consideration to the possible range of human behaviours within personal, societal and institutional contexts. van Langenhove and Harré (1999a) described positioning theory as a tool applied to the analysis of everyday conversations conducted in clinical settings in which student midwives are engaged, whereby identities (individual and social), societal issues, and culture may be determined.

POSITIONING THEORY DEFINED

A 'position' is a metaphorical concept in which an individual 'positions' himself/herself within three social entities encompassing people, institutions, and societies, where discursive practices are conducted either privately or publicly. Moghaddam (1999) explained that the application of the word 'position' rather than 'role' is to bring to attention the "dynamic and negotiable aspects of interpersonal encounters" (p. 74). Harré and van Langenhove (1999c) support this claim stating that "adopting or being assigned a role fixes only a range of positions, positions compatible with that role" (p. 196). It is apparent that the notion of 'position' in an institution or society has a more fluid connotation in regard to participation in conversations (van Langenhove & Harré, 1999a; Tan & Moghaddam, 1995; Gillett & Harré, 1994; Davies & Harré, 1990). The word 'position', therefore, takes on a specific meaning in regard to standpoints, either on a personal level or as a group representative.

Davies and Harré (1999) explained that positioning "... is the discursive process whereby people are located in conversations as observably and subjectively coherent participants in jointly produced storylines. There can be interactive positioning in which what one person says positions another" (p. 37). The concept of position is manifested by a certain set of rights, duties and obligations as a speaker whereby each episode of everyday life can be seen as the development of a storyline (Gillett & Harré, 1994; van Langenhove & Harré, 1994). The literature more recently emphasized the importance of local moral orders or obligations that are implicit within social structures and interactions through conversations (Harré & van Langenhove, 1999a; van Langenhove & Harré, 1999b; Davies & Harré, 1999; Moghaddam, 1999; Gillett & Harré, 1994).

Moral orders are upheld within linguistic practices performed either privately or publicly (Tan & Moghaddam, 1995), frequently supported by the application of metaphors and images (Howie & Peters, 1996) to facilitate positioning within conversations. These inherent features exemplify the ontological model for positioning theory that comprises people, speech acts, rules, and storylines. Rules within this context are applied as descriptions to operationalise the range of possible responses that are unique to participating individuals within specific situations, language, and communication processes (Gillett & Harré, 1994). Howie (1999) emphasized the relationship between the moral capacity to position another individual and the skill applied to undertake this effectively with variables such as the individual concerned, situation, intended outcomes, and issues associated with power and parity, which were explained fully by Johnston and Kerper (1996).

Although it is acknowledged that interactive positioning can occur, generally positions are relational. For example, when one is positioned as powerful, others may be positioned to feel powerless. Conversely, one may feel confident simply because another individual has positioned himself/herself as confident. Davies and Harré (1999) warned that it would be a mistake to assume that positioning is intentional since "one lives one's life in terms of the kind of person one takes oneself to be, whoever or whatever might be responsible for its production" (p. 37). This is understood to mean that positioning theory is dynamic and dependent upon situations which individuals find themselves in and how they manage these situations. In the following, van Langenhove and Harré (1999a) explained:

Positioning is thus to be understood as a procedure of making determinate a psychological phenomenon for the purpose at hand. But positions can and do change. Fluid positionings, not fixed roles, are used by people to cope with the situation they usually find themselves in.

(van Langenhove and Harré, 1999a, p. 17)

Importantly, it is within discursive practices that the 'social world' is formed and, according to van Langenhove and Harré (1999a), it is "within conversations, [that] social acts and societal icons are generated and reproduced" (p. 15). This means that social actions can be recognized or 'determined' by others, whereas some actions may not be understood and are described within the literature as 'indeterminate'. Obviously individuals choose whether or not they wish to respond to being positioned within institutional settings. Choices may not exist for individuals subjected to positioning by those who have, for example, a foremost function of authority within an organization. In essence, positioning theory employs the mutually determining triad of position, speech-act, and storyline (Harré & van Langenhove, 1991; van Langenhove & Harré, 1999a).

SOCIOLOGICAL, PSYCHOLOGICAL CONTEXTS AND POSITIONING

The sociological and psychological background of the social world occurs when individuals are active in the production of social relations with events in which they are involved. The notion that the social world is a social construction was developed during the 1970s (Gillett & Harré, 1994; van Langenhove & Bertolink, 1999). Harré and van Langenhove (1999a) described how two basic principles underpin social constructionism with positioning. Firstly, what individuals do, publicly and privately, is intentional; and secondly, what individuals are to themselves and others is a result of interpersonal interactions developed over a lifetime. Davies and Harré (1999, p. 33) referred to the "immanentist stance" that makes acknowledgment of conversations conducted within social rules, whereas van Langenhove and Bertolink (1999) emphasized that individuals are responsible for the construction of their social reality.

Social constructionism, as argued by van Langenhove and Bertolink (1999), is crucial for social phenomena to be considered and generated in and through conversations and conversation-like activities. As such, discursive processes are considered to be the place where many, if not most psychosocial constructions are jointly created (Harré & van Langenhove, 1999a). Positioning theory focuses on understanding how psychological phenomena are produced in discourse. The constant flow of everyday life in which we all take part is fragmented through discourse into distinct episodes that constitute the basic elements of our biographies of the social world.

Harré and van Langenhove (1999a) viewed the social world comprising one basic realm: conversations and analogous patterns of interaction in which psychological and sociological phenomena are generated within complex interpersonal relations and belief systems such as social class. A 'social world' is also understood to consist of a network of interactions framed within some relatively stable repertoire of rules and meanings. Within this context, Harré and van Langenhove (1999a) promoted positioning theory as a most valid analytical tool to facilitate understanding within many and varied institutional discursive processes. This can also be applied to the societal and cultural influences within midwifery education and practice.

PERSONAL IDENTITY IN SOCIAL EPISODES

According to Gillett and Harré (1994), Harré and van Langenhove (1999a), and Sabat and Harré (1999), personal identity is one's sense of being located in a position and moral order and may be recognized in autobiographical stories. For example, when an individual assumes accountability for actions and this is evident in application of the first person indexicals such as 'I', 'me', 'myself', 'my' or 'mine'. Personal identity, as explained by Harré and van Langenhove (1999b), is connected with personal agency and is related to the assumed responsibility for actions taken. The literature also refers to 'selfhood', 'personhood' and 'self' in which Gillett and Harré (1994) proposed that shared meanings and relationships are connected with personal identity, agency and autobiography. For most individuals, personal identity is related to many multifaceted factors such as culture and time, which are subjected to change, within the parameters of personal and social attributes of discourse in which there are many contradictions and paradoxes. Individuals position themselves by means of either oral discourse or written discourse. Personal identity can be expressed by representation of a biography to indicate the individual's position at that particular moment in time (Harré & van Langenhove, 1999a; Harré & van Langenhove, 1999b). The necessity for individuals to have both a personal identity and social identity in order to be perceived as complete is emphasized by van Langenhove and Harré (1999a). Sabat and Harré (1999) clarified that social identity means the notion of 'selves' that are presented socially and publicly, but yet within this context, 'self' presents as a contradiction to collectivism practiced by non-western societies (Berman, 1999).

Autobiographical accounts produced in either public (speech-acts) or private (thoughts), enhances persona development upon which the cooperation of others in discursive practices is critical with many possible outcomes, either positive or negative (Gillett & Harré, 1994). Sabat and Harré (1999) explain that personas "… serve to create the public impression of a type, a persona or character, from a local repertoire" (p. 93), clearly demonstrating that personas are typically joint productions. Recognition of a persona may impose profound effects on society or individuals, whereby the persona and related behaviour is open to scrutiny and has the potential to attract appropriate or inappropriate responses or actions by participants. Harré and van Langenhove (1999a) emphasized that positioning theory is reliant upon the moral and personal attributes of participants to provide guidelines or rules for discursive practices.

LANGUAGE AND DISCURSIVE PRACTICES

Language, according to Davies and Harré (1990), is a public institution and, as a consequence, is the foundation upon which social structures and interactions are developed and generally referred to as either the social force, or illocutionary force. Gillett and Harré

(1994) explained that discourses are constructed jointly by individuals within socio-cultural groups as important components of the framework for interpretation, whereby symbols, interactions, relationships, and rules are applied. The discursive act of positioning involves a reconstruction of the biographies related to the individual being positioned and the positions that may be subject to rhetorical re-descriptions. Individuals, therefore, construct stories about institutions or events that are intelligible and become, as pointed out by Harré and van Langenhove (1991), 'societal icons'. Three methods assist in the expression of personal identity within discursive practice: (a) agency (assuming responsibility); (b) statement on the point of view; and (c) evaluation of a past event as a contribution to one's biography (Harré & van Langenhove, 1999a; Howie & Peters, 1996).

Oral presentations may also be referred to as stories or autobiographies. Harré and van Langenhove (1999b) and Davies and Harré (1999) referred to stories as the result of interactions between the audience and the narrator who is compelled to speak in accordance with the demands of his/her audience. For this demand to be met adequately, the narrator requires an effective memory. When a story is written the reader can only grasp the meaning of the text whereas, in oral presentation, can "... intervene to change the text" (Harré & van Langenhove, 1999b, p. 67). Stories serve as a critical means by which individuals make themselves intelligible within a social world. Harré and van Langenhove (1999b) referred to the 'discursive triad' that incorporates storylines, the positioned speaker, and the social force of narration, as contributing to the construction of storylines. Clearly, written stories generate a great deal of information about the author concerned and, according to Moghaddam (1999), also reveal the speaker's favoured forms of autobiographical presentation. Activities such as letters, memos, or research proposals can also be regarded as conversations because invariably decision-making processes occur in this way (van Langenhove & Bertolink, 1999).

Position, storylines, and relatively determinate speech acts are three key factors inherent within discursive practices or conversations, and play an influential part in human behaviour (Harré & van Langenhove, 1999a; van Langenhove & Harré 1999a). Discourse is considered as a central concept in the theoretical development for social constructions and, in particular, the relationship of discourse with powerful influences such as psychic and social phenomena. Harré and van Langenhove (1999a) explained that "... some basic issues from social constructionism and discourse analysis in order to frame positioning theory as one possible conceptual apparatus that allows for social constructionist theorizing based on a dynamic analysis of conversations and discourses" (p. 2). Other factors that should be considered when engaging in discursive constructions include history, culture, and social differences that are individually unique and require thoughtful, sensitive negotiation (Carbaugh, 1999; Berman, 1999; Moghaddam, 1999; Sabat & Harré, 1999; Tan & Moghaddam, 1999).

CULTURAL DIFFERENCES

Harré and van Langenhove (1999a) also promoted positioning theory as an analytical tool for societal issues on a cultural level. Moghaddam (1999) explained reflexive positioning applied to moral and personal attributes of the self to encompass culture, cultural ideals, and symbolic meanings. Culture, in this context is applied to environmental, social, political, and spiritual forces that act as direct influences within an individual's culturally embedded narratives. Carbaugh (1999, p. 160) stated that every social interaction "invokes culture, intelligible forms of action and identity" and cautioned that conflicts and confusion may occur as a result of variation within cultural meaning systems specific for each cultural group. Although culture is intrinsic within all individuals, the positioning framework presents as an active and dynamic view of the self "… while being mindful that fundamental aspects of intrapersonal positioning practices may vary widely with culture" (Moghaddam, 1999, p. 75).

In the application of the term 'intrapersonal positioning', Moghaddam (1999) described this as an extension of positioning from 'self', (typical of western society), to encompass the 'collective', (typical of non-western society). This allows cultural differences to be accommodated and allow individuals to utilize, for example, moral orders, metaphors, and storylines within their narratives specific for them and their lived experiences. In reference to positioning in 'intergroup relations', Tan and Moghaddam (1999), explained that positioning is not exclusively for individuals and may be applied to members, representatives, and mediators of groups. In support for the acknowledgement of cultural differences and positioning, three examples developed by Moghaddam (1999), and presented in the following, provide explanation of how they can vary with:

1. Cultural ideals and the desire by a particular group of people to move toward through positioning;
2. Particular dimensions in which a group of people find relevant (sic) in positioning themselves and others in discourse;
3. Preferred forms of autobiographic telling, which may influence the types of stories people tell themselves about themselves in the process of positioning.

(Tan and Moghaddam, 1999, p. 80).

With the acknowledgement of cultural differences and the potential impact upon discourse and social interactions, the types of positioning presents as a critical component of this literature review.

TYPES OF POSITIONING

Several types of positioning have been identified by van Langenhove and Harré (1999a, pp. 20-23) who explained 'modes of positioning theory', which are summarized in the following:

1. First order positioning (refers to the way an individual locates herself or himself and others).
2. Second order positioning (occurs when the first order positioning is questioned and has to be negotiated) must be intentional.
3. Third order positioning (occurs when accountive positioning occurs outside the initial discussion) must be intentional.
4. Performative and accountive positioning (refers to one's own or others conflation).
5. Moral and personal position (positioning with regard to the moral orders in which they perform social actions).

6. Self and other positioning (positioning constitutes the initiator and others in certain ways, and is also a resource through which all persons involved can negotiate new positions).
7. Tacit and intentional positioning (includes three typical kinds of positioning talk: (a) the first kind refers to the positioning assumed by individuals, how they position others and are positioned by others; (b) the second kind includes discursive practices in which acts of positioning where the first kind becomes a topic or target; and (c) the third kind refers to discursive practices in which the positioning-talk has as a topic first or second order positioning.

The modes of positioning theory are offered as discrete categories and concede certain flexibility. The categories raise questions in regard to possible constraints on spontaneous social acts that occur within conversations, devoid of motive or intention.

The application of intentions within positioning theory is subject to further examination when an individual decides to express personal identity, in a number of ways. For example, the individual may choose to apply any one of the four categories of positioning as outlined by van Langenhove and Harré (1999a), supported by elaborations to exemplify positioning within midwifery education and practice. Figure 6 provides a diagrammatical representation of the types of intentional positioning.

	Deliberative positioning	Accountive positioning
Self-positioning	Performative self-positioning	Forced other positioning
Other-positioning	Performative positioning of others	Forced positioning of others

Adapted from "Introducing positioning theory" (p. 24), by van Langenhove and R. Harré. In R. Harré and L. van Langenhove (Eds.)., 1999a. *Positioning Theory: Moral Contexts of International Action*. Oxford: Blackwell Publishers Ltd.

Figure 6. Types of intentional positioning in midwifery practice.

Intentional positionings (van Langenhove & Harré, 1999a, pp 24-28) that can be assumed in midwifery practice have been summarized below:

1. **Situations of deliberative self-positioning**: Occurs when an individual wishes to express his/her personal identity and present a course of action. A student, for example, discusses with her preceptor/midwife, the care of a childbearing woman based on needs that have been identified by the student. The student recognizes her limitations within midwifery practice.
2. **Situations for forced self-positioning**: This is applied when the initiative lies with somebody else rather than the individual involved. For example, a student reporting all aspects of care to the preceptor/midwife, who is responsible for the delivery of safe midwifery practice.
3. **Situations of deliberative positioning of others**: Frequently this type of positioning occurs when a student positions a midwife who she/he holds in high esteem and tends to actively engage the attention of the midwife as often as possible and whenever possible, in order to learn about professional development.

4. **Situations of forced positioning of others**: This may be demonstrated within student groups when one group member is identified by his/her peers as the person who needs, for example, additional support and care. In regard to this final point, the social force of the speech-acts depends to some extent on the positions an individual being positioned decides to take, whereby the individual may reject all offers of assistance from peers.

REFLEXIVE POSITIONING

Davies and Harré (1999) referred to reflexive positioning as the process by which individuals choose to position themselves privately (thoughts) or through internal discourse that promotes both intentional and unintentional positioning with the production of storylines. It also influences an individual's local moral capacity and personal attributes to influence speech acts (Harré & van Langenhove, 1999b; Tan & Moghaddam, 1995). According to Moghaddam (1999), reflexive positioning is a pragmatic practice because there are various mechanisms to produce one's autobiography.

Moghaddam (1999) explained that an individual's story might be retold as a new experience, thereby suggesting that autobiographies following a process of reflexive positioning may be altered to produce mutual storylines and meanings for particular occasions and participants. Harré and van Langenhove (1999b) supported this viewpoint when they observed that positioning theory embodies "... a reconstructive element: the biographies of the one being positioned and the positions may be subject to rhetorical redescriptions" (p. 62). This sets the scene, as Howie and Peters (1996) noted, for both positioning theory and reflection in which creative, dynamic, collaborative storylines, and meanings are developed. Within this, opportunities exist for the individual to reflect, position him or herself or others, to apply appropriate images, metaphors, and storylines for that particular social episode.

Positioning therefore, enables a study of relationships between participants as well as the rich detail that occur even with the most fleeting moment of interactions between individuals. Even in these brief episodes of interaction can provide invaluable opportunities for positioning (Winslade, 2005). This is the case of midwifery education where professional conversations are encouraged (Phillips & Hayes, 2006). Positioning is therefore an effective tool for analyzing the dynamics of conversations through the emerging patterns of speech acts and storylines (Harré, 2005).

POSITIONING THEORY AND MIDWIFERY EDUCATION

In positioning theory, speech patterns in everyday conversations in institutions indicate the local moral order, the local system of rights, and duties and obligations within which both public and private intentional acts are performed. While the meanings are clear to individuals involved in conversation, the location of the individuals, using the variety of discursive positions available to them, may also be easily recognized within the social context. A typical example is when a new student positions herself (self-positioning) as a neophyte in midwifery practice. This neophyte status is easily identified by the midwife in conversation, even if the student was previously unknown to her. The student may be 'positioned' and identified in discursive practice (accountive positioning) as one who requires supervision and support in practice.

Types of positioning: One distinction in positioning refers to first and second order positioning applied to the discursive practices conducted between students and their preceptors in this study. The distinction refers to the manner in which individuals locate themselves and others. A characteristic example of first order positioning normally occurs when a preceptor, who has the moral capacity to position the student, requests in conversation that the student provide a component of midwifery care. The student accepts this, either consciously or unconsciously, by locating the preceptor/midwife as a trusted partner of care. Second order positioning occurs when the first order positioning is challenged and requires further negotiation. Third order positioning occurs when for example, "accountive positioning" (van Langenhove & Harré, 1999a, p. 21) takes place outside of the initial discussion.

Indexical Use to Demonstrate Storylines in Positioning

The concepts of 'position' and 'positioning' within conversations make "… a person's actions intelligible and relatively determinate as social acts and within which the members of the conversation have specific locations" (van Langenhove & Harré, 1999a, p. 16). The application of 'indexicals' bring attention to the storyline and facilitate analysis of reflection and positioning theory within the psycho-sociological interactions that are typical of everyday professional conversations conducted in institutional settings.

Through the application of personal pronouns such as 'I', 'we', 'me', 'my' and 'you', speakers can demonstrate responsibility for their own actions (agency), a sense of personal identity, and commitment. In conversations when the first person is employed, the meaning applied is simply to claim a personal action or responsibility. Harré and van Langenhove (1999a) referred to these applications of 'indexicals' as 'personas', which all individuals at some point might choose to employ in the course of a conversation.

'I' is applied to express 'personal identity', while 'we' is expressed to create "… a double singularity of public personhood" (Harré, 2002; Harré & van Langenhove, 1999a, p. 7). Personhood or personal identity is demonstrated when an individual takes responsibility for an action (agency). The application of, 'me' and 'my' constantly draws attention to the constructionist accounts that may be used to disclose personal identity (Harré & van Langenhove, 1999a). The use of the pronoun 'you' is another frequently used expression that may be applied when an individual applies another persona within a particular context, for reasons that are known only to themselves (Harré & van Langenhove, 1999a). Within a culture of 'caring' in midwifery practice, 'I', 'we', and 'you' demonstrate attitudes and relationships that existed between students, midwives, childbearing women and their families. In regard to such relationships, the expression 'you know' was typically employed with the interviewer, thereby bringing the interviewer into the storyline. The pronoun 'they' can be used in the context of "intergroup positioning" (Tan & Moghaddam, 1999, p. 183) and where responsibilities are shared.

EVERYDAY MIDWIFERY CONVERSATIONS

Everyday midwifery conversations presented as autobiographical dialogues are considered to represent personal experiences and meanings constructed by students and their respective preceptor/midwives using a case study approach. The overarching goal was to "… catch the complexity of a single case" (Stake, 1995, p. xi), where the ontological and phenomenological significance for the person presented in various social episodes and where each participant's descriptions and interpretations of their accounts in conversations could be carefully studied. The presentation of specific storylines within everyday midwifery conversations is to depict the subjective meanings of experiences and their intentionality (Eberhart & Pieper, 1994), as well as transformational learning for the participants of conversations.

Within in the culture of midwifery education and practice, use of indexicals such as 'I', 'we', 'my', 'you' and 'they', pertain to the relationships between midwives, students and their preceptor midwives, educators and consumers of care, women and their families. The conversations of students and their conversations partners were all women and this is acknowledged as not being unusual in midwifery education as it has been found that the number of men enrolling midwifery education tends to be exceptionally low. Examples of excerpts of professional conversations of three students from a cohort of ten were selected as they presented diverse professional and learning experiences and where understanding, according to Stake, (1995) is a critical component of case study design. The respective storylines of three students are presented in the following along with those of their preceptor/midwives, including a storyline analysis (Phillips, 2002). The indexicals of 'I', 'we', 'my', 'you' and 'they' have been underlined to highlight their application in storylines.

Student One

They let <u>you</u> do more things. For example, when <u>I</u> was on night duty a new lady came in [admitted], <u>they'd</u> say go and do baseline things [perform a maternal and fetal health assessment] and come back and tell me what <u>you</u> think. And so that's what <u>I</u> did. **[Forced positioning by others]**.

And yes, it was really good. <u>They</u> would only assess the woman when the doctor went in there to see her [woman] and <u>they'd</u> acknowledge what <u>you</u> know, what <u>you</u> thought. **[Self and other positioning]**.

In that regard there are still other things. Like midwives showing <u>you</u> one delivery [assisting with birth]. Things like that and with my last delivery, "Oh <u>you</u> don't do it like that!" Yes, <u>I</u> just think, "Oh my goodness!" **[Forced positioning by others]**.

Storyline Analysis – Student One

The use of the third person 'you' indicates the student's perception of herself as a subordinate member and the struggle for limited autonomy within the local moral order. In reference to the comment by the midwife, "Oh you don't do it like that!" (third order positioning), the student in her response used the first person of 'I' to indicate how she felt about this statement. This is in contrast to the preceding texts where there is reference to 'they' and where it is implied that the midwives are responsible and accountable for care.

Midwife One: (Preceptor/Midwife for Student One)

I guess in the last couple of weeks we had talked a little bit as we were on night shift. We had quite a few hours to fill in. So we had general discussions. We had five midwives on night shift so we had quite a few discussions with people with different incidents that they would talk about. She would listen. **[Deliberative self-positioning]**.

I was quite happy to let her conduct the cases [assist women during labour and birth] and I was just there more as a sounding board. If she had anything that she was worried about or any concerns at all … [she could access the midwife]. But I was quite happy letting her do the appropriate care and I was just there to check you know, nothing was going out of the ordinary, which I didn't think it would. Because as I said, I was quite confident she would run the case okay. **[Accountive other positioning]**.

Storyline Analysis – Midwife One

Storylines within the selected excerpts with Midwife One placed emphasis upon the adaptation to discursive action in which social representation and institutional forces influenced professional appraisal of technical competence and decision-making related to safe practice. Use of 'I' and 'we' were used within these 'performative' and 'accountive' storylines as a consistent presentation of the student's confident self and other positioning. Implicit in these texts was the midwife's positioning as a competent preceptor of the student.

Student Two

I'm still thinking about it [reflective practice] all the time, in a positive way. Not in a stressful manner. I don't feel stressed by what you know. I went through a period in the course where I felt quite stressed by certain events that occurred. But certainly now, I seem to cope, you know. Sometimes it doesn't always work out the way you want it to and I cope. I think to myself and I still think a lot and think about now, should have I done that or did I do the right thing and you know, did so and so do the right thing? I still reflect a lot on best practice, I guess. You know, what is [the] best practice in certain situations. **[Deliberative self-positioning]**.

Storyline Analysis – Student Two

The first person 'I' was predominately used by the student throughout this selected excerpt. The focus in this interview was the transformation in her reflective practice from simply 'thinking' to extending this process to encompass learning and developing a role as a future midwife by reference to best practice.

Student Two Continued

Yes, I think I always questioned my own ability I guess. But guess with midwifery the buck stops a lot more with the midwife. I found more in general nursing that there were times that you were following orders or you were always calling the doctor for an opinion. I was always calling the doctor for an opinion, I guess. And there was always somebody else that was checking up on you (the midwife with whom the student works with in a model of supervision). For instance, blood results. That type of thing. Whereas now, I feel I have the knowledge and the ability to take more responsibility for my own practice. I think not only as a midwife but also as a general nurse. **[Deliberative forced positioning]**.

Storyline Analysis – Student Two

The reference point used as a measure for professional development was the comparison of her practice as a registered nurse in a rural setting and how her learning throughout the course had also strengthened her perceptions of her role as a nurse. The use of the second person 'you', indicates a detachment from the responsibility in the provision of care within institutional practices in which procedures and policies required a secure position in the local moral order for professional practice. Of particular note in this excerpt is the positioning assumed by the student in the dual role of both nurse and midwife.

Midwife Two

I couldn't class her as an equal [partner of care] at this stage. Unfortunately because she doesn't have, I suppose the clinical expertise that I need in my unit because it is so small. I need somebody perhaps who has a few years of experience behind them, to make her an equal partner [of care]. We're talking partnership because there is only two [midwives] working in the area. However, she has such, such insight that she can manage as much and when she needs help she comes and gets it. So that she knows when is stepping over the mark at this stage. **[Accountive other positioning]**.

Storyline Analysis – Midwife Two

In this text with Midwife Two, frequent use of the first person 'I' and 'we' demonstrated a concerned and caring practitioner but acknowledging the limitation of resources such as experienced midwives employed available at her small unit.

Student Three

I feel relieved. Like I feel a weight has been lifted off my shoulders because you know, I guess for me, academically things are finished [academic course requirements had been successfully completed at the time of this interview]. Excited. Because it is something that I wanted to pursue. I'm glad now to be moving into women's health. You know, it would be nice to keep up my general [nursing] skills but I can really see my future, career wise, in women's health. Each clinical day and work day, whatever, is constantly rewarding. So it is very fulfilling as well. Hard sometimes. Very emotional sometimes, but satisfying. **[Deliberative positioning]**.

Storyline Analysis – Student Three

In this particular storyline, the student applied first order positioning, demonstrated by her use of the first person 'I' to express her relief that she had completed all of the academic work required for the course, the Graduate Diploma of Midwifery. The phrase 'you know' was applied, co-opting a casual but familiar approach to convince the interviewer in this storyline that her future is within women's health.

Student Three Continued

A lot of my girlfriends at the moment are talking about getting pregnant and a couple of them have asked me for advice just about planning for their pregnancy and what not. And just the way that I talk to them you know, let them talk about their attitudes and it's just like you would jump in and say blah, blah, blah. But this time I found myself sitting back and listening more to them and where they're coming from and what is important to them and their partner and then I'll give advice. **[Deliberative self-positioning].**

Storyline Analysis – Student Three

In this text there is an overt self-positioning presented as discursive acts of declarations in the storyline in which the student asserts herself as midwife in the use of 'I' and in giving advice to her friends.

Midwife Three

I think with a lot more experience she will be a very good midwife. Yes definitely. Especially with her fantastic communication skills! She is really good and I think that's a lot and the key to it. I mean you hope to be able to communicate very well to be a good midwife. I mean, the clinical skills will come but she's had limited exposure to all the clinical areas so far. **[Deliberative positioning of others].**

Storyline Analysis – Midwife Three

This midwife identified the student's strengths of communication skills but at the same time made acknowledgement of the student's limited experience in midwifery practice settings. Despite this limitation the midwife's position was one of confidence in that the student would develop her practice as a very good midwife. In this the midwife positioned herself as a supportive and caring preceptor for the student.

These selected excerpts supported by the storyline analyses provide an example of the social episodes conducted in midwifery practice settings to influence professional identity formation and induction into professional practice.

DISCURSIVE ACCOUNTS OF EMOTIONS

A strong sense of emotion is offered in the discursive accounts of these interpersonal exchanges in which collegial relationships developed between the three student participants, their peers and midwives. Bateson (1989) stated, "We grow in dialogue, not only in the rare intensity of passionate collaboration, but through a multiplicity of forms of friendship and collegiality" (p. 94), to reflect the intensity of these relationships. This statement also draws attention to the intimacy of conversational relations and powers revealed amongst students in the program in which the three students were enrolled. The retrospective accounts were often identified as 'debriefing' by the students and midwives, and were understood as a discussion of social episodes in which their positioning in midwifery practice was reviewed. Typically, debriefing was implemented to gain support in conversations from peers or other midwives, (as well as myself as researcher/mentor), outside the initial episode for validation of their social discursive acts or actions.

DEBRIEFING

Debriefing promoted discursive practices with others and ensured that through work place conversations there was a mutual exchange of information, questions, and answers. These episodes were encouraged to foster reflective practice. In a number of episodes, 'oral' constructions and 'written' reflexive practices were referred to as strategies by each of the three students to create meanings from spontaneous or unpredicted events that developed into challenging experiences (Yost et al., 2000). This is in opposition to problem-based learning developed upon structured situations (Boud & Feletti, 1991; Ross, 1991) and where there is a distance from discursive acts or activities in terms of time and space. Watson (1998) and Heath (1998), however, argued for dialogical support.

Students claimed that dialogical support offered by preceptors/midwives was mainly serendipitous, rather than being conscious and planned events. It seemed that personal professional identity formation also depended upon forms of particular friendships and collegiality, which preceptors/midwives often engaged in during frontline action or cultural agency. In the debriefing conversations researched here, students were in the frontline action and cultural agency. The restrictive availability of preceptors in maternity services meant that the notion of 'preceptorship' tended to operate in the collective/accountive spaces rather than individual/deliberative psychological spaces (figure 4) of students in their personal professional identity formation. Students, therefore, occupied these psychological spaces in debriefing conversations with significant others. Conversations are therefore imperative for professional learning.

In reference to Gonzalez Rodriguez and Sjostrom (1998), it is argued that discursive practices employed by the students were the types of reflective practices characteristic of adult learners who utilized learning opportunities. This aspect of adult learning is interpreted as a skill innate for discursive positioning in the deliberative and accountive locations of oneself and others in conversations. Thompson and Rebeschi (1999) noted that adult learners tend to be primarily concerned with their capacity and predisposition to apply critical analysis and thinking in their professional practice.

Implicit in the positioning and repositioning adopted in the storylines of the three students was their intentionality of practice development in the many spontaneous clinical events cited by each of them. Although many examples have been presented in the narrative chapters, perhaps the one that is most compelling is by Student One, in her account, was told by her clinical educator to observe a birth in which intervention was required.

> I was pushed into observing a birth and felt it was impersonal. [**Forced self-positioning**] I felt that I was invading the woman's privacy because she looked at everyone present in the room. I felt unwanted in the room. She (woman) was also crying and was very distressed by what was happening to her. There should not have been so many people and I felt powerless because I had to observe. If I had a choice, I would not have been in the room because of her (woman) distress. Urgent action was needed by the obstetrician, registrar, resident medical officer, two paediatricians, and a midwife to assist the paediatricians, the midwife to assist the lady, the doctor delivering the baby and two students. [**Deliberative self-positioning**]

This was a most disturbing incident for Student One to observe because she empathized with the woman's distress and subsequently positioned herself as the 'unwilling observer'. In this situation, the student positioned herself as being disempowered and unable to seek support from either the clinical teacher or midwives present in the birth room.

In another storyline, positive positioning occurred when a midwife complimented Student Two on how well she assisted a woman during birth.

> One midwife said to me "Oh you can deliver my baby any day!" I took this as a compliment. She (midwife) also said "I would be very happy for you to look after me when in labour". So, I thought that was good. So I thought that was good. I have had very positive feedback from the Unit Manager from the postnatal ward. This reinforces the fact that often clients have expressed to her (Unit manager) the support that I have given to them and enable them to move and improve the quality of care with their babies. **[Deliberative positioning by self and others]**

On the other hand, Student Three's culturally sensitive positioning with women from other cultural groups is exemplified in the following selected text.

> The woman was a multigravid who had a daughter of two and a half years of age in Bali before migrating to Australia. Her husband and daughter were present at the labour and delivery. I was present for some of her first stage of labour … I had the opportunity to build a rapport with the woman and her family and establish their cultural beliefs and traditions related to the birth and their birth plan. The family requested to keep the placenta and take it home. It was so interesting to hear about their customs related to the placenta and the blessing ceremony they will perform at home, to honour the birth of their child. I was able to ascertain their expectations of the birth and how it differed from their experience in Bali. The woman commented on how well she had been treated and that the staff had been sensitive to her needs and made her feel in control ... **[Accountive positioning]**

The illocutionary force employed by each of the students in their psychological positioning has been demonstrated in their pronoun grammar. Their repositioning is demonstrated in the reconstruction of grammar, as well as in the reconstruction of meaning and understanding in their storylines. In the application of their tacit understanding, positioning skills, and personal professional identities, these students transformed their discursive actions in various social episodes throughout the year.

PROFESSIONAL CONVERSATIONS WITH PRECEPTORS

In their function as preceptors, midwives as employees of maternity services were obliged to supervise and appraise students in practice, while students were expected to identify with the rules, regulations, and local moral order in which they continued to be positioned as the least effective members of the chain of authority. Students' discussions of interactions and relationships with the preceptor/midwives were developed from the perspective of 'other' in this research. The relationship differences have been taken to be complimentary because particular interactions in a community of professional practice places emphasis upon a concrete (ethical) (Lineham & McCarthy, 2000) and caring participation, rather than collaboration and friendship as institutional norms or standards.

The impact of conversations broadly defined between preceptor/midwives, (including those midwives who were not preceptors), is an important consideration in professional education. The psychological mechanism argued is one that is conducted through institutionally embedded frontline conversations with midwives and debriefing with significant others, and where complex meanings were appropriated, internalized, published, and conventionalized over time. Within such culturally embedded practices, it is argued here that midwives, through their positioning acts or activities, projected the social force of their storylines. These storylines occupied multiple identity possibilities within the institutional moral order in which the students encountered other students, for example, medical students, undergraduate student nurses, and allied health workers. As part of their employment within maternity services, it is expected that midwives fulfill this obligation in the promotion of interdisciplinary relationships and teamwork.

The actual moral authority and power exercised by midwives in their function as preceptors have been acknowledged in the many recalled discursive episodes of the students who provided testimonies of both positive and negative positioning. In reference to forced positioning of students, many sources of power exist but the one that stands out most in this research is institutional authority which, according to these students, is not always used appropriately. In its association with organizational hierarchy, institutional authority is usually held by virtue of an institutional appointment to a role, which Hatch (1997) observed "… exists within the relationship between social actions [discursive practices] rather than residing within the actors [roles] themselves" (p. 282). By contrast, and in application of positioning theory, authority is assumed by discursive participants on the basis of their moral capacity on any level within an organization. This applied not only to midwives in their function as preceptors, but to students as well, because they were also employed by the same health care network within maternity services on a part-time basis throughout the duration of the course.

PROFESSIONAL IDENTITY FORMATION AND INDUCTION INTO PROFESSIONAL PRACTICE

Personal identity formation and induction into professional practice was supported by students' experience in practice settings and where they were supported in a model of supervision called preceptorship. The social episodes occurred within the social structures of maternity services and recalled conversations were generally around the interactions between the students and their preceptors/midwives. Clinical learning was framed within the 'private/public' and 'self/shared' dimensions of acts and actions. These acts/actions were held to both inform and maintain professional practice at a personal and social organizational level.

Figure 7 shows how conversation (social act) and quasi conversation (reflexive action) have been defined in this research to sustain the professional identity formation of students within institutional practices. This is characterized as four phases in a personal professional identity formation projection that include, appropriation, internalization, transformation, and conventionalization, as shown previously in figure 5.

It is assumed that the process of personal professional identity formation is a dynamic interaction or reconciliation between private and public thinking. In reference to van Langenhove and Harré (1994) however, they did not project this process as a linear method of individual socialization into a role. On the basis of their social constructivist interpretation, individuals may move back and forth between public and private speech acts in particular episodes, rather than being limited to one phase in the cycle.

Midwifery setting (critical incidents)	Reflective practice (oral and written)	Phases in personal identity formation
PRIVATE (self)		
After participation in a clinical incident in which a student consults the preceptor/midwife or peers for advice.	Following a clinical incident, a student thinks about the events that had occurred. May be reflexive (internal reflection) or involve written reflection.	**Appropriation** of social understandings, grammar; institutional practices and societal rhetoric.
Participation in a clinical incident in which a student does not consult the preceptor/ midwife or peers for advice.	Self-other positioning/ repositioning in conversation initiated by the student concerned with a peer, preceptor/midwife and/or lecturer.	**Internalization** of professional expectations through conscious or unconscious reflexive positioning.
Midwifery setting (critical incidents)	**Reflective practice** (oral and written)	**Phases in personal identity formation**
PUBLIC (shared)		
Public presentation following a clinical incident: Documentation is made in a woman's history. For example, the administration of medication in an emergency situation.	The performance/ demonstration of the construction of professional identity with the student's preceptor/midwife, lecturer, other midwives, peers, family, or significant other.	**Transformation** of professional practice following professional repositioning of the student concerned.
Report time (handover), meal breaks, tea breaks or quiet times in a midwifery unit provide an ideal opportunity for midwives to tell their stories about midwifery related experiences. It is also an opportunity for assessments of students by preceptors to occur.	Self-other positioning/ repositioning in conversation initiated by the student concerned with a peer, preceptor/midwife and/or lecturer.	**Conventionalization** of institutional midwifery culture and formation of a professional identity.
	Such opportunities facilitate discussion about care where students are expected to make increasingly identifiable and singular constructs.	

Figure 7. Codifying the psychological spaces in discursive acts in clinical learning.

During clinical placements, the students were exposed to events that promoted explorations of their life space through both public and private speech acts/actions, which they sought engagement in to influence their personal professional identity formation.

As three agents, each student positioned themselves pertaining to their personal attributes such as their physical and dispositional skills and powers, as well as personality and temperament (Harré & van Langenhove, 1999c). In this context, the notion of agency has been designated to include the capacity of each individual to influence professional judgments in the domain of midwifery practice. In essence, the focus of the conversations was on the relationship between what these students believed they could perform and what they could not perform in midwifery practice under the supervision of their preceptor/midwives. Here, the sense of professional agency is formed and the social structure of midwifery practice is reconstructed.

Phillips' research was also concerned with the analysis of the ontological levels of discursive acts that incorporated the meaning of actions and whether or not the participating students fully understood midwifery gestures and signs in social episodes. It drew attention to their claims that they could correctly identify and understand the meaning of symbols for safe midwifery practice and the application of such meanings in the correct context. What they were permitted to do on any occasion within midwifery practice was taken from a small but a rapidly expanding repertoire of categories and subcategories of actions, which were always subject to the discretion of the preceptor/midwife to whom they were each assigned. The moral dimension of personal professional identity formation has not been identified in terms of a set of moral principles or rules, but rather in terms of the moment-moment 'oughtness', in which each of the students responded in particular situations. The application of "oughtness" according to Lineham and McCarthy (2000, p. 452) means, "… selfhood emerges and is enacted in particular moments in a given community of practice". Each student therefore, undertook certain actions based upon the belief that they possessed the right or the moral duty or responsibility to engage in. Such personal actions projected their selfhood and agency.

It was through discursive actions as social actors that for each of the three students, whose selected excerpts of their storylines from interviews, came to the realization they too embodied the rituals of safe midwifery practices that, over time, led to a wider understanding of institutional policies and procedures. The social discourses they engaged in with their preceptor/midwives, peers, and significant others were made determinate in the public reality and impacted on their public performance as a student (both academic and practice development). The social episodes that they selected in their everyday conversations with midwives and others were unfolded, analyzed, and synthesized through discursive psychology. It is within these accounts of social episodes that the flux of social life in midwifery education and practice was researched. It was here in the social episodes of midwifery practice settings that the local moral order and authority of maternity services, course requirements, and the local authority (NBV), were also determinate in the transformation of each student's personal professional identity. This research has also emphasized the necessity to demarcate and protect the 'discursive space' where the personal and social meanings are acquired, as well as interpretation of Benner's stages of skill acquisition. In this commitment to a new ontology in midwifery research and practice based on discursive space, taking conversation as the starting point of social theorizing is important to attend to the particularities of intimacy. This claim is to maintain individual differences and nuances in the local expressive order related to the language systems of institutions such as maternity services.

POSITIONING AND REPOSITIONING PROCESSES

In positioning theory, 'conversation' is important for human behavior where individuals are active in the production of social interactions. The social world of midwifery practice embraces the ontological levels of semiotics, agency and cultural structures through professional conversations and where positioning and re-positioning occurs (Phillips, Fawns & Hayes, 2002). Further, human behavior and personality traits are taken to be inherent in power relationships amongst individuals (Bradley, 1999), to influence or even transform the cultural environment. As observed by Fahy (2002) and McKenzie and Carey (2002), this occurs in patriarchal settings of maternity services and presented in the social episodes of each of the three students.

Kanter (1981) noted that women in female groups tend to be more oriented toward immediate relationships than men in male groups. This was certainly an expectation of the three students (all women) who often sought closer working relationships with their nominated preceptor/midwives, all of whom were also women. Their early accounts were often interwoven with expressions of dissatisfaction with immediate relationships with their preceptor/midwives who positioned them as less supportive than expected. It was in conversations students assumed positions that were associated with their view of their professional life-world at that given time. It is argued here that the students' positions in the social world were continually being constructed and reconstructed in conversations. This is consistent with the feminist post-structuralist stance and its relationship to positioning is explained by Davies and Harré (1990, p. 46) who stated

> Once having taken up a particular position as one's own, a person inevitably sees the world from the vantage point of that position and in terms of the particular images, metaphors, storylines and concepts, which are made relevant within the particular discursive practice in which they are positioned.

Conversational relationships with midwives were and continue to be potent for students linked to the fascination of childbearing and the miracle of birth. At times, the tenuous links of life appear fragile and sometime death of either a woman or fetus/newborn can occur as a result of birth. These factors may impose incredible demands on midwives to deliver responsible, effective, and appropriate care that can be matched with the corresponding need to debrief with colleagues to verify and validate professional actions. The impact of the social setting in which the midwife is the significant other and through social interactions is pivotal in the personal professional practice identity formation of students.

PROFESSIONAL IDENTITY FORMATION

The application of positioning theory and discursive psychology together has afforded a better understanding of indeterminate interactions that present during induction into professional practice of midwifery. It does this through combining attention to midwifery practice as the social world in which the rapid dynamics of social interactions coexist with consideration of the personal rights and obligations in the local moral order of preceptor/midwives and students. Discursive positioning processes have been elaborated in the cognitive apprenticeships of the three students, identified through their experiences of professional practice in midwifery. Their storylines projected an understanding of selfhood developed from moment-by-moment interactions in practice.

Another powerful and yet paradoxical example of the influence of the workplace discourses with midwives is in the appropriation of 'midwifery language' and metaphors. In the curriculum for the Graduate Diploma of Midwifery, the word 'birth' is consistently applied because it reflects the language used by women and is consistently voiced through childbearing consumer groups. Academics use the word birth, and yet many midwives in practice continue to apply the word 'delivery' to mean birth. This application is also used by students thereby demonstrating the influence and authority of those engaged in professional practice.

This semiotic device continues to prevail within social institutions where midwives have a direct influence upon students. This continued use of the word 'delivery' by midwives within maternity services could be related to the traditional influence of medicine through 'obstetric language' applied to childbirth practices by obstetricians. Johansen, Newburn and Macfarlane (2002) stated that, from an international perspective, midwives have contributed to the medicalisation of childbirth and disempowerment of midwifery as a profession. Clearly, this has been achieved through semiotic devices such as the word delivery, which is at the expense of midwifery heritage and culture that identify it as a separate profession from that of medicine. Both Giddens (1984) and Bhaskar (1986) observed that social reproduction is an unintended consequence of social action and discursive action. It is central to the argument of this research that semiotic interactions can inform, in a powerful way, the understanding of cultural agency and transformational models of social action.

Many midwives have frequently stated that when they talk about aspects of care, it is typically presented in a broad context that is impersonal. Frequently these low-level insights, given to the childbearing woman and her family about midwifery care, can also be extended to students. Students continue to report that preceptors/midwives and non preceptors, usually exercise their authority over them in practice settings and in the delivery of care, but despite their shortcomings in student supervision, they were highly valued. The three students also reported on a number of occasions, that learning experiences were often left to chance and this continues to be the case. This outcome for students is often reflected in the episodic nature of frontline experiences, coupled with the inability to predict workloads. Most childbearing women are normally admitted to maternity units for their birthing experiences, that in terms of duration and time, are not always predictable.

The phenomenological and ontological framework for interpretation of social behaviour provides a heuristic structure for the description and interpretation of discourse in midwifery practice and research elaborated in the various psychological spaces. These are afforded by different situated learning opportunities operating in response to appropriate pedagogies in midwifery education, as depicted in figure 8. These pedagogies pertain to situated cognition in social episodes in professional identity projects with educators, preceptors/midwives, other midwives, and health professionals, as well as significant others (such as family members), in public debriefing conversations and maintaining written accounts in their clinical logs. In their role as preceptors, midwives were expected to both formally and informally encourage discourse by engaging in conversations related to frontline social episodes of professional practice. In all cases, the students and preceptor/midwives located each other in conversations as objectively and subjectively coherent participants in jointly produced storylines about midwifery where positioning theory is inherent.

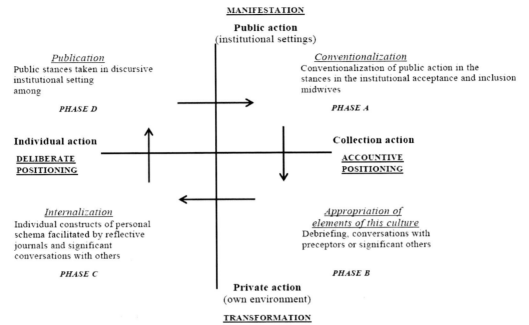

Adapted from "Cultural stereotypes and positioning theory", by L. van Langenhove and R. Harré, 1994, *Journal for the Theory of Social Behaviour, 24*, (4), p. 365.

Figure 8. The psychological spaces in discursive action in a cycle of professional identity formation.

Figure 9 relates positioning to learning settings through the cycle of professional identity formation. For example, *Phase A* (conventionalization) represents socialization of students through discursive actions during their clinical placements in maternity service settings, whereas in *Phase B* students move to appropriate their agency as emerging midwives during their induction into midwifery. This was achieved through positioning and repositioning themselves for best possible learning opportunities in practice. It can be seen, for instance, that writing in clinical logs needs improved scaffolding to be more effective in cognitive transformation, rather than complete reliance upon descriptive accounts normally provided in professional education.

Positioning theory can be applied as an analytical tool in explaining cultural stereotyping of postgraduate students during their clinical placements. Its application in midwifery education emphasizes the significance of both cultural factors and symbols of professional practice through the formally sanctioned social dialogical practices conducted within institutional settings. Here they can seek to transform and maintain the local moral order through their committed actions. In their own way, each of the three students exhibited relational positions within social settings, significant for analysis and construction of meanings relevant for their personal professional identity formation and organizational transformation. Social positioning theory has been applied as a framework for explaining the manner in the three students engaged in information seeking behaviours to influence their personal professional identity formation.

individual action	collective action
phase d	*phase a*
Contribution in the collective experience through the participation of care under the supervision of preceptors/midwives. Application of self and other/forced and deliberative repositioning to obtain learning opportunities. Comparison and analysis of practices according to, for example, the policies and procedures of maternity services and requirements for endorsement as stated by the Nurses Board of Victoria.	Participation in social/collective experiences through the delivery of care for childbearing women by, for example: listening and using midwifery language, technology use in frontline care delivery conversations with midwives, women, and others related to care contribution to reports about the care of childbearing women. Skills and knowledge accepted/rejected by preceptors/midwives.
phase c	*phase b*
Comparison, analysis and evaluation of practice development through private thoughts and/or clinical logs. Identification of personal goals for personal professional identity formation. Implementation of actions to achieve learning goals.	Engagement in second and third order positioning, reflecting upon discursive acts or actions with preceptors/midwives related to social episodes in midwifery practice. Review of own actions in midwifery practice and the practice of others. Reference to preceptors/midwives for expert knowledge and debriefing. Engagement in debriefing with peers or significant others.

Figure 9. Codification of repositioning operations conducted by students.

A TRANSFORMATIONAL MODEL OF SOCIAL ACTION

Midwives, as cultural agents in maternity services, enact and embody cultural ideological resources and institutional rules and regulations to uphold safe practices. This research has framed professional education as a social behaviour that affords interactions at various ontological and phenomenological levels in workplace semiotics. Bhaskar (1989) conceded that humans are the only moving force in history because events occur through their own actions. He argued that the choices for actions are usually based on pre-existing structures but does not, however, acknowledge the causal effects of social actions. Explicit in Archer's dynamic elaboration of Bhaskar's transformational model of social action (TMSA), is the social and cultural transformation undertaken by agents (Archer, 1995). The responsibility of a systematic transformation of social and cultural agency lies with each agent. The accounts of the three students illustrated that this has been the case and anchors morphogenesis of agency. The data from this research along with Archer's morphogenetic TMSA have provided the analytic tools to begin to explain the complex agential interchanges between the macro and micro ontological levels which elaborate change in a system's structural form or state.

When agential morphogenesis occurs, interactions will be different from earlier actions because of the impact of elaborated consequences of prior action. This claim has been supported by the many examples presented in the accounts of the three students, and especially those of their respective preceptors/midwives related to the students' professional identity formation. Inherent in these accounts are the reflective practices and positioning in which all students engaged. The morphogenetic perspective is not only dualistic but is also sequential, dealing in endless three-part cycles: structural conditioning, social interaction, and structural elaboration (Archer, 1988). Throughout their various clinical placements during the course, the three students engaged in this transformational cycle, which required analysis at both macro and micro levels. Implicit in the transformation process were the reflective practices (both public and private expressions), and positioning accounts of all participating students (and their preceptors/midwives), which demonstrated the trajectories of their social expectations and intersected into transformational action.

DISCURSIVE AND CULTURAL VIEWS OF AGENCY IN MIDWIFERY EDUCATION

Through the discursive accounts of students the concepts of structure and culture are intrinsic within institutions, but they are contingent upon social agents and their interactions to influence different generations of people (Harré, 1983; Archer, 1988; 1995). In the transformational journey of the three students as active participants in their professional education, the culture of midwifery practice was also revealed. Within this culture, each student actively researched their positioning, and the positioning of others, in their discursive acts in midwifery practice to advance their personal professional identity formation as a midwife. During clinical placements, each student's agency was conducted as a "... causal intervening in the world, subject to continuing possibility of reflexive self-awareness only analytically separable into episodes" (Bhaskar, 1989, p. 82). As agents, these students positioned and repositioned themselves, as well as others, to meet specific needs throughout their induction into midwifery practice. It became clear that they responded to these needs by negotiating their professional lifestyle through various interpersonal dialogues and, at times, they constructed their psychological 'life spaces' through intrapersonal dialogues.

The notion of cultural agency in professional discourse related to social conditions encompassed factors such as power, technology, physical environment, and institutional bureaucracy. These factors were considered by preceptors/midwives to be part of the 'routine' of maternity services within the institutional practices of the health care service are also explicitly acknowledged by each of the three student participants as important influences during their induction into midwifery practice. It is argued that the case for agency operates inside society where linguistic entities create institutions through structures. Structures include institutional behaviours and dynamics that influence the structure of students' psychology through rules, policies, and procedures, and predispose their personal professional identity formation. A function of professional education is to influence personal change, but usually the concept of social psychology is overlooked because it is here that personal change is effected through organized cultural processes. If change is difficult to effect amidst broader social constraints in a community of practice, individual change is even more difficult to achieve in isolation. This means that to effect substantial psychological change, major alteration is required in the formative social relations, conditions, and institutions. The linguistic sociability of the midwives in this research project contributed to a defined culture that was generated and reproduced within the institutional setting of maternity services where specific rules, policies, and procedures are applied.

Institutional practices, societal rhetoric, and discursive positioning also facilitated a dynamic social 'structuration' achieved through language, rules, and signs that all contributed to a reproduction of culture. Each of the three students and their preceptors/midwives frequently stated that they found these factors to be often unpredictable and inexplicable. The students presented many structural and cultural entities in their selected accounts of the conversations with their preceptors/midwives and others. In these conversations they also provided social representations of their meanings and interpretations of these entities. This was the process in which cultural psychologists, such as Ratner (2000), see all individuals subjugating their conscious or unconscious individuality to the group or work unit and act as cultural agents through their expressions of significant opinions and viewpoints. The students frequently indicated strong concerns in their accounts about denied recognition, appreciation, and inclusion by midwives in workplace discourse. These accounts, and those of their preceptors/midwives, have together demonstrated a professional culture rich in discursive practices and relationships.

While this cultural aspect of personal agency within professional practice is shared, questions remain. These relate to inherent cultural factors of individual professional practitioners and social constructions, ethnicity, and family values that influence social actions. In addition to class and gender, Bradley (1999, p. 21) argued that concepts such as ethnicity and age, assist individuals "… to make sense of the way in which members of societies differ from each other" and where identity is influenced by ancestry, culture, language, or religion. In this instance, reference is made to Student Three's vibrant accounts of her need for symbolic interchange with her peers, midwives, family members, and significant others for her personal professional identity formation.

Conversely, both Student One and Two, on the other hand, presented more familiarly stoical accounts that were concentrated on care and any technical issues in which they participated. They described their management of clinical learning opportunities as part of course requirements, with a view to their future practice as midwives within their respective communities. It could be argued that as more technically minded individuals, these two students reduced components of the course to essential elements to conceptualize insights into their practice development. Over the duration of the course, all three students built on their prior knowledge, experiences, and dispositions to connect episodes together into a biography, supported by situated learning with midwives, other health care professionals (obstetricians and general medical practitioners) and significant others.

The manner in which the three students conducted their social lives through their discursive practices and rhetorical skills, led them to particular locations to enforce meanings and narratives anteceding social structures. Antecedent social structures in this context constituted the control in which discursive interactions took place. What is required is a more elaborate social framework in which clinical educators and academics can give adequate weight to social structures and the value of discourse or professional conversations.

Midwives, clinical educators and academics as social agents need to acknowledge the influence and impact of social structures through conversations. It is through conversations that social structures and human agency are not only presupposed by they are also revealed. In the interviews with each of the three students and their respective preceptors/midwives, their accounts were filled with social episodes in which structures and human agency were innate.

Harré (1983) espoused different causal influences over the course of social episodes in 'macro' social structures the impact upon individuals. In the case of students who have particular needs such as the completion of practice requirements, a powerful macro-social structure within maternity services was economic pressures that often limited opportunities for students to engage in particular social episodes with their preceptors/midwives who frequently had other concurrent responsibilities. These issues were expressed in the accounts of the three students and their respective preceptors/midwives.

A TRANSFORMATIONAL MODEL OF SOCIAL ACTION IN MIDWIFERY EDUCATION

Practice and research in professional education often lacks a transformational model of social action to embrace the social ontological levels of cultural purposes or semiotics, agency, possibilities or structure. This is specifically in reference to the location of agency in the social world and the way social structures are reproduced and transformed. In midwifery education, clinical educators and academics have generally overlooked the organized social life of professional practice where the moment-to-moments interactions are both intentional and interpersonal. These interactions are those conducted in the provision of care. Instead, educators and academics have promoted the more restrictive reflective narrative approaches founded on individualistic conceptions of cultural agency in professional education. An individualistic view of agency and culture in professional education in universities is a form of scholasticism, but ignores the demands and constraints with professional practice.

A transformational model of midwifery education developed from discursive practices can fill many gaps in the theory of reflective practice by adopting an understanding of the clinical learning context where internal or private purposes and public or social activities intersect. This model will also offer a more dynamic theory of socially situated learning in codifying the ontology of experiences and concepts because it fosters production of meaning in the non-rational and non-cognitive aspects of tacit learning. In doing so, it offers a more coherent analysis of relationships between interactions that occur through a public semiotic system of practices, gestures, and both private and public speech. Features of a transformational model of midwifery education and research (Phillips, 2002) are summarized in the following:

- Preceptors/midwives, educators in practice settings as well as academics need to invite students into situated learning experiences that are understood as personal professional identity projects for learning.
- Preceptors/midwives, educators in practice settings as well as academics through their mutual and open discursive practices support student discussions related to

specific public responsibilities and duties within the local moral order of the institutional framework of maternity services for safe practice.

- Student placements in maternity need to be developed in systematic approach to provide diversity of experiences of pertaining to technical procedures, cultural settings and support debriefing discussions between students and preceptors/midwives.
- Reflective practices conducted through debriefing activities in a one-to-one activity or in a group and or a private journal are generally considered by academics, professional organizations such as the ANMC Australian Nursing and Midwifery Council (2006) and the literature, contribute to the cycles of personal professional identity formation in different ways and at various stages. In practice settings there are abundant learning opportunities that should promote dynamic interactions between public (conversations) and private (thinking) reflections.
- Students needs to be seen as active participants of their learning and should be encouraged to participate and present in various collegial settings for the purpose of assessing their own emerging perceptions, positioning and repositioning skills in conversations with others in practice settings.
- The transformation of a student's cultural agency can be self-monitored through their reflective practices encouraged in courses such as the Graduate Diploma of Midwifery. Through entries in each student's private space using online modalities, or even written entries, each student is well placed to chart their professional learning. Regular conversations between preceptors/midwives, educators, academics and students can be used to judge formative and summative competence in technical and cultural practice.

Professional conversations clearly contribute to the personal professional identity formation of students through the social structures of maternity services. Educators need to move from didactic approaches in midwifery education and fully embrace the tacit potency of moment-by-moment frontline conversations into their strategic planning processes of teaching and debriefing activities.

CONCLUSION

As social cultural agents in various practice settings of maternity services where there are defined structures such as rules and regulations are upheld for safe practices, midwives also provide supervised support and care of students. It is within these settings that the actions and conversations of midwives influence students in their professional identity formation as future midwives by learning about the delivery of care on a one-to-one basis. This is achieved through the work related conversations that are both intentional and interpersonal, often resulting in reflective practices that are promoted in academic programs.

It is generally claimed that reflection serves as a mechanism for individuals to identify, problem solve, and transform their learning through processes that could be seen as psychological or sociological entities, but rarely both. Positioning theory is a psycho-sociological ontology in which individuals metaphorically position themselves within three entities: people, institutions, and societies, where discursive practices are conducted either privately, as thinking, or publicly expressed through conversations. Three principal concepts in positioning theory include position, speech-act, and storyline developed from conversations where meanings are constructed and impact upon the social world. In the complex but dynamic social world of professional practice, positioning can be applied in midwifery practice settings as an analytical tool to disentangle and understand the conversations related to the delivery of care. In applying this, students can reflect upon their identified learning need in practice settings and position themselves to fill their knowledge gap by engagement in deliberate conversations with their midwife. Academics need to acknowledge the potential of conversational interactions between students and midwives in practice settings and embrace them in their teaching and learning activities. Reflective positioning is therefore, the way forward in promoting active student learning in preparation for professional practice development in the social and cultural environment of midwifery practice settings.

REFERENCES

Archer, M.S. (1988). *Culture and agency: The place of culture in social theory.* Cambridge: Cambridge University Press.

Archer, M.S. (1995). *Realist social theory: The morphogenetic approach.* Cambridge: Cambridge University Press.

ANMC Australian Nursing & Midwifery Council. (2006). *National Competency Standards for the Midwife.* Dickson, Australian Capital Territory: ANMC Australian Nursing & Midwifery Council.

Bateson, M. (1989). *Composing a life.* New York: Plume Book.

Benner, P. (1984). *From novice to expert: Excellence and power in clinical nursing practice.* Menlo Park, California: Addison-Wesley Publishing Company.

Benner, P., Tanner, C.A. & Chesla, C.A. (1996). *Expertise in nursing practice: Caring, clinical judgment, and ethics.* New York: Springer Publishing Company.

Berman, L. (1999). Positioning in the formation of a 'national' identify. In R.Harré & L. van Langenhove (Eds.), *Positioning theory: Moral contexts of intentional action* (pp. 138-159). Oxford: Blackwell Publishers Ltd.

Bhaskar, R. (1978). *A realist theory of science.* Sussex, Great Britain: The Harvest Press Limited.

Bhaskar, R. (1986). *Scientific realism and human emancipation.* London: Verso.

Bhaskar, R. (1989). *The possibility of naturalism: A philosophical critique of the contemporary human sciences* (2nd ed.). New York: Harvester Wheatsheaf.

Bolton, G. (1999). Stories at work: Reflective writing for practitioners. *The Lancet, 354* (9174), 241. Retrieved March 22, 2000 from http://web2.infotrac.galegroup.co..._A55989149&bkm_8_4?sw_aep=monash

Boud, D., & Feletti, G. (1991). Part 1. What is Problem-based learning? In D. Boud & G. Feletti (Eds.), *The challenge of problem based learning* (pp. 21-22). London: Kogan Page.

Boud, D. Keogh, R., & Walker, D. (Eds.). (1985). *Reflection: Turning experience into learning* 9pp. 7-17). London: Kogan Page.

Bradley, H. (1999). *Gender and power in the workplace: Analyzing the impact of economic change.* New York: St Martin's Press.

Brookfield, S. (1990). Using critical incidents to explore learners' assumptions. In J. Mezirow & Associates, *Fostering critical reflection in adulthood: A guide to transformative and emancipator learning* (pp. 177-193). San Francisco: Jossey-Bass publishers.

Brown, H.N. & Sorrell, J.M. (1993). Use of clinical journals to enhance critical thinking. *Nurse Education, 18* (5), 16-19.

Butler, J. (1992). Teacher professional development: An Australian case study. *Journal of Education for Teaching, 18* (3), 221-237.

Carbaugh, D. (1999). Positioning as display of cultural identity. In R. Harré & L. van Langenhove (Eds.), *Positioning theory: Moral contexts of intentional action* (pp. 160-177). Oxford: Blackwell Publishers Ltd.

Collier, S.T. (1999). Characteristics of reflective thought during the student teaching experience. *Journal of Teacher Education, 50* (3), 173. Retrieved March 22, 2000 from http://web2.infotrac.galegroup.co...7!xrn_6_OA54709098?sw_aep=monash

Davies, B. & Harré, R. (1990). Positioning: The discursive production of selves. *Journal for the Theory of Social Behaviour, 20 (1), 43-63.*

Davies, B. & Harré, R. (1999). Positioning and personhood. In R. Harré & L. van Langenhove (Eds.), *Positioning theory: Moral contexts of intentional action* (pp. 32-52). Oxford: Blackwell Publishers Ltd.

Davis, M. (1998). The rocky road to reflection. In C. Johns & D. Freshwater (Eds.), *Transforming nursing through reflective practice* (pp. 206-213). Oxford: Blackwell Science.

Dewey, J. (1933). *How we think: A restatement of the relation of reflective thinking to the educative process.* Boston: D.C. Heath and Company.

Dreyfus, H.L., & Dreyfus, S.E. (with Athanasiou, T.) (1986). *Mind over machine: The power of human intuition and expertise in the era of the computer.* New York: The Free Press.

Eisner, E. (1979). *The educational imagination: On the design and evaluation of school programs.* New York: Macmillan Publishing Co., Inc.

Eberhart, C.P., & Pieper, B.B. (1994). Understanding human action through narrative expression and hermeneutic inquiry. In P.L. Chinn (Ed.), *Advances in methods of inquiry for nursing* (pp. 41-58). Gaithersburg, Maryland: An Aspen Publication.

Fahy, K. (2002, March). Reflecting on practice to theorise empowerment for women: Using Foucault's concept. *Australian Journal of Midwifery, 15* (1), 5-13.

Fawns, R. (1984). The sources of theoretical principles for science method programs: A new setting explored. *Research in Science Education, 14,* 173-180.

Ferrell, L. (1998). Doing the right thing. Customary vs reflective morality in nursing practice. In C. Johns & D. Freshwater (Eds.), *Transforming nursing through reflective practice* (pp. 32-42). Oxford: Blackwell Science.

Fitzgerald, M., & Chapman, Y. (2000). Theories of reflection for learning. In S. Burns & C. Bulman (Eds.), *Reflective practice in nursing: The growth of the professional practitioner* (2nd ed., pp. 1 – 27). Oxford: Blackwell Science.

Giddens, A. (1979). *Central problems in social theory: Action, structure and contradiction in social analysis.* London: The Macmillan Press Ltd.

Giddens, A. (1984). *The constitution of society: Outline of the theory of structuration.* Cambridge: Polity Press.

Gillett, G., & Harré, R. (1994). *The discursive mind.* Thousand Oaks: Sage Publications.

Gonzalez Rodriguez, Y.E., & Sjostrom, B.R. (1998). Critical reflection for professional development: A comparative study of nontraditional adult and traditional student teachers. *Journal of Teacher Education, 49* (3), 177 (10). Retrieved March 30, 2000 from http://web7.infotrac.galegroup.co..._A2064699&bkm_207?sw_aep=monash

Greenwood, J. (1998). The role of reflection in single and double loop learning. *Journal of Advanced Nursing, 27* (5), 1048-1053. Retrieved April 6, 2000 from http://www.gilbert.cc.monash.edu.au....1+Text&D=nursing&S=NHNDEPCPFPALBP

Gustafsson, C. & Fagerberg, I. (2004). Reflection, the way to professional development? *Journal of Clinical Nursing, 13* (3), 271-280.

Habermas, J. (1976). *Communication and the evolution of society* (T. McCarthy, Trans. 1979). Toronto, Canada: Beacon Press.

Hanfmann, E., & Vakar, G. (Eds.) (1962). *Thought and language: L.S. Vygotsky.* Cambridge: Massachusetts Institute of Technology.

Harré, R. (Ed.). (1976). *Life sentences: Aspects of the social role of language.* London: John Wiley & Sons.

Harré, R. (1983). *Personal being: A theory for individual psychology.* Oxford: Basil Blackwell Publisher Limited.

Harré, R., & van Langenhove, L. (1991). Varieties of positioning. *Journal for the Theory of Social Behaviour, 21* (4), 393-407.

Harré, R. (2002). Public sources of the personal mind; Social constructionism in context. *Theory & Psychology, 12* (5), 611-623

Harré, R. (2005). Positioning and the discursive of categories. *Psychopathology, 38,* 185-188.

Harré, R., & van Langenhove, L. (1999a). The dynamics of social episodes. In R. Harré & L. van Langenhove (Eds.), *Positioning theory: Moral contexts of intentional action* (pp. 1-13). Oxford: Blackwell Publishers Ltd.

Harré, R., & van Langenhove, L. (1999b). Reflexive positioning: Autobiography. In R. Harré & L. van Langenhove (Eds.), *Positioning theory: Moral contexts of intentional action* (pp. 60-73). Oxford: Blackwell Publishers Ltd.

Harré, R., & van Langenhove, L. (1999c). Epilogue: Further opportunities. In R. Harré & L. van Langenhove (Eds.), *Positioning theory: Moral contexts of intentional action* (pp. 195-199). Oxford: Blackwell Publishers Ltd.

Hatch, M.J. (1997). *Organization theory: Modern symbolic and postmodern perspectives.* Oxford: Oxford University Press.

Hatton, N., & Smith, D. (1995). Reflection in teacher education: Towards definition and implementation. *Teacher & Teacher Education, 11* (1), 33-49.

Heath, H. (1998). Reflections and patterns of knowing in nursing. *Journal of Advanced Nursing, 27* (5), 1054-1059. Retrieved April 6, 2000 from http://www-gilbert.cc.monash.edu...1+Text&D+nursing&S=NHNDEPCPFPALBP

Howie, D. (1999). Preparing for positive positioning. In R. Harré & L. van Langenhove (Eds.), *Positioning theory: Moral contexts of intentional action* (pp. 53-59). Oxford: Blackwell Publishers Ltd.

Howie, D., & Peters, M. (1996). Positioning theory: Vygotsky, Wittgenstein and social constructionist psychology. *Journal for the Theory of Social Behaviour, 26* (1), 51-64.

Johanson, R., Newburn, M., & Macfarlane, A. (2002, April 13,). Has the medicalisation of childbirth gone too far? *BMJ, 324,* 892-895.

Johns, C. (1998). Illuminating the transformative potential of guided reflection. In C. Johns & D. Freshwater (Eds.), *Transforming nursing through reflective practice* (pp. 78-90). Oxford: Blackwell Science.

Johnston, M., & Kerper, R. (1996). Positioning ourselves: Parity and power in collaborative work. *Curriculum Inquiry, 26* (10, 5-24.

Kanter, R.M. (1981). Women and the structure of organizations: Explorations in theory and behavior. In O. Grusky & G.A. Miller (Eds.), *The sociology of organizations: Basic studies,* (2nd ed., pp. 395-424). New York: The Free Press.

Kemmis, S. (1985). Action research and the politics of reflection. In D. Boud, R. Keogh, & D. Walker (Eds.), *Reflection: Turning experience into learning* (pp. 85-90). London: Kogan Page.

Knights, S. (1985). Reflection and learning: the importance of a listener. In D. Boud, R. Keogh, & D. Walker (Eds.), *Reflection: Turning experience into learning* (pp. 85-90). London: Kogan Page.

Koch, T. (1998). Story telling: Is it really research? *Journal of Advanced Nursing, 28* (6), 1182-1190.

Kuiper, A. & Pesut, D.J. (2004). Promoting cognitive and metacognitive reflective reasoning skills in nursing practice: self-regulated learning theory. *Journal of Advanced Nursing, 45,* (4), 381-391. Retrieved July 16, 2004 from http://ejournals.ebsco.com/Articles.asp? ContributionID=5662945

Langer, M.M. (1989). *Merleau-Ponty's phenomenology of perception: A guide and commentary.* Tallahassee: The Florida State University Press.

Lineham, C. & McCarthy, J. (2000). Positioning in practice: Understanding participation in the social world. *Journal for the Theory of Social Behaviour, 30* (40, 435-453.

Lukinsky, J. (1990). Reflective withdrawal through journal writing. In J. Mezirow and Associates, *Fostering critical reflection in adulthood: A guide to transformative and emancipator learning* (pp. 213-234). San Francisco: Jossey-Bass Publishers.

Lumby, J. (1998). Transforming nursing through reflective practice. In C. Johns & D. Freshwater (Eds.), *Transforming nursing through reflective practice* (pp. 91-103). Oxford: Blackwell Science.

McKenzie, P.J., & Carey, R.F. (2002). "What's wrong with that woman?" – Positioning theory and information-seeking behavior. Dimensions of a global information science. *Canadian Association for Information Science Proceedings of the 28th Annual Conference.* Retrieved August 27, 2000 from http://www.slis.ualberta.ca/ cais2000/ mckenzie.htm

Magnussen Ironside, P. (1999). Thinking in nursing education. Part1. A student's experience learning to think. *Nursing and health care perspectives, 20* (5), 238. Retrieved April 6, 2000 from http://web2.infotrac.galegroup.co..._A57042247bkm_16_5?sw_aep=monash

Mezirow, J. (1991). *Transformative dimensions of adult learning.* San Francisco: Jossey-Bass Publishers.

Mezirow, J. (1994). Understanding transformative theory. *Adults Education Quarterly, 4* (4), 222-232.

Mezirow, J. (1996). Contemporary paradigms of learning. *Adult Education Quarterly, 46*(3), 158-173.

Mezirow, J. (1998). On critical reflection. *Adult Education Quarterly, 48* (3), 185-198.

Moghaddam, F.M. (1999). Reflexive positioning: Culture and private discourse. In R. Harré & L. van Langenhove (Eds.), *Positioning theory: Moral contexts of intentional action* (pp. 74-86). Oxford: Blackwell Publishers Ltd.

Paterson, B.L. (1995). Developing and maintaining reflection in clinical journals. *Nurse Education Today, 15,* 211-220.

Phillips, D. (2002). *A discursive model of professional identify formation and cultural agency in midwifery education: A framework to guide practice and research.* Unpublished doctoral thesis.

Phillips, D., Fawns, R. & Hayes, B. (2002). From personal reflection to social positioning: The development of a transformational model of professional education in midwifery. *Nursing Inquiry, 9,* 239-249.

Phillips, D. & Hayes, B. (2006). Moving towards a model of professional identity formation in midwifery through conversations and positioning theory. *Australian Journal of Adult Learning, 46* (2), 224-242.

Phillips, D. & Morrow, J. (2008). Reflective practice in postgraduate midwifery education. *British Journal of Midwifery, 16* (7), 463-467.

Polanyi, M. (1958). *Personal knowledge: Towards a post-critical philosophy.* London: Routledge and Kogan Paul Limited.

Ratner, C. (2000). Agency and culture. *Journal for the Theory of Social Behaviour, 30* (4), 413-434.

Rich, A., & Parker, D.L. (1995). Reflection and critical incident analysis: Ethical and moral implications of their use within nursing and midwifery education. *Journal of Advanced Nursing, 22* (6), 1050-1057. Retrieved March 23, 2000 from http:www_gilbert.cc. monash.edu....ull+Text&D=ncall&S=NHNDEPCPHPADBP

Rolfe, G. (1998).Beyond expertise: Reflective and reflexive nursing practice. In C. Johns & D. Freshwater (Eds.), *Transforming nursing through reflective practice* (pp. 21-31). Oxford: Blackwell Science.

Ross, B. (1991). Towards a framework for problem-based curricula. In D. Boud & G. Feletti (Eds.). *The challenge of problem based learning* (pp. 34-41). London: Kogan Page.

Sabat, S., & Harré, R. (1999). Positioning and the recovery of social identity. In R. Harré & L. van Langenhove (Eds.), *Positioning theory: Moral contexts of intentional action* (pp. 87-101). Oxford: Blackwell Publishers Ltd.

Schön, D. (1983). *The reflective practitioner: How professionals think in action.* England: Ashgate Publishing Limited.

Schön, D. (1988). *Educating the reflective practitioner: Toward a new design for teaching and learning in the profession.* San Francisco: Jossey-*Bass Publi*shers.

Schön, D. (1991). *The reflective practitioner: How professionals think in action.* England: Ashgate Publishing Limited.

Shulman, L.S. (1987). Knowledge and teaching: Foundations of the new reform. *Harvard Educational Review, 52* (1), 1-22.

Shulman, L.S. (1998). Theory, practice, and the education of professionals (John Dewey: The Chicago Years). *The Elementary School Journal, 98* (5), 511. Retrieved March 22, 2000 from http://web2.infotrac.galegroup.co...!xrn_15_0_A20903584?sw_aep=monash

Silverman, H.J. (Ed.). (1991). *Continental philosophy 1V: Gadamer and hermeneutics.* New York: Routledge.

Smith, A. (1998). Learning about reflection. [Issues and innovations in nursing education]. *Journal of Advanced Nursing, 28* (4), 891-898. Retrieved April 6, 2000 from http://www-gilbert.cc.monash.edu....1=Text7D=nursing&S=NHNDEPCPFPALBP

Sockett, H. (1993). *The moral base for teacher professionalism.* New York: Columbia University.

Stake, R. (1995). *The art of case study research.* Thousand Oaks, California: Sage publications.

Tan, S.L., & Moghaddam, F.M. (1995). Reflexive positioning and culture. *Journal for the Theory of Social Behaviour, 25* 94), 387-400.

Tan, S.L., & Moghaddam, F.M. (1999). Positioning in intergroup relations. In R. Harré & L. van Langenhove (Eds.), *Positioning theory: Moral contexts of intentional action* (pp. 178-194). Oxford: Blackwell Publishers Ltd.

Taylor, B. (1998). Locating a phenomenological perspective of reflective nursing and midwifery practice by contrasting interpretive and critical reflection. In C. Johns & D. Freshwater (Eds.), *Transforming nursing through reflective practice* (pp. 134-150). Oxford: Blackwell Science.

Taylor, B. (2000). *Reflective practice: A guide for nurses and midwives.* St. Leonards, New South Wales: Allen and Allen.

Taylor, B.J. (2006). *Reflective practice: A guide for nurses and midwives.* (2nd ed). Maidenhead, Berkshire, England: Open University Press.

Thompson, C., & Rebeschi, L.M. (1999). Critical thinking skills of baccalaureate nursing students at program entry and exits. *Nursing and Health Care Perspectives, 20* (5), 248. Retrieved March 30, 2000 from http://web7.infotrac.galegroup.co...7!xrn_4_ A57042249/sw_aep=monash

van Langenhove, L., & Bertolink, R. (1999).Positioning and assessment of technology. In R. Harré & L. van Langenhove (Eds.), *Positioning theory: Moral contexts of intentional action* (pp. 116-126). Oxford: Blackwell Publishers Ltd.

van Langenhove, L., & Harré, R. (1994). Cultural stereotypes and positioning theory. *Journal for the Theory of Social Behaviour, 24* 94), 359-372.

van Langenhove, L., & Harré, R. (1999a). Introducing positioning theory. In R. Harré & L. van Langenhove (Eds.), *Positioning theory: Moral contexts of intentional action* (pp. 14-31). Oxford: Blackwell Publishers Ltd.

van Langenhove, L., & Harré, R. (1999b). Positioning as the production and use of stereotypes. In R. Harré & L. van Langenhove (Eds.), *Positioning theory: Moral contexts of intentional action* (pp. 127- 137). Oxford: Blackwell Publishers Ltd.

Van Manen, M. (1994). Pedagogy, virtue, and narrative identity in teaching. *Curriculum Inquiry, 24* (2), 135-170.

Walker, D. (1985). Writing and reflection. In D. Boud, R. Keogh, & D. Walker (Eds.), *Reflection: Turning experience into learning* (pp. 52-68). London: Kogan Page.

Watson, J. (1998). A meta-reflection on reflective practice and caring theory. In C. Johns & D. Freshwater (Eds.), *Transforming nursing through reflective practice* (pp. 214-219). Oxford: Blackwell Science.

Wellington, B., & Austin, P. (1996). Orientations to reflective practice. *Educational Research, 38* (3), 307-316.

Winslade, J.M. (2005). Utilising discursive positioning in counseling. *British Journal of Guidance & Counselling, 33* (3), 351-364.

Yost, D.S., Sentner, S.M., & Forlenza-Bailey, A. (2000). An examination of the construct of critical reflection: Implications for teacher education programming in the 21st century. *Journal of Teacher Education, 5* (1), 39. Retreived March 30, 2000 from http://web7.infotrac.galegroup.co...0_A59125227&bkm_3_?sw_aep=monash

In: Social Development
Editor: Lynda R. Elling

ISBN: 978-1-60741-612-8
© 2009 Nova Science Publishers, Inc.

Chapter 2

DEVELOPMENT OF NORTHERN IRISH CATHOLIC AND PALESTINIAN MUSLIM NATIONAL IDENTITIES AND THE ROLE OF COMMON HISTORIES

Stephen Vertigans
Robert Gordon University
Aberdeen, UK

ABSTRACT

In this paper, comparative analysis of the processes behind the social development of Catholic and Muslim nationalist identities in Northern Ireland and the Palestinian territories respectively is undertaken. This is designed to try to enhance levels of understanding about the maintenance and duration of nationalist conflicts and ultimately the likelihood of resolution. Particular attention is placed on the social processes that recreate and reinforce 'common histories' and religio-nationalist identities. Important commonalities are identified including the role of historical memories, religious institutions, education, family members and peers in transmitting messages and images about the 'other' and physical divides that collectively contribute to geographical and social demarcation.

INTRODUCTION

Considerable research has been undertaken into the multifarious religious, historical, economic and political reasons behind the nationalisation of Northern Irish Catholics and Palestinian Muslims. Comparative analysis between the social processes through which their collective identities develop and are internalised have been neglected. This paper seeks to contribute to addressing this neglect by examining the social development of religio-nationalist identities and the interwoven 'common histories.' Particular attention is placed upon processes that result in the social development and transmission of historical memories and the roles of religious institutions, schools, family members and peers in connecting with the past, explaining the present and providing solutions for the future. To establish the significance of history, the paper examines the evolution of the conflicts. There is not the scope to undertake this exploration in depth; instead a brief review of the major developments which have remained instrumental or became repositioned within modern settings is provided. More detailed readings are recommended for any reader wishing to gain a more thorough knowledge. Catholic and Muslim experiences in Northern Ireland and the Palestinian territories respectively, are explored throughout. Important commonalities are identified, including the role of similar socialising agents in transmitting messages and images about the 'other', physical divides that collectively contribute to geographical and social demarcation and the impact of 'legitimising' factors. Yet despite these similarities, the peace process in Northern Ireland has become widely accepted within the province while few are confident that the conflict over the Palestinian territories will be resolved in the foreseeable future. Developing upon the preceding points, the paper concludes by identifying the significant differences in the social development of common identities and feelings of belonging that have been instrumental in these different outcomes.

THE DEVELOPMENT OF NATIONAL IDENTITIES

Without wishing to engage heavily in the primordialist[1] and modernist[2] debate, this section aims to explore the development of Western societies, nationalism and subsequently other nation-states. The modern nation-state is strongly associated with industrial modernisation and the associated processes of technological advancement, growth of commerce, urbanisation, rapid expansion of bureaucracy, the division of labour and increased literacy. Modernists like, Anderson (2006), argue the development of 'print capitalism' was instrumental in 'national consciousness.' However if printed material was to become so influential, it had to be accompanied with growing rates of literacy, which required educational programmes. Through the widespread introduction of schools' curricula and other forms of socialisation, national identity was diffused throughout the designated region (Halliday 2000). Crucially, for modernists, despite the modern nature of national identities, these forms of consciousness share a sense of collective belonging that is connected to the past. The extent to which this past is mythologized is part of the debate within the studies of nationalism, but for the purposes of this chapter the accuracy is secondary. For this study, the primary importance is allocated to the W.I. Thomas (1928) maxim, if people think a situation is real then it is real in its consequences. This study is much more concerned with the processes through which people connect with 'historical memories' rather than their accuracy and extent of selection, reformulation and fabrication. Nevertheless there is considerable evidence to suggest that the events that are described occurred; the precision of the interpretations and their significance maybe somewhat more contested. Across the debate within nationalist studies, it is generally agreed that collective consciousness around a 'nation' was solidified through symbols and narratives with the printed history of the nation which connected the past and present, the living and dead, around discrete parameters. For

---

[1] Primordialism is most commonly associated with Shils (1957) and Geertz (1963).

[2] Anderson (2006) is the foremost proponent of the modernist approach. A discussion of the academic struggle over the origins of nationalism can be found within (Guibernau 2004, Halliday 2000, Smith 1991, 2003) Vertigans (2009)

Smith (2003) these interconnections are essential: people's perceptions of the past are instrumental to them understanding the present. If perceptions are to be widely shared and part of a collective consciousness, a common history is required that revolves around memories of battles, poets, heroes and heroines, and very often a 'Golden Age'. This is a period that is considered to consist of culture, religion, moral purpose and knowledge which are drawn upon in the present. For groups encountering oppression or division, these connections to 'historical memories' are crucial and can be noticed in nationalist attempts to generate popular support for independence by emphasising a cultural legacy, national characteristics and associated territory (Dieckhoff 2005).

Because of the strong association between nationalism and Western modernity, there is a tendency to only categorise secular groups as nationalists, even though there are innumerable examples of religious organisations who share common consciousness around the concept of a 'nation' with defined boundaries. Religio nationalist groups are also proficient at connecting with the past with the intended additional benefit of theological justification. For example, militant Islamic groups emphasise the origins of Islam and the activities and rhetoric of Muhammed and the four *caliphs* and their consequences when the religion quickly developed to become the dominant regional power. Contrary to McCrone (1998, discussed below) militants tend to emphasise the primacy of their designated discourse, and to which other loyalties e.g. family, gender, socio-economic, should be subsumed (Vertigans 2009).

Looked at from this perspective, Catholic and Islamic nationalism or transnationalism discourse associated with 'al-Qa'ida' provides a sense of identity around an 'imagined community' that places emphasis upon shared similarity and distinctions from others. By implication, emphasis upon similarities as the basis for collective solidarity excludes the different 'other,' people, groups and 'nations' that do not possess the requisite characteristics. As Mennell (2007: 40) suggests, 'the intellectual and emotional construction of a group's "we-image" and "we-feelings" always takes place in tandem with the construction of a "they-image" about some other group or groups of people, and with the development of feelings about them.' This process is also accompanied by explicit denunciation of the 'other', whether Jews, Protestants, Israelis, Westerners or 'Brits' or even moderate nationalists or Muslims. Yet this behaviour is consistent with, and shares similarities to the historical involvement of earlier, applications of their discourse within struggles against colonial control.

At this point, it should be emphasised that the national identities are not simply a consequence of the application of history to the present day. On the contrary, nationalism has to connect with contemporary experiences. Consequently collective loyalties that are prominent today within Palestinian and Northern Irish religious and nationalist groups are partly a consequence of recent developments within societies, international relations and processes of globalisation. Socialisation processes, for example through peers and the media, are utilised by groups to try to shift levels of allegiance and belief and often embed the heroes and sacrifices of the 'Golden Age' within contemporary discourse. Nevertheless despite considerable efforts to integrate nationalist loyalties, identities remain diverse. This is not unusual. McCrone (1998: 183) suggests that 'the power of nationalism in the modern world lies in its capacity to reconfigure personal identities and loyalties in a way more in tune with the social, cultural and political realities... .' But this is not to state that nationalism is inevitably the paramount form of identity. Instead McCrone acknowledges that nationalism may not have priority over multiple identities and other forms of social identity like socio-economic class or gender.

Within both Northern Ireland and the Palestinian territories, and it should be stressed, other parts of the world, people hold a multitude of beliefs and loyalties with different forms of behaviour that can overlap and yet be distinctive. For example, in both regions people belong to a range of collectivities, including religious, ethnic, national, gender and socio-economic. There is, as Todd et al. (2006: 329) remark with regards to Northern Ireland, a complex national identity that incorporates hybridity and fluidity in identification. Some individuals have internalised values that support the use of violence on behalf of a struggle for independence. Examples in the case studies include the republican IRA and INLA and loyalist UVF and UFF in Northern Ireland[3] and to varying degrees, Hamas, Islamic Jihad and Fatah in the Palestinian territories.[4] In this sense, members of opposing groups may share views about the justification of violence and willingness to undertaken activities. Others within the same regions have abhorred acts of violence committed, the protagonists argue, on behalf of their community. Yet despite these differences it is being argued that people within the communities share common norms and values that provide them with a collective sense of identity and often part of a broader movement.[5] Such people will also be differentiated through other collective groupings to which they belong and possibly disagree over aspects of group members' identities. Through different forms of communication, shared activities and spatiality, commonalities and feelings of belonging develop and are transmitted across generations that revolve around existing characteristics, namely a combination of religious, ethnic and national loyalties. For the purposes of this study, across Catholics in Northern Ireland and Muslims in the Palestinian territories, there are shared, whether real or imagined, allegiances based upon aspects of religion, ethnicity, nationalism and/or encounters that contribute to feelings about who people are as individuals and groups. Such a collective framework for identification is meaningful to its members, providing reference points that are the basis for distinguishing between people who share these values and 'others' who do not. And the classifications frequently exaggerate both 'flattering' similarities between members and derogatory and distinctive characteristics of 'others'. Barth (1969, 1981) develops the significance of this for ethnic identities, suggesting that messages about identity have to be accepted by both individual and 'significant others'. And on the reverse of this identification,

---

[3] Republican groups are defined as those that used violence in order to achieve a united Ireland, loyalists are organisations using violence to prevent a united Ireland and generally to remain part of the United Kingdom.

[4] Both Hamas and Islamic Jihad are associated with militant forms of Islam. Hamas is currently the elected 'governing' party within the territories, although power tends to be concentrated within the Gaza Strip, and has a military wing, the al-Qassam Brigades. Islamic Jihad tends to concentrate upon military activities. The Fatah Party, until recently the dominant party, is more secular, placing greater emphasis upon more secular forms of nationalism (Frisch 2005). Nevertheless the party is associated with the al-Aqsa Brigade which Cunningham (2003) and Saikal (2003) note, utilises Islamic rhetoric and symbols, thereby blurring the religious/secular divide. Further details can be found in Abu-Amr (1994), Esposito (2002), Tamimi (2007) and Vertigans (2008).

[5] Within the Palestinian territories, the struggle for independence is increasingly associated with Islam, albeit with differing interpretations and practice, often broken down by allegiance to the political parties and groups discussed in footnote 4. In Northern Ireland, there have been two distinct broad, opposing movements. The Unionists generally seek to retain the status of the province as part of the United Kingdom and are overwhelmingly Protestant. Across the spectrum of Unionism, most people do not use violence but the more extreme level would include loyalists. By comparison, nationalists seek a unified Ireland and are predominantly Catholic. Again most people have not used violence but the broader movement includes republicans who share similar goals with different means of attaining them.

Cohen (1986) argues that groups are also categorised by 'outsiders' which contributes to a strengthening of boundaries and inner loyalties and external distancing. Therefore, as will be discussed later, how the group is considered and categorising by the 'other' will impact upon collective identities.

In demarcated territories, mutual identifications, categorisations and reinforcements are quickly apparent within physical and psychological barriers. Within these environments, history, which is always embedded within collective memories, becomes even more significant. As Jenkins (2004: 26) elucidates, 'the past is a particularly important resource upon which to draw in interpreting the here and now and forecasting the future.' In situations where that history is associated with 'grave injustice' narratives reverberate throughout environments. Consequently children have been growing up within these communities, immersed within social relations and activities that are embedded with images, symbols and the narrative of collective identities, highlighting common descent, injustices and value orientations. And the criterion for group membership becomes a form of social constraint, heavily influencing individuals' beliefs and behaviour in both their relations within the group and perceptions and interactions with the 'other'. To behave in a manner in which the 'other' was considered the 'same' would challenge the foundations on which the group was based and, without shifting allegiances, would make continued membership difficult and could, in certain situations, result in punishment. This explanatory and experiential framework becomes the basis for individual and collective identification and the categorisation of the 'other'.

Before the social development of these frameworks within the respective regions is outlined, it is important to discuss the approach to identity formation that is being applied. My starting point is that identity forms through social interaction in processes that are both intentional and unintentional. We may wish for children, employees, students or citizens to be responsible, trustworthy, hard working, humane individuals and instigate methods and institutions that are designed to cultivate people with these characteristics. However beyond extreme instances of isolation and incarceration, socialisation can never be completely controlled and no agent irrespective of the extent of their power and authority can prevent interaction with other socialising agents. As Barth (1969) explains, identities are socially constructed during interaction within and across boundaries that are shared with other identities. Nor can any agent precisely determine the extent to which their messages will be internalised by individuals who will interpret the missives alongside those transmitted by family members, friends, work colleagues and the media. And of course, all these messages will also interact with the individual's existing personality and levels of cognition.

Historical Roots of Palestinian and Irish Catholic Collective Identities

Both nationalist struggles are long-standing and considerable research[6] has been undertaken into contributing economic and political factors. There is not the scope in this

---

[6] Important texts include, for Northern Ireland, Bishop and Mallie (1988), Bruce (1992), Coogan (1995), Crawford (2003), Cusack and McDonald (1997), English (2003), McDonald and Cusack (2005), Moloney (2002), Taylor (1998 and 2000), Toolis (1995) and the Palestinian-Israeli conflict, Bregman and Jihan (1998), Cohn-Sherbok and Dawood, (2003), Fraser (2007), Gresh and Vidal (1990), Oren (2002), Said (1994), Smith (2007) and Tessler (1994).

chapter to explore the issues in depth. Instead it is intended to provide enough information about the historical evolution of the conflicts in order to make recent violence and the role of common memories understandable. The analysis commences with Northern Ireland where multiple events have been symbolised, redefined to give meaning to the present, including for nationalists, the plantations, Potato or Great Famine, Bloody Sunday and Hunger Strikes and for unionists, King Billy, the Apprentice Boys and Bloody Friday. In terms of chronology, the struggles in Northern Ireland have the longest historical origins, arguably stemming from the twelfth century when King Henry II of England established control in an area close to Dublin. For the next four centuries, the English sought to impose their rule and by the sixteenth century, this had been achieved over large sections of the island. One area that was not under English control was the northern province of Ulster. To strengthen their dominance over the region, the Plantation of Ulster was introduced in 1609 which encouraged predominantly Protestants from England, Scotland and Wales to migrate. The migrants were attracted by the promise of land with previous Catholic landowners exiled to the mountains or less fertile ground. From this point, the Protestants were competing for limited resources with the indigenous Catholics who were disadvantaged by the implementation of discriminatory penal laws which favoured the migrants (Bishop and Mallie 1988, Coogan 1995). This quickly led to the physical and psychological separation of the two 'communities' which was reinforced by different languages and cultural pastimes. Both sides viewed the 'other' negatively; Catholics, resentful about the loss of their territory, periodically rebelled, while Protestants lived in fear of attack. In 1800 the relationship between Britain and Ireland was formalised in the Act of Union which allocated responsibility for the governing of Ireland to the British Parliament. Despite the ongoing discrimination, most notoriously during the 1840s famine, and early republican groups aiming for independence, including the United Irishmen, the Fenians and Irish Republican Brotherhood, the union remained in place over one hundred years later. Nevertheless it was becoming apparent to the British government that concessions were required in order to quell republicanism. Although these failed to overcome discriminatory practices, Protestants were concerned that their advantages were being threatened and formed their own military groups.

When Home Rule for Ireland was proposed, the island was to be granted its own parliament with the power to govern within the broader British framework. Unionist concerns rose dramatically, resulting in the formation of the Ulster Volunteer Force (UVF) to resist the forecasted Irish independence. However with the intervention of the First World War, the UVF enlisted as a division in the British Army and many of their soldiers were killed, especially during the 1916 Battle of the Somme. In the same year, Sinn Féin, at that time a small republican group, led by Padraig Pearse and James Connolly, seized the General Post Office and declared themselves to be the provisional government of the new republic. The Easter Rising, as it became known, was not widely supported, was badly planned and quickly defeated. A number of republicans were killed and some of the leaders including Pearse and Connolly were executed. At the time Pearse predicted that through their willingness to sacrifice themselves for a united Ireland they would be 'remembered by posterity and blessed by unborn generations' (Bishop and Mallie 1988: 26). This was to prove prescient because the rebellion and the British reaction raised levels of awareness about republicanism and support for Sinn Féin increased. And when general elections were held, after the end of the war, the party won an overwhelming majority of seats in the island and abstained from attending Westminster. Seemingly with a popular mandate, an Irish

Parliament was established and a declaration of independence issued. This was rejected by the British and Irish unionists and between 1919 and 1921 the Anglo-Irish war was fought. Ultimately the war ended in a stalemate and a settlement was agreed that in 1922 portioned Ireland into Northern Ireland and the Irish Free State.[7] The former was to consist of six counties in the north east that were part of the county of Ulster which had previously consisted of nine. By selecting six counties where Protestants were a majority, unlike in the excluded areas, Protestant dominance was guaranteed and Britain retained ultimate control. The remaining 26 counties of the island became part of the republic. Initially the division was not universally accepted by nationalists and a civil war ensued between the Irish government military and the Irish Republican Army (IRA). With limited popular support, the IRA lost and became marginalised within Irish politics. Yet the matter of a unified and independent island was not discarded, indeed there was a widespread belief based in part upon the Government of Ireland Act, passed by the British Government, that an Irish parliament for the whole island would be established.

After partition, the demarcation boundaries promptly became embedded and optimism that a united island could be achieved peacefully began to disappear. The geographical division was also instrumental in the fracture of Irish nationalism. Morag (2008) comments on the different impact of being an overwhelming majority having autonomy to create national identity through state institutions in the 'south' and experiences in the 'north' where people were part of a minority subjected to British and Protestant control. Unsurprisingly in these contexts, very different forms of Irish nationalism developed, with militarism increasingly stemming from the northern counties. The IRA sought to connect to the diminished hopes and organised violent campaigns between the 1920s and 1960s. During the 1930s, the struggle with the republican government which had lingered after the civil war, was formally ended and subsequent campaigns concentrated upon British and Northern Irish targets. Throughout this period, the IRA proved ineffective and after the failure of their Border Campaign (1956-62), the group de-militarised and concentrated upon Marxist ideology and discursive consciousness. The lack of popular support for armed conflict should not however be construed as Catholic popular support for the Northern Irish construct. Catholics remained discriminated against across political representation, employment, housing and human rights. In order to address the rising Catholic protests, which connected into growing awareness of ethnic and egalitarian tensions in other parts of the world, a number of concessions were made by the Northern Ireland government (Bruce 1992, Coogan 1995). Overall, the concessions were part of an approach that had raised Catholic hopes that were not fulfilled, described by Moloney (2002: 53) as 'cosmetic, patronizing, and at times insulting'. Feeling that electoral politicians were not going to deliver structural reforms, many Catholics chose to participate within the burgeoning demonstrations that were to become incorporated within the civil rights movement led by the Northern Irish Civil Rights Association. Conversely, Unionists were fearful about the implications both of the concessions and the mobilisation within NICRA which largely attracted Catholic support despite many Protestants sharing similar experiences. The association of NICRA with sectarianism[8] resulted in confrontation between the demonstrators, the Royal Ulster

---

[7] The Free State was nominally a part of the British Empire until 1949 when it became a Republic.

[8] Contrary to this popular perception, the movement only campaigned on civil rights issues (Disturbance in Northern Ireland).

Constabulary and protesting unionists. Rallies became scenes of violence between the competing groups and spiralled to rioting, intimidation, firebombing and house burning, often engaging children (Cairns 1987). Attacks were particularly venomous in mixed residential areas where the minority group, both Catholic and Protestant, were forced to leave, creating thousands of refugees who relocated to their 'own' communities for security and lack of other alternatives. These experiences were to contribute to the radicalisation of the respective communities, and recruitment to the emerging paramilitary groups increased rapidly (Fairweather et al. 1984, MacDonald 1991, Taylor 1998, 2000).

Levels of violence escalated in part due to developments catching the British government by surprise; a problem that was magnified by the lack of attention that had been placed upon the province. Subsequently this meant that there was inadequate understanding about the nature of the problems and a range of ill-advised policies was introduced that further inflamed the troubles. When British troops were deployed to assist the RUC who were failing to control the violence, it has been well documented that Catholics were supportive, considering the army an important means to achieving peace. This perception was influenced by the relative weakness of the IRA who struggled to react following their disarmament in 1962. Following an internal disagreement over the use of violence, the organisation split into two groups, the Official IRA who wanted to concentrate upon democratic solutions and the Provisional IRA "the Provos" who argued that the armed struggle must be allocated prominence. As the Provos became dominant and the British army was increasingly considered to be invasive and pro-Unionist, feelings changed. Now the Provos were becoming embedded within communities, patrolling streets, leading Martin Meehan, an IRA leader, to declare that the role in defending Catholic areas legitimised the paramilitaries,[9] because 'the whole broad spectrum of nationalist people actually supported what the IRA were doing.'[10] The extent to which the whole community supported the paramilitaries is somewhat contestable. Nevertheless there does appear to be a widespread belief that neither the police nor the army could be relied upon to protect Catholics against loyalist attacks. Therefore the IRA rose in prominence to become viewed as defenders of the community. By comparison, the British military were considered to be part of the problem, unfairly imposing unjust restraints; an obstacle to a united Ireland.

Republican and loyalists sectarian emphasis upon the requirement for defence unsurprisingly contributed to a strengthening of community unity and collective effervescence in the face of fear, threats and attack, arguably in the name of communal protection. At the same time that people like Brendan Hughes were joining the IRA because 'we had to do something to protect ourselves with ... I wanted to be involved too because our whole community felt that we were under attack,'[11] opposing loyalist paramilitaries like William Smith 'believed that if loyalists did not take on that [proactive] role, then eventually the Provos would have their way because the British government would just bow to the pressure.'[12] Thus a vicious circle emerged of attack and retaliation where loyalists felt threatened by the rising numbers of, and activities by, Republican paramilitaries and felt

---

[9] In Northern Ireland, members of the armed groups were called, although by no means universally, 'paramilitaries'. This term is used throughout while acknowledging that for many people, these are 'terrorists'.

[10] Meehan is quoted in Taylor (1998: 74).

[11] Hughes is quoted in Taylor (1998:53).

unable to trust the British army and government which led to more people joining loyalist groups. Concomitantly increasing actions by, and support for, loyalist groups and a deepening distrust and hatred of the British army, contributed to growing recruitment to the IRA. Levels of support grew still further after 'Bloody Sunday' when the British Parachute Regiment shot dead 13 civilians in January 1972. This event became hugely symbolic, with many joining the republicans in the emotive aftermath (Bishop and Mallie 1988, Coogan 1995, Moloney 2002, Taylor 1998). Later that year, the IRA killed nine people in a serious of explosions on what became known as 'Bloody Friday' and was equally influential in the mobilisation of recruits to loyalist groups (Crawford 2003, Cusack and McDonald 1997, Dillon 2004 and McDonald and Cusack 2005). Within this environment, retaliation became the tactic of both sides, although it was not always apparent who had committed the initial attack.

The escalation of violence obviously impacted upon communities and feelings of conflict fatigue became notable. Some among the IRA leadership began to question the effectiveness of the violent campaign and called a truce. During this period, republicans began to negotiate with the British government while the loyalists fearing British concessions continued with their campaign. However the peace talks failed to achieve progress and from 1976 the republicans re-introduced the campaign of violence. 1976 was also notable because of the removal of the 'special status' category of paramilitary prisoners in order to criminalise rather than politicise. Over the longer term, the policy was to be instrumental in the formulation of a new type of republican politics which became prominent during, and particularly in the aftermath of, the Hunger Strikes. Following the changed status, attention shifted away from military operations to the prisons. Republican prisoners imprisoned after the policy had been introduced, rejected the criminalised status and initially refused to wear prison clothes. Instead the prisoners clothed themselves in blankets, a practice that became known as living 'on the blanket'. The campaign became extended into the 'dirty protest' when republicans prisoners refused to wash and smeared excrement on the walls of their cells. Considerable media and public attention was attracted by these actions which were to gradually diminish. After four years it was decided that a new approach was required and the hunger strikes were introduced. The first strike commenced in 1980 and although it was driven by secular demands, the symbolism of sacrifice and fasting connected with, and interwove, republican and Catholic history (Coulter 1999, Fairweather et al. 1984 and McKeown 2001). On believing that the British government would be making necessary concessions the strike was ended without loss of life. However the concessions failed to materialise and a second fast began in 1981 led by Bobby Sands. Shortly after he first refused food, Frank Maguire, the nationalist MP for Fermanagh-South Tyrone died and there was considerable debate within the republican movement over contesting the vacant seat. Eventually it was agreed to nominate Bobby Sands and to campaign on the prisoners' demands. Sands was duly elected and his victory, alongside the symbolism and sacrifice of the hunger strike, reignited nationalism. In total ten men died in the hunger strike commencing with Sands. His death attracted massive media attention and his funeral was attended by tens of thousands of mourners. However the strike's impact diminished with each death and when nationalist support for them decreased and some families authorised medical attention, in October 1981,

---

[12] Smith is quoted in Taylor (2000: 79).

they were stopped. The prisoners' demands had not been met[13] but by this stage the significance of the strike went way beyond prison boundaries. Impressed by the strikers' dedication and sacrifice, support for the republican movement was energised and many new recruits joined the IRA and INLA (Irish National Liberation Army who were also represented in the strike). In addition to the mobilising of armed members, the strike was also instrumental in the politicisation of the nationalist struggle and the twin track approach of 'armalite and ballot box'. Finally global media coverage was instrumental in internationalising the conflict, arousing awareness and support, especially among Irish Catholic Americans, and increasing criticism of the British approach.

Conversely the roots of peace were firmly planted at this time, although few would have confidently declared this. During the strike, support for loyalist groups had also risen with new members and former paramilitaries rejoining. As Billy Giles, a UVF member, stated, 'Protestants were fearful of what was going to happen... . They feared there was going to be an uprising and they were all going to be slaughtered ... . Many of us who had left, came back.' The opposing paramilitaries continued to engage in their perceived retaliatory actions and the IRA pursued attacks against British targets, including most notoriously in 1984 blowing up the Brighton hotel where the governing Conservative Party were staying. Nevertheless, over time the seemingly endless cycle of violence and lack of any obvious progress contributed to feelings of conflict fatigue. This had a particular impact upon the republicans who were facing more concerted loyalist attacks and effective counter-terror tactics by the British army. Consequently when the Enniskillen bomb detonated prematurely killing civilians and causing widespread Protestant and Catholic anger, the republicans' position had been significantly weakened and they could not rely on uncritical community support for the continuation of the violent struggle. And with the British government also encountering public opposition and a desire to end the conflict, peace talks commenced, initially clandestinely and then openly culminating in the Good Friday Agreement (Taylor 1998). Despite stalemates, tortuously slow progress at times and continuing paramilitary activities, the peace has largely held.

Disputes between Palestinian Muslim, Christian[14] and Jews became prominent in the aftermath of the First World War. Prior to this time period, as Mansfield (1978) points out, the region was not a geographical or political entity with defined borders. Yet before the region became immersed in local, national and international tensions, relations between Arab Muslims, Christians and Jews had been relatively harmonious. Neither religion nor nationalism were prominent sources of conflict, with different religious denominations sharing common identification with a sense of 'Arabness'. However through integrated processes, tensions and national and religio ethnic identities emerged, solidified and became embedded over the first half of the twentieth century and have not improved since.

Demographic data for the period is lacking and studies have tended to rely upon estimates. Before 1914, there was calculated to be 600,000 Arab Muslims and Christians and 60,000 Jews. With the formation of the Zionist movement, led by Theodor Herzl, in the late nineteenth century, the demand for a home in the 'Land of Zion' became pronounced,

---

[13] Gradually and covertly paramilitary prisoners were subsequently granted special privileges that may have satisfied the hunger strikers.

[14] In 2006 there was an estimated 205,000 Palestinian Arab Christians (CIAa and b) or approximately five percent of the population, overwhelmingly concentrated in the West Bank. This paper focuses upon Palestinian Muslims.

although disputed within Judaism. Zionist activities became more noticeable, with Jewish businessmen spending millions of dollars in purchasing land and property, often from Arab and Turkish absentee landlords (Armstrong 2004) and developing communities. Relations between Arabs and Jews deteriorated. At this time, the region was governed by the Ottoman Empire who fought unsuccessfully alongside Germany and Austria-Hungary in the First World War. During the war, the victorious allies put forward three contradictory proposals in the event of the Ottomans being defeated and losing this territory:

1. The 1916 Syke-Picot agreement that was to dismember the Ottoman land. Part of Palestine was to be controlled by the British with the remainder controlled by a joint Allied government;
2. In order to attract Arab support in the war, Britain agreed to support Arab demands for independence;
3. Finally, the 1917 Balfour Declaration introduced the establishment of a 'Jewish national homeland in Palestine' with British backing.

At the end of the war, Britain gained a mandate over Palestine and the wider area, Transjordan, which was to gain independence as Jordan.

In 1918, a British census calculated that there were 700,000 Muslims and 56,000 Jews. Jewish immigration rose and by 1931 stood at 175,000 and surged during the 1930s, partly in reaction to developments in Germany and rising levels of anti-semiticism[15] Gradually reciprocal suspicion and fear of the two increasingly distinctive communities rose and the scale of violence escalated throughout the 1930s and 1940s. To try and resolve the conflict and address humanitarian and moral concerns that arose following the defeat of Germany in the Second World War, a resolution was passed by the United Nations to divide Palestine into two nation-states; Arab and Israeli. The former rejected the proposal which was accepted by the latter and in 1948 an independent state of Israel was declared and the British withdrew. Neighbouring Arab nations, Egypt, Jordan and Syria, under the pretext of saving the Palestinians[16], fought the first war with Israel and lost in 1949. Israel's victory led to an increase in Israeli territory and the end of the proposed Palestinian state with the remaining territory becoming the responsibility of Egypt and Jordan. At this point, 716, 678 Jews lived in what had become Israel compared to 1.3 million Muslims and Christians who lived within the previous Palestinian boundaries of whom over 700,000 were now refugees.[17]

The extent of the Jewish migration is highlighted by Behar (2007) who reports that over 90 per cent of Jews living in Israel at this time were of European origin. And in an interesting comparison, Behar observes that Jews who were living in the Middle East did not have similar experiences to recent European co-religion migrants, like racism, xenophobia and pogroms. In addition, European Zionism was formulated on Eurocentric principles that did not engage with non European Jews. Consequently and somewhat ironically there was a much less developed sense of a national Jewish consciousness in the region that became Israel. Cross cutting loyalties could also be noticed within the majority of 'Arabized-Jews' who lived in other parts of the Middle East, and continued to do so after 1948, although by this

---

[15] Figures provided in Mansfield (1978).

[16] Although there are clear indications that the Arab forces had their own designs on the land.

[17] Reported in Behar (2007).

stage, Arab nationalism was becoming consolidated and embedded with anti-Jewish sentiments.

Following the loss of land and the absorption of the remaining territory, Palestinians initially believed that the international community would be mobilised by the magnitude of the perceived injustice they had encountered. Onus was therefore placed upon other nation-states and agencies rectifying 'the Catastrophe' and restoring the territory and properties to the Palestinians. Additionally expectations were high that the Arab nation-states could resolve the problem, partly of their making, either through military conflict or diplomacy. These hopes were closely intertwined with the increasingly popular Arab nationalism during the 1950s and 1960s. In some respects the restoration of 'Palestine' was subsumed within the broader framework for a unified Arab nation, to be led by the Egyptian leader, Gamal Abdel Nasser. However neither the international community nor Arab governments provided solutions that were acceptable to the Palestinians. Gradually, Palestinians decided that independence could only be achieved by the actions of Palestinians, a process that arguably formally commenced with the formation of Fatah in 1959 and whose founders, including Yasser Arafat, were to subsequently be instrumental in the Palestinian Liberation Organisation (PLO) (Abdallah 2003, Halliday 2002, Saikal 2003). Towards the end of the 1960s the shift in allegiance accelerated through growing dissatisfaction with secular nationalism that stemmed predominantly from the 1967 defeat by Israel of Arab forces from Egypt, Jordan and Syria. At the end of the war, Israel occupied the Sinai Peninsula, the Golan Heights, Gaza and the West Bank, with the latter two areas overwhelmingly occupied by Palestinians and considered part of the Palestinian nation-state in the 1947 intended demarcation. Following Israel's victory, the United Nations passed a resolution calling for peace and the withdrawal of Israel from the land won in the war. Subsequently however prospects for peace, except for a period of optimism in the 1990s have been limited, and influenced by increasingly religious and nationalist political groups, Israel commenced its settlement policy[18] which resulted in property being built for Jews on the disputed territory in Gaza and the West Bank. Confidence in outside forces was further diminished following the peace treaty between Egypt and Israel in 1979 which undermined broader Arab unity on occupied territories.

Perhaps surprisingly, as Tamimi (2007) observes, in the decade after Israel assumed responsibility for the now disputed Palestinian territory, in socio-economic terms, the Palestinian's position, especially in Gaza, improved. Border controls were relatively lax, there were considerable higher paid employment opportunities in Israel and communications and transportation between the two separate Palestinian areas improved. Gradually however through interrelated developments like the introduction of the settlement policy, increased influence of the religio, right-wing in Israeli politics, rising Palestinian radicalism, most noticeable in terror groups like the PFLP, more invasive and restrictive controls and rising community surveillance, tensions became increasingly noticeable.

Since 1967, there have been numerous attempts to attain peace, with the closest following the 1993 Oslo Peace Process. This agreement outlined that in return for the Palestinians recognising Israel as a nation-state, there would be a phased Israeli withdrawal from the territories. The most difficult issues, namely the creation of a Palestinian nation-state, the Jewish settlements in the occupied territories, the rights of refugees, the status of Jerusalem

---

[18] The policy was not formally announced until 1977.

and the distribution of water were to be resolved during a five year interim period. Despite the principles being widely supported by most Palestinians (Oliver and Steinberg 2005, Tamimi 2007) militant groups continued to attack Jewish targets. Simultaneously Jewish radicals were also mobilised by the 'threat of peace' and attacked Muslims[19] and ultimately the Israeli Prime Minister, Yitzhak Rabin, who had been instrumental in the process. The death of Rabin, against a backdrop of rising tensions and volatility on both sides was in many ways the end of the peace process. Subsequent Israeli leaders, Binyamin Netanyahu and Ehud Barak, met with Arafat under American-sponsored talks. However none of these leaders possessed the necessary political support to be able to address the outstanding difficult issues that were now becoming exacerbated by increased violence by Palestinian groups and the Israeli army and ongoing settlement building. Palestinian frustrations were to be more broadly translated into anger and militancy following the controversial visit by Ariel Sharon to the extremely sensitive al-Aqsa/Temple Mount complex, prior to his election as Israeli Prime Minister. Mass demonstrations followed and quickly escalated to the al-Aqsa *intifada*. Unlike the first *intifada* (1987-1993), which was initially a civilian uprising, the second *intifada* was dominated by militants. Violence and not diplomacy became the main method of communication with militants undertaking terror attacks, most prominently suicide bombs and Israel adopting a more militaristic approach and aggressive role for their armed forces. At the time of writing, the latest peace proposal, the 'road map' which provided a timetable for negotiation has been driven off the tracks and a stalemate ensues. The Israeli 'wall' built inside the West Bank for 'security purposes' is arguably proving successful in terms of limiting the number of suicide attacks. However the 'wall' is hugely controversial, not least as further Palestinian land has been claimed by Israel, local populations have been greatly inconvenienced and there is a suspicion that the barrier is part of a longer term strategy to demarcate the West Bank. With conditions deteriorating inside the territories, anger and resentment remain prominent. Furthermore the wall's 'success' is contributing to the loose allegiances that had formed around national Palestinian consciousness fracturing as traditional divides between Gaza and the West Bank, city dwellers, refugees and rural areas re-emerge. In the political arena, this is most noticeable in the violent disputes between Hamas and Fatah supporters and has contributed to a further undermining of national unity with neither group possessing sufficiently broad support in order to address the obstacles to peace.

RELIGION IN THE TERRITORIES

Religion within the Catholic and Muslim communities has become integral to their ethnic nationalism, a main determiner of status and loyalties and dividing factor from the 'other.' Both Islam and Catholicism have been able to evoke senses of the sacred and provide explanations, frameworks of meaning and theological justification for actions. Religious symbols, rituals, doctrinal teachings and organisations are instrumental in processes of ethnic identification. Similarly the prevalence of religion impacts upon the identity formations of Catholics and Muslims and their senses of collective belonging to the Palestinian or Irish "nation". For the Catholics, since reformation religious denomination has been interwoven

---

[19] Prior to the death of Rabin, the most notable attack was undertaken by Baruch Goldstein who killed 29 Muslim worshippers in 1994.

with Irish ethnicity as the main source of demarcation and basis for national identity. For the Palestinians emphasis was also placed upon Arab ethnic identity which has gradually diminished through greater religiosity which is increasingly bound with Palestinian nationalism. In these instances both Sunni[20] Islam and Catholic Christianity and the struggles for independence can be described collectively as forms of 'religio-nationalism'. The religious and ethnic values interconnected within this form of nationalism become, to varying degrees, integral components of supporters and activists' identities, helping to shape their beliefs and behaviour (Vertigans 2008).

As in other parts of Western Europe, sectarianism in Ireland became an integral part of the society following the Reformation but unlike other regions, 'the specific conditions of political and religious movements... resulted in ingrained communal divisions, where the lines of religious division ran almost parallel to political divisions' (Morrow 1995: 153). By the nineteenth century, political divisions had been consolidated according to religious loyalties and today people are inclined to classify themselves according to denomination. Even older children and young adults, whose formative years have largely been more peaceful than other generations over the last 35 years, continue to overwhelmingly identify with being either 'Catholic' or 'Protestant' and around 80 per cent believe that religion will always impact upon how people in Northern Ireland consider each other (Young Life and Times Survey 2004, 2005).

The influence of religion differs within the Catholic and Muslim communities. Catholicism has been a main source of collective identification in Northern Ireland, holding a symbolic role within the 'Troubles' as they are euphemistically called. Arguably the influence of religion upon identities, operating outside the interwoven relationship with nationalism and, impacting upon moral behaviour and political influence, has diminished as part of broader processes of secularisation and the secular nature of Northern Irish society. Yet a close relationship between religion and culture remains. Protestants continue to associate acts of violence by republicans and nationalist symbols with Catholicism whilst Catholics will make similar associations with loyalist attacks and unionist marches (Murray 1995). By comparison, Islam within the Palestinian territories has become more prominent, grounded within versions of history and growing in significance across religious, cultural, economic, legal and political spheres. Religious behaviour and support for political Islam has grown markedly since the 1980s. Today both Hamas, the leading religious organisation, governing party and, widely considered outside the territories, 'terrorist' group, and the more secular Fatah Party, utilise Islam to arouse nationalist support and justify actions.

Contrary to popular perceptions of the region as being one dominated by religious allegiance, arguably religion did not become politicised until the aftermath of Israel's victory in the 1967 war. Within Israel and the Jewish diaspora, many Jews considered the victory to be a sign from God of support for their endeavours and the captured territory, particularly the West Bank, was considered to be part of the biblical Land of Israel. Consequently the success of the secular military became interwoven with historical territory and the 'Golden Age' of Judaism, resulting in the strengthening of religious and nationalist ties. At a pragmatic level, Jews were relocated to the occupied land as part of the settlement programme. In the West Bank, settlements attained significance for political, economic and religious factors. The association with the Land of Israel has become embedded within perceptions of the territory,

---

[20] The overwhelming majority of Palestinian Muslims belong to the Sunni denomination.

particularly amongst the ultra nationalist parties, making discussions about the withdrawal or deconstruction of the settlements hugely emotive. Within the Knesset there is neither the inclination nor authority to challenge this association and withdrawal looks extremely unlikely for the foreseeable future.

For Muslims in the region, the war was also viewed through the prism of religion with very different conclusions drawn. Instead of their actions and political developments being considered to be legitimised by God, for many Muslims the defeat was the opposite: namely, that the humiliating loss proved the moral bankruptcy and inappropriateness of secular Arab nationalism, which was epitomised by the defeated Egyptian leader, Gamal Abdel Nasser. Contrary to the Jewish response, Muslims therefore considered the defeat to be the outcome of the weakness of Islam across Arab societies and concomitant attempts to modernise based upon Western models. The solution was therefore to be found with greater piety and integration of religion within the nation-state and civil society. Thus the 1967 war was to legitimise both Judaism and Islam (Vertigans 2008).

The widespread political shift to greater religiosity was not immediate. Secular structures remained, and largely remain, in place. Policies that were predominantly secular in intention continued to be implemented by Israeli governments and Palestinian movements. For the latter, defeat did not initially result in the same degree of mobilisation of religious sentiments that occurred in neighbouring parts of the Arab Middle East. This is in part because prior to the war, the primary representative of the Palestinians was the secular Palestinian Liberation Organisation (PLO). The PLO had been established by the Arab League in 1964 and was dominated by 'Arabs'. After the 1967 war, younger Palestinians gained control and shifted the emphasis from the now discredited Arab to Palestinian nationalism. Even allowing for this, within these 'secular' groups and Israel, greater reliance was placed upon their respective religions to justify actions and to denounce the 'other.' This political utilisation of the religions connected into, and enhanced, rising levels of religiosity amongst the respective populations.

During the period of the Palestinian Liberation Organisation's (PLO) secular dominance, religious norms, values and practices continued to form the basis for many aspects of personal life and identities. By comparison, towards the latter stages of Yasser Arafat's leadership (1969–2004), secular nationalism associated with Fatah and the then Palestinian Authority (PA) was undermined by a multitude of factors that included the failure of the peace process, and association with corruption, human rights' violations, bureaucratic ineptitude and failing public services.[21] The extension of religion from individual consciousness to political identification happened as people became disillusioned both with the PA's policies and more broadly Arab nationalism. For the first time the conflict with Israel became Islamicised. Today, Hamas is the leading political party in the territories and Islam is central to individual, social and political behaviour. Within militant groups and government justifications of military actions or attempts at recruitment, religion and politics are entwined. Abu-Surur, a leading figure within Hamas, provides a good example of this interrelationship when outlining how Palestinians should 'make our blood cheap for the sake of Allah and out of love for this homeland... in order that Palestine remains Islamic, and be liberated.'[22] People are encouraged to die altruistically for religion and the homeland and egotistically for

---

[21] A more detailed discussion of these points can be found in Abu-Amr (1994), Reuter (2004).

[22] Abu-Suror is quoted in Oliver and Steinberg (2005).

salvation (Pedahzur et al. 2003, Sutton and Vertigans 2005). And this use of religion to mobilise support and justify violence is not restricted to Islamic militant groups like Hamas and Islamic Jihad. For example, Frisch (2005: 398) notes how the main secular party within the Palestinian Authority, Fatah, 'uses religious belief and emotion as a mobilizing tool on behalf of Palestinian nationalist goals... Fatah recognizes the significance of Islam as an important component of the collective identity and culture of Palestinians.' The party is also linked to the al-Aqsa Brigade militant group that emerged during the second intifada. Despite these secular links, the group also utilises Islamic rhetoric and symbols as the basis for resistance (Saikal 2003) and as Cunningham (2003) notes the lines between secularists and Islamists have become blurred.

By comparison Catholicism has been integral within Irish nationalism since the earlier stages of the conflict and the manner in which religious denomination was used to distinguish ethnicity and privilege. Both Catholic and the rival Unionist nationalisms have, as MacLaughlin (2001) has argued, provided real meaning for many 'ordinary people', informing attitudes towards identity, community and work. Kelly and Sinclair (2003) suggest that religious identity provides a strong basis for community or political affiliation. Religion is immersed within versions of Irish history, nationalist discourse and sacramental references with symbols noticeable within loyalist and republican rhetoric and murals. And in one of the most influential events of the Troubles, the republican prisoners' hunger strikes, while ostensibly for secular demands, utilised the symbolism of sacrifice and fasting within nationalist history and Catholicism to enhance support and levels of legitimacy (McKeown 2001, Fairweather et al 1984, O'Malley 1990).

The ongoing impact of religion within Northern Ireland is noticeable within studies of rates for church attendance which is considerably higher than in other parts of the UK.[23] But as Coulter (1999) points out the conflict is not primarily a Holy War as is widely perceived outside Northern Ireland. This is supported by research (Fairweather et al 1984, Toolis 1995, Mitchell 2006) into the perceptions of Protestants and Catholics who report making and remaining friends with the other denomination and stress that the conflict is political and economic and not religious. However as Coulter remarks, the involvement of religion should not be understated. While religion is not the cause of the troubles, 'it has exercised a palpable influence. Religious belief and practice within the six counties have served to promote those secular identities and disputes that form the basis of the "Northern Ireland problem"' (Coulter 1999: 58). And both Catholic and Protestant nationalisms, and the history on which they are based, have utilised religion to provide legitimacy for sectarianism and the reinforcement of nationalist loyalties.

In summary, therefore as McLaughlin et al. (2006: 599) remark with regards to the Northern Irish conflict but which also applies to Palestinian Muslim communal identities, religion acts as 'a socially determined boundary. However religion is only one dimension of the conflict.' The remainder of this chapter concentrates on the other dimensions.

---

[23] A SOL survey (2002) identified that 67 per cent of Catholics attend religious services at least once per week compared to 39 per cent of Protestants. The figures for daily prayer were 58 per cent and 41 per cent respectively.

COMMUNITY RELATIONS

Within working class divided communities in Northern Ireland, the influence of unionist and nationalist groups is immediately apparent. For many children and young adults these communities are where their encounters occur and levels of knowledge about events and other groups with whom they have at best limited contact internalised. Strong networks of inter generations and extended families in areas consolidated by perceived threats of attack add to peoples' attachment and sense of identity embedded within the locality (Connolly and Healy 2004). Spatially, within these communities, opposing British and Irish flags are prominent, streets are decorated in red, white and blue or green, orange and white and murals decorating house gable end walls depict slogans and scenes of mythology, martyrdom, heroes and victory and demonise the 'other' (Dillon 2004, Rolston 1991). Graffiti is also prominent in the Palestinian territories. Particular groups and actions are promoted and rivals, Jews, Israel and the United States denounced (Abu-Amr 1994, Oliver and Steinberg 2005). Violent deaths have become part of common experiences, graphically represented within local cultures that are permeated with the concept of martyrdom. Across the Palestinian territories, suicide bombers posthumously become heroes and heroines, commencing with a public funeral. On walls and lampposts, 'martyr of the month' calendars and pocket sized cards showing images of martyrs are prominent and individuals immortalised within pre attack visually recorded 'living wills' and children's chanting. These rituals of communal affirmation are designed to translate into collective effervescence, to develop and reaffirm collective identifications based both upon the heroism and sacrifice of 'our' heroes' and the brutality and injustices of the 'other'. Such symbolism is therefore strengthening identification with the 'we' community and distance from the 'other'.

There are numerous social consequences to these developments within communities. Over time, ways of thinking and behaving about 'our' communities and the 'other' has become routinised, permeating the local culture and is a major influence upon formative development. There is particular concern over the extent these influences affect the development of children's identity and the challenges this causes to contemporary perceptions of childhood. As Cairns (1987), Connolly and Healy (2004) and Fraser (1974) have shown, these processes have had a significant impact upon both Protestant and Catholic working class children. These children possess negative attitudes and prejudices towards the 'other' and play games depicting localised violence. In the past they frequently progressed to undertaking the activities for real as they become older. Lanclos (2003) notes how children's play provides training that is often applied immediately or in the near future within the environment. Crucially internalisation commences very early in the child's life. Children aged between three and four were discovered by Connolly and Healy (2004: 63) to recognise 'certain cultural events and symbols associated with their own community and are internalising preferences towards these.' The impact of the environments continued throughout childhood resulting in children, particularly boys, identifying strongly with particular paramilitary groups. For these children segregation determined by sectarian categories was considered to be inevitable. And although the children were exposed to new information and encounters and gained greater awareness of historical events and political issues and ideologies as they matured, these tended to be interpreted 'in a way that tends to confirm and explain their existing experiences' (Connolly and Healy 2004: 64).

The socialisation processes of children in the Palestinian territories also develop and reinforce social divisions, demarcations that are arguably even more firmly rooted and rigid than their Northern Irish peers. There are a number of reasons for this. Many children become involved in youth groups associated with militant groups, are playing *Intifada*, fantasizing over their deaths and becoming martyrs. Children are growing up with the constant fear of attack, sharing the sense of incapacitation, with disrupted education and limited career prospects. These conditions result in many children developing post-traumatic stress disorder which can cause severe emotional problems and lead to neuroticism, high risk taking and low self-esteem (Elsarraj 1997, Moughrabi, Post *et al* 2003, Victor 2004). It is also worth noting that important formative stages of today's younger adults occurred when they were children of the first *Intifada* with many participating in stone throwing and demonstrations. Within these environments violence has been normalised. Relationships with Israelis are dominated by perceptions of the conflict with little or no opportunity for Palestinians in the territories to meet Israeli citizens which would help breakdown the stereotypes and ignorance that exist between the two populations.

PHYSICAL DIVISIONS AND BEYOND

Across the two regions, demarcations exist within rural areas, towns and cities, as mentioned above, that create physical separation between communities and contribute to the ethnic religious processes of identification being applied to specific geographic milieu. Spatial divisions of the populations can also be found within particular regions and sub regions reducing opportunities for everyday social contact. Within Northern Ireland, religious denominations are concentrated in particular areas. Catholics are based in parts of Belfast and western parts of the province, and Protestants tend to be located within other areas of Belfast and Antrim, Down and Armagh in the eastern part of the province. Perhaps surprisingly, the physical separation has not reduced markedly since the cessation of violence, exemplified by the existence in 2004 of 26 barriers, 'peace walls.' The barriers are designed to physically divide the two populations with most of the walls being erected after the Good Friday Agreement (McDonald and Cusack 2005). Demarcation is not restricted to geography. On the contrary it continues to extent into childhood friendships and later relationships with the overwhelming majority of marriages in the province being endogamous. Within sporting activities, the denominations tend to engage in different sports, with Catholics associated with Gaelic games and Protestants with cricket, rugby and hockey which are closely connected to British traditions. There are some sports in which both populations participate. Football is the most popular but is riddled with sectarianism with teams divided according to community loyalties and intense rivalry often spilling over into violence that involves not only opposing teams but supporters (Coulter 1999).

Within the Palestinian territories, social relationships between Muslims and Jews are severely restricted, dominated by military/militia or military/civilian interactions with little or no mechanisms for social or cultural interaction. The physical divisions have been rigorously applied across the territories with Jerusalem split according to religious denomination and Jewish settlements heavily fortified. In the Palestinian territories, the restricted mobility across socio-economic categories and heavily concentrated populations means that the middle classes are also closely integrated within the conflict; a point reflected by the high proportion of well educated people who become suicide bombers. And following the collapse of the peace process, the onset of the second *Intifada* in 2000, construction of what is variously called the "separation barrier," "security fence" or "apartheid wall" and concomitant collapse of economic interaction and employment opportunities, mutual contact points between Palestinians and Jews in the territories have further receded. For all the communities involved in both territories, this physical separation has contributed to greater ignorance, 'suspicion, fear and ultimately the potential for sectarian violence' (Murray 1995: 219). After violence became commonplace, siege mentality formed within the communities and created a further rigid division to overcome.

TRANSMITTING RELIGIO-NATIONALISM

Across the respective communities, people have internalised religio-nationalist values and beliefs in conditions that place considerable emphasis upon communal identities and loyalties. With limited geographical mobility, particularly for the poorly educated, peoples' social networks tend to be restricted to their area and consist of religious institutions and family and friends who share similar experiences and life chances (Vertigans 2008). The intensity of these localised networks contributes to the development of strong attachments both to the areas and social relations and conversely maintains de-attachment from the 'other' across generations. The longevity tends to contribute to its legitimacy becoming part of local customs and integral to social identity that emphasises inner group similarity and outer difference. Religion is the most immediate source both of unity and division and is taught most explicitly through religious institutions.

Within the Palestinian territories, the physical landscape is dominated by mosques and associated buildings. After generations of diminishing authority, these religious institutions have an increasingly important socialising role. Buildings, like churches, are meeting places for cultural, political and religious purposes and are integral parts of the social and community infrastructure. Within mosques, collective memories and myths are shared with many *imams* undertaking socialisation, lambasting the West and Israel and advocating the fight for Islam. Hamas and Islamic Jihad both have arrangements in place to recruit members at religious institutions (Burdman 2003). It should however be stressed that many *imams* are not militants and oppose acts of violence. Mosques more generally also have an important role to play within the broad spectrum of religiosity with worship and religious festivals generating bonds of solidarity and symbolism across the territories. They are also environments in which people meet and socialise within an atmosphere of religiosity. Both militant and moderate preachers are therefore contributing to greater range and depth of religiosity within the territories.

Involvement by religious leaders and preachers within the Catholic clergy is by comparison more ambivalent. Protestant unionists[24] tend to consider that 'the Roman Catholic Church...dominates Irish politics and social life,' (Davis 1994: 118). Yet republicans have largely viewed the same institution to be antagonistic to the cause since the nineteenth century

---

[24] The most vitriolic and consistent critic of Catholic clergy has been Ian Paisley. Perhaps most notoriously, in 1972 he claimed that the Roman church was 'drunk with martyrs' blood' (quoted in Davis 1994: 132).

(Davis 1994, Morrow 1995). These differing perspectives highlight the dilemmas that the Roman Catholic hierarchy face within Northern Ireland. Davis (1994) suggests the clergy's engagement with national governments and the nationalist community restricts their options and they cannot be seen to either defend the union with Britain or support a united Ireland. And when exploring the past, ambiguities can be noticed. When under British control, at one level, there was intense pride in the achievements of Catholicism. Nevertheless as Fitzpatrick (1988) remarks, this did not result in inevitable support for nationalism. At a senior level the bishops tended to be extremely conservative and were more concerned about secular nationalism than they were about British governance. Yet contrary to opinions within loyalism and republicanism, employees of the Catholic Church have not responded homogenously to the Troubles. For example, republicanism has been endorsed by some priests. Overall though, sentiments tend to reflect the difficult balancing of opposing interests and criticism has been directed across this spectrum at Republican, loyalist and British army acts of violence,[25] particularly from cardinals, bishops and on occasion Pope John Paul II.

Conversely the Church of Ireland has contributed to the maintenance of sectarianism despite this lack of active support for republicanism and to a lesser extent nationalism. The church's functions, processions and celebrations have tended to be embedded within symbols and procedures, emphasising common religious identities within gatherings, and by extension in Northern Ireland, nationalist. Symbolically Catholicism in Northern Ireland is also strongly associated with dying and mourning processes which are again designed to solidify community ties and loyalties. When the cause of death is violent attack by a member of the 'other' the church becomes integral to the process of mourning, bringing together people under the auspices of God to remember and mourn. And against a conflict and emotive backdrop, through services and collective gatherings, both fear and hostility can be generated, usually unintentionally. As Irvine (1991) MacDonagh (1983) and Morrow (1995) detail, priests share dilemmas and connect with the concerns, experiences and prejudices of congregations but rarely address them. Yet ironically this lack of confrontation has resulted in loyalists arguing that the performance of the last rites on paramilitaries and the reluctance to excommunicate, awards these people implicit Catholic church approval.

Beyond the mosque and church, religion has also permeated other social processes involved in identity formation, commencing with the family. Within the Palestinian territories, children are exposed to Islam from birth, with people 'born Muslim'. Since 1948, there has been widespread support for national liberation which is communicated from adults to children. After religion became more widely practised during the 1980s, children were exposed to greater piety and devotion. Signs of religiosity are more noticeable beyond the growing number of mosques and increased attendance levels. 'Morality squads' have become visible, patrolling the streets and confronting perceived irreligious behaviour, appearance and institutions, for example, places of gambling and alcohol (Oliver and Steinberg 2005). Bearded men and veiled women are much more prominent and religious practices are more noticeable within social relations. Family lives, and the perceived role of women within, have increasingly been influenced by Islamic interpretations and religion provides behavioural frameworks for adults and children. And because Islam has grown in popularity as a political

---

[25] For example, during the 1980 Hunger Strike, Davis (1994) points out that there was support for some of the aims of the strikers but not the methods. This instance highlighted one of the central disputes between the clergy

discourse, there is also considerably more emphasis upon religion beyond individual identity and outside the private sphere. At a practical level this can be noticed in the widespread penetration of Islamic social services and at an extreme political level, through the emergence of groups like Hamas and Islamic Jihad and their association with acts of violence.

Across the territories, the ways in which childhood is penetrated with images, and rhetoric, of violence is striking. Oliver and Steinberg (2005) report on babies and toddlers dressed and photographed as suicide bombers, children marching with 'toy' bomb belts attached to their chests and emotive posters of children in distress facing death and freedom that are widely displayed. These factors have contributed to children being socialised in more radical contexts. Normative levels of religious practice within familial environments have shifted to standards that would previously have been considered immoderate and incorporate strong opposition to the role of Israel and Jews and its perceived contribution to the problems that Islamic believers were encountering. Unsurprisingly enhanced religiosity and associated denigration of the 'other' has permeated familial socialising processes and in many instances has resulted in various family members recruiting relations to be suicide bombers (Victor 2004).

A number of studies have highlighted how Irish history and sense of 'Irishness' interwoven with Catholicism and cultural values are transmitted across generations by families. These processes help to perpetuate and reinforce hostility against the 'other' (Fairweather 1984, MacDonald 1991). It is the family that first introduces children to Catholicism and often this introduction also includes discussion about Protestants. A Young Life and Times Survey (2004) showed that the family was the most important source of information about the 'other' religious community. Different studies discovered that family members have introduced children to the Troubles in a prejudicial manner, teaching them negative aspects of the religious 'other' and encouraging sectarianism. A number of young people have recalled how their parents encouraged them to participate in riots and petrol bombings, for example, 'My father told me stories of when he was younger he bricked da prods (British] now it has passed down through the generation to me and my brothers and sisters' (McLaughlin et al. 2006: 610).[26] Within these conflict areas, McLaughlin et al. (2006: 611) suggest that the inter-generational transmission of 'opinions and beliefs was often construed as a form of protection and aimed at maximizing family safety and security.' Taylor and Quayle (1994: 42) remark that 'the family connections that emerge when discussing terrorist organisations are considerable.' This is borne out when examining the republican linage of the prominent paramilitaries of the Troubles, particularly within the IRA with the parents and grandparents of many being involved in previous IRA military campaigns and the Anglo-Irish war. Gerry McGeough, a convicted IRA member, provides an illuminative account when describing his childhood where Republican resistance,

> was something which I certainly was very conscious of from a very early age and something which instilled considerable pride in me. The fact was that I was of this Gaelic Irish stock which had for generation after generation resisted foreign rule in our country (quoted in Taylor 1998: 37).

---

and republican movement, namely the willingness of the latter to accept death for the broader social goal while the former emphasise the sacredness of life.

[26] See also Smyth et al (2004).

The significance of extensive family ties is expounded by Taylor and Quayle (1994: 42) who suggest that events carried out within families, often across generations, connect the past with the present. Such events and accompanying narrative can become the cornerstone for legitimising terrorism. 'The present therefore has continuity with the past, and the young person growing in this environment absorbs the ethos of terrorism as part of his early socialisation.' However transmission of nationalist, religious or republican values and behaviours were not necessarily intended. McLaughlin et al. (2006: 610) report on their research into Catholic adolescent views about religion, ethnicity and group identity. In their study, they discovered that parents were often not deliberately trying to teach their children about religion and ethnicity. Instead 'everyday activities assisted in inadvertently reinforcing difference and division.'

Like the processes of socialisation in non conflict regions, the radicalisation of younger Catholics and Muslims is not simply an intergenerational phenomenon, not least as children are actively involved in the construction of their identities. Post *et al* (2003) discovered that the majority of both secular and Islamic Palestinian 'terrorists' came from families whose levels of activism were average or less. In the study, it was discovered that just over 30 per cent of militant Muslims and 15 per cent of secular 'terrorists' attained similar beliefs from their families. Thus close to 70 per cent of militant Muslims developed their more extreme religious interpretations from other socialising agents. In Northern Ireland, many members originated from families that were apolitical, unsupportive of republicanism and who were subsequently shocked and even horrified when they found out about their relatives' involvement (Dillon 2004, MacDonald 1991, McDonald and Cusack 2005). And in many instances, as McDonald and Cusack (2005) report, in this example with respect to loyalists but which applies also to Catholic and Muslim communities, children can hold more sectarian views than the older generations, in part because unlike their parents and grandparents, they have rarely interacted with the 'other'.

Peer groups are also important socialising agents at various stages of radicalisation. Within these groups, individuals share encounters and discuss events. Peers are also influential within processes of identification and stigmatisation because of the different dynamics that form between individuals of similar ages. Across Muslim and Catholic communities young children play exclusively in the company of their religious and ethnic peers and quickly develop a sense of 'us' and 'them' that connects with familial messages. With little opportunity for less insular and more integrative interactions, this distinction becomes reinforced by other agencies like education and the media as the child matures. Social loyalties become associated with religious divisions and interactions within groups encourage conformity to sectarianism. For example, Ewart et al's (2004) study of Northern Ireland's young people identified that sectarianism resulted in them having 'restricted social spaces' with limited opportunities to develop cross community friendships. Peer pressure was also instrumental in the participation of sectarian behaviour and the formation of same-religion friendships. Decisions to join clubs, societies, cults and even 'terrorist' organisations can also be influenced by peers. Recruitment into Palestinian 'terror' cells is also strongly influenced by friendship networks, with friends often responsible for introducing individuals into militancy, vouching for their trustworthiness and reliability. For example, Olimpio[27] reports on the Hebron football club that provided eight suicide attackers out of its team of

---

[27] Olimpio's study is discussed in Ricolfi (2006).

eleven players. Attacks on friends by the 'other' have also been important motivating forces behind individual processes of radicalisation through generating feelings of anger, hatred and a desire for revenge.

Imprisonment has also been instrumental in strengthening collective nationalist and religious identities. Abu-Amr's (1994) examination of Palestinian Islamic extremism, including recruitment in prisons and Post *et al*'s (2003) study of prison found that the peer group was of considerable influence in the intensification of religious belief and for some the decision to undertake 'terror' activities. Similarly the imprisonment of republican paramilitaries within Northern Ireland resulted in 'political' prisoners freely associating, with the time and opportunity to discuss and develop political issues and ideologies that may not otherwise have been possible outside. In these environments, loyalties and commitment to the cause were often further strengthened (Adams 1996, Dillon 2004, Taylor 1998).

Educational institutions like schools, adult education centres and libraries across communities are also important in the transmission of religious and associated nationalist norms and values that become integral components of identities, particularly for younger generations. Governments sought to implement secular criteria that needed to be internalised with particular levels of competence achieved and measured through qualifications. These systems of learning would deliver graduates capable of undertaking the required roles that would enable the nation-state to develop. And at the level of the hidden curriculum, they would contribute to the development of modern, rational identities. The internalisation of these forms of knowledge became central to individual progression. McCrone (1998: 47) adds that the main purpose of schooling was to 'imbue pupils with the new patriotism... . This can be seen in the mobilisation of "national" history, geography and the "national curriculum." The continuing, and in the Palestinian territories increasing, influence of religion and opposing ethnic loyalties can be noticed within a range of national school curricula. Smith (2003) identified that within these settings, religion is used to help define and underpin ideas and policies and reinforce national loyalties. In some respects, the intentions connect with Gellner's (1983) view that cultural homogenisation occurs as schools are introduced across territories teaching the dominant language and emphasising national loyalties.

For the two case studies, it is immediately noticeable that the forms of nationalist doctrine that are espoused contradict that of the dominant 'other'. This is because within these settings social boundaries are routinised or institutionalised, overwhelmingly segregated according to religious affiliation and include sectarian images and messages. For example, Burdman's (2003) study into Palestinian children and martyrdom discovered numerous anti-Semitic statements demonising Jews and references to a religious obligation to sacrifice and the fight for 'Palestine' within school literature. When discussing why people joined the first *Intifada* MacDonald (1991: 85) was informed, 'Everyone was angry, especially at school because there we learned that the whole world was free except us.' Some teachers have also been associated with the recruitment of pupils to undertake acts of political violence (Victor 2004). In higher education, many student associations are dominated by militant Muslims and leaflets and posters are widely distributed within campuses. Both lecturers and student movements have central roles in recruiting support amongst their peers in places of higher education like al-Najah University.[28] Radical teachers are employed in private and public

---

[28] Al-Najah University is considered to be the most radical institution, supplying at least 135 suicide bombers between 2000 and 2003 (Victor 2004).

schools and prove instrumental in providing meaning and explanation for religious and Palestinian experiences. Lessons often discuss past and recent events, the superiority of Islam and denunciation of Israel, Jews and the West. At the opposing end of the learning spectrum, Oliver and Steinberg (2005: 60) discuss revolutionary fervour within kindergartens and songs and chants that children are taught that promote violence against America and Israel and identify the Jews as having stolen 'our country.'

Within the Palestinian territories, political parties and religious groups place considerable emphasis on controlled learning. This connects into Islamic groups' emphasis upon *da'wa*, 'a call to God' through preaching and proselytising that seeks to reshape individual consciousness. As part of this remit, Hamas has delivered religious education through mosques, schools, summer camps, evening classes, sports clubs and youth groups as a long-standing integral part of its approach to conflict (Abu-Amr 1994, Esposito 2002, Levitt 2006). For Hamas, *jihad* to attain independence requires 'the propagation of Islamic consciousness among the masses on all local, Arab and Islamic levels... It is necessary to instil in the minds of the Muslim generations that the Palestinian problem is a religious problem and should be dealt with on that basis.' Children are given 'an Islamic education based on the implementation of religious precepts, on the conscientious study of the Book of Allah...' (Hamas 1988). As part of this approach, there is considerable penetration of Islamic learning institutions within the territories. Religion is now prominent across types of learning institution with schools[29] and universities heavily influenced by militants.

Education and the broader schooling experience have also been instrumental in the formation of sectarian identities within Northern Ireland. For Whyte (1986) defining and reproducing ethno-religious demarcations is endemic within the education system. Over the last 30 years, there has been a dramatic increase in opportunities within higher and further education. However within schooling, the demarcations to be found within wider society continue to be replicated and have been prominent within institutions of education since at least the 1820s. And when the island was partitioned, separate schools were established in the north. Each denomination became associated with different sports, music and literature and both the formal and hidden curricula connected explicitly with the respective populations (Coulter 1999, Davis 1994, Gallagher *et al* 2003). Eighty years after partition, these divides remain with 96 per cent of primary educated Protestant children attending a Protestant school and 94 per cent of their Catholic peers attending Catholic schools (reported in Gallagher *et al* 2003).[30]

In Catholic schools pupils are informed, as one respondent told Cañás Bottos and Rougier (2006), 'right from the start: "Catholics are right and Protestants are wrong...[the priests] were very cumbersome, the majority of them and they instilled a fairly anti-British idea.' These schools are 'imbued with a Catholic religious atmosphere and imbibe an Irish nationalist version of history' (Irvine 1991: 193). It is therefore unsurprising that alongside the formal school curriculum Catholicism litany and scripture is espoused. Songs, ballads, dances and stories continue to be performed grounded in nationalist traditions and customs. And at what may initially appear to be a more superficial level, school uniforms are distinctive between the denominations. The significance of this however goes beyond differences in colours or

---

[29] The PA's Ministry of Education estimated that in the Gaza Strip, 65 per cent of educational institutions below secondary level were provided by Islamic institutions (International Crisis Group 2003).

[30] For secondary school attendance the figures were slightly reduced.

design, the uniforms strengthen collective identification and expose individuals to sectarian attacks (Smyth et al 2004). The impact of the curricula within schools is much debated and shares some commonalities with the broader debate about the role of formal education. However in Northern Ireland, Gallagher (1995) argues that irrespective of this wider debate, segregation in schools emphasises group differences and reinforces ignorance and suspicion. It has since been acknowledged that 'unless the children meet and learn about each others' traditions at school, the odds are against a peaceful and secure future in this country' (Integrated Education Fund 2003: 2). In order to achieve this, integrated schools have been introduced. However the policy has struggled, with limited popular appeal and only three per cent of primary school children are attending these institutions.

The last socialising agent to be discussed is the media which has been influential in the development of distinct ethnic religious identities since the development of 'modern' printing forms and the advent of publishing houses. By the middle of the nineteenth century, Donnelly (1980) identifies the roles of Catholic Irish and Ulster British publishing houses and widespread availability of newspapers, pamphlets and books in the development and reinforcement of distinctive identities. During the Troubles, the media has provided images and information and many paramilitaries, particularly republican, have delved into history books to help understand and legitimise their struggles. Today while international types of media are prominent within Northern Ireland, newspapers, magazines and books that are predominantly designed for one of the populations remain popular and widely available. Media sources have also been utilised and owned by paramilitary organisations to communicate with their supporters and to generate greater community support. In addition to the intentional purposes of the media, there is the unintentional consequence of news reporting. Cairns (1987) analysed television news reporting and found that the emphasis on incidents associated with the Troubles led to an over concentration of violent images and terms with inadequate attention placed upon contextualising the items resulting in inflated fears and hatreds. This would not necessarily be problematic if the media was not many children's main source of information about the Troubles (Cairns 1987 and Connolly and Maginn 1999).

Similarly within the Palestinian territories, the media has been influential in identity formation generating support for greater religiosity and nationalist commitment. From the 1990s onwards, advancements in communicative technology have aided the transmission of images, reports and discussions through satellite technology that have mobilised support both within the region and beyond. Today, in addition to more traditional forms of media like newsletters, newspapers and children's magazines, which tend to portray America and Israel negatively (Frisch 2003), militant religious groups also communicate through their own satellite station like Hamas' al-Aqsa television. This is part of an attempt to overcome what is seen as global American and Zionist media control. Radio and television programmes are transmitted that support their religious discourse, providing narrative and images that reinforce the justification for greater religiosity within individual and collective identities and the nationalist struggle. Programmes are aimed at both adults and children, with the latter catered for by specialised programmes, cartoons, songs and music videos that promote violence,[31] the symbolism of childhood martyrdom[32] and glorify suicide bombers (Oliver and Steinberg 2005, Victor 2004). Modern technology has also provided further opportunities to communicate messages, values and through the internet within websites and chat-rooms (Aouragh 2003, Bunt 2003). Through these different methods of communication, Palestinians, like the majority of the world, are now provided with information and graphic images about events and policies that can contribute to the widespread feelings of anger and incapacitation whilst reinforcing religious loyalties and antagonisms (Vertigans 2008).

LEGITIMISING FACTORS

Socialisation processes can be seen to be providing Palestinian Muslims and Catholics in Northern Ireland with religious loyalties that are connected to political and community allegiances and the maintenance of Jewish and Protestant 'others.' However, these processes do not operate in isolation. To be instrumental in the psychological separation between groups, messages and symbols have to be legitimised (Vertigans 2008, 2009). In the Palestinian territories this happens through interpretive knowledge about a combination of historical and recent events. These include at a broader level the formation of Israel, the inability or reluctance of the international community or Arab nations to address concerns diplomatically or through warfare and the failure of secular ideologies to achieve Palestinian liberation and deliver sustainable development in the territories. At an individual level, religious and political messages have been legitimised by personal or friends' experiences including humiliation at omnipresent roadblocks, death, arrest or detention of family members and friends, employment restrictions, malnourishment and poverty and desire for revenge.[33] The cross cutting nature of these issues helps explain the diverse support base[34] for more radical forms of Islam.

Across Catholic communities, religio-nationalist loyalties are legitimised and strengthened within a range of similar similarities in experiences. These include pervasive patrols and partisan military operations, curfews and internment which were often experienced as 'raiding and wrecking homes and precious possessions, dragging children from their beds, abusing women, beating men and boys' (Fairweather *et al* (1984: 15). Because of this emphasis upon the roles of the British army and RUC, nationalists felt their communities to be under siege. In these circumstances in Northern Ireland and elsewhere, solidarity was reinforced as a defensive mechanism and on the reverse, British policy and

---

[31] For example in a Palestinian TV programme recorded on 2 May 2001 the narrator tells seven and eight year old children that 'The time for toys and games is over, throw away your toys, pick up rocks' (quoted in Burdman 2003: 103).

[32] Burdman (2003: 104) draws attention to a clip shown on PATV in 1998 which showed a military camp for children who repeated after the coach 'Children of my country, I am the suicide squad.' The highly sensitive death of Mohammed al Dirrah at the start of the second *intifada*, has also been dramaticized on Palestinian television. In the post death scenes the boy informs his father 'I shall go to my place in heaven, how sweet is the fragrance of the Martyrs'.

[33] Further information about these feelings can be found in Khosrokhavar (2005), Post et al. (2003) and Victor (2004).

[34] For instance the popularity of Hamas is spread across poor areas, municipal and professional associations, chambers of commerce and student associations with leaders including religious officials, professionals and technocrats.

presence was de-legitimised and animosity of the Protestant 'other' enhanced. Donohue (2000) explains that measures like arbitrary detention and the demarcation of a suspected community sustained Catholic grievances, deterred many individuals from assisting the British and contributed to the radicalisation of others. These events and encounters tended to be concentrated within working class zones which were predominantly divided according to denomination. Nevertheless although middle class homes were less likely to encounter such extensive army presence and police tactics, their effects crosscut socio-economic boundaries. The relatively small population and geographical proximity means that most people, irrespective of socio-economic classification, have known people who have been harassed, injured, arrested and in some instances killed and adversely affected by the economic problems and limited employment opportunities that occurred throughout the Troubles. In summary, the mobilisation of support and legitimisation of paramilitary actions and rhetoric, was a consequence of multiple factors that included economic, social, cultural, political and military experiences.

SOCIAL BOUNDARIES FOR PERSONAL EXPERIENCES AND COMMON HISTORIES

Within Northern Ireland and the Palestinian territories, the above analysis identified a range of social processes through which a sense of communal identity formed for the 'excluded' groups. This is not to state that the individuals involved shared the same identity. What they did share was a sense of collective identity based values derived from ethnicity and religion interwoven within a framework of nationalism. In other respects there is considerable difference between individual identification that includes gender, racial, socio-economic, habits, emotions, education and generational loyalties. These allegiances also influence discursive consciousness and have to be negotiated along with national connections and very different perceptions of what that means and how these feelings are to be extended from individual and groups into territories.

Common history across the regions is also widely shared and contested by the 'other'. Indeed interpretations of history can often be traced as the roots for the stigmatisation of the rival group. Elias and Scotson (1965) have outlined how perceptions of the past can be instrumental both in sustaining a sense of group solidarity in the present and the longevity of social and psychological boundaries. By connecting with the past, groups' discourse gains continuity and feelings of shared fate that transcend generations, ensuring that the socially constructed barriers and unifiers continue, in many instances, long after the original cultivators have died. For Elias and Scotson these distinctions became embedded within stereotypes which were used by the powerful 'established' to denigrate the 'outsiders' based around characteristics of 'group disgrace' in order to protect their identities and status and to which could be added resources. 'Outsiders' were all categorised according to the 'minority of the worst' with the behaviour of the least desirable characters applied to the whole group. The reverse of this negative stereotyping, is unsurprisingly positive. The established based their self-perceived superiority upon their common histories and a 'minority of the best' that stemmed from the most highly regarded aspects associated with the group; less desirable features were overlooked. Consequently the 'established' collective identity was based both upon their own identified sources of 'group charisma' and characteristics applied to outsiders who compared unfavourably and which became the basis for their stigmatisation. Gossip was an integral part of these dynamics, reinforcing positive group feelings and negative images about the 'other'. In Elias and Scotson's study of a town in the English midlands the emphasis was upon informal social dynamics between two distinctive groups within the working class. One group 'the villagers' were able to retain a sense of superiority over people who lived in the 'estate' and who in some respects, internalised the 'established' perceptions. Sutton and Vertigans (2005) adapted this explanatory framework to help illuminate some of the processes behind the stigmatisation of radical Muslims but extended the application because it was argued that attempts to create 'group disgrace' can be unsuccessful and often unintentionally contributed to a greater sense of 'group charisma' among 'outsiders'. Some parallels can be drawn with the development of conflict in the two territories.

Both in Northern Ireland and the Palestinian territories, common memories revolve around lost territory, the 'others' aggression, international injustice and hypocrisy and are fused within 'group disgrace' and processes of stigmatisation that are very much based upon the 'minority of the worst'. For the Palestinians, the Israeli Defence Force became representative of Israel. Hass (2003: 151) suggests that 'for this generation, Israel is no more than a subsidiary of an army that knows no limits and settlements that knows no borders.' Similarly for Irish nationalists, loyalist paramilitary and the British army were to exemplify Protestants and the British. The categorisations share a tendency to concentrate upon perceived levels of violence, discrimination and excessive and unwarranted intrusions into lives and communities that arouse emotions which provide further stimuli for collective solidarity and distinctions. The same processes have also been instrumental in creating and strengthening 'outsider' group solidarity and a sense of communal identity frequently around the legacy of 'common history', symbols and cultural ways of life that are considered to be attacked or threatened. By formulating group allegiance in part through comparison with the 'other,' unity is achieved and means that internal differences reduced in magnitude through the emphasis on the 'minority of the best' and minimised by comparison with the "others' minority of the worst." And unlike Elias and Scotson's outsiders, Palestinian Muslims and Northern Irish Catholics have not internalised negative self-images. Instead from positions of weakness with regards to national power, they formulate superior self identification that connects closely to common histories. Even during colonialism, as O'Farrell (1975) remarked, while the English sought to emphasise the alleged inferior, uncivilised barbarity of the Irish Catholics in order to justify their domination, such attempts at stigmatisation tended to fail. On the contrary, Irish Catholics would respond by emphasising their levels of religiosity, scholarship, saints and monasticism. Arguably by challenging British attempts to impose 'group disgrace' the Catholics' 'group charisma' strengthened and became established within nationalist culture. Furthermore this occurred when Ulster became the dominant and prosperous part of pre partition Ireland and Protestants prospered, considerably assisted by discrimination in education, employment and legislation. By comparison, Catholics' resources and positions had both diminished and were underdeveloped. In this context, connections are made with periods when their ethnic and religious group was dominant and events which were emphasised military or moral superiority. Emphasis upon morality and sacrifice is particularly interesting because these are images that are drawn not from episodes that are successful in a military context but as examples of sacrifice and the willingness of group members to give up their lives on behalf of the wider community. An obvious example would be the 1981 hunger strikes in Northern Ireland, discussed above. The deaths reinvigorated the republican movement and as a consequence mobilised massive support for the opposing loyalists whose own interpretations of the event as 'common history' were very different. By focussing upon the reciprocal dynamics that interweave historical and contemporary common memories, the outsider groups are able to establish the markers of identification for their own 'charisma' and the established's 'stigma'. The same processes provide mechanisms through which to understand and explain the perceived injustices and atrocities encountered and help reinforce the processes of collective solidarity and enmity and by extension the prospects for peace. In addition to the experiences of subjugation and perceived injustices, images and narrative of 'Golden Ages' can also be invoked which connect with peoples 'common histories' and which provide the basis for the future.

PROSPECTS FOR PEACE

Within Muslim and Catholic communities, it has been established that religio nationalist identities have been socially constructed through a range of socialising processes that provide the basis for identification. Nevertheless nationalist identities are not immutable or as Todd et al. (2006: 341) point out polarisation and conflict 'is not rooted in a primordial and unchanging ethnicity: it is rather a question of the triggers and resources for identity shift … .' National identities may be rooted individually and socially but within flexible, evolving relations and communities that both enable and constrain. Consequently identities alter through reflexivity and negotiating local, national and international cultural, economic, political and social processes and activities. In other words, shifting figurations within ongoing socialisation can result in changing perceptions of self and common history, levels of national consciousness, group demarcations and commitment to peace. What were once clearly defined and widely accepted boundaries of identification can become blurred and the distance between groups diminishes.

Today, Northern Ireland is slowly progressing along a route to peace. It is extremely unlikely that peace between the Palestinians and Israelis will be achieved for the foreseeable future. Optimism is greater within Northern Ireland, in part because paramilitaries representing both Catholics and Protestants were losing community support, experiencing conflict fatigue and high profile acts of violence were increasingly seen to be counter productive. Neither the Israeli government nor leading Palestinian groups have reached this conclusion. In addition, Northern Irish society is more closely integrated with, and influenced by, the international community, immersed within the European Union and processes of globalisation. Kerr (1996) comments on how the globalisation of culture has impacted on the province, with much music, literature and sporting allegiances originating externally and being shared across the communities. Globalisation has also impacted upon greater integration within employment. Sectarian employers like the ship builders are increasingly disappearing and multi-national organisations locating to the region have no interest in religious loyalties. Consequently these incoming organisations are not making appointments based upon sectarian connections. McLaughlin et al's (2006) study reflects this, identifying that religious identity is no longer considered to be significant in relation to employment or workplace behaviour. Therefore the extent of discriminatory practices within employment has significantly reduced. By comparison, international investment in the Palestinian territories is low, there is little confidence and trust in international political institutions and global cultural representations are increasingly dominated by religious images and symbols. These factors have contributed to feelings of anger, frustration and desperation that exceed the excesses encountered during Northern Ireland's Troubles. These feelings and experiences are allied to increasingly widespread interpretations of Islam that seek to legitimise violence in the cause of Palestinian nationalism with militants extolling the virtues of martyrdom and salvation on behalf of the nation.[35] The growing influence of absolutist forms of Islam makes compromise even harder to attain. Religion is therefore instrumental in the conflict in a way that is not noticeable in Northern Ireland, although Catholicism has contributed to an atmosphere of distinction, separation and maintenance of the collective identities that paramilitaries emerged from and utilised.

The strengthening of religio-national identities within socialising processes in conditions that are seen to justify violence, suggest that the Israeli-Palestinian conflict will not be resolved without major international engagement and shifts in approach both from the Israelis and Palestinians. In Northern Ireland, socio-economics and the political situation have improved yet there are grounds for considerable caution. Sectarianism remains prominent across generations as Leonard's (2006) study of teenagers in Belfast showed. The Peace Agreement has not addressed these processes, indeed on the contrary it has been criticised for providing the two communities with 'autonomy over matters of central concern to their sense of identity ... endorses social segregation ... giving equal legitimacy to "British" and "Irish" cultural identities ... in "separate but equal" terms (Wilford 2001: 60-1). And while McLaughlin et al. (2006) showed that employment practices had changed, religious identity remained instrumental within the individual, familial and group spheres. Mutual processes of stigmatisation have been routinised within everyday life and continue to be communicated daily through gossip and institutions across generations. This is partly because physical separation between communities continues and impressions of the 'other' are based upon 'common histories', indirect relations or the behaviour of the 'minority of the worst'. Yet in both regions demarcations have been recently reinforced by the increase in the 'peace walls' and apartheid/security wall/fence. Segregation across communities, schools and cultural activities are reinforcing exclusivity and difference when inclusion and commonalities are required if peace is to become firmly embedded. Peaceful overtures have to also overcome generations of socialisation processes that provide senses of support and belonging and social barriers. People have internalised a fusion of religion, historical events, images and symbols and recent cultural, political, social and economic experiences and widespread destruction, injuries and killings committed by the 'other'. In other words much greater attention needs to be placed on addressing the social processes that continue to contribute towards the internalisation of fundamentally opposing norms and values across the regions.

---

[35] Discussed in more detail in Khosrokhavar (2005), Vertigans (2008; 2009) and Victor (2004).

CONCLUSION

Recent experiences within Northern Ireland and the Palestinian territories have clearly differed. While the former appears to be on a peace trajectory, the latter remain firmly rooted in conflict. Both territories have concentrated peoples in relatively small geographical areas. In such environments, it is easier to identify and communicate what the people share and how they differ from the 'other' than within huge nation-states or across the world in transnational organisations. Through regular interaction, intermingling and shared experiences and memories, social processes become embedded with narratives and practices and collective identities can be reinforced and sustained. The nature of the related socialising processes is non conformist in comparison with universally recognised nation-states whose socialisation aims for individuals to internalise dominant norms, values and practices on which the stability of societies rely. However in the discussed regions, the outsider processes of identification construe and define beliefs and behaviour that challenge the established status quo while conversely remaining loyal to localised expectations. The legitimacy of this opposition and the breadth of nationalist support are heightened if contemporary experiences connect with 'common history' that helps to construct and constrain experiences and behaviour and the attribution of charisma and stigma. In the process, previous and long lasting accounts of repression and injustice and a lineage of protest and sacrifice are provided that justify the challenge.

Religious institutions, norms, values, behaviour and perceptions are integral to these community loyalties, group unification and the struggle for national independence. Processes commence during childhood with children exposed to deeply rooted beliefs that are communicated by a range of institutions including family, friends, media and schools. Many children have, and continue to, internalise sectarian discursive consciousness because this has been legitimised at a number of levels and remains so throughout adulthood. And because of the pervasive nature of the nationalisms, the level of internalisation of these challenging, if not confrontational, precepts will determine the extent to which the individual will be assimilated within the outsider group. Thus it is only by holding values that would ensure their ostracism from the established that individuals will attain acceptance and a sense of solidarity with outsiders. If peace in Northern Ireland is to become permanent and introduced within the Palestinian territories, groups must become convinced that peaceful political participation is the most appropriate way forward, be willing to negotiate with the support of their communities and in the longer term breakdown the stereotypes of the 'minority of the worst'. In Northern Ireland the first two stages have been reached yet concerns remain about the likelihood of overcoming rigid divides and different common histories when the communities continue to be separate. By comparison, the prospects for peace over the Palestinian territories have regressed with no Israeli or Palestinian political party possessing the popular mandate to be able to resolve the seemingly intractable problems which are further complicated by the increasing religiosity and the inherent difficulties of negotiating over matters through the prism of absolutism. This intractability is further reinforced by the ongoing evidence both sides accumulate about the 'minority of the worst' which strengthens still further their processes of stigmatisation. In other words, the prospects for the Palestinian territories look extremely bleak.

REFERENCES

Abdallah, A.M. (2003). 'Causes of Anti-Americanism in the Arab World: A Socio-Political Perspective', *Middle East Review of International Affairs,* Vol. 7(4) 62-73.

Abu-Amr, Z. (1994). *Islamic Fundamentalism in the West Bank and Gaza.* Indiana University Press, Bloomington.

Adams, G. (1996). *Before the Dawn: An Autobiography.* London: Heinemann.

Aouragh, M. (2003). Cyber Intifada and Palestinian Identity. *International Institute for the Study of Islam in the Modern World.*

Armstrong, K. (2004). *The Battle for God: Fundamentalism in Judaism, Christianity and Islam.* London: Harper Perennial.

Barth, F. (1969). 'Introduction.' In Barth, F. (ed.) *Ethnic Groups and Boundaries: The Social Organisation of Culture Difference.* Oslo: Universitetsforlaget.

Barth, F. (1981). *Process and Form in Social Life: Selected Essays of Frederic Barth, vol. 1.* London: Routledge and Kegan Paul.

Behar, M. (2007). 'Palestine, Arabized Jews and the Elusive Consequences of Jewish and Arab National Formations', *Nationalism and Ethnic Politics* 13, 581-611.

Bishop, P and Mallie, E. (1988). *The Provisional IRA.* London: Corgi.

Bregman, A. and Jihan El-Tahri, (1998). *Israel and the Arabs, An Eyewitness account of War and Peace in the Middle East,* New York: TV Books.

Bruce, S. (1992). *The Red Hand: Protestant Paramilitaries in Northern Ireland.* Oxford: Oxford University Press.

Bunt, G. (2003). *Islam in the Digital Age.* London: Pluto Press.

Burdman, D. (2003). Education, Indoctrination, and Incitement: Palestinian Children on their Way to Martyrdom. *Terrorism and Political Violence.* 15(1): 96-123.

Cairns, E. (1987). *Caught in Crossfire: Children and the Northern Ireland Conflict.* Belfast: Appletree Press Ltd.

Caños Bottos, L. and Rougier, N. (2006). 'Generations on the Border: Changes in Ethno-National Identity in the Irish Border Area', *Nationalism and Ethnic Politics,* 12(3-4): 617-642.

Central Intelligence Agency (CIAa). "The World Factbook: Gaza" https://www.cia.gov/ cia/publications/factbook/geos/gz.html#People Last accessed 12 November 2006.

Central Intelligence Agency (CIAb). "The World Factbook: West Bank," https://www.cia. gov/cia/publications/factbook/geos/we.html#People. Last accessed 12 November 2006.

Cohen, A.P. (1986). 'Of symbols and boundaries, or does Ertie's greatcoat hold the key'. In A.P. Cohen (ed) *Symbolising Boundaries: Identity and Diversity in British Cultures.* Manchester: Manchester University Press.

Cohn-Sherbok, D. & Dawood, E. (2001). *The Palestine-Israeli Conflict: A Beginner's Guide.* Oxford: Oneworld.

Connolly P., and McGinn, P. (1999). *Sectarianism, Children and Community Relations in Northern Ireland.* Coleraine: University of Ulster, Centre for Study of Conflict.

Connolly, P. and Healy, J. (2004). *Children and the Conflict in Northern Ireland: The Experiences and Perspectives of 3-11 Year Olds.* Belfast: Office of the First Minister and Deputy First Minister Research Branch.

Coogan, T.P.(1995). *The I.R.A.* London: HarperCollins Publishers.

Coulter, C. (1999). *Contemporary Northern Irish Society: An Introduction*. London: Pluto Press.

Crawford, C. (2003). *Inside the UDA: Volunteers and Violence*. London: Pluto Press.

Cunningham, K. (2003). Cross-regional Trends in Female Terrorism. *Studies in Conflict and Terrorism*. 26(3): 171-195.

Cusack, H. and McDonald, J. (1997). *UVF*. Dublin: Poolbeg Press.

Davis, R. (1994). *Mirror Hate: The Convergent Ideology of Northern Ireland Paramilitaries, 1966-1992*. Aldershot, UK: Dartmouth Publishing Company Ltd.

Dieckhoff, A. (2005). 'Beyond Conventional Wisdom: Cultural and Political Nationalism Revisited'. In Dieckhoff, A. and Jaffrelot, C. (eds). *Revisiting Nationalism: Theories and Processes*. London: C.Hurst & Co.

Dillon, M. (2004). *The Trigger Men*. Edinburgh: Mainstream Publishing.

Donahue, L. (2000). "Civil Liberties, Terrorism, and Liberal Democracy: Lessons from the United Kingdom", Belfer Center for Science and International Affairs. Available at http://belfercenter.ksg.harvard.edu/files/esdp00-01_donohue.doc

Donnelly, J.S. (1980). 'Propagating the Cause of the United Irishmen,' *Studies*, 69(2), 5-23.

Elias, N and Scotson, J.L. (1965). *The Established and the Outsiders: A Sociological Enquiry into Community Problems. London: Frank Cass Ltd.*

Elsarraj, E. (1997). Palestinian Children and Violence. *Palestine-Israel Journal*. 4(1): 12-15.

English, R. (2003). *Armed Struggle: A History of the IRA*. London: MacMillan.

Esposito, J. (2002). *Unholy War: Terror in the Name of Islam*. New York: Oxford University Press.

Ewart, S. et al (2004). *Voices behind the Statistics: Young People's views of Sectarianism in Northern Ireland*. London: National Children's Bureau.

Fairweather, E. McDonough, R. and McFadyean, M. (1984). *Only the Rivers Run Free: Northern Ireland: The Women's War*. London: Pluto Press.

Fitzpatrick, B. (1988). *Seventeenth-century Ireland: The war of religions*. Dublin: Gill & Macmillan.

Fraser, M.. (1974). *Children in Conflict*. Harmondsworth: Penguin.

Fraser, T.G. (2007). *The Arab-Israeli Conflict*. Basingstoke: Palgrave.

Frisch, H. (2003). 'The Palestinian Media and Anti-Americanism: A Case Study', *Middle East Review of International Affairs*. 7(4): 74-82.

Frisch, H. (2005). 'Has the Israeli-Palestinian Conflict become Islamic? Fatah, Islam and the Al-Aqsa Brigades', *Terrorism and Political Violence* 17, 391-416.

Gallagher, A. (1995). *Majority Minority Review 1: Education in a Divided Society*. Coleraine: University of Ulster.

Gallagher, A. Smith, A. and Montgomery, A. (2003). *Integrated Education in Northern Ireland: Participation, Profile and Performance*. Coleraine: UNESCO Centre, University of Ulster.

Geertz, C. (ed.) (1963). *Old Societies and New States*. London: The Free Press of Glencoe.

Gresh, A. and Vidal, D. (1990). *An A to Z of the Middle East*. London: Zed Books.

Guibernau, M. (2004). 'Anthony D. Smith on Nations and National Identity: a critical assessment,' *Nations and Nationalism* 10 (1-2): 125-41.

Halliday, F. (2000). *Nation and Religion in the Middle East*. London, Saqi Books.

Halliday, F. (2002). *Two Hours that Shook the World.* London: Saqi Books.

Hamas. (1988). *The Charter of Hamas*. www.hamasonline.com/indexx.php?page= Hamas/hamas_convenant.

Hass, A. (2003). *Reporting from Ramallah*. Los Angeles: Semiotext(e).

Integrated Education Fund (2003). *Northern Ireland: A Divided Society*. Available at http://www/ief.org.uk/files/history/dividedsoicety.asp

International Crisis Group (ICG), (2003). 'Islamic Social Welfare Activism In The Occupied Palestinian Territories: A Legitimate Target?' *ICG Middle East Report N°13*. 2 April.

Irvine, M. (1991). *Northern Ireland: Faith and Faction*. London: Routledge.

Jenkins, R. (2004). *Social Identity*. Routledge: London.

Kelly, B. and Sinclair, R. (2003). *Children from cross-community Families in Public Care in Northern Ireland*. London: National Children's Bureau.

Kerr, A. (ed) (1996). *Perceptions: Cultures in Conflict*. Derry: Guildhall Press.

Khosrokhavar, F. (2005). *Suicide Bombers: Allah's New Martyrs*. London: Pluto Press.

Kimmerling, B. and Migdal, J.S. (2003). *The Palestinian People: A History*, Cambridge, Harvard University Press.

Lanclos, D. (2003). *At Play in Belfast: Children's Folklore and Identities in Northern Ireland*. New Brunswick, New Jersey: Rutgers University Press.

Leonard, M. (2006). 'Teenagers Telling Sectarian Stories'. *Sociology*. 40(6): 1117-33.

Levitt, M. (2006). *Hamas: Politics, Charity, and Terrorism in the Service of Jihad*. New Haven: Yale University Press.

MacDonagh, O. (1983). *States of Mind: A Study of Anglo-Irish Conflict 1780-1980*. London: George Allen and Unwin.

MacDonald, E. (1991). *Shoot the Women First*. London: First Estate.

MacDonald, M. (1986). *Children of Wrath: Political Violence in Northern Ireland*. Cambridge: Polity.

McLaughlin, J. (2001). *Reimagining the Nation-State: The Contested Terrains of Nation-building*. London: Pluto Press.

McLaughlin, J., Trew, K. and Muldoon, O. (2006). 'Religion, Ethnicity and Group Identity: Irish Adolescents' Views', *Nationalism and Ethnic Politics* 12(4): 599-616.

Mansfield. P. (1978). *The Arabs*. Harmondsworth: Penguin.

McCrone, D. (1998). *The Sociology of Nationalism*. London and New York: Routledge.

McDonald, H. and Cusack, J. (2005). *UDA: Inside the Heart of Loyalist Terror*. Dublin: Penguin Books.

McGarry, J. and O'Leary, B. (1995). *Explaining Northern Ireland: Broken Images*. London: Blackwell.

McKeown, L. (2001). *Out of Time: Irish Republican Prisoners, Long Kesh 1972-2000*. Belfast: Beyond the Pale.

Mennell, S. (2007). *The American Civilizing Process*. Cambridge: Polity Press.

Mitchell, C. (2006). 'The Religious Content of Ethnic Identities,' *Sociology*. 40(6): 1135-52.

Moloney, E. (2002). *A Secret History of the IRA*. London: Penguin Books.

Morag, N. (2008). 'The Emerald Isle: Ireland and the clash of Irish and Ulster-born nationalisms', *National Identities*, 10 (3): 263-280.

Morrow, D. (1995). Church and Religion in the Ulster Crisis. In Dunn, S. (ed), *Facets of the Conflict in Northern Ireland*. London: MacMillan.

Moughrabi, F. *A Nation at Risk: The Impact of Violence on Palestinian Children*. http://www.gcmhp.net/File_files/NationAtrisk.html

Murray, D. (1995). Culture, Religion and Violence. In Dunn, S. (ed.) *Facets of the Conflict in Northern Ireland*. London: Macmillan.

O'Farrell, P. (1975). *England and Ireland since 1800*. London: Oxford University Press.

Oliver, A-M, and Steinberg, P. (2005). *The Road to Martyrs Square*. Oxford: Oxford University Press.

O'Malley, P. (1990). *Biting at the Grave: The Irish Hunger Strikes and the Politics of Despair*. Belfast: Blackstaff Press.

Oren, M. (2002). *Six Days of War: June 1967 and the Making of the Modern Middle East*. Oxford: Oxford University Press.

Post, J., Sprinzak, E. and Denny, L. (2003). The Terrorists in their Own Words: Interviews with 35 Incarcerated Middle Eastern Terrorists. *Terrorism and Political Violence*. 15(1): 171-84.

Reuter, C. (2004). *My Life is a Weapon*. Princeton: Princeton University Press.

Ricolfi, L (2006). Palestinians: 1981-2003. In Gambetta, D. (ed) *Making Sense of Suicide Missions*. Oxford: Oxford University Press.

Rolston, B. (1991). *Politics and Painting: Murals and Conflict in Northern Ireland*. Rutherford: Associated University Press.

Said, E. (1994). *The Politics of Dispossession,* New York: Random House.

Saikal, A. (2003). *Islam and the West*. Basingstoke: Palgrave Macmillan.

Sakr, N. (2001). *Satellite Realms*. London, I.B.Tauris.

Shils, E. (1957). 'Primordial, Personal, Sacred and Civil Ties', *British Journal of Sociology*, 8(2): 130-45.

Smith, A. (1991). *National Identity*. Harmondsworth: Penguin Books.

Smith, A. (2003). *Chosen Peoples*. Oxford: Oxford University Press.

Smith, C. (2007). *Palestine & the Arab-Israeli Conflict*. (Basingstoke: Palgrave).

Smyth, M. et al. (2004). *The Impact of Political Conflict on Children in Northern Ireland*. Belfast: Institute for Conflict Research.

SOL. (2002). Surveys Online, *European Social Survey 2002*. Available at http://www.ark.ac.uk/sol/surveys/gen_social_att/ESS/2002/website/Identity/RLGATND. html

SOL. (2005). Surveys Online, *Community Relations: Identity*. Available at http://www.ark.ac. uk/sol/surveys/community_relations/time_series/CRencyidentity.htm

Sutton, P. and Vertigans, S. (2005). *Resurgent Islam: A Sociological Approach.* Cambridge: Polity Press.

Tamimi, A. (2007). *Hamas: Unwritten Chapters*. London: Hurst & Co.

Taylor, M. and Quayle, E. (1994). *Terrorist Lives*. London: Brassey's Defence Publishers.

Taylor, P. (1998). *Provos: the IRA and Sinn Fein*. London: Bloomsbury Publishing.

Taylor, P. (2000). *Loyalists*. London: Bloomsbury Publishing.

Tessler, M. (1994). *A History of the Israeli-Palestinian Conflict (Indiana Series in Arab and Islamic Studies)*. Bloomington: Indiana Univ Press.

Thomas, W.I. (1928). *The Child in America*. New York: Alfred. A. Knopf.

Todd, J., O'Keefe, T. Rougier, N. and Caňos Bottos, L. (2006). 'Fluid or Frozen: Choice and Change in Ethno-National Identification in Contemporary Northern Ireland', Nationalism and Ethnic Politics. 12(3-4): 323-346.

Toolis, K. (1995). *Rebel Hearts*. London: Picador.

Vertigans, S. (2008). *Terrorism and Societies*. Aldershot: Ashgate.

Vertigans, S. (2009). *Militant Islam: A Sociology of characteristics, causes and consequences.* Abingdon: Routledge.

Victor, B. (2004). *Army of Roses.* London: Constable & Robinson.

Whyte, J. (1986). How is the Boundary Maintained Between the Two Communities in Northern Ireland. *Ethnic and Racial Studies.* 9(2): 219-234.

Wilford, R. (2001). 'The Assembly.' In R.Wilson (ed.). *Agreeing to Disagree? A Guide to the Northern Ireland Assembly*, Norwich: The Stationery Office.

Young Life and Times Survey (YLT) (2004, 2005). *YLT, Northern Ireland Young Life and Times.* Available at http://www.ark.ac.uk/ylt/2004/Identity/NINATID.html.

In: Social Development
Editor: Lynda R. Elling

ISBN: 978-1-60741-612-8
© 2009 Nova Science Publishers, Inc.

Chapter 3

BIOSPHERE RESERVES AS LEARNING SITES OF SUSTAINABLE DEVELOPMENT (A CASE STUDY OF THE CZECH REPUBLIC)

Drahomíra Kušová[*], Jan Těšitel and Michael Bartoš

Institute of Systems Biology and Ecology, Academy of Sciences of the Czech
Republic,v.v.i. Na Sádkách 7, 370 05 České Budějovice, Czech Republic
and
University of South Bohemia, Faculty of Agriculture,
Studentská 13, 370 05 České Budějovice, Czech Republic

ABSTRACT

Established under the UNESCO's Man and the Biosphere (MAB) Programme, biosphere reserves represent protected areas intended to demonstrate well balanced relationship between a high level of nature protection and an appropriate local development, as articulated in the Seville Strategy and reinforced by the Madrid Declaration. According to their definition, biosphere reserves are to simultaneously fulfill four functions – conservation of biological diversity, ecological education, research and promotion of sustainable forms of socioeconomic activities. They can be theoretically considered learning sites of sustainable development. The chapter contributes primarily to the discussion on social part of the relationship between nature protection and socioeconomic development, namely on quality of life of local population living in protected areas, problems of social acceptance of biodiversity conservation measures and institutional arrangements applied when biosphere reserve concept is aimed to be practically implemented. Comparative analysis was conducted in three selected Czech biosphere reserves in order to challenge a cliché on nature protection and socioeconomic development to be a priori in contradiction as well as the belief in state nature protection being the exclusive leader in the process of the concept of biosphere reserve implementation. Triangulation approach was applied as a fundamental frame for empirical data acquisition and analysis, combining spatial analysis of data describing socioeconomic parameters of particular municipalities, semi-standardized interviews with key personalities, extensive questionnaire survey addressing general public, content

---

[*] e-mail: draku@usbe.cas.cz

analysis of regional periodicals and case study analysis focused on success and failure factors in the process of a concrete project implementation. The research results suggest that biosphere reserves did not differ in quality of life of their inhabitants compared with surrounding areas. In some cases, the existence of biosphere reserve was even seen as a comparative advantage – certificate of high quality nature as a base for local tourism development. In the Czech legislative environment, biosphere reserves are institutionally associated with administration of protected landscape areas. Such an institutional arrangement enables executing of state nature protection, providing public with ecological education, and guaranteeing research on a satisfactory level. There are problems, however, in supporting of sustainable forms of development. Goal oriented network, projects driven, of engaged stakeholders is suggested as a more efficient organizational form in this respect. Evidence of a still ongoing process of learning by interacting, aimed at using biosphere reserve as a trade mark of some kind, indicates that the biosphere reserves could as well in practical terms be considered learning sites of sustainable development. The chapter intends to contribute to the debate on ideas of the UN Decade on Education for Sustainable Development 2005-2014.

Keywords: biosphere reserve, sustainable development, social learning, triangulation

INTRODUCTION

Nature protection has evolved over time, gradually stressing special themes – the progress can be seen from those starting with protection of particular species to protection of ecosystems until today, when an appropriate management of large scale landscape areas has become a focal point. The focus on landscape scale has brought about also a shift in the role local communities are expected to play in this type of nature protection – satisfaction of their socioeconomic aspirations has begun to be perceived as an inevitable part of management of protected areas. Such a tendency is evident in Central Europe, where areas having a status of being protected cannot be considered pristine landscapes (Getzner & Jungamier, 2000; Paavola & Adger, 2005). On the contrary, they are permanently populated cultural landscapes having passed century long transformation by human activities. As a result modern nature protection measures count with needs of local population in order not to make areas under protection a priori disadvantaged from socioeconomic viewpoint (Těšitel et al., 2006). Very important in this context is a definition of nature protection as it was formulated by IUCN in its World Conservation Strategy. In fact it was anthropocentric as it considered nature protection to be a management of air, water, soil, mineral resources and living systems, including man, aimed at achieving sustainable quality of life (IUCN, 1980). Later on, the strategic shift was reflected by the UNESCO concept of biosphere reserves as it was articulated in the Seville Strategy and reinforced in the Madrid Declaration. According to its guiding idea biosphere reserve is to strengthen general awareness of mutual interrelations between humankind and biosphere by ensuring its four functions - enabling high-level biodiversity protection[1], supporting research and education, and promoting sustainable forms of socioeconomic development (UNESCO, 1996, 2001, 2002, 2008).

---

[1] We are aware of the fact that the conservation function is a prerequisite for the biosphere reserve existence, the chapter, however contributes primarily to the discussion on social part of the relationship between nature protection and socioeconomic development.

Multiplicity of functions associated with biosphere reserve refers to the concept of sustainable landscape (Antrop, 2006). Though we can agree with the argument that the whole notion of sustainable landscape development may involve some contradictions, merging landscape and sustainability may yield at least two positive results. Discussion on sustainability acquires spatial dimension (e.g. Price, 2002); on the other hand, the theoretical concept of cultural landscape (Antrop, 2001; Naveh, 2001; Palang et al., 2005) is translated" into a more or less effective political scheme, suitable as a basis for practical decision making. In this context, sustainable landscape can be considered as a landscape where trade-offs between nature protection and socioeconomic aspirations of local communities are expected to be well balanced. In economic terms it presumes balancing three types of capital – natural, social and cultural (e.g. Farina, 2000; Garrod et al., 2006). In the rhetoric of sustainable development these capitals play the role of an internal potential of a particular region (Jehle 1998), the potential that can be realized when it meets an appropriate external context (e.g. Kušová et al., 1999; Těšitel et al., 1999).

An attempt to address the interdependence between human economies and natural ecosystems has been articulated in ecological economics, among others, in terms of ecosystem services (e.g. Costanza et al., 1997; Brock & Xepapadeas, 2003; Imhoff, 2004; Millennium Ecosystem Assessment, 2005; Faber, 2008). Though we can consider ecological economics to represent a paradigm shift (Kaval, 2006), it is evident that the discussion has primarily a form of an academic debate. As already Constanza (1997) stated in one of the pioneering articles in the field of ecological economics, because ecosystem services are not fully 'captured' in commercial markets or adequately quantified in terms comparable with economic services and manufactured capital, they are often given too little weight in policy decisions. Since, only a little has changed. As a result, the historically rooted stereotype in thinking, adopted by experts as well as general public presuming nature protection measures to be in contradiction with socioeconomic development has been surviving. For nature protectionists, "marketing" of protected areas is something "dirty", "commercial", not "suitable" for the field of nature protection (Roth, 2007). On the other side, nature protection in general and large scale protected areas in particular have a poor image as they are seen mainly as a burden for regional development by local and regional entrepreneurs and general public (e.g. van Kooten & Wang, 1998; Paiders, 2007)[2].

The UNESCO concept of biosphere reserve, in the first instance, is a policy objective aimed at reconciling conservation of biodiversity and biological resources with their sustainable use, backed up by internationally agreed upon conventions. The concept itself is

---

[2] They are not only nature protection enthusiasts or developers, however, who view the relation in terms of contradiction. Such a setting is sometimes taking for granted also by people whose profession is to conserve the nature. The seminar organized by the Czech Ministry of Environment in autumn 2004, as an event acompanying the film festival titled Ekofilm" devoted to problems of environment annually organised in the towns of České Budějovice and Český Krumlov in the Czech Republic, could be used as one of practical examples. The issue to be discussed was a relation between nature protection and local socioeconomic development. The point was that organizers, representing official position of the top administrative body of nature protection, titled this event by use of the word "contra" – "Nature protection contra socioeconomic development of local communities". As a result, notion of conflict was introduced at the very outset between representatives of nature protection and local mayors participating in the seminar (Těšitel et al., 2005a).

appealing, however its practical application is a subject of wide range of institutional and administrative challenges (e.g. Parto, 2005; Stoll-Kleemann et al., 2006). One might even question whether the concept is compatible with the current institutional environment premised on centralized control over nature protection. By promoting the idea that the management of each biosphere reserve should be essentially formulated as a 'pact' between the local community and the society as a whole, the concept invites all interested groups and sectors for participation in a partnership approach. Doing so it acknowledges the fact that the capacity (e.g. knowledge, power and resources) to solve complex problem related to the implementation of the biosphere reserve concept is often widely dispersed across a set of actors located on different scales (e.g. Imperial, 1999). Such and approach seems to fully reflect the general tendency of the last decades embodied in the gradual shift from government towards governance, where responsibility for policy-making spans public and private sectors, promoting thus increased interest in networks as an organizational concept when conducting joint action (Parto, 2005). Though networks are interpreted many ways (e.g. Murdoch, 2000; Gunjan, 2005; Dredge, 2006), they are as a rule supposed to be open-ended, often unusual, ad hoc arrangements that demonstrate remarkable problem-solving capacity and open up opportunities for learning and change (Hajer, 2003 a). Policy making under the new conditions has become a matter of defining an agreed upon package of actions to be taken by variety of stakeholders, often supported by "soft law" such as conventions or agreements (Hajer, 2003). In this perspective, network structures are built upon social interactions and relationships which provide security and trust (e.g. Lowe, 1988; Tait & Lyall, 2004)[3]. Biosphere reserves, fundamentally concerned with whole-of-landscape processes, across a variety of land tenures and uses can be thus seen vehicles for managing the social, cultural and institutional change and capacity-building at the multiple scales (Amin & Thrift, 1994; Storper, 1997; Maskel & Malmberg, 1999; MacLeod, 2001; Brunghorst, 2001).

Main ambition of the chapter is to challenge the two cliché - firstly that nature protection and socioeconomic development are a priori in contradiction, and secondly that state nature protection should be considered an exclusive leader in the process of the concept of biosphere reserve practical implementation. In this context the discussion primarily addresses issues related to quality of life of local population living in protected areas, mutual attitudes of local inhabitants and administration of protected landscape areas, and institutional arrangements applied when biosphere reserve concept is aimed to be practically implemented. Finally, conditions under which biosphere reserve could be considered a learning site for practicing rules of sustainable development are discussed (e.g. Price, 2002; Stoll-Kleemann et al. 2006; Kušová et al., 2006, 2008).

Triangulation approach was applied as a principal scheme of the analysis. It can be defined as a combination of concepts, methods and dates used in order to get several viewpoints upon the topic to be studied (e.g. Olsen, 2004). It refers to the fact that reality is a complex matter and you need more than one single explanatory framework or data set to understand it at a reasonable level. The main advantage of triangulation approach lies then in its ability to depict multifaceted picture of a reality at hand. In our case, we combined concept of quality of life, issue of social acceptance of nature protection measures, and a problem of

---

[3] The Madrid Declaration (UNESCO, 2008) in this context suggests forming of effective partnerships through cooperation among state administration bodies, private sector, media, local communities, and scientific and educational institutions.

adequacy of biosphere reserve institutional arrangement as the main theoretical viewpoints. Empirical data for the analyses were acquired by a set of respective research techniques. In order to make a coherent picture, these techniques were not applied in isolated way. Step by step process was used instead, which made individual techniques to complement each other (Figure 1). We started with the content analysis of regional periodicals. Based on the knowledge gained about medial image on the relationship between nature protection and local development, structure of questionnaire was refined to address more precisely how local public perceives its socioeconomic situation as well as to reveal attitude of local inhabitants to nature protection representatives. Once main conflicts as well as examples of mutual cooperation between nature protection and local inhabitants were identified, as reflected by local public and media, one module of semi-standardized interview was structured with the aim to address local key personalities and get their opinions on these issues. It was complemented with another one asking about their experiences with practical implementation of the biosphere reserve concept. Spatial analysis of local socioeconomic conditions was relatively independent part of the research in this respect, framed however by the general scheme of the concept of quality of life. Case study analysis was applied in the end to identify concrete factors of success and failure in the process of practical implementation of a project aimed at promotion of the concept of biosphere reserve in one of model area.

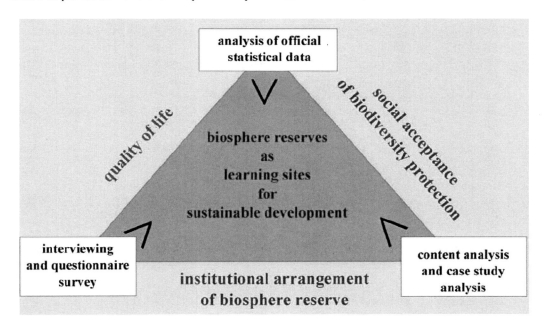

Figure 1. Scheme of the triangulation approach – a combination of concepts and techniques used to address the research topic.

Three Czech biosphere reserves (BR) were used for the empirical analysis (Figure 2). They were The Šumava Mountains[4], Třeboňsko characterized by many wetlands[5] and

---

[4] The Šumava Mountains represent the least damaged and best preserved mountain forest ecosystems and peat bogs in Central Europe. In the course of the 20th century this area was peripheral and the main economic activities were agriculture and forestry. The post-1948 period was characterised by the presence of the "Iron Curtain" and establishment of a military training area which made the area

Křivoklátsko dominated by the valley of the Berounka River[6] (Figures 3, 4, 5). They vary in their natural parameters as well as in their latest socioeconomic history, representing thus a relatively broad array of aspects to be taken into consideration when analyzing their functioning. Institutionally they are associated with the administration of Protected Landscape Areas (PLA), in the case of the Šumava Mts. with administration of PLA and National Park (NP).

Figure 2. Model areas – three Czech biosphere reserves.

---

almost inaccessable for 50 years. Marginality of the region has helped to sustain natural attractions, and led to the designation of the Šumava Protected landscape area in 1963 and the Šumava National park in 1991. The biosphere reserve was declared in 1990, and includes the National Park and the Šumava Protected Landscape Area (PLA), the total area being 1, 671 km2. Thanks to its geomorphological characteristics and mainly glacial relics, the Šumava Mountains area is listed in the IUCN Red Book of Ecosystems and Šumava wetlands are on the list of Ramsar Convention. Since 2004 most of the territory has become part of the European network Natura 2000. (http://www.npsumava.cz)

[5] This area was declared biosphere reserve in 1977, two years before Třeboňsko PLA was proclaimed. The area of 700 km2 of drained lake basin includes a mosaic of varied wetlands as well as dry biotopes with significant diversity of animal and plant species. The dominant landscape phenomenon consists in 465 fishponds, more than 500 pools and old meanders of the rivers Lužnice and Nežárka. This area has been under intense human management roughly since the 12th century but reached secondary biological balance. This fact allows for unique close coexistence of internationally significant wetlands protected by Ramsar Convention (Třeboň ponds and Třeboň peat bogs), and typical keeping of traditional carp as well as other economic activities (extraction of raw materials, agriculture, building construction). Since 2004 most of the area belongs to the European network Natura 2000. (http://www.trebonsko.ochranaprirody.cz/)

[6] The area of 628 km^2 was named after the royal castle of Křivoklát, which dominates over the valley of the Berounka River. Even nowadays, thanks to the fact that the territory belonged to the Czech crown till the 17th century and was thus used mainly for hunting, large deciduous and mixed forests thrive in this area. Steep slopes of the deep Berounka River valley are covered with natural vegetation of different communities, with sporadic rock outcomes hosting xerothermic fauna and flora. Many localities host beautiful meadows of different types, which occurred in the place of original forests and which represent an important part of landscape due to their richness of species. The castle and game park in Lány, a residence of the president, is connected with modern history of the Czech Republic. The factor influencing the land use in the biosphere reserve is the vicinity of the capital city, Prague. Due to its qualities, Křivoklátsko area has been listed among UNESCO biosphere reserves since the Czechoslovak proposal was accepted on March 1, 1977. One year later the area was proclaimed PLA with its own administration. Since 2004 most of the area belongs to the European network Natura 2000. (http://www.krivoklatsko.ochranaprirody.cz/)

Figure 3. Šumava Mts. scenic view.

Figure 4. Fishponds – a typical feature of the Třeboňsko basin.

Figure 5. Berounka river valley – the axis of the Křivoklátsko biosphere reserve.

QUALITY OF LIFE

Quality of life has been acknowledged as one of important idicators measuring level of sustainability of development, on local to national scales (e.g. Collados & Duane, 1999; Wilson et al., 2007). Double optics should be applied when we study quality of life - the objective and subjective ones. The former as a rule reflects social consensus on the level of satisfaction of what is considered to be a standard of living. Objectivity in this case means that the standard is defined externally. The latter, subjective one, on the other hand presumes to represent personal experiences and aspirations of individual people. Both views can be applied to describe situation of individual people, communities, and once spatial aspect is considered, they can be used to give evidence about localities or regions (Mareš, 1999). It refers to regional economic theories, in particular to the discussion on driving forces that may lead to differentiation among particular regions during the course of their historical development (Blažek & Uhlíř, 2002.). Our empirical research hypothesized that biosphere reserves will differ in quality of life of their inhabitants from the surrounding areas[7]. To test the hypothesis, twenty two objective parameters were used as it can be seen in the legend of figures 7 and 8.

Subjective dimension of life quality was defined in terms of physical, mental and social wellness and wholesomeness, referring thus to the theory of subjective well-being (Massam,

---

[7] Different approaches can be traced in pertinent professional literature on how to measure unevenness between regions by use of objective statistical data. In order to identify poor regions in Britain, for example, eight indicators were used. Townsend (1987) refers to another approach. It is based on measuring of degree of poverty of regions as a degree of material deprivation, by use of five criteria. Analogically, Jarman (1984) designs score of unprivileged regions by assigning individual indicators of deprivation by their specific weights.

2002). Empirical research tried to find out how practical implementation of nature protection measures in the three concrete biosphere reserves is perceived to have affected the nine respective aspects of quality of life of local population - physical well-being, mental well-being, value system, place they live in, human relations, availability of services, everyday activities, free-time activities, their career (Těšitel et al. 2005).

Data provided by the Czech Statistical Institute were used to describe the status of quality of life objectively. All results were visualized by use of GIS technology. In order to test our hypothesis on unevenness the model areas were extended to include also municipalities that form their surroundings. It consisted of a stripe around studied protected areas having width of 20 km. Municipalities of interest formed then three groups – lying completely within the protected areas; being in between, i.e. intersected by borders of protected areas; and those having its cadastres completely out of protected areas (Figure 6). Two sets of variables describing our three biosphere reserves as well as their surroundings were used. The first set consisted of ten variables representing type of land use, expressed in terms of share of particular land-use categories within a basic statistical unit. The second set characterized socioeconomic milieu in the territory by use of basic demographic variables - variables describing material well-being of inhabitants as well as those on availability of infrastructure and services. All variables were related to municipality level as the basic statistical unit. Individual municipalities were twice processed by use of *principal component analysis (PCA)* – according to the data on land use (Figure 7)[8] and according to the relative socioeconomic parameters (Figure 8)[9]. Based on results of both ordinations a new variable - "normalized socioeconomic status" of municipalities - was derived[10]. It was then used to test the significance of differences between protected areas and their surroundings. Values of the variable were calculated for all the municipalities forming our broader model areas. The difference between values assigned to municipalities inside the protected areas and those

---

[8] Analysis of land use was done by use of PCA ordination. The first two ordination axes (PCA1 and PCA2) were used. These axes account for 41% of variability of the data set. Two new parameters were calculated - "degree of urbanization", URBA = PCA1+PCA2 – describing a gradient from rural to urbanized areas, and "share of agriculture" AGRI = PCA1-PCA2 – quantifying the position on gradient between prevailing forested areas to prevailing agricultural land. An arbitrary division of the space of these variables was then used as a basis for municipality classification.

[9] The socioeconomic data were processed in an analogical way. One third of data variability was described by the first ordination axis (PCA1), while the second one (PCA2) accounted for the next eleven per cent. Further decline was smooth and continuous. Two factors appeared to explain the position of a municipality in ordination space formed by two first axes – level of education and age structure. Four arbitrary classes were identified on this basis. The first class can be characterized as one comprising "normal" municipalities with population living in relatively well equipped local urban centers. The second one represents municipalities with an aging population, even "dying out spots" in some cases. Municipalities of the third class are populated by relatively young people, not enough educated, however, suffering from unemployment. The fourth class is composed of municipalities with young educated and growing population.

[10] The calculation of the normalized socioeconomic status was based on two principal presumptions. Firstly, we presumed that land use types were related to the nature conditions of a particular locality and the character of a municipality (formed by prevailing economic activity in both contemporary and historical perspectives), and secondly that the socioeconomic conditions were influenced by land use practices. The relationship between land use and socioeconomic parameters was searched for by use of correlations among several first axes for both mentioned PCA ordinations. Thanks to the statistically significant dependence between the first ordination axis of the socioeconomic parameters (PCA1) and degree of urbanization (URBA), it was possible to use, instead of the score of the first ordination axis, the difference between its value and the value expected, which was calculated by use of the linear regression model (for i^{th} municipality): $PCA1_i = (a + b\ URBA_i) + e_i$, where "a" and "b" are regression parameters and "e" is an error. Differences between real and expected values were then calculated as values of variable $DIF\_PCA1 = PCA1 - (a + b\ URBA)$, that we called "normalized socioeconomic status" of a municipality. The higher its value, the better living conditions occur in a municipality.

lying outside was tested by F-test in analysis of variance with a three-level factor: municipalities within the protected area (group A), on the border of this area (group B) and placed completely outside the protected area (group C). The difference proved to be statistically insignificant. Based on this we can conclude that protected areas do not differ from the "normal" surrounding areas as to socioeconomic conditions, at least those described by the first ordination axes (Figure 9).

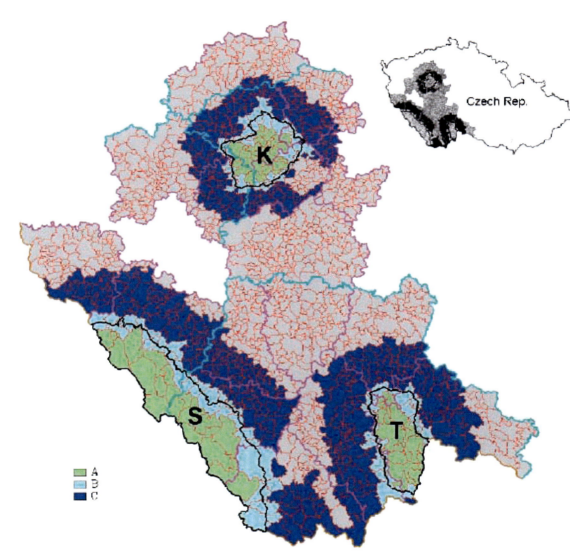

Legend: K - Protected landscape area Křivoklátsko, S - National park and Protected landscape area Šumava, T - Protected landscape area Třeboňsko; protected areas are marked by black lines. Municipalities were divided into three groups according to border of the protected area (A - completely within the area, B - on the border, C - surrounding of the area).

Figure 6. Model areas for testing differences between protected areas and their surroundings.

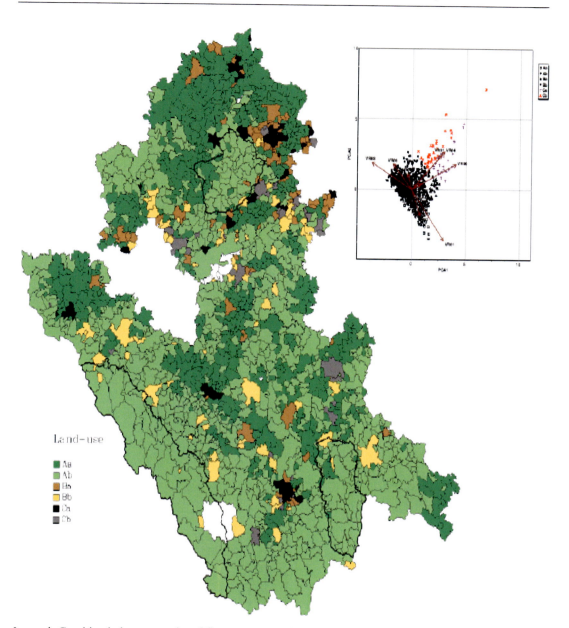

Legend: Combined classes consist of first uppercase character for municipalities within rural landscape (A), intermediate landscape (B) and urbanized landscape (C) - classes are derived from degree of urbanization. Lowercase character represents agricultural land type (a) or forest land type (b).

Accompanying figure shows ordination biplot of first two PCA axes based on data (Czech Statistical Institute, municipality statistic database, 2002): share of arable land (vr81), hop gardens (vr82), vineyard (vr83), gardens (vr84), orchards (vr85), grasslands (vr86), forests (vr88), waters (vr89), build-up areas (vr90), other plots (vr91).

Not filled units – white color: Data not available (military training area).

Figure 7. Classification of municipalities according to land-use data.

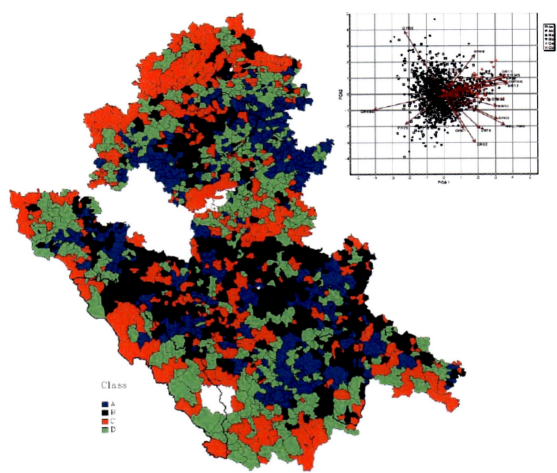

Legend: Municipalities are divided into classes A - with standard human population (PCA1 ≥ 0, PCA2 ≥ 0), B - with aging population (PCA1 < 0, PCA2 ≥ 0), C - with young low-qualified population (PCA1 < 0, PCA2 < 0), D - with growing "perspective" population (PCA1 ≥ 0, PCA2 < 0).

Accompanying figure shows ordination biplot of first two PCA axes based on relative data (original data - Czech Statistical Institute, Census 2001): Calculated out of total number of houses: permanently inhabited houses (dr02), houses owned by physical person (dr03). Calculated out of total population size: number of persons having a car in the family (er04s), having a phone line in a family (er08), having a mobile phone in the family (er10), having phone or mobile in the family (er12), having a personal computer in the family (er14s), with recreational house ownership in the family (er18), with possibility to use some recreational building (er20s), "well appointed" persons (er22), youngs of 0-14 years old (or01), adults (or02), seniors above 64 years old (or03), peoples without secondary level education (or08s), peoples reached second level education (or10s), university graduates (or11), students commuting for a school (xr02). Relative change in inhabitants number per year within period 1960-2000 (REL_REG). Calculated out of adult population size: economically active peoples (vr78), unemployed peoples searching for job (vr79), peoples commuting for a job (xr01), commuting at a long distance - out of the district (xr07s).

Not filled units – white color: Data not available (military training area).

Figure 8. Classification of municipalities according to socioeconomic parameters.

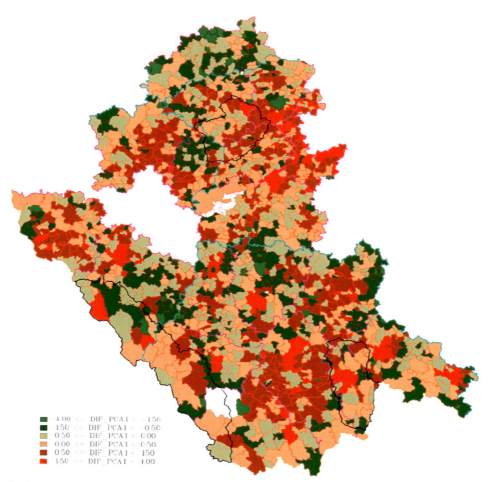

Legend: The higher value of DIF_PCA1, the better living conditions in a municipality.
Not filled units – white color: Data not available (military training areas).

Figure 9. Classification of municipalities according to the normalized socioeconomic status.

The opinions of local population related to their everyday life and their attitude to the administration of protected areas and, consequently to nature protection in general was mapped by *questionnaire survey technique*. Adult people over fifteen permanently living in the model areas formed the basic set. The sample was then derived by use of the combination of quota and random sampling, the quota being based on the size of municipality. Altogether, 1 150 respondents were addressed. The share of the sample in the basic set was 1, 86%, which made the sample representative enough for our purposes[11].

When analyzing the behavior of local people and their attitude to the locality they live in, including its nature quality, level of their "rooting" proved to be one of key determinants. Viewed from this perspective, people who live in our model areas can be characterized as members of a stabilized population. They seem to be deeply rooted in the territory, most of

---

[11] The field survey was conducted in summer 2004. Data were statistically analyzed by use of the first and second order contingency tables method and graphical outputs were produced by Excel 2000 for Windows.

them have been living there for a long time, or they were even born there. Besides their affinity to nature, it is primarily social relations that make them feel tied to the locality - family, friends, job opportunities, flat and ownership of real estate. After all, the majority of them do not have to commute for a job or school out of the model area. They do not want to move out of the territory at all (Figures 10 and 11).

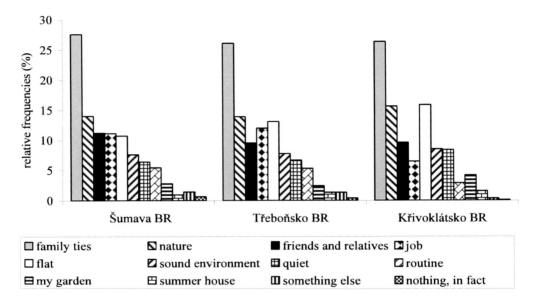

Figure 10. Ties to the territory.

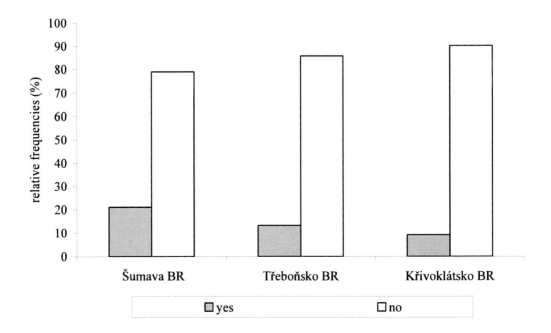

Figure 11. Intention to leave the territory.

The perception of the present socioeconomic situation as it is viewed by locals does not differ from the picture drawn by official statistical data. When evaluating the quality of facilities in their municipalities, most of them have been convinced that available services as well as infrastructure are appropriate in the sense that they reflect the size of a particular municipality and its history. As to their own current economic situation, the majority of inhabitants seems to be content with it (Figures 12 and 13).

"Sound environment" and "well-preserved nature" can be considered as two principal attributes of the territory. The present-day popularity of areas offering high quality environment can be partly related to the need of modern people to live, or at least to relax, within relatively unspoiled landscape, which is often explained by human phylogenetic attachments to nature (e.g. Orians, 1980; Wilson, 1984)[12]. Recognition of biosphere reserves as tourist destinations means in fact setting them into the context of the nation-wide or international market by use of which the internal potential of biosphere reserves can be commodified. In parallel, these attributes were recognized as comparative advantage for further socioeconomic development, when assessed from inside of the biosphere reserve. In all the model areas there is a commonly shared positive opinion among people as to the role of protected and certified environment in tourism development (Figure 14). The "tourist" potential is perceived as not being fully exploited yet (see Figure 15). Once we agree with locals and assume that sustainable tourism can be considered the base of the local economy in protected areas, we can go even further in the defence of nature protection measures. As sustainable tourism can be characterized, among others, as one that commodify local natural capital of certain quality (Jenkins, 2001; Kušová et al., 2002; Ira, 2005; Nolte, 2005), we can formulate a theoretical statement, to some extent paradoxical, that it is the nature protection, as a guardian of certified nature, that can guarantee local economic development in long run as it keeps promoting comparative advantage of an area (e.g.Bartoš et al. 1998, Těšitel et al. 1999, Sharpley, 2000, Vos and Klijn, 2000).

Based on the analysis both of objective data and subjective reflection of the situation by local population we can generally conclude that there is no statistically significant difference between protected areas and their surroundings in terms of objectively measured parameters describing material well-being. Nor the inhabitants of protected areas feel themselves handicapped. Natural capital in terms of "certified" nature, such as biosphere reserve, plays an ambivalent role. The status of being protected can be seen simultaneously both as limitation and comparative advantage. On one hand, nature protection really poses limits to some economic activities as to their type, intensity or localization concerns.

---

[12] This theme has also been taken up in the Czech professional literature, and in some studies aimed at explaining our desire for outdoor recreation (Honzík, 1965; Librová, 1987, 1988; Maršálková & Todlová, 1983), where home and countryside have been separated by urban expansion. The 'escape from the city' has now been a phenomenon for several decades, as the constraints of time, money and transport have been relaxed, whilst expanding urban areas have meant that people have had to travel further to escape city life. This has created situations in which more people seek unspoiled landscape settings within a diminishing rural area. This imbalance seems to result, at least in Czech conditions, in the increasing importance of preserved areas as a recreational hinterland for towns.

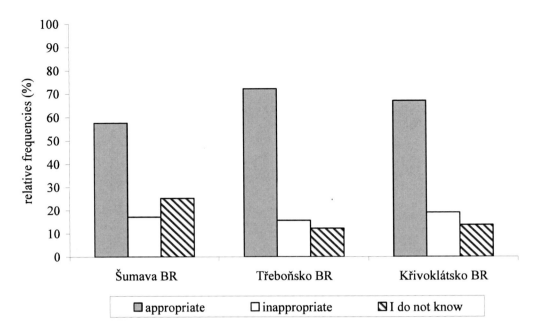

Figure 12. Quality of services and infrastructure related to scale of municipality.

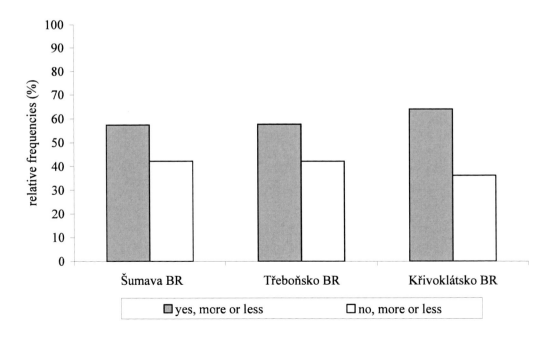

Figure 13. Contentment with personal economic situation.

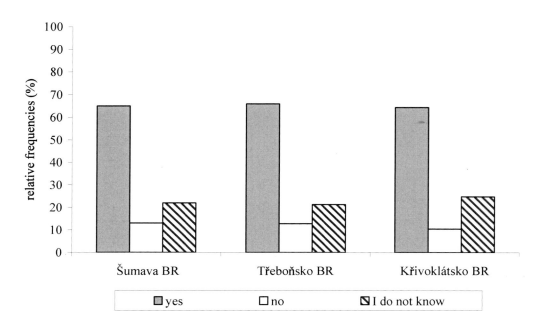

Figure 14. Does the existence of protected area increase tourist attractiveness of the region?

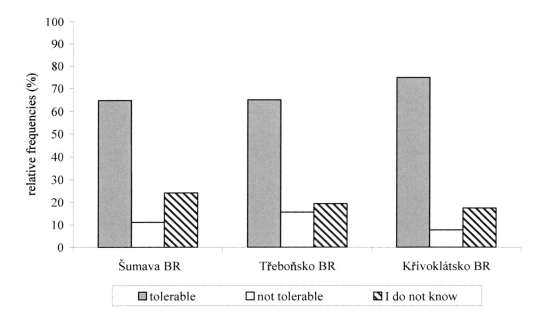

Figure 15. Tourist pressure on the region as perceived by local people.

On the other hand, these areas have been successful in converting the internal potential of "certified" high-quality nature into a key agent in local tourism development. Furthermore, thanks to the state policy of nature protection and regional development policy, protected areas are eligible for special funds which cannot be applied for by other regions (e.g. Bartoš et al., 1998). The success in such a trade-offs depends on many factors, including local personalities and their activities. Anyhow, this ambiguity challenges the generally widely spread cliché considering protected areas as ones being handicapped a priori as to the quality of life of local population concerns (e.g. Zemek and Heřman, 1998; Bartoš et al., 2005; Zemek et al., 2005).

SOCIAL ACCEPTANCE OF BIODIVERSITY PROTECTION MEASURES

Public opinion can be considered an important factor in nature and environment protection. It has changed evidently in the Czech Republic when we compare current situation with that at the beginning of 90's, shortly after the "Velvet Revolution"[13]. At that time, fundamentals of market economy as well as nature protection policy, which was then seen as something quite important, started to be shaped. Quality of environment and necessity of its improvement was being subject of public debate, and measures aimed at nature protection were discussed within this context. After almost twenty years of practicing market economy the situation has changed profoundly. Environment as such has definitely lost its attractiveness of being a subject of political debate. Its measured parameters are supposed to have already met desirable limits (e.g. OECD, 2005). As to the nature protection concerns, a myth has generally spread that there is a clash of interests between nature protection and socioeconomic development; public opinion being as a rule pro-development oriented (e.g. Rolston, 1997; Těšitel et al, 2005).

Nature protection bodies seem thus to be caught in a bit paradoxical situation as to their social status concerns – as a representatives of state administration they are in charge of promoting measures that goes against value system of the most of the Czech society[14]. Cooperation should be thus desired modus operandi rather then power driven behavior which is likely to trigger conflicts. Empirical research, in this context, was aimed at revealing of attitudes local population had to the protected areas administration as well as at identifying of the most representative examples cooperation or conflicts among these players. Mutual behavior of local population and administration of the particular protected areas was empirically analyzed by use of questionnaire survey technique already mentioned above, combined with content analysis of regional periodicals aimed at identifying of medial image of this relationship.

Results of *questionnaire survey* suggest that everyday life of local population in all the studied areas does not seem to be much influenced by the fact that they lived in a protected area. In fact, only a minority of inhabitants has encountered representatives of the protected

---

[13] The "Velvet Revolution" (November 16 – December 29, 1989) refers to a non-violent revolution in Czechoslovakia that saw the overthrow of the Communist government and intorduced democracy.

[14] When evaluating social acceptance of activities executed by the state nature protection bodies, direct comparison with other similar structures of state administration, specialized in other fields of expertise but facing in fact situations of the same type (decisions, approvals, fines imposing, inspections, etc), such as the Police of the Czech Republic, Czech Trade Inspection, Hygienic service, and others, may be misleading. Activities of these institutions, though frequently criticized, correspond with public opinion. As being socially accepted as self-evident, they can fully focus (and limit) their activities at execution of the state administration. Nature protection bodies are facing much more complicated situation, compared to them. Besides performing state administration itself there is a lot of other things they should do, aimed at shifting value system of the society towards a "more friendly" perception of nature, and consequently to changing behavioral patterns

landscape area administration in person; they are as a rule those who have had to deal with some legal or bureaucratic procedures in which the administration of PLA participates. On the other hand, most people living in the area use some facilities run by the administration, and participate in voluntary activities related to nature protection. They also highly appreciate the fact that the "label" of a protected area increases tourist attractiveness of the whole territory (Figures 16 and 14). As to their relationship to nature protection, they perceive it in a "peaceful way"; in some cases they even have been able to find a way how to make some kind of profit from it. The relatively "peaceful" coexistence is primarily based on the fact that representatives of the municipalities as well as the administration of protected areas had a time to overcome the initial contradiction, evident when protected areas had been established, and have come to the point of building a joint vision of future coexistence. Sustainable tourism, as an activity acceptable by both parties, seems to have become the key point of the above mentioned common vision.

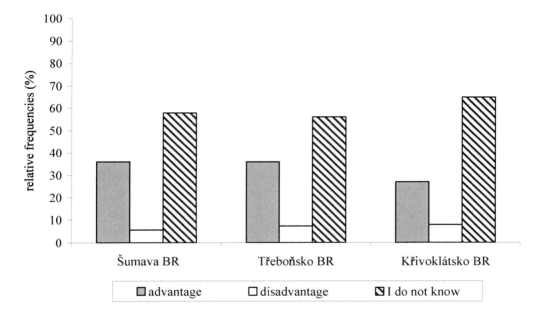

Figure 16. Role of protected area in regional development as perceived by local people.

Content analysis was based on the general presumption that the press reacts to real-life problems, and is also an intermediary of social control of the institutions which are in charge of it. Medial image is then supposed to represent a reflection of expected interest of the public in particular problems (e.g. MacLuhan, 1991; DeFleur & Ball-Rokeach, 1996; Blažek, 1998). Quantitative analysis, identifying frequency, ratio and context of a pertinent messages in selected media, was complemented by qualitative content analysis that offered a more detailed interpretation of the process in which media constructed reality in relation to problems at hand (Disman, 1993). By use of this technique, comparative monitoring of the regional periodicals was carried out in all the three model areas[15].

---

[15] Daily newspapers were used as contextual units for content analysis. The period of monitoring was seven years, from January 1998 to September 2004, and the main aim consisted in documenting "the medial presentation of the relationship between nature protection and communal development". It was made operable by use of the

Individual BRs proved to differ as to their medial image. Viewed from this perspective, Třeboňsko and Křivoklátsko can be seen as areas where the problems of nature protection do not stir public opinion. Content analysis documents "conflicts" between nature protection and communities as usually belonging to the sphere of the routine administrative agenda. On no account they do have a character of ⌐fatal" problem considering any of the parties involved. In both areas, the image presented in the press includes more examples of successful cooperation between nature protection authorities and communities. If we were to formulate a hypothesis summarizing the situation, we could probably say that in the course of the previous twenty years, "both the systems got accustomed to each other". In this respect, the area of the Šumava Mts. is different compared to the above mentioned protected areas. It is hardly possible to state that this area is free from medially presented conflicts. The consensus between the Šumava NP and the communities is hindered by a large number of various circumstances. The national park came to the existence relative short time ago (in 1991); furthermore its activities overlap with those of protected landscape area. The PLA, as well as the NP, are situated on the territory belonging to two administrative regions; the final version of the Act on the Šumava National Park has not yet been accepted; the communities strive for financial funding of their budgets and for compensations, and at the same time they struggle to reduce unemployment. On the other hand, nature protection bodies have adopted traditionally defensive strategy towards any potential economic activity as their general communication pattern, referring to the principle of precaution (similar results see e.g. Jeník, 2006). In this case, the conflicts presented in the press can be considered ⌐fatal". The decision of one actor in a dispute can have serious consequences for the other actor involved[16]. That is why the relationships between both actors are tenser. However, here too, the points of view are gradually converging. Tourism plays pivotal role in this process, more specifically its sustainable forms whose development seems to be acceptable for both sites, making thus platform for mutual communication (Kušová et al. 2005). The above mentioned hypothesis could be thus slightly reformulated – How much time is needed for both systems to get used to each other? Maybe in 20 years' time the Šumava Mts. area will be presented in press in a way resembling the current articles on Křivoklátsko and Třeboňsko – very much like an "idyll".

INSTITUTIONAL ARRANGEMENTS OF BIOSPHERE RESERVE

Biosphere reserve is not recognized as a legal category of protected areas by the Czech environmental legislation. The Nature Conservation and Landscape Protection Act does not include biosphere reserve when defining six national protected area categories: national park, protected landscape area, national nature reserve, national nature monument, nature reserve and nature monument. Biosphere reserve is then perceived as an international label sticked on an area already protected according to the national environmental legislation, that does not have any legal support (Urban, 2006). Institutionally, the management of biosphere reserve is

---

following key words: Třeboňsko, Křivoklátsko, Šumava, Biosphere Reserve, communities, enterprise, cooperation, support, coexistence and conflict. As recorded units, entire articles were used that contained the name of a particular PLA or NP together with at least one of the remaining key words.

[16] Reduction of the Park area versus preventing construction of a bridge over Lipno lake, for example.

associated with the administration of protected landscape area, or national park. Due to low compatibility of the concept of biosphere reserve with the Czech legislation the space to manoeuvre of the protected area administration in its effort of the biosphere reserve concept implementation is a relatively narrow one. The manoeuvreing space varies, however depending on individual particular functions to be fulfilled as some of them are regulated by law whereas the others not.

The *technique of semi-standardized interviews* was applied as the principal method for information gathering on present institutional arrangements related to the management of biosphere reserve. Altogether thirty four key informants were addressed in each model area by use of semi-standardized interview, being staff members of protected areas administration, mayors of local municipalities, key local entrepreneurs as well as experts in nature protection and regional development. While in general, the interviews focused on their years lasting experiences with practical implementation of all the four basic functions biosphere reserve is expected to fulfill – nature protection, research, education and promotion of sustainable development, main attention was paid to the last one.

Qualitative analysis of the empirical material gained by interviews suggests that the administration bodies of the protected areas are employing plenty of legislation tools for nature protection. Basically, these tools are of restrictive and compensational character. The former still prevail in practical situations, which is also evident in a relatively long list of the competences the administration has as an indisputable participant in territorial proceedings (see the Act 114/1992 of the Law Code, on Nature Conservation and Landscape Protection). However, the administration authorities are not dependent exclusively on restrictions. Since 1996 there has been the Programme of Landscape Cultivation, which is executed by the administration on behalf of the Ministry of the Environment CR. Non-restrictive tools also include the compensation of possible economic drawback caused by nature conservation. The principle of compensation is just being tested but its operation aroused interest among administration representatives as to expected improvement of their position in negotiations with other land users. Generally speaking, the execution of state administration in nature conservation is not hindered by any serious problems and runs relatively smoothly in the framework of legislative rules and provisions. The space for administration to manoeuvre is clearly and unambiguously defined and successfully utilized. In case there are conflicts in communication, they can be mostly viewed as ⌐normal" interpersonal conflicts emerging due to advancing of different interests.

Compared to nature conservation, the activities connected with education and training are framed by legislation only in a general way. Each administration body chose a different strategy to perform their tasks. In the Šumava Mts. it is the national park that plays an important part. Due to the fact that it runs its own public relation department, the national park performs almost all educational activities including those pertaining to the administration of the protected landscape area. The activities are varied – e.g. there are eleven frequently visited well functioning information centers within the territory[17]. Educational activities of the protected landscape area are thus limited to founding and maintaining educational tracks and information boards. As to Třeboňsko and Křivoklátsko Protected Landscape Areas, apart from founding educational trails they focus on two types of educational activities and programs. They combine issuing information brochures and

---

[17] see www.npsumava.cz

running an information and educational centre. The brochures and other printed materials target partly on visitors coming to the territory, and partly on local people. It can be said that within the delimited space the administration bodies do their best. And the public highly appreciate their effort (Kušová et al., 2005a; Těšitel et al, 2005).

As a matter of fact, the protected areas are subject both to internal and external research. The situation in particular places of interest is practically the same. The internal research is carried out in the form of more or less regular surveys conducted by the employees of the administration authorities. These surveys mainly consist of monitoring or inventory. They are usually done periodically in five-year intervals. All administrative authorities are well equipped to carry out such internal surveys. However, the protected areas also fulfill the functions of model areas for specific research projects and diploma theses elaborated by various external institutions. These external subjects focus on their own research objectives, which are reflected in the definitions of the themes. Considering the usefulness of results of these projects for the protected areas administrative bodies, our results show that the administration usually lacks relevant information on the results. The cooperation with research institutions is mostly based on individual professional contacts with the colleagues dealing with similar themes. There is a lack of systematic approach to scientific research. The imbalance between scientific and social research represents another problem. The situation has not changed since 1993, when the worldwide MaB session emphasized that man should be in the centre of interest within the program, but in fact it is paid little attention (e.g. Oszlányi, 2001). The scientific research still strongly prevails in the protected areas. Much still has to be done in this respect, however social dimension of sustainability has already started to gain recognition.[18]

Support of sustainable development is the fourth function to be fulfilled by the biosphere reserves. Considering our model territories, the biosphere reserve is institutionally associated with the administrative authority of the protected area. It allows for viewing this function as a share of the administrative body activities on the life of the local community. Some activities affecting the communal life were already mentioned. The execution of the state administration definitely belongs to them as well as the educational activities. Nevertheless, the discussed theme surpasses this framework and concerns the administration as engaged and participating in ⌐generally beneficial projects", i.e. the projects which do not primarily focus on nature conservation but more on the adequate socioeconomic development in the area. While in many cases the results applicable to protected landscape areas did not differ from those applicable to the national park, in the case of the participation of the protected areas administration bodies in the projects it is reasonable to differentiate. At present the administrative bodies of the protected landscape areas participate in development projects mainly indirectly. Being experts in many aspects of the territory in question, their employees provide the applicants with factual information. They provide their know-how during the formulation of the project proposal and issue supportive references increasing the applicant's chances that the project is admitted. When the project is getting implemented, these experts join the process as indisputable participants in administration procedures. However, this form of participation seems to be limited in time. The main partners in the mentioned cooperation

---

[18] It can be documented, among others, by the shift from the Long-term Ecological Research (LTER) to the Long-term Socioecological Research (LTSER) with its focus on coupled socioecological system (Haberl et al., 2006). Biosphere reserves are expected to play the role of research platforms within this program.

system are communities and microregions, whose representatives have successfully acquired the necessary skills or they hire professional agencies for the preparation of project proposals. Direct participation in the development projects is problematic. When applying the BR concept to practice we must face incomplete, poor compatibility with the system of Czech environmental legislation. One of the consequences is thus the lack of unambiguous legislative rules defining direct participation of the protected area administration, as a state administration body, in such projects. Quite naturally it results in neutral, indifferent attitude of the administrative bodies to the projects, which can be easily explained by their fear from the conflict of interests if they were direct participants. Their representatives are afraid of the situation when, in the competence of state administration, they might have to assume an attitude towards themselves as implementing bodies. Another argument in favor of their indifference is the ever busier state administration agenda. Besides that, individual administrative bodies of protected areas are not legal entities. The status of legal entity applies only to their headquarters. The Šumava National Park (ŠNP) displays a different situation. Firstly, it has a different legislative status compared to protected landscape areas. Šumava National Park is a sovereign subject having its legal identity. Secondly, as an allowance organization, it can make its own decisions on the allocation of funds. The third important difference bases on the fact that within the ŠNP organizational structure, the execution of state administration has been separated from its other activities. Moreover, it has established a public relation department. Besides that there are further ⎡stimuli" fostering its pro-active approach. The ŠNP raises considerable financial means due to its right of forest management. The funds can be subsequently invested in particular projects. At the same time, all its activities are permanently "monitored" and checked by the public, which creates permanent pressure in the broadest sense. The park administration has already realized activities which can be called ⎡good will projects", the examples of such projects being ⎡Our Peatbog", and ⎡Cultural Heritage Renewal". Considering the theory of cultural capital (e.g. Bourdieu & Passeeron, 1990; Garrod et al., 2006), it is a gesture reinforcing the national park administration in its effort to define its status towards other stakeholders in the territory.

Despite the differences in the status between the national park and protected landscape area administration bodies it can be stated that all these authorities are primarily representatives of the state administration which influences to a great extent their mode of operation. The existing institutional setting motivates employees of these bodies only a little to perform any activity beyond the scope of current legislation. Generally speaking, the current institutional model ensures that they can actively carry out only three of four BR functions – biodiversity protection, education and training and, to some extent, performance of scientific research. The fourth function – support of sustainable development through participation in activities improving socioeconomic standard of local communities – can be accomplished only partially and indirectly. Active participation of protected areas representatives in developmental activities, though sustainable, seems to be hardly possible mainly due to the fact that these activities are perceived as being intermingled with the execution of state administration (Kušová et al., 2007).

In addition we applied *case study analysis* to assess a project aimed at promoting principles of the biosphere reserve concept in the Šumava Mts. region, in terms of identifying of success and failure factors of their practical implementation. More specifically we tried to reveal if the way they were implemented could contribute to overcoming of the current institutional limits and make the biosphere reserve a learning site of sustainable development.

The project titled ⌐Conservation and Sustainable Use of Biodiversity through Sound Tourism Development in Biosphere Reserves in Central and Eastern Europe"[19], rephrased in the region as "Sound Tourism – A Chance for the Šumava Biosphere Reserve" financially supported by the UNEP-GEF, was initiated by the ŠNP administration and had actually a form of a gesture. The end-user of the project outputs, however, was defined as the entire territory of the Šumava Biosphere Reserve. The mission of the project was twofold – besides producing outputs of its particular activities, it was intended to be a tool facilitating communication between the protected area administration and other stakeholders involved in the project. That is how it was functioning since the very beginning. The project proposal was elaborated by a team consisting of the representatives of all local groups interested in relevant fields - nature conservation, local entrepreneurs, communities, representatives of regional governments and NGOs. Considering our point of view, it is important to mention the Local Steering Committee of the project, comprising those who were in charge of the project preparation. In the period of project implementation its members participated in the project management as well as in lobbying for widening the scope of the project activities, and for further fundraising.

The project could be considered a set of nine interlinked activities which span from those having very practical outputs to activities producing strategic planning materials. "Establishment of a System of Cross Border Tourist Trails", "Training of Local Guides" and "Identification of a Potential of the Šumava Biosphere Reserve for New Touristic Activities" (Figures 17 and 18) can be seen as the most practical outputs of the project, having immediate impact on the territory. There were two activities within the project directly supporting sustainable forms of tourism – "System of Financial Incentives", having a form of local grant scheme aimed primarily at improving small scale touristic infrastructure (Figure 19), and "System of Certification of Local Products and Services"[20]. Among the strategic activities we can count participation of the project in preparation of the "Concept of Sustainable Tourism Development in the Šumava Region" (Figure 20), "Institutional Analysis of the Šumava Biosphere Reserve" and designing of an electronic "Database on Cultural Heritage of the Šumava Biosphere Reserve". Designing of platform for information exchange among local mayors, representatives of nature protection authorities and other key stakeholders became an inseparable part of the project, manifested in the form of series of round tables and training courses (Figure 21).

As indicated by the questionnaire survey and key informant interviewing, the relationship between NP and PLA, and biosphere reserve is perceived as being confusing for many people (Figure 22). Evaluated in this context, the project seemed to play a pivotal role in the process of forming the notion of the biosphere reserve concept among local as well as regional public.

---

[19] www.oete.de/tourism4nature/index.htm
[20] www.domaci-vyrobky.cz

Biosphere Reserves as Learning Sites of Sustainable Development 111

Figure 17. Potential of the Šumva BR for mountain biking (after Pavlásek, 2006).

Figure 18. Cover page of the study "Hippoturistics in the Šumava BR" elaborated within the project.

Figure 19. Educational trail in Dešenice built with the financial support of the grant scheme.

Figure 20. Cover page of the Concept of Sound Tourism Development in the Šumava Mts., elaborated with contribution of the project.

Biosphere Reserves as Learning Sites of Sustainable Development 113

Figure 21. Round table with mayors of the Šumava BR municipalities, Modrava village, July 3. 2007.

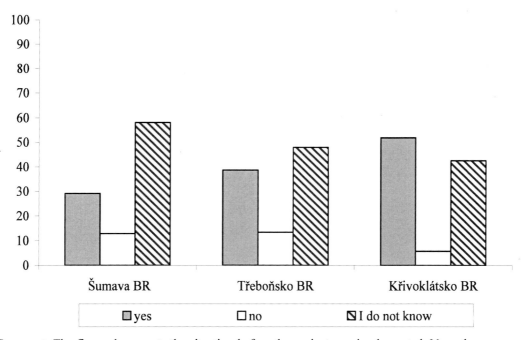

Comment: The figure documents the situation before the project was implemented. Nowadays we can presume that the awareness on BR is likely to be higher in the Šumava Mts. as the UNEP-GEF project was heavily informed about in the region by varied promotional materials, and circa 500 local personalities were, in some way, directly involved in the project implementation.

Figure 22. Do you think that the protected area has the status of biosphere reserve?

The scope of the project was to complex to be executed by one expert or institution. As a result, one of its main "social by-products" was an establishment of several social networks, partly overlapping, by use of which particular project activities were realized. Šumava National Park and Protected Landscape Area Administration, Regional Development Agency Šumava, Regional Environmental Centre Czech Republic, as well as NEBE Agency formed a core of these networks, coordinated as a rule by the Institute of Systems Biology and Ecology AS CR. In parallel to forming social networks, network of projects emerged around individual activities. In this manner, the UNEP-GEF project was linked with two INTERREG-type projects – PANet (Protected Areas Networks – Establishment and Management of Corridors, Networks and Cooperation) and Certification of Local Products in the Šumava Mts., pooling thus experts, know-how and financial resource with the aim to use them as much as effectively (Těšitel et al., 2007)[21].

The complexity of the problems solved by the projects has resulted in time chaining. Viewed from this perspective, the projects network proved to be an efficient impetus to start solving the problems, delivering however, neither financial sources nor time enough to accomplish the task in its full extent. As the networks of interested partners has already been established, some projects activities are expected to continue in the future, supported however by another grants, both running and applied for. The projects network thus spans far beyond the "lifetime" of particular projects, setting a base for a long term activities related to the concept of biosphere reserve. In particular, the system of local guides (Figure 23) was adopted by the Šumava National Park Administration and included into its regular agenda. Building of data base on cultural heritage (Figure 24) is expected to continue in terms of integrating information sources from the Czech, German (Bavarian) and Austrian side, financially supported by the South Bohemia regional government and EU Structural Funds.

It was a fortunate coincidence of facts that caused the network of projects fulfilled two types of expectations – that it produced outputs excellent by themselves, and that contributed substantially to the discussion on the notion of the biosphere reserve in the region, in fact introducing the term into strategic planning documents as well as into more practical discussions around tables.

First of all, the issue itself – sustainable tourism – has been a relatively consensual theme[22]. Secondly, the project yielded concrete and visible outputs, aimed at promoting of sound forms of tourism development. Though the national park was an important project partner, in fact it itself initiated formulation of the project and applied for it, officially the project was coordinated by an independent body (the academician institute) and thus perceived as not being directly linked to the national park and its rather restrictive policy.

---

[21] For example, thanks to this cooperation, certification system ŠUMAVA–originální produkt® originally focused on local products was extended to include as well services related to sound tourism. As a result, Šumava Mts. can be considered a region where the process of certification has been most advanced, compared to the other regions within the Czech Republic where the system was implemented.

[22] Tourism was recognized as key factor for local development as early as at the beginning of nineties, both by local elite and general public (e.g. Těšitel et al., 2003, 2003a). As to the form, tourism has developed in a more or less sustainable way in the Šumava Mts., which is a fact valued by nature protection representatives.

Biosphere Reserves as Learning Sites of Sustainable Development 115

Figure 23. Leaflet promoting local guides in the Šumava BR (2007).

Figure 24. Home page of the electronic database on cultural heritage of the Šumava BR.

The "trade mark" of the biosphere reserve was used as being in "legislative vacuum", which was perceived as a weak point at the beginning of the project, namely by the representatives of state nature protection. In the end, however, the legislative vagueness proved to be an advantage as it "liberated" all the stakeholders from their bred-in-the-bone schematic viewpoints. The project seemed to "break the behavioral stereotypes", of particular personalities involved. Being mentally "free" from a legal framework, they behaved rather cooperatively, concentrating on achieving concrete output instead of pushing forward official doctrines of particular institutions they were expected to represent. Formal independence of the projects network from the Šumava National Park and Protected Landscape Area Administration led to the situation when all the partners, including representatives on nature protection themselves, ceased to prejudice and started actively cooperate. The projects network formed thus concrete out-of-official-policy-standing platform of cooperation among experts, not biased by official doctrines. As a result, sound tourism ceased to be viewed as being a-priori in contradiction with nature conservation. In this perspective the concept of biosphere reserve itself proved to have a big potential of becoming a good trade mark. Referring to the concept allowed representatives state nature protection "not to loose their face" when discussing "developmental issues" with other stakeholders. The process of achieving desired project outputs proved to be as much important as the outputs themselves, in some perspective even more important, as it enabled linking stakeholders and forming flexible alliances, both formal and informal. Gradual building and reconstructing of the network-like arrangements could be thus explained in terms of learning by interacting process (e.g. Lundvall, 1997; Gunjan, 2005; Kušová et al., 2008a) on mutual communication among stakeholders involved about the innovative concept of biosphere reserve.

Successful realization of the projects, more specifically the way the process of implementation was guided, suggests that the project based management could yield success in achieving the biosphere reserve functions, at least its fourth one – promotion of sustainable development. Goal oriented network of interested stakeholders, permanently reconstructed, seems then to be a more adequate organizational form to be applied when attempting to implement the BR concept into practice.

CONCLUSION

On the Method

The mosaic depicted by the triangulation approach was rather complex. Picture about quality of life in biosphere reserves drawn by use of objective statistical data did not differ from that we got when analyzing the data gained by questionnaire survey. Both views, objective and subjective ones, overlap to a great extent. Sustainable tourism as the most promising factor fostering local development appeard as an output of content analysis of media, questionnaire survey as well as key informant interviewing. While all the three model areas can be viewed as similar in most aspects content analysis revealed fundamental diferences between Šumava BR and the remainig two model areas as to the relationship between nature protection bodies and local communities. Different positions on the scale between conflict and cooperation, occupied by particular biosphere reserves introduced a question of time necessary in order local economic activities with nature protection to be reconciled. By use of interviews and case study analysis we were able to analyze behavioural strategies of individual stakeholders and assess effectiveness of institutional setting of biosphere reserve, which led us to the suggestion of network like organizational arrangement as a complement to an existing hierarchical scheme of state nature protection.

Biosphere Reserve as a Learning Site

Biosphere reserves are poised to take on a new role in nature protection. Not only they are expected to be a means for the people who live and work within and around them to attain a balanced relationship with the natural world. As they do not operate in isolation but form a network of global scale, individual biosphere reserves are supposed to serve as pilot sites or "learning places" to explore and demonstrate approaches to conservation and sustainable development, providing lessons which can be applied elsewhere[23].

On the other hand, it is recommended by the Seville Strategy that the general concept should be implemented in many different ways in order to meet local needs and conditions. In fact, one of the greatest strengths of the biosphere reserve concept has been the flexibility and creativity with which it could been realized in various situations. Hence, each biosphere reserve could be a context-specific experiment in sustainable development at varying scales.

Learning from each other, or to come to more general conclusions, seems thus to be to a great extent dependent on level of similarity in terms of internal conditions as well as external

---

[23] (http://www.unesco.org/mab/faq_br.shtml#functions

(regional and national) milieu particular biospheres share. When we are to asses our outcomes from this perspective, it is necessary to point out two aspects.

Firstly, we have to state that, all the three biosphere reserves studied are embedded in a very similar regional milieu, being situated in regions where serious social conflicts are not present. This is mainly thanks to the relatively low unemployment rate occurring there (Figure 25). This type of external milieu cannot be, however applied to the remaining three Czech biosphere reserves that have to operate in regions facing more complicated socioeconomic situation[24]. As the attitude of people to nature, and consequently to nature protection, is presumed to be dependent on particular socioeconomic situation, more precisely on the level of satisfaction of what is perceived as appropriate level of material needs (e.g. Ingelhart, 1990; Librová, 1994) we should be cautious when trying to generalize results and apply them nation-wide.

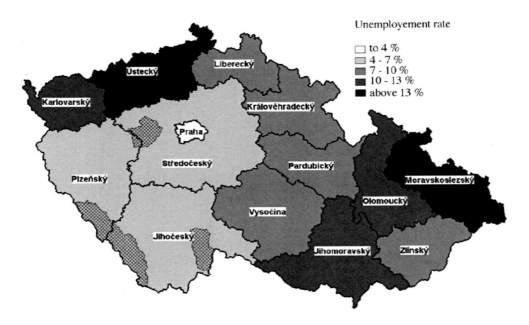

Figure 25. Regional distribution of unemployment—Czech Republic, 31-12-2004 (after Ministry of Labour and Social Affairs of the Czech Republic).

Secondly, the BR concept builds upon cooperation among stakeholders in the locality or region. Jointly shared vision on what could be considered common ground for discussion around the future coexistence of biodiversity protection and acceptable forms of its sustainable use can be viewed as condition necessary, making implementation of the concept likely, at least. In our case, sustainable tourism has played the pivotal role, which, as a branch of local economy, seems to be more flexible, compared to the more traditional and conservative economic activities such as agriculture and forestry. The need for cooperative approaches arises from a change in the competitive strategies that are influenced by the volatility and sensitivity of tourism industry (Gunjan, 2005) that requires key actors to think

---

[24] The Krkonoše BR, Bílé Karpaty BR and Dolní Morava BR are located in Liberecký region, Zlínský region and Jihomoravský region respectively

about which of their resources and activities are most sensibly combined (Crompton, 1990; Palmer, 1998). Having this in mind we can conclude that the example discussed above should be thought as being limited to sound tourism related activities as flexible networks are most likely to appear there.

At the very end it can be stated, that the chapter indicated possibilities and limitations of the BR concept implementation in the Czech Republic. Generally speaking, the concept proved to be an efficient tool supporting platform of communication on local as well as regional levels aimed at harmonizing of diverse interests. Viewing from this perspective, presented results may become an inspiration for other biosphere reserves. As the chapter tries to interpret biosphere reserve, among others, in terms of the process of social learning, it can be seen as a contribution to the debate on ideas of the ongoing UN Decade on Education for Sustainable Development 2005-2014.

ACKNOWLEDGMENTS

The study was based on the following research projects: Participative management of protected areas – a key to minimization of conflicts between biodiversity protection and socioeconomic development of local communities (VaV 610/3/03), funded by the Ministry of Environment CR; Research project of the Institute of Systems Biology and Ecology – AV0Z60870520 – Spatial and functional dynamics of biological, ecological and socioeconomic systems in interaction with the global change of climate; Conservation and sustainable use of biodiversity through sound tourism development in biosphere reserves in Central and Eastern Europe. Grant United Nations Environment Programme, Global Environment Facility Medium Sized Project, GFL/2328-2714-4829, PMS: GF/4020-05-01; PANet 2010-Protected areas network-Establishment and Management of Corridors, Networks and Cooperation. INTRREG IIIB CADSES.

REFERENCES

Amin A. & Thrift N. (1994): Living in the global. In: Amin A. & Thrift N. (Eds.): *Globalisation, institutions and regional development in Europe* (pp 1-22). Oxford: Oxford University Press.

Antrop, M. (2001). The language of landscape ecologists and planners. A comparative content analysis of concepts used in landscape ecology. *Landscape and Urban Planning, 55,* 163-173.

Antrop, M. (2006). Sustainable landscapes: contradiction, fiction or utopia. *Landscape and Urban Planning, 75*(3-4), 187-197.

Bartoš, M., Kušová, D. & Těšitel, J. (1998). Integrated endogenous regional development concept and the role of Šumava National Park administration. *Silva Gabreta, 2,* 385–394.

Bartoš, M., Kušová, D. & Těšitel, J. (2005). Life in Large Scale Areas with Specific Regime. *Životné Prostredie, 39*(2),76–79 (in Czech).

Blažek, B. (1998). *Venkov, města, média [Countryside, cities, media].* Praha: SLON (in Czech).

Blažek, J. & Uhlíř, D. (2002). *Teorie regionálniho rozvoje [Theories of regional development]*, Praha: Karolinum (in Czech).

Bourdieu P. & Passeron J. C. (1990). *Reproduction in education, society and culture. Second Edition.* London: Sage.

Brock W.A, & Xepapadeas A. (2003). Valuing Biodiversity from an Economic Perspective: A Unified Economic, Ecological, and Genetic Approach. *The American Economic Review, 93*(5), 1597-1614.

Brunckhorst, D. (2001). Building capital through bioregional planning and biosphere reserve. *Ethics in Science and Environmental Politics,* 19-32.

Collados, C. & Duane, T. P. (1999). Natural capital and quality of life: a model for valuating the sustainability of alternative regional development paths. *Ecological Economics, 30*(3), 441-460.

Costanza, R., d'Arge, R., de Groot, R., Farber, S. C., Grasso, M., Hannon, B., Limburg, K., Naeem, S., O'Neill, R. V., Paruelo, J., Raskin, R. G., Sutton, P. & van den Belt, M. (1997). The value of the world's ecosystem services and natural capital. *Nature, 387* (6630), 253-260.

Crompton J. L. (1990). Attitude determinants in tourism destination choice. *Annals of Tourism Research, 17*, 432-448.

DeFleur, M. & Ball–Rokeach, S. (1996). *Teorie masové komunikace [Theory of mass communication]*. Praha: Karolinum (in Czech).

Disman, M. (1993). *Jak se vyrábi sociologická znalost [Way to produce sociological knowledge]*. Praha: Karolinum (in Czech).

Dredge D. (2006). Policy networks and the local organisation of tourism. *Tourism Management, 27*, 269-280.

Faber, M. (2008). *How to be an Ecological Economist. Discussion Paper Series No. 454,* University of Heidelberg.

Farina, A. (2000). The Cultural Landscape as a Model for Integration of Ecology and Economics. *BioScience, 50*(4), 313-320.

Garrod B., Wornell R. & Youell R. (2006). Re-conceptualising rural resources as countryside capital: the case of rural tourism. *Journal of Rural Studies, 22,* 117-128.

Getzner, M. & Jungmeier, M. (2000). Conservation policy and the regional economy: the regional impact of Natura 2000 conservation sites in Austria. *Journal of Nature Conservation, 10*(1), 25-34.

Gunjan S. (2005). Relationships, networks and the learning regions: case evidence from the Peak District National Park. *Tourism Management, 26*, 277-289.

Hajer, M. (2003). Policy without polity? Policy analysis and the institutional void. *Policy Sciences, 36*, 175-195.

Hajer, M. (2003 a). A frame in the fields: policymaking and the reinvention of politics. In: Hajer, M. & Wagenaar, W., (Eds.), *Deliberative Policy Analysis* (pp. 88-110). Cambridge: Cambridge University Press.

Honzík K. (1965). *Tvorba životniho stylu [On the creation of lifestyle]*. Prague: NPL (in Czech).

Imhoff, Marc L. (2004). Global patterns in human consumption of net primary production. *Nature, 429*(6994), 870–73.

Imperial, M. T. (1999). Institutional Analysis and Ecosystem-Based Management: The Institutional Analysis and Development Framework. *Environmental Management, 24*(4), 449-465.

Ingelhart, R. (1990). *The culture shift in advanced industrial society*. Princeton.

Ira, V. (2005). Sustainable development, quality of life and tourism. In: Hesková M., Šittler E. & Dvořák V. (Eds.), *Tourism, regional development and education. Reviewed proseedings of the 10th International conference „Tourism, regional development and education"*, Tábor, 12–13. May 2005. Katedra cestovního ruchu Tábor, Jihočeská univerzita České Budějovice, 51–56.

I.U.C.N. (1980). *World Conservation Strategy: Living Resources Conservation for Sustainable Development.* Gland: I.U.C.N.

Jarman, B. (1984). Identification of Underprivileged Areas. *British Medical Journal, 289,* 1587-1592.

Jehle, R. (1998). Pojetí endogenního rurálního rozvoje a jeho zavádění do regionální politiky České republiky. [The concept of endogenous rural development in the framework of its introduction in the regional policy in the Czech Republic.] *Zemědělská ekonomika, 44*(1), 9-12 (in Czech).

Jeník, J. (2006). Polarita přírody a kultury v teorii a praxi. [Polarity of Nature and Culture in Theory and Practice.] *Životné Prostredie, 40*(5), 234-237 (in Czech).

Jenkins, T. (Ed.) (2001). Integrated tourism: a conceptual framework, Deliverable 1, Ms. Supporting and Promoting Integrated Tourism in Europe's Lagging Regions, 64 pp, online reference http://sprite.econ.upatras.gr/.

Kaval, P. (2006). Valuing Ecosystem Services: A New Paradigm Shift. *Working Paper in Economics 1/6.* University of Waikato.

Kooten, C. G. & Wang, S (1998). Estimating Economic Costs of NatureProtection: British Columbia's Forest Regulations. *Canadian Public Policy – Analyse De Politiques, 24*(2),63-71.

Kušová, D., Bartoš, M. & Těšitel, J. (1999). Potential development of the right shore of Lipno Lake area – comparison of landscape and urban planning documentation with ideas of local inhabitants. *Silva Gabreta, 3,* 217–227.

Kušová, D., Bartoš, M. & Těšitel, J. (2002). Role of traditions in tourism development in the Czech part of the Bohemian Forest. *Silva Gabreta, 8,* 265–274.

Kušová, D., Těšitel, J. & Bartoš, M. (2005). The media image of the relationship between nature protection and socio-economic development in selected protected landscape areas. *Silva Gabreta, 11*(2),123–133.

Kušová, D., Těšitel, J., Matějka, K. & Bartoš, M. (2005a). Nature protection and socio-economic development in selected protected landscape areas. *Ekológia (Bratislava), 24,* (Supplement 1), 109-123.

Kušová, D., Těšitel, J., Matějka, K. & Bartoš, M. (2006). Socio-economic conditions in selected biosphere reserves. *Silva Gabreta, 12*(3), 157–169.

Kušová, D., Těšitel, J. & Bartoš, M. (2007). Možnosti využití konceptu biosférické rezervace na Šumavě. [Implementation possibilities of the BR concept in the Bohemian Forest]. In: Dvořák L., Šustr P., Braun V. (Eds.): *Aktuality šumavského výzkumu III. [Research actualities in Bohemian/Bavarian Forest]*, Správa Národního parku a Chráněné krajinné oblasti Šumava, Srní, 4.-5.10. 2007, 139 – 143 (in Czech).

Kušová, D., Těšitel, J., Matějka, K. & Bartoš, M. (2008). Biosphere reserves – an attempt to form sustainable landscape (A case study of three biosphere reserves in the Czech Republic). *Landscape and Urban Planning, 84*(1), 187-197.

Kušová, D., Těšitel, J. & Bartoš, M. (2008a). Biosphere reserves – learning sites of sustainable development ? *Silva Gabreta, 14* (3), 221-234.

Librová, H. (1987). *Sociální potřeba a hodnota krajiny. [Social need and landscape value.]* Brno: UJEP (in Czech).

Librová, H. (1988). *Láska ke krajině? [Love for landscape?]* Brno: Blok (in Czech).

Librová, H. (1994). Pestří a zelení: kapitoly dobrovolné skromnosti. [The colorful and the green: chapters on voluntary modesty] Brno: Veronica (in Czech).

Lowe, A. (1988). Small Hotel Survival: An inductive approach. *The International Journal of Hospitality Management, 7*(3), 197-223.

Lundvall, B. Å. (1997). Information Technology in the Learning Economy. *Communications & Strategies, 28*, 117-192.

MacLeod, G. (2001). New Regionalism reconsidered: Globalisation, regulation and the recasting of political economic space. *Internatioinal Journal of Urban and Regional Research, 25*, 804-829.

MacLuhan, M. (1991). *Jak rozumět médiím. Extenze člověka. [To understand media. Human dimension.]* Praha: Odeon (in Czech).

Mareš, P. (1999). *Sociologie nerovnosti a chudoby. [Sociology of unevenness and poverty.]* Praha: SLON (in Czech).

Maršálková, M. & Todlová, M. (1983). *Podklady, informace a náměty pro další rozvoj rekreace v ČSR. [Information materials and proposals for further development of recreation in the Czech Republic.]* České Budějovice: ÚKE ČSAV (in Czech).

Maskell, P. & Malmberg, A. (1999). Localised Learning and Industrial Competitiveness. *Cambridge Journal of Economics, 23*(2), 167-186.

Massam, B. H. (2002). Quality of life: public planning and private living. *Progress in Planning, 58*, 141 – 227.

Millennium Ecosystem Assessment. (2005). *Ecosystems and Human Well-being:Synthesis.* Washington, DC: Island Press.

Murdoch, J. (2000). Networks – a new paradigm of rural development? *Journal of Rural Studies, 16*, 407-419.

Naveh, Z. (2001). Ten major premises for a holistic conception of multifunctional landscapes. *Landscape and Urban Planning, 57*, 269-283.

Nolte, B. (2005). *Tourism in Biosphärenreservaten Ostmitteleuropas. Hoffnungen, Hindernisse und Handlungsspielräume bei der Umsetzung von Nachhaltigkeit.* Berlin: Mensch&Buch Verlag.

OECD (2005). *Report on policy, state and development of the environment: the Czech Republic.* Praha: Ministry of Environment of the Czech Republic.

Olsen, W. (2004). Triangulation in social research: Qualitative and quantitative methods can really be mixed. In: Holborn, Ormskirk (Eds.): *Developments in Sociology.* Ormskirk: Causeway Press.

Orians, G. H. (1980). Habitat selection: general theory and application to human behavior. In: Lockard, J.S. (Ed.), *The Evolution of Human Social Behavior.* New York: Elsevier.

Oszlányi, J. (2001). Research in UNESCO Biosphere Reserves as one of the elements of the Seville Strategy. *Ekologia (Bratislava), 20*(Supplement 3), 36-45.

Paavola, J. & Adger, N. W. (2005). Institutional ecological economics. *Ecological Economics, 53*, 353-368.

Paiders, J. (2007). How nature protection restrictions affect economic development? An example of municipalities from the North Vidzeme Biosphere Reserve, Latvia. *Working paper*, University of Latvia.

Palmer, A. (1998): Evaluationg the governance style of marketing groups. *Annales of Tourism Research, 25*(1), 185-201.

Parto, S. (2005). "Good" Governance and Policy Analysis: What of Institutions?. Maastricht Economic Research Institute on Innovation and Technology. *MERIT-Infonomics Research Memorandum series 2005-001.*

Palang, H., Helmfrid, S., Antrop, M. & Alumäe, H. (2005). Rural Landscapes: past processes and future strategies. *Landscape and Urban Planning, 70*, 3-8.

Pavlásek, Z. (2006). Netradiční aktivity v Biosférické rezervaci Šumava (studie možnosti rozvoje netradičních sportovních a turistických aktivit). [Non-traditional activities in the Šumava Biosphere Reserve – study on development potential of non-traditional sport and touristic activities]. Vimperk, České Budějovice: NP Šumava and ÚSBE AV ČR, v.v.i. http://www.npsumava.cz/storage/setr_aktivity1.pdf (in Czech).

Price, M. F. (2002). The periodic review of biosphere reserves: a mechanism to foster sites of excellence for conservation and sustainable development. *Environmental Science & Policy, 5*, 13-18.

Rolston, H. (1997). Feeding People versus Saving Nature. In Gottieb, R. S. (Ed): *The Ecological Community* (208-225). New York, London: Routlege.

Roth, S. (2007). Summary of Outcomes of the Workshop on NATURA 2000 and Tourism. Bonn: Ecological Tourism Europe (ETE).

Sharpley, R. (2000). Tourism and Sustainable Development: Exploring the Theoretical Divide, *Journal of Sustainable Tourism, 8*,1-19.

Stoll-Kleemann S., Bender S., Berghöfer A., Bertzky M., Fritz-Vietta N., Schliep R. & Thierfelder B. (2006). Linking Governance and Management Perspectives with Conservation Success in Protected Areas and Biosphere Reserves. *Discussion paper 01 of the GoBi Research Group*. Berlin: Humboldt-Universität.

Storper M. (1997). *The regional world: Territorial development in a global economy.* London: Guilford Press.

Tait, J. & Lyall, C. (2004). A New Mode of Governance for Science, Technology, Risk and the Environment ? *Innogen Working Paper 17* (November 2004).

Těšitel, J., Kušová, D. & Bartoš, M. (1999). Non marginal parameters of marginal areas. *Ekológia (Bratislava), 18*(2), 39–46.

Těšitel J., Kušová D. & Bartoš M. (2003). Tourist's reasons for visiting mountain areas: a case study of the Šumava Mountains. *Landscape Research, 28*(3), 317 – 322.

Těšitel J., Kušová D. & Bartoš M. (2003a). Role of tourism in development of rural marginal areas (region Šumava Mts., Czech Republic). In: Banski J., Owsinski J. (Eds.): *Alternatives for European Rural Areas* (81-91) Warsaw: European Rural Development Network, Institute of Agricultural and Food Economics, Institute of Geography and Spatial Organization, Polish Academy of Sciences.

Těšitel, J., Kušová, D., Matějka, K. & Bartoš, M. (2005). *Lidé v biosférickiých rezervacích [People in biosphere reserves]*. České Budějovice: Institute of Systems Biology and Ecology, Academy of Sciences (in Czech).

Těšitel, J., Kušová, D., Matějka, K. & Bartoš, M. (2005a). Protected landscape areas and regional development (the case of the Czech Republic). In: Florianczyk, Z., Czapiewski, K. (Eds.): *Rural Development Capacity in Carpathian Europe* (113-126) Warsaw: European Rural Development Network, Institute of Agricultural and Food Economics, Institute of Geography and Spatial Organization, Polish Academy of Sciences.

Těšitel, J., Kušová, D. & Bartoš, M. (2006). Rural areas development – local needs or external forces. In: Florianczyk, Z., Czapiewski, K. (Eds.): *Endogenous factors stimulating rural development* (87-97). Warzaw: European Rural Development Network, Institute of Agricultural and Food Economics, Institute of Geography and Spatial Organization, Polish Academy of Sciences.

Těšitel, J., Kušová, D. & Bartoš, M. (2007). *Šetrný turismus v biosférických rezervacích – nástroj formování sítí spolupráce: případová studie Biosférické rezervace Šumava. [Sound tourism in biosphere reserves – a tool to form a network of cooperation: a case study of the Šumava Biosphere Reseve.]* Klagenfurt: Úřad vlády Korutan, (in Czech).

Townsend, P. (1987): Deprivation. *Journal of Social Policy, 16*(2), 87-103.

UNESCO, (1996). *Biosphere Reserves: The Seville Strategy and the Statutory Framework of the World Network.* Paris: UNESCO..

UNESCO, (2001). *MAB Report Series No. 69.* Seville+5 International Meeting of Experts in Pamplona (Spain, 2000), Proceedings. Paris: UNESCO.

UNESCO, (2002). *Biosphere reserves: Special places for people and nature.* Paris: UNESCO.

UNESCO, (2008). *The Madrid Declaration.* Paris: UNESCO.

Urban, F. (2006). *Institutional and management frameworks in the Biosphere Reserve Šumava.* Bonn: ETE..

Vos, W. & Klijn, J. A. (2000). Trends in European landscape development: prospects for sustainable future. In: Klijn, J. A., Wos, W. (Eds.): *From landscape ecology to landscape science* (13-30). Wageningen: Kluwer Academic Publishers.

Wilson, O. E. (1984). *Biophilia - The human bond with other species.* Cambridge: Harvard University Press.

Wilson, J., Tyedmers, P. & Pelot, R. (2007). Contrasting and comparing sustainable development indicator metrics. *Ecological Indicators, 7*(2), 299-314.

Zemek, F., Heřman, M. (1998). Socio-economic potential of landscape integrated in GIS frame. *Ekológia (Bratislava), 17,* (Supplement 1), 232–240.

Zemek, F., Heřman, M., Mašková, Z. & Květ, J. (2005). Multifunctional land use – a chance or resettling abandoned landscapes? (A case study of the Zhůří territory, the Czech Republic). *Ekológia (Bratislava), 24,* (Supplement 1), 96–108.

In: Social Development
Editor: Lynda R. Elling

ISBN: 978-1-60741-612-8
© 2009 Nova Science Publishers, Inc.

Chapter 4

SOCIAL DEVELOPMENT NEEDS BETTER POLITICS

Paul E. Smith
School of Geography and Environmental Studies,
University of Tasmania, Australia

ABSTRACT

Social development is a public good and therefore likely to depend at least partly on the performance of government. However, liberal democracies have basic structures that appear to make them act with some irresponsibility and ignorance. This challenges us to replace or alter these structures or introduce new institutions to counter their effects. The latter approach may be the most feasible as its initiation may not require the assistance of the existing political establishment. Research into institutional design is still in its infancy, which points to a need for experimentation, so a new institution is proposed for trial. The structural dysfunction noted above indicates that this could be a forum based on an opinion poll designed to cultivate deliberative public participation in democratic government. Two of the many elements of this design are that the poll is run regularly, say at the same time each year, and it repeats the same questions in each poll. This institution could be initiated without official support and may then develop a public demand that compels politicians to make it a permanent part of democratic government. This should improve the delivery of public goods, thereby fostering social development.

INTRODUCTION

A major challenge to social development is that of improving the effectiveness of large groups of people making competent choices about what they want for themselves as a group, including what they want their group to do. In other words, politics or government should be made to work better, so that public goods of many types may be produced where currently they are either ignored, or provided in inadequate quantity or quality. An example of the need for this is the problem of global warming. For developed, politically advanced nations such as the US, this problem is not just whether it reduces its greenhouse gas emissions, but whether it provides leadership and other assistance to the rest of the world.

Is Democracy up to It?

Liberal democracy is touted by the western hemisphere as delivering the best form of government, but inspection of its fundamental institutions reveals that it is constructed to behave with a degree of irresponsibility and ignorance. As the function of government is to provide public goods (Olson 1965; Taylor 1987, 1), this means that liberal democratic types will under provide these goods. A detailed description will not be given here of how this irresponsibility and ignorance is generated, but in broad terms, it happens in three ways. One is that the electoral process of selecting legislators produces an element of uncertainty about who it is, that is actually in charge of government – is it politicians, or is it the electors who influence them through their vote? Any confusion about who leads means that no one is really sure who has the responsibility to determine policy, so each party leaves some of it to the other and the job tends to get neglected - especially where policy is difficult to devise, or to implement. The second source of irresponsibility and ignorance is that the system of selecting representatives forces them into incessant competition with each other for electoral success, so they sacrifice the development of good policy in order to focus on gaining and retaining power. The third source is that universal suffrage and equality of the vote often expresses, on any particular issue, the ignorance of the disengaged majority of citizens rather than the wisdom developed by some. Political candidates who reflect this ignorance of the majority are those who usually achieve electoral success. These three problems are primary dysfunctions: they are direct results of the basic structures of liberal democracies. The irresponsibility and ignorance that these structures produce may be considered to be secondary dysfunctions and the resultant undersupply of public goods is a tertiary dysfunction.

Just how much tertiary dysfunction occurs is difficult to say and it will tend to vary from one type of liberal democracy to another, but it is suggested that it is sufficiently bad to call for institutional change that would reduce irresponsibility and ignorance. If democracy - that is, government by the people - is to survive such changes, then these reforms must facilitate public participation in government while expressing the talents and knowledge possessed by the people instead of their ignorance and apathy. It should be noted that the Scandinavian democracies have relatively good public participation, for example their voluntary voting turnouts for elections are very high. Part of the reason for such engagement is likely to be that the proportional representation they employ assists the expression of diverse points of view in both the public and the parliamentary arenas. This may provide some incentive for citizens to think about political issues, to debate them and to vote (Milner 2002, 89).

The Possibility of Designing a New Institution to Improve Democratic Politics

Australian political scientists Ian Marsh and Lindy Edwards (2004, 82) have identified serious inadequacies in the development of policy in Australian democracy. In presenting their paper on this problem at a seminar at the University of Tasmania in August 2008, Marsh assessed reform as an "impossible dilemma" of two problems. The first is that the established emphasis on developing policy or strategy within the executive limits its effectiveness: it restricts options and makes implementation difficult. The second is that separating strategy from the executive is a paradigm shift in governance and therefore virtually impossible. However, it is suggested that it may be possible to achieve such a paradigm shift by establishing a new institution that forms strategy outside the executive and does so in a manner that creates an expectation by the public that the executive must implement it. A design for this purpose is outlined in the next section.

Two scholars of public administration and management, Erik-Hans Klijn and Joop F. M. Koppenjan (2006, 158), have noted that research into procedures for the design of political institutions is still in its infancy, so such design is limited to a process of "pushing and pulling with uncertain results". This trial and error approach should be guided by collective action theory, but as political scientist Elinor Ostrom (2007, 203) observes,

> a key lesson of research on collective action theory is recognizing the complex linkages among variables at multiple levels that together affect individual reputations, trust, and reciprocity as these, in turn, affect levels of cooperation and joint benefits. Conducting empirical research is thus extremely challenging.... The reason that experimental research has become such an important method for testing theory is that it is a method for controlling the setting of many variables while changing only one or two variables at a time... the theory of collective action is not only one of the most important subjects for political scientists, it is also one of the most challenging.

Ostrom's advocacy of experimental research is another expression of the need for "pushing and pulling". This comprises the devising of a theory describing how democracy or collective action malfunctions and then testing it by setting up and running an institution that the theory indicates would improve the responsiveness and quality of collective action. This should show whether the theory accurately describes the malfunction. If the result is unsatisfactory, another 'push' and 'pull' should be tried, in which the push is the development of a new theory and its application to design a new institution, while the pull is the running of this innovation to see if it works.

A PROPOSED DESIGN – THE PEOPLE'S FORUM

The theory of democratic dysfunction outlined above may be seen as the start of a 'push' in an iterative push-pull process of designing a political institution to improve democratic politics. The remainder of this 'push' is to use the theory to devise a design. The 'pull' in this process would be the trialling of this design in the real world of democratic politics. Some of the features of this proposed institution, as described below, are specified for its implementation in Australia but it should be easy to adapt it to other democracies. It could be run in provinces or states, across nations and even globally. If a trial proved successful, it would indicate that the theory is substantially accurate and perhaps no further push-pull is needed.

This proposed institution is called the People's Forum. The major elements of its design are described below and these are selected to make it address the three primary democratic dysfunctions identified by the theory given above. Leadership would be clarified by placing it unambiguously in the hands of the people, as this Forum would offer them a facility for developing strategic policy and then advocating it, even to the point of instructing politicians (by developing a specific pressure of public opinion) to implement it. This facility for strategic leadership would also counter the excess of competition between politicians; because it would reduce the arena in which this is possible. Politicians would have less scope to compete with each other in advocating policy because strategic issues are taken over by the people. The People's Forum would thereby replace some competition between politicians with competition between citizens as it invites them to debate public policy. But this replacement would also have a cooperative aspect, as the Forum invites citizens to compare their reasons for, and feelings about, their ideas on policy. This restriction of competition between politicians over policy also restricts their competition with each other for leadership of the state, as it clearly relegates them to the role of executives who are directed by the people. Excessive compromise and the resultant ignorance in the behaviour of the polity would also be reduced by the People's Forum. This would be achieved in two ways: the Forum would give a more influential voice to the knowledge and wisdom possessed by citizens and it would stimulate the development of this sophistication.

The People's Forum would really only be the foundation for a forum, because its major function is to offer an agenda to the public. However, this agenda would be presented in a way that stimulates and assists debate and deliberation. It is presented as a ballot paper for a poll on public issues that is open to all electors and held at regular intervals, say once a year. This ballot paper could list a virtually unlimited number of issues and would have the same ones in each poll, repeating the same questions on these until the public opinion registered by the poll shows that its voters have ceased to change or develop their views. Such stabilization would be demonstrated by the trends in the way voters are thinking on each question, over successive polls. So this institution should create a public forum by presenting an agenda of questions as a ballot paper, by taking a vote every year and by publicising the results, which invites the people to discuss these and vote again next time, to reaffirm or change them.

In addition to helping to develop the opinions of many citizens in this way, the People's Forum is also designed to develop political influence for the opinions it registers as majority views in its polls. In order to achieve both the development of opinion and political influence, the Forum must do three major things. First, as indicated above, its poll must employ *voluntary voting* to take a self-selected sample, not a random sample, so that only those who are interested in its issues and questions participate. Such participants are likely to be those who will debate the issues in response to the presence of the poll and thereby further develop their thinking on them. These polls will therefore reflect the views of those in the community who are most likely to have well developed opinions. A growing public awareness of this should give results of the People's Forum some public status and therefore a possibility of political influence. The second thing that this poll must do is restrict itself to *issues that are long-running*, so that it can ask the same questions for a number of years to give time for thorough public debate and for citizens' opinions to develop in response to this engagement. Over a number of successive voting events, the poll results will therefore be registering views that are increasingly well considered. This effect should also become well known, giving People's Forum polls more status in the eyes of the general public. The third major requirement is to focus on *fundamental questions*. This should give these poll results even more public standing, so they should become politically influential, especially as the general public develop awareness that these polls probably reflect much more wisdom than random sample opinion polls. Any such status and influence that the People's Forum develops will encourage more people to vote in it, in an effort to use this influence. Greater numbers of voters will further enhance the influence of the Forum, while these numbers and this influence will focus more attention on the issues that it deals with, so that debate and deliberation of these by all citizens is encouraged.

To assist the People's Forum to produce effective deliberation and thereby help to create political influence, very careful attention must be given, not only to the selection of the issues, but to how each is described on the ballot paper, to the choice of the questions that deal with each issue, and to the menu of answers offered for the voter's choice on each question. This attention must be the responsibility of the managers of the People's Forum, for they are in a position to ensure that relevant experts are engaged and that the whole ballot paper is always kept under review. Highly developed skills in issue identification, issue analysis, issue evaluation and question technique are essential. Issues should be chosen that help public debates on other issues in the poll and questions should be chosen that help the debates on other questions in the poll, for many issues are interrelated and public opinion will develop more constructively if the Forum's ballot paper can point to these relationships and invite voters to think about them before they finalize their vote. The voluntary, self-selecting nature of the vote would place the managers of the People's Forum under constant public pressure to be seen to be producing a balanced, comprehensive, competent and relevant ballot paper. If a public suspicion develops that this is not the case, citizens will boycott the poll and it will collapse. With this in mind, the managers will invite suggestions from the public for new issues, questions and menus of answers, in order to use such input to help improve the scope and quality of the ballot paper and to give it more political influence.

The People's Forum would publicize its polls and may let each voting event run for a week with progressive daily tallies on all questions, to stimulate public interest before the poll closes. As it runs on self-selection, voting would be made as accessible as possible by employing voting by phone and internet. This technology also makes daily tallies possible. Hardcopy versions of the website ballot paper should be made available to anyone, free of cost and at any time of the year. It seems preferable that this system should be able to accept votes made on impulse, with no prior registration, in order to maximize participation. Ensuring that voters are eligible and that they only vote once in each poll may make impulse voting difficult to allow without the cooperation of the state or national government in making their electoral rolls available. The People's Forum may have to require that voters register prior to each poll during the introduction of the system, but after two or three years this demonstration phase may develop a public support that pressures politicians into cooperating by providing electoral rolls and perhaps funding, making this device an integral part of democratic government. Such an introductory demonstration may depend on finance from philanthropic sources or a public subscription, perhaps organised by NGOs that are concerned with public issues.

As indicated above, the progress of a People's Forum poll would be publicized each day of the week that it took place, in order to stimulate interest and to encourage people to vote before the poll closed. This daily publicity would show the trends over previous years of People's Forum voting on major questions and compare them with the current progress of the tally. Similar analyses would be publicized after the conclusion of the poll and these could deal with all the questions voted on. Where post-poll analysis shows that majorities in these polls are consistently pressing for new laws or government policies (or steadily advancing towards such advocacy), it should mean that serious public pressure is building for politicians to introduce these laws or policies. This may be the case if even only a tiny minority of the population voted on those Forum questions, because it should eventually become widely appreciated that a People's Forum vote represents those in the community who are interested in those issues and it should therefore exhibit much more wisdom than a vote in a conventional opinion poll. On any particular issue the latter is likely to represent a disengaged majority. People's Forum votes that call for reforms of policy or law could be confirmed as acceptable to the whole community if the government declared its intention to introduce new policies or laws to comply with the Forum, unless its next poll starts to show a slackening or reversal of the relevant trends.

A crucial feature of the People's Forum is that a trial may be initiated irrespective of whether government supports this or not. This would acquaint citizens with its potential and may thereby build public pressure for the government to support it by financing it and making electoral rolls available for its polls. Such an experiment depends on funds being found for this purpose. For example, to demonstrate this system in the Australian state of Tasmania, a small team of perhaps five people may be needed and the operation might cost around Aus$4M to run for three years. A period of this length may be needed to familiarize the public with the People's Forum and start to get a significant proportion of them involved in its polls. In view of the potential benefits if such a demonstration was successful and led to a widespread copying of of the Forum around the world, this initial expenditure could be very productive. Such developments could improve the provision of public goods of all types in many countries and even globally. They may make democracy more comprehensible and attractive to citizens of less liberal regimes. Such an investment in innovation would be much less than that of a great deal of experimentation in medicine, electronic technology, fundamental physics, and many other fields, yet yield much more pervasive benefits. By improving our system for providing public goods we would be starting to get our societies under more sensible control, radically expanding the possibilities for social development.

CONCLUSION

The focus of this problem-solving attempt is on liberal democratic governments rather than on repressive regimes because the former appear to be the hope of the world for the freedom and dignity of people. If democracies are faltering they offer poor guidance and incentive for the reform of less liberal systems.

The People's Forum is not envisaged as the ultimate improvement for democratic government, merely the form of improvement that appears to be possible in the circumstances that liberal democracies provide at present. If they use this institution, liberal democracies may then be able to further improve their structure, because the standard of public debate that the Forum produces should improve their ability to understand and use expert advice. For example, such advice might be that elections should be based on proportional representation of electorates that have a number of representatives, perhaps around ten, so that minority views are expressed and debated in parliament and thus better heard by the public at large. Another example is that the People's Forum could deliberate the possibility of avoiding primary democratic dysfunctions by replacing elections with sortition. This might be a partial replacement in which some hundreds of representatives are selected at random, who then get to know each other to some degree before voting to elect a cabinet or government of especially able and informed people. This election could take candidates either from the randomly selected representatives, or from a pool of candidates consisting of these representatives and other citizens that the representatives nominate. Another innovative proposal that the People's Forum could assist the public to assess is ParPolity, a system of representation proposed by political scientist Stephen Shalom (2005) that employs nested councils. The Forum could also consider the proposal by another political scientist, Kevin O'Leary (2006), for a randomly selected national assembly that in the US would comprise 435 deliberating groups of 100 citizens. Each of these groups would represent a congressional ward, so they may guide its representative in the House. This 43,500 strong sample of the population would have to be established by legislation or citizen initiated referenda and it would initially have only an advisory role. O'Leary envisages that it could be strengthened by constitutional amendment to become a 'People's House' that helps set the legislative agenda and has the power to veto bills passed by the House or the Senate.

Each of these four reforms would depend on popular political will for their implementation, but the establishment of the People's Forum does not rely on this, at least for its initial phase. If funds can be found to get it up and running, its exposure to the public may develop the political will to convert this demonstration into a permanent, fully functional institution. This would give liberal democratic government a real capacity to critically reflect on itself, so it could reform policy on its own structure, such as the four examples given above, as well as develop better considered policy on issues external to itself. Part of the latter might be that the People's Forum helps society examine its culture in order to make rational choices about its future development.

REFERENCES

Klijn, Erik-Hans and Koppenjan, Joop. F. M. 2006. "Institutional Design: Changing institutional features of networks." *Public Management Review* 8(1): 141-160.

Marsh, Ian & Edwards, Lindy. 2008. "Dilemmas of Policy Innovation in the Public Sector: A Case Study of the National Innovation Summit." http://www.airc.net.au/extras/927. ArticleSummitCase.doc [Accessed 20 August 2008].

Milner, Henry. 2002. *Civic Literacy: How Informed Citizens Make Democracy Work.* Hanover NH: University Press of New England.

O'Leary, Kevin. 2006. *Saving Democracy: A plan for real representation in America.* Stanford CA: Stanford University Press.

Olson, Mancur. 1965. *The Logic of Collective Action..* Cambridge MA: Harvard University Press.

Ostrom, Elinor. 2007. "Collective Action Theory." In *The Oxford Handbook of Comparative Politics* eds. Carles Boix and Susan C. Stokes. Oxford UK: Oxford University Press, 186-208.

Shalom, Stephen. 2005. "ParPolity: Political Vision for a Good Society." http://www.zmag. org/shalompol.htm. [Accessed 8 June 2007].

Taylor, Michael. 1987. *The Possibility of Cooperation.* Cambridge UK: Cambridge University Press.

In: Social Development
Editor: Lynda R. Elling

ISBN: 978-1-60741-612-8
© 2009 Nova Science Publishers, Inc.

Chapter 5

WATER POLICY REFORMS IN BRAZIL: THE CONTRADICTION BETWEEN ECONOMIC APPROACHES AND SOCIONATURAL NEEDS

Antonio A. R. Ioris[*]

Lecturer, Department of Geography and Environment
& Aberdeen Centre for Environmental Sustainability (ACES),
University of Aberdeen, UK

ABSTRACT

In the last two decades, water use and conservation have been the object of an intense process of institutional reforms, which have helped to introduce new approaches to the assessment of problems and the formulation of solutions. According to the international doctrine, the responses to water management problems should normally include a combination of regulatory requirements and market-based incentives. Nonetheless, despite improvements in some areas and changes in discourse, there are growing evidences that mainstream approaches have largely failed to deal with the degradation of water systems and promote different bases of water use. The Brazilian experience is a case in point, where a new regulatory framework was recently implemented, but it is restricted to calls for environmental governance, integrated measures and, crucially, the recognition of the economic value of water. Related adjustments in the provision of public services have facilitated the involvement of private companies in water supply and in hydroelectricity generation, without enough consideration of environmental and social demands. Making use of empirical and secondary data, this paper argues that the new regulatory framework have so far failed to prevent the multiplication of environmental impacts and the maintenance of social inequalities in the water sector. The overall conclusion is that effective alternatives to water problems will require a more organised reaction from water user and local communities, together broader political and economic reforms.

Keywords: water management, water reforms, political ecology, environmental economics, economic instruments, ecosystem services, Brazil.

---

[*] Department of Geography and Environment, School of Geosciences, Elphinstone Road, Aberdeen, AB24 3UF, Scotland, UK; Phone: +44 1224 273703 Fax: +44 1224 272331; e-mail: a.ioris@abdn.ac.uk

1. Introduction: The Reform Agenda

Allocation and use of water are among the most pressing issues of the contemporary search for better standards of life, social justice and environmental conservation. To a large extent, this debate has evolved around the need to expand water infrastructure, as a requirement for economic growth, and the ecological degradation and selective provision of water services often associated to such projects. If during most of the 20th Century large sums of public money were invested in water engineering, with time it became increasingly evident that traditional interventions were also responsible for water pollution and altered river flows, without necessarily satisfying essential public demands. The realisation of the shortcomings of conventional approaches to water infrastructure led, since the end of the 1970s, to a review of water policies and government priorities. Emerging environmental awareness and public mobilisation, particularly in the political north, also added pressure on national governments and multilateral agencies to gradually shift from single engineering initiatives to more comprehensive responses. Informed by concepts such as 'sustainable development' and 'systemic thinking', new ways of dealing with water problems started to shape the global water agenda. Public policies have been particularly influenced by the goals of integrated water resources management (IWRM), which include the formulation of 'holistic' solutions to water management problems, the reconciliation of multiple demands and, crucially, the appreciation of the economic value of water (Mitchell, 2005).[1]

Because of the more explicit recognition of the economic value of water, calls for economic efficiency and market exposure have occupied centre stage in the agenda of water reforms. It represents a move in favour of hybrid mechanisms of environmental governance and beyond the divisions between state-market-society that allegedly caused most of the mistakes in the previous decades (Lemos and Agrawal, 2006). It is now claimed that adequate solutions to old and new management problems should include not just the direct costs related to project implementation, but also the calculation of the monetary value of water in order to "eliminate inefficiencies and express its full economic potential" (WAAP, 2006). According to this position, "a major weakness of past approaches to the water sector has been the excessive reliance on overextended government agencies to manage water resources" while the new agenda calls for "greater reliance on pricing and incentives" (The World Bank, 1993: 47). The the application now of market-based solutions to environmental problems is expected to foster economic rationality and promote management efficiency. Interestingly, the international pressures for the adoption of market-inspired reforms have induced a homogenisation of water policies around the world, despite major social, cultural and economic differences between countries. For that reason, it is worth asking whether the ongoing reforms have actually resulted in any meaningful solutions to highly contingent and localised water problems. Considering the environmental and social statistics available in various UN reports and national assessments, it is evident that recent policies have largely failed to secure environmental restoration or implement more equitable basis of water allocation and use. Notwithstanding a change in the discourse, in the countries where the (so-

---

[1] Water management comprises multilayered measures carried out by public and private organisations in order to assess, allocate, use and preserve water stocks, aquatic processes and catchment systems. Water policy includes the set of guidelines, legal instruments and economic incentives used by public organisations to

called) 'new management paradigm' has been applied, the outcomes of the reforms have been restricted to some bureaucratic improvements and, at best, the removal of isolated, circumstantial problems.

The Brazilian experience is a case in point of the inherent limitations of the global water reforms and this essay intends to discuss the contradictory influences of neoclassical economics on the ongoing reorganization of water management in Brazil. It will be shown that, with the approval of a new water law in 1997, an extensive regulatory apparatus was put in place, mostly influenced by the goals of integrated management, but so far it achieved only marginal results in terms of environmental restoration and conflict resolution. Although the legislation delegated to catchment committees the approval of plans and the reconciliation of spatial differences, the core element of new policies has been the expression of the monetary value of water. It will be argued that, despite the rhetoric of environmental sustainability, official initiatives continue to subject socionatural water systems to economic exploitation and unfair distribution of opportunities. The recent announcement of irrigation and hydropower projects by the national administration, in spite of strong public opposition, evidentiates the priority of 'economic growth at any price'. In the same way, newly formed decision-making forums have been dominated by the same oligarchic political groups that always controlled economic and social opportunities related to water use and conservation (Valêncio e Martins, 2004). It means that, instead of promoting a genuine change in public policies, the new approaches have largely preserved the hegemonic interests of landowners, industrialists, construction companies and real estate investors, at the expense of the majority of the population and ecological recovery. This text will eventually contend that effective responses to water problems require new basis for the use and conservation of water, which should be necessarily constructed according to social justice and environmental sustainability requirements, but also free from the pervasive influences of market rationality.

2. THE ECONOMIC SPECTRE OF THE WATER REFORMS IN BRAZIL

In the 20th Century, some of the largest water projects in the world were built in Brazil to generate electricity, regulate river flow and assist irrigation and urban growth. "Exploiting perceived abundance for economic development has been the dominant historical premise of Brazilian policy toward water and rivers" (Conca, 2006: 311). The construction of dams and the expansion of water infrastructure were part of a national programme of industrialisation and economic development that marked the period between 1930s-70s (Ioris, 2007), during which there was timid enforcement of the environmental legislation, demonstrated by the fact that contentions issues were only superficially considered at the very end of the planning application process (Salvador, 1999). Weak environmental regulation was also used as a deliberate policy to attract foreign investments, particularly directed to intensive and highly polluting industries (May, 1999). The official response to the social and environmental impacts of water projects started to be articulated in the 1980s, when a group of avant-garde civil servants and academics pressed for reforms and for the adoption of the (aforementioned)

---

influence social institutions and personal decision-making. Both water management and water policies express political disputes and the balance of power between social groups, and between society and the state.

IWRM principles (Conca, 2006). This reaction 'from within' was initially stronger in the State of São Paulo, but before too long it passed to influence the debate on water reforms in other parts of the country. The discussion eventually reached the National Congress and culminated in the approval, in 1997, of a new legislation on water policy (Law 9,433) that replaced the previous Water Code of 1934. Since then, an extensive structure of policy-making and water regulation has been implemented in the federal and state (provincial) levels of government. At the same time, more than 140 catchment committees were established as the official forums for local stakeholder representation.

Notwithstanding the number of events and campaigns, a more careful examination of the first ten years of the new legal framework reveals disappointing results in terms of reducing impacts and improving the management of water systems. Such gloomy picture is formally acknowledged by the Ministry of the Environment (MMA, 2006), in particular the widespread sources of pollution in urban areas (e.g. only 47% of the municipalities have sewerage systems and only 18% of the total sewage is treated) and in the countryside (e.g. around 70% percent of the watercourses between Rio Grande do Sul and Bahia are polluted by agro-chemicals used in intensive crop production). In addition, resource availability has been compromised by the over-extraction of water and the continuous construction of large dams. The failures of the new water policies suggest that the theory of integrated water management has been mechanically pushed through by multilateral agencies to grant functions to a system yet to be constructed (Abers and Keck, 2006). Most authors, nonetheless, continue to praise the quality of the water legislation on the grounds that there has not been enough time yet for the full expression of the 'sophisticated' principles ingrained in the law (Machado, 2006) and, despite remaining problems, the 'modern governance' of water has come to be increasingly institutionalised in Brazil (Conca, 2006).

However, the overall trends of water degradation and, more importantly, the selective involvement of the public in the decision-making seem to suggest a more fundamental weakness on the ongoing water reforms. Decisions about water use and conservation in Brazil remain intrinsically linked to systems of political and economic control long established in colonial times (Bryant, 1998) and associated to the old patrimonialistic operation of the Brazilian State.[2]. In effect, the legal reforms have privileged the influence of private agents in the formulation of water projects (e.g. hydropower schemes and public water companies), at the same time that raised novel opportunities for capital accumulation via, now, the adoption of ecological conservation measures. It is certainly not a coincidence that the introduction of new water management happened together with the wider liberalisation of the Brazilian economy, which has consisted of declining public investments, high interest rates, labour market reforms, high unemployment and attraction of foreign capital (cf. Mollo and Saad-Filho, 2006). In this case, the water sector reproduces the same contradictions and conflicts of other public areas subjected to the influence of the neoliberal agenda of development. Despite this pervasive influence of neoclassical economics on the ongoing water institutional reforms in Brazil, there has been insufficient analyses of the expanding economic rationality underpinning the assessment of environmental impacts and selection of conservation measures. It means that the association between the new approaches to water problems and the hegemonic influence of market-based policies remains largely ignored and

---

[2] Patrimonialism, in the Weberian sense, has been a fundamental characteristic of the public sector in Brazil, a phenomenon with roots in organisation of the old Portuguese State (Faoro, 2001).

undertheorised. As a contribution to the debate, this text organises the economic pressures under three separate headings, namely the 'modernisation' of the public sector, monetary valuation of water and payment for ecosystem services. It should be noted that, in practice, these are closely interrelated processes that constantly reinforce each other.

2.1. Public Sector 'Modernisation'

The redesign of the Brazilian public sector started in 1995 with the publication of the 'White Paper on The Reform of the State Apparatus', which included a new set of criteria for investing in infrastructure and the management of public utilities (MARE, 1995). The justification was, on the one hand, the lack of public funds to modernise and expand public services and, on the other, the supposedly ineffective and wasteful operation of state-owned enterprises. The overall reorganisation of the public sector had also important repercussions for water regulation. Within the structure of the Ministry of the Environment, a new water secretariat was created in 1995 to coordinate national policies and influence the legal reforms under debate in the parliament. With the approval of the new legislation in 1997, the National Water Resources Management System (SINGREH) was established to bring together various public agencies and consultative committees. The structure was completed in 2001 when the National Water Authority (ANA) was installed to be responsible for water use permits and the implementation of technical programmes. Notwithstanding the consolidation of a professional bureaucracy to deal with environmental policies in Brazil, still only a small fraction of the public budget has been spent on environmental issues (around 0.4%), most of it used on administrative rather than on core functions (Young, 2005).

A more substantial limitation of the regulatory structure is the systematic concession to economic growth priorities. From local to national initiatives, the passive acceptance of the idea of economic development 'at any cost' has remained a strong feature of the decision-making process (for instance, new techniques developed for the assessment of water projects maintain that the design of new hydropower schemes should include the environment as merely a 'variable in the equation', e.g. Tolmasquim et al., 2001). The recent years have shown politicians always too keen to force the authorisation of new public or private initiatives on the grounds of raising taxes and job creation, even when the actual results are evident and widespread social and ecological disruption. In 2005, the Ministry of the Environment was forced to approve a questionable project of water transference from the São Francisco River to northern catchments in the semi-arid region. This inter-basin project has been vehemently criticised on the grounds that the benefits of water transference are likely to be appropriated by political leaders at the expense of socionatural impacts on both the source and the receiving catchments. Likewise, in 2007 the Ministry was compelled to grant licences for the construction of two large hydropower schemes along the Madeira River, in the heart of the Amazon region, regardless of the direct disapproval by its senior staff and technical experts. In other regions of Brazil, hydraulic projects continue to be approved and implemented even if they violate traditional community rights over common resources (Ribeiro et al., 2005).

Another significant element of the conservative 'modernisation' of the public sector is the programme of public utility privatisation, which is among the largest in the world. The privatisation of electricity and basic sanitation companies represented around a quarter of that total assets transferred into private hands (approximately US$100 billion were transferred into private hands, either through the full divestiture or through operational concessions of public utilities).[3] Because around 90% of the electricity generated in Brazil comes from hydropower schemes, the privatisation of energy has in effect been an indirect form of water resources privatisation. So far, most of the electricity distribution companies and around 40% of the generation companies owned by the state were sold-off to private operators. In nominal terms, the transfer of electricity utilities to private hands attracted US$ 23.5 billion (Anuatti-Neto *et al.*, 2003). Around 48% of the payments made by private investors to acquire electricity companies were financed by government-owned banks (particularly via the national development bank BNDES). The involvement of private operators was also facilitated by changes in the legislation that removed the difference between domestic and foreign firms. Privatisation was further encouraged by reducing investments in public utilities prior to the sell-off (i.e. to reduce political opposition due to the deteriorating performance of state-owned utilities), contractual clauses that protected privatised companies against changes in the exchange rate, electricity tariffs rising above inflation and the removal of compensatory subsidies to low income families (Pistonesi, 2005, quoted in Solanes and Jouravlev, 2006). Since 2003, the current federal administration has reduced the emphasis on the full divestiture of public electric utilities, but has maintained other traditional options of private sector involvement by contracting out services and public-private partnerships (see below).

Different that the hydroelectric sector, the privatisation of water supply and sanitation has been more restricted and faced higher political resistance. One fundamental obstacle is the hybrid responsibility that characterises water services in Brazil: according to the constitution, municipal authorities are in charge of water services, whereas the great majority delegated the operation to companies owned by the state (provincial) governments. The agreements between municipal and state authorities were formalised in the 1970s, during the military dictatorship, when the national policy was to concentrate resources and power in the state utilities. Under the influence of the liberal policies of the 1990s, some states (provinces) dissolved or demobilised their water companies, unilaterally returning the responsibility to the municipal administrators. That gave the opportunity to some municipal administrators to transfer the local water services to private companies (mostly foreigners). Privatisation was further encouraged by the reduction of investments by the central government, which is responsible for managing the main investment fund (i.e. FGTS): between 1995 and 1998, only R$ 1.8 billion was invested in the sector, while R$ 7.4 billion of past loans were paid back to the central government.[4] It means that a surplus of R$ 5.7 billion was retained in the investment fund, regardless of the urgency of social demands (Oliveira Filho, 2006). During this period, a specific agreement was signed with the IMF committing the Brazilian government in 1999 to broaden the scope of the privatization of water services. The result is that the annual average public investments between 1995 and 1998 totalised R$ 680 million, but the same average reached only R$ 68 million between 1999 and 2002 (it was zero in 2001).[5] In parallel, while the central government reduced the access of public utilities to

---

[3] Public irrigation schemes have also been increasingly transferred to private enterprise, normally through a fixed term concession of land and infrastructure.

[4] 1.00 US$ is approximately R$ 1.80.

[5] Under the current administration of President Lula (2007-2010), there have been additional resources allocated to sanitation infrastructure under the Accelerated Growth Programme (PAC). However, the rate of investments has been significantly lower than initially announced due to operation delays, disputes between states and

governmental funds, incentives and loans were made available to attract the attention of private operators (Oliveira Filho, 2006). Nonetheless, because of lengthy negotiations and legal disputes, only 3% of the water supply and sanitation utilities were privatised, which serve around 5% of the national population (Britto and Silva, 2006).

The privatisation of water supply and sanitation is only one element of a very complicated sector that still fails to serve 24.2% of the population with drinking water and 46.2% with sewerage services (cf. IBGE, 2004). If in the previous decades water supply and sanitation was restricted to the wealthier cities and neighbourhoods, the recent privatisation of publicly owned companies little improved the situation. Instead of higher investments and efficiency, privatised companies have been criticised for charging more for a worse, less reliable service. In many situations, privatisation has shifted "the burden for providing services to the poor from society as a whole and back to the poor themselves" (Mulreany et al., 2006). Privatisation has also raised a range of conflicts between private operators, public regulators and customers, as well as evidences of wrongdoings (Mello, 2001).[6] The concession process has been far from transparent, despite steady increase of tariffs and charges (for instance, the charge to connect to the water network system in the city of Limeira increased from 65% to 176% of the official minimal month salary after privatisation, with no discounts for low income families, cf. Vargas, 2005). Similarly to what happens in other countries, privatisation in Brazil faces growing scepticism about the actual motivations of companies that are more accountable to the shareholders than to their customers and, at this point in time, the future of the water sector is uncertain, with an unclear legislation and ambivalent policies. While the new legislation on basic sanitation passed in the year 2007 (Law 11,445), which emphasises the provision of services as a basic human right, it also stimulates the formation of 'public-private partnerships', which is nothing else than a disguised form of utility privatisation.

2.2. Environmental Charges and the Monetary Value of Water

The very first article of the 1997 water law established the primacy of the neoclassical economic theory over water management in Brazil. The article recognises that: "(…) water is a scarce natural resource, which has economic value". There is here an unambiguous resemblance with the fourth UN Dublin Principle (approved at the 1992 International Conference on Water and the Environment) which stated that "water has an economic value in all its competing uses and should be recognized as an economic good". This phrase encapsulates the two fundamental tenets of the neoclassical paradigm of environmental management: the idea of a scarce resource and the (economic) value of water. In effect, the expression of the economic value of water has been the main concept supporting the formulation of subsequent policies and initiatives in the last decade in Brazil. As repeatedly mentioned in the official publications, because of quantitative scarcity and declining quality, water is no longer a 'free good', but has clear economic value. In other words, because water

---

municipalities, and the macroeconomic instability associated with the international financial crisis. At the same time, PAC has been politically exploited, especially because it has been coordinated by the minister appointed by the president to succeed him in office (Dr. Dilma Rousseff).

[6] In 2001, a political activist was murdered in the State of Mato Grosso after having denounced corruption in the privatisation of the municipal water utility (reported by Hall and Lobina, 2006).

is (or was made) scarce, it now requires an economic treatment to address existing and future problems. Once the monetary value of water is determined (what requires the application of neoclassical methods of environmental economic, cf. Serôa da Motta, 1998), it can be managed as any other economic factor of production that has marketable costs, effects and benefits. The ideological affirmation of its scarcity transforms water into an economic factor and a profitable commodity rather than a human right with vital ecosystem functions (Swyngedouw, 2004 and 2005).

The most relevant expression of the monetised value of water in Brazil has been the imposition of water user charges under the 'user-pays principle' (or the related 'polluter-pays principle'). According to mainstream economic approaches, those wanting to extract water or dilute effluents in watercourses should pay a charge proportionate to the negative impacts caused (i.e. environmental externalities). In theoretical terms, the introduction of water user charges in Brazil has aimed to minimise social costs through the determination of the optimum scale of operation and induce rational economic behaviour, but also to generate revenues for environmental restoration and law enforcement (Garrido, 2004). However, since the early days of the new legal regime in the end of the 1990s, the imposition of water charges has grown into controversy on the national and local scales. In many catchments, the political maelstrom related to the controversial introduction of water charges has hijacked the broader debate on environmental restoration and prevention of impacts. The perverse consequence of water user charges is evident in the areas where it has already been adopted, in particular the split of stakeholders into confrontational groups and the widespread suspicion about hidden agendas. The poisoning of stakeholder dialogue is further aggravated by the official policies supporting the introduction of water charges only in catchments where water conflicts exist or are likely to emerge (cf. GEO Brasil, 2007: 54).

What is more, instead of improving the environmental condition of catchments and places, the payment for water charges tacitly validates the operation of activities that cause large environmental impacts. Because industries, electricity operators and irrigators now pay for water use, they can claim to be legally entitled to continue to impact the aquatic environment as before the new legislation was passed. That has been the case with industrial effluent discharges in the Paraíba do Sul catchment, where the industrial sector has been able to preemptively manipulate the approval of water charges so suit their demands for soft regulation. At the same time, larger industries have opportunistically used their payment for water use to improve their commercial image as corporately responsible (Féres et al., 2005). Since industries are now officially involved in the system of environmental regulation, there is scarce room for calling into question their responsibility for the poor environmental quality of the catchment. In spite of the 'inclusive negotiation' that, according to Formiga-Johnsson et al. (2007), characterises the local experience, there is also an official acknowledgement that the implementation of water charges in the Paraíba do Sul catchment has not progresses as expected in part because of the absence of participatory consultations with the various stakeholder sectors (UNEP, 2004). The result is that the introduction of bulk water charges has contributed little in terms of environmental restoration in the Paraíba do Sul: the official statistics show that, between 2003 and 2006, the charging scheme was responsible for collecting a total of R$ 25.4 million, which is considerably less than the estimated need to restore the catchment (i.e. an annual investment of R$ 360 million or R$ 4,600 million by 2025, cf. Coppetec, 2006).

2.3. Payment for Environmental Services

Apart from the 'modernisation' of the public sector and monetary valuation, the market-based solutions that underpin the ongoing institutional reforms have increasingly facilitated the adoption of other indirect mechanisms of water commodification. One of these new forms of converting nature into tradable commodities is the payment for environmental services (PES), which includes 'services' related to watershed conservation such as the maintenance of clean water supply and protection against soil erosion (Kosoy et al. 2007). The rationality of PES is directly inspired in the neoclassical concepts that free market operations can guarantee the most efficient solution to environmental externalities. The justification is that those who benefit from ecosystem services should be prepared to make direct payments to the local people more closely associated to the conservation of the ecosystem. For instance, if the protection of an upstream forested area helps to maintain river flows, the environmental service (in this case, the guarantee of water availability by the protection of the forest) should be paid by downstream water users. PES entails a full interchangeably between the market inputs used by the industries and agriculture and the non-market service of maintaining the river flow. The first requirement before PES can be adopted is obviously the calculation of the monetary value of the environmental services. The calculation is normally processed through ecosystem valuation methods, which normally produce significant inconsistencies. For example, Fearnside (1997) estimated that 10% of the Brazilian agriculture depends on rainfall originated from the evapotranspiration in the Amazon, which would correspond to an environmental service (i.e. guarantee of rainfall) that is worth US$ 7 billions per year for the entire rainforest. On their part, Seidl and Moraes (2000) calculated that water supply and regulation in a single watershed in the Brazilian Pantanal amounts to US$ 6.3 billions per year.

Regardless of those methodological difficulties, many Brazilian academics and policy makers have embraced the payment for environmental services as an ingenious option for dealing with water management problems. The National Water Authority (ANA) launched the "Water Producer Programme", an initiative that offers financial compensation for soil conservation interventions that potentially increase or maintain water availability. One of the catchments covered by the programme, located in the municipality of Extrema, contains the freshwater supply to the city of São Paulo and, in 2007, landowners started to receive financial support to adopt soil conservation measures that indirectly protect watercourses. Another similar initiative is the Catchment Pollution Removal Programme (PRODES), which 'buys' the treatment of sewage by private or public operators (instead of the direct financing of the sewage works). The attractiveness of PES is demonstrated by two 'private member's bills' recently introduced and currently under discussion in the National Congress (bill 142/2007 in the Senate and 792/2007 in the House of Representatives). Similar propositions were presented in various state assemblies to further regulate the payment for ecosystem services in areas under local jurisdiction (e.g. in the State of Acre). For many academics and politicians, the win-win promise of PES seems the ultimately proof of the perfection of the market, which is capable of finding inventive solutions to the very problems it causes. In view of that, PES would not only introduce a 'sophisticated' response to environmental degradation, but also generates new commercial opportunities related, for example, to the certification and monitoring of environmental services.

On paper, the certification of environmental services has the ability to promote environmental protection, since water uses would become more aware of the economic value of ecosystems (cf. Silvano et al., 2005). In practice, however, the success of PES in terms of protecting and restoring the environment has been close to nothing. The disappointing outcomes of the PES experience can be explained by various operational and conceptual incongruities. First of all, it is extremely difficult to relate the provider of the service with those willing to pay for it. It has been reported the limitations of PES in watershed conservation in India due to high transaction costs and the intensification of poverty problems (Kerr et al., 2007). The adoption of PES has been also prevented by demand-side limitations and a lack of supply-side know-how (Wunder, 2007). Secondly, PES only works in situations where the threat of environmental degradation is extremely high. That is because it requires an irrefutable proof of the environmental risk to persuade beneficiaries to accept the payment for the service. If the PES regime becomes more widely adopted, it can even induce the artificial 'fabrication' of environmental threats in order to justify the payment. In other words, the implementation PES can divert the attention away from environmental protection towards profitable market transactions. Thirdly, in the few cases where it has bee adopted, the price of the environmental service payment is not the outcome of free market bargain, but on the contrary it is created by the regulatory demands and opportunistic behaviour of private firms (Robertson, 2007). Fourthly and more important, the market logic behind PES is fundamentally based on a utilitarian relation between people and nature that ignores the capacity of local populations to appreciate the value and spontaneously protect their ecological base. This rationale assumes that human beings are naturally inclined to convert the natural resource into cash and, therefore, people need to be paid to avoid causing environmental harm (this is, for example, the argument of Vosti et al., 2003 for the protection of the Amazon Basin). It overlooks the fact that local populations have a long-term history of skilful interaction with the environment and that the pressures over natural resources are, to a large extent, created by economic globalisation, the same process that new encourages the adoption of artificial schemes like PES.

3. THE REFORM GRIDLOCK

The reform of water policies has occupied a central stage in the environmental agenda of Brazil in the last decade. The new water regulatory regime supposedly contains 'advanced' tools of environmental governance, including utility privatisation, water user charges and the payment for ecosystem services. Nonetheless, the environmental results of the new water regulation have been, at best, disappointing. The regime has similarly aggravated stakeholder conflicts while it legitimises the negative impacts of more intensive water users (i.e. via operation licences and bulk water charges). It means that, in practice, little has changed: the stability of water systems and the fundamental rights of deprived social groups continues to be forfeited under the need for more dams or the exploitation of catchment resources. Even in catchments with meaningful public mobilisation and solid structures of public representation, the degrading trends remain unaffected (paradigmatic examples are the river basis of Sinos, São Francisco, Piracicaba and Paraíba do Sul, among others). This apparent paradox of novel legal approaches that reproduce old constraints can only be explained by the bureaucratisation of the relations between society and nature under hegemonic market-based policies (i.e. the dynamics of power and rationalisation described by Foucault). The persistence of water management problems is certainly acknowledged by many scholars (e.g. Abers and Keck, 2006; Conca, 2006; Machado, 2006), however there is still limited scrutiny of the systematic failures of the new water regulatory regime. It is rare to see authors willing to investigate why technological improvements, public participation and mitigation measures have been systematically sidestepped by the accumulation strategies of contemporary capitalism.

As in other countries undertaking similar institutional reforms, a brief search in the academic bibliography and policy documents reveals the powerful economic 'mantra' that underpins the ideas about the ongoing water reforms in Brazil. An intriguing example is provided by the recent National Water Plan, which explicitly claims that economic growth is a precondition for the solution of water-related problems. The plan describes three future scenarios for water sector, which as described as 'water for all', 'water for some' and 'water for few'. The main difference between those scenarios is the projected annual rate of GDP growth, respectively 4.5%, 3.5% and 1.5% per year (MMA, 2006, Vol. II). According to these scenarios, water access would be universalised in Brazil only with a higher rate of economic growth, at the same time that environmental restoration depends on the good performance of the economy. Here, as in other documents, the association between water management and economic growth ultimately instils a particular pattern of social relations that are fraught with tensions and contradictions. If in the past, the emphasis was on the construction of engineering works, the current water management reforms aim to remove obstacles to economic production (e.g. river pollution and water scarcity), at the same time that raise new alternatives for capital accumulation (e.g. environmental consultancy and the payment for ecosystem services). The same way that economic agents need to invest in technology to increase relative surplus value and also contain the workforce, there is a need to remove ecological degradation in order to restore accumulation conditions and contain the threats to the stability of economic systems. As pointed out by Smith (2007), surplus value is extracted from the dead labour dormant in the degraded watercourse via the 'excavation' of the relations between nature and society under capitalism. Crucially, before those accumulation responses can be adopted, it is essential that the monetary value of water be quantified and discursively normalised, which is achieved by the imposition of water charges (i.e. the sophisticated approaches developed by mainstream economists to estimate water charges have, as a direct consequence, the institutionalisation of a common monetary basis among water users).[7] The powerful symbolism of the monetary value of water makes possible the reinsertion of degraded environmental systems into production relations via the commodification of restoration and conservation measures.

There are common similarities between the exacerbated influence of mainstream economics over the reform of the water sector in Brazil and experiences of the majority of Latin American countries (see Solanes and Jouravlev, 2006). New forms of dealing with water management started to be implemented in the region after the end of the military dictatorships in the 1980s, when the approval of liberalising laws to regulate environmental conservation and utility operation coincided with a whole range of market-friendly measures. That included the closure of government departments, the privatisation of government-owned

---

[7] In Brazil, water user charges are normally calculated according to three main factors: volume extracted, rate of use and quality of the returned flow.

assets and the aggressive attraction of foreign investors. The commonalities between the Brazilian experience and what happens elsewhere in Latin America is not simply a coincidence, but attest the exogenous origins of the ongoing water reforms. In the same way that development banks and multilateral organisations encouraged the expansion of water infrastructure after the Second World War, the current water reforms are fundamentally grounded on concepts that emanate from universities and think-tankers based in the North. That is the fundamental cause of the systematic difficulty to connect local demands and the values of local populations with the language and the targets of the centralised regulatory agencies. Even with a large proportion of the freshwater available in the planet, the water sector in Latin America merely reproduced the pulses of investment and reorganisation imposed by the leading economies. Such reforms are not happening in a vacuum, but intimately related to the patterns of economic production and consumption promoted by economic globalisation. For those than can pay, the globalised economy can provide wasteful lifestyles, which increasingly depend on large volumes of water and electricity. For the poorer strata of the society, however, globalisation has brought new threats to their livelihood and additional pressures over shared natural resources (Newell, 2007). The consequence is that the ongoing water reforms continue to stir conflicts and provoke bitter reactions among poorer citizens and environmentalists across the region (Liverman and Vilas, 2006).

By and large, contemporary water policies have been contained by their technocratic insistence in the internalisation of costs and the optimisation of resources, while social justice and collective responsibilities for the degradation of shared water resources are left out of the agenda. The priority of economic rationality for the solution of water problems in Brazil only propagates a system of environmental exploitation and social exclusion related to water management that historically characterised water management in the country. It has been mentioned elsewhere that market solutions are inadequate to deal with stochastic and complex ecological systems, because it creates a 'policy lock-in' that precludes dynamic adjustments (Bromley, 2007). In other words, the priority given to the economic dimension of water management is nothing else than the mainstream political paradigm reflecting its view of itself. As Bowels (2004) observes, market forces have more than only an allocative role, but also exert a disciplinary function that in reality operates through the asymmetric use of power. At the same time, while acknowledging the harmful impacts of market pressures, it is also important to avoid explaining all problems of the new water regime in Brazil as solely the result of broader economic priorities. On the contrary, there are other fundamental factors that locally contribute to management failures. As observed by Prudham (2004), only the juxtaposition of the hegemonic character of market society with the specific political ecological contradictions can "reveal the crisis tendencies of environmental neoliberalism". It is exactly this powerful articulation between the hegemony of market-based regulation and local power asymmetries that have ultimately responded for the insufficient results of the water reforms in Brazil.

4. THE WAY FORWARD?

The water regulatory regime introduced in the 1990s in Brazil attempted, but largely failed to bring straightforward responses to multilayered water questions. The fundamental shortcoming of the new approaches is the ideological separation between environmental degradation and social inequalities. Because of that fundamental dichotomy, the policies derived from the new water legislation have neglected the social and political context where decisions are made and projects implemented. It has overlooked the crucial fact that water problems in Brazil are closely related to rural land tenure, uneven urban development and socioeconomic opportunities, issues that are mostly excluded from the scope of the water reforms. Policy instruments of the new regime, which include water charges and flexible water regulation, were superimposed to a political system based on discriminatory practices on the national and local scales. Almost all the changes are restricted to the top-level of policy-making, with very limited repercussions on the local problems of water use and conservation. Some improvements in terms of public participation and environmental restoration represent no commitment by politicians or public agencies, but are convenient mechanisms for minimising public opposition against the implementation of the new regulatory regime. Public mobilisation in catchment committees has been systematically neutralised by disputes involving water charges, while economic pressures continued to degrade watercourses and displace local communities. Only the more organised social groups have been able to understand the intricacies of the new system and have cleverly used their position to maintain and expand privileges.

The overall conclusion is that alternatives to the current management of water reforms require, first and foremost, denouncing the rationality of neoclassical economics and its commanding influence over public water policies. It means that water management problems can only be resolved by bringing together the local (catchment) demands and a national and international resistance to the pervasive commodification of nature. Alternatives to the ecological crisis can only emerge from the linking of all anti-systemic social movements against the endless accumulation of capital (cf. Wallerstein, 2003) that has been facilitated by the globalisation of the markets. In other words, improvements in the water sector make no sense without relating it to the totality of the globalised economy and, therefore, the construction of new basis for the relation between nature and society. In strategic terms, critical groups should be able to make use of all opportunities of political resistance, which necessarily includes the official channels currently available in the environmental regulatory system, as a first step in the construction of a genuine agenda of reforms. Even if the social movements cannot immediately keep nature out of the hegemony of neoliberal policies, grassroots mobilisation can advance a robust critique of the unfair and unsustainable appropriation of ecological resources, water in particular.

REFERENCES

Abers, R.N., & Keck, M.E. (2006). Muddy waters: The political construction of deliberative river basin governance in Brazil. *International Journal of Urban and Regional Research*, 30(3), 601-622.

Anuatti-Neto, F., Barossi-Filho, M., Carvalho, A., and Macedo, R. (2003). *Costs and benefits of privatization: Evidence from Brazil*. Washington, D.C.: IADB.

Bowles, S. (2004). *Microeconomics: Behavior, institutions and evolution*. New York: Russell Sage Foundation.

Britto, A., and Silva, R. T. (2006). Water management in the cities of Brazil: Conflicts and new opportunities in regulation. In *Urban water conflicts: An analysis of the origins and nature of water-related unrest and conflicts in the urban context* (pp. 39-51). Paris: IHP/UNESCO.

Bromley, D.W. (2007). Environmental regulations and the problem of sustainability: Moving beyond 'market failure'. *Ecological Economics*, 63, 676-683.

Bryant, R.L. (1998). Power, knowledge and political ecology in the Third World: A review. *Progress in Physical Geography*, 22, 79-94.

Conca, K. (2006). *Governing water: Contentious transnational politics and global institutional building*. Cambridge, Mass., and London: MIT Press.

Coppetec. (2006). *Plano de recursos hídricos da bacia do Rio Paraíba do Sul*. Resende: AGEVAP.

Faoro, R. (2001). *Os donos do poder: Formação histórica do patronato político brasileiro* (2nd edition). São Paulo: Globo.

Fearnside, P.M. (1997). Environmental services as a strategy for sustainable development in rural Amazonia. *Ecological Economics*, 20(1), 53-70.

Féres, J., Thomas, A., Reynaud, A., & Serôa da Motta, R. (2005). *Demanda por água e custo de controle da poluição hídrica nas indústrias da bacia do Rio Paraíba do Sul*. Document No. 1084. IPEA: Rio de Janeiro.

Formiga-Johnsson, R.M., Kumler, L., & Lemos, M.C. (2007). The politics of bulk water pricing in Brazil: Lessons from the Paraíba do Sul Basin. *Water Policy*, 9, 87-104.

Garrido, R.J. (2004). Reflexões sobre a aplicação da cobrança pelo uso da água no Brasil. In C.J.S. Machado (ed.), *Gestão de ágas doces* (pp. 105-133). Rio de Janeiro: Interciência.

GEO Brasil. (2007). *Recursos hídricos*. Brasília: MMA, ANA & PNUMA.

Hall, D., & Lobina, E. (2006). Agua, privatización y ciudadania. In *La gota de la vida: Hacia una gestión sustentable y democrática del agua* (pp. 288-309). Central America, México & Cuba: Fundación Heinrich Böll.

IBGE. (2004). *Atlas de saneamento*. Rio de Janeiro: IBGE.

Ioris A.A.R. (2007). The headwaters of water problems in Brazil: Commodification and exclusion. *Capitalism Nature Socialism*, 18(1), 28-50.

Kerr, J., Milne, G., Chhotray, V., Baumann, P., & James, A.J. (2007). Managing watershed externalities in India: Theory and practice. *Environment Development and Sustainability*, 9, 263-281.

Kosoy, N., Martinez-Tuna, M., Muradian, R., & Martinez-Alier, J. (2007). Payments for environmental services in watersheds: Insights from a comparative study of three cases in Central America. *Ecological Economics*, 61, 446-455.

Lemos, M.C., & Agrawal, A. (2006). Environmental governance. *Annual Review of Environment and Resources*, 31, 297-325.

Liverman, D., & Vilas, S. (2006). Neoliberalism and the environment in Latin America. *Annual Review of Environment and Resources*, 31, 327-363.

Machado, C.J.S. (2006). O mundo da administração pública das águas do Estado do Rio de Janeiro segundo o olhar de um antropólogo. *Horizontes Antropológicos*, 25, 171-190.

MARE. (1995). *Plano diretor da reforma do Estado*. Brasília: MARE.

May, P.H. (1999). O setor financeiro privado internacional e o meio ambiente: O caso do Brasil. In C. Cavalcanti (Ed.), *Meio ambiente, desenvolvimento sustentável e políticas públicas* (2nd edition, pp. 299-313). São Paulo: Cortez.

Mello, M. (2001). *Privatização do setor de saneamento no Brasil: Quatro experiências e muitas lições*. Document No. 447. Rio de Janeiro: Economics Department, PUC.

Mitchell, B. (2005). Integrated water resources management, institutional arrangements, and land-use planning. *Environment and Planning A*, 37, 1335-1352.

MMA. (2006). *Plano nacional de recursos hídricos*. Brasília: Ministry of the Environment.

Mollo, M. L. R., and Saad-Filho, A. (2006). Neoliberal economic policies in Brazil (1994-2005): Cardoso, Lula and the need for a democratic alternative. *New Political Economy*, 11(1), 99-123.

Mulreany, J. P., Calikoglu, S., Ruiz. S., & Sapsin, J.W. (2006). Water privatization and public health in Latin America. *Revista Panamericana de Salud Publica*, 19(1), 23–32.

Newell, P. (2007). Trade and environmental justice in Latin America. *New Political Economy*, 12(2), 237-259.

Oliveira Filho, A. (2006). Institucionalização e desafios da política nacional de saneamento: Um balanço. *Proposta*, 110, 12-23.

Prudham, S. (2004). Poisoning the well: Neoliberalism and the contamination of municipal water in Walkerton, Ontario. *Geoforum*, 35, 343–359.

Ribeiro, E.M., Galizoni, F.M., Calixto, J.S., Assis, T.P., Ayres, E.B., & Silvestre, L.H. (2005). Gestão, uso e conservação de recursos naturais em comunidades rurais do Alto Jequetinhonha. *Estudos Urbanos e Regionais*, 7(2), 77-99.

Robertson, M. (2007). Discovering price in all the wrong places: The work of commodity definition and price under neoliberal environmental policy. *Antipode*, 39(3), 500-526.

Seidl, A., & Moraes. A.S. 2000. Global valuation of ecosystem services: Application to the Pantanal da Nhecolandia, Brazil. *Ecological Economics*, 33, 1-6.

Serôa da Motta, R. (1998(. *Manual para valoração econômica de recursos ambientais*. Brasília: MMA.

Silvano, R. A. M., Udvardy, S., Ceroni, M., & Farley, J. (2005). An ecological integrity assessment of a Brazilian Atlantic Forest watershed based on surveys of stream health and local farmers' perceptions: Implications for management. *Ecological Economics*, 53, 369-385.

Smith, N. (2007). Nature as accumulation strategy. In L. Panitch, & C. Leys (Eds.) *Socialist register: Coming to terms with nature* (pp. 16-36). London: Merlin Press.

Solanes, M., and Jouravlev, A. (2006). *Water governance for development and sustainability*. Serie Recursos Naturales e Infraestructura, Document No. 111. Santiago, Chile: CEPAL.

Swyngedouw, E. (2004). *Social power and the urbanization of water: Flows of power*. Oxford Geographical and Environmental Studies. Oxford: Oxford University Press.

Swyngedouw, E. (2005). Dispossessing H_2O: The contested terrain of water privatization. *Capitalism Nature Socialism*, 16(1), 81-98.

The World Bank. (1993). *Water resources management: A World Bank policy paper*. Washington, D.C.: IBRD.

Tolmasquim, M.T., Serôa da Motta, R., La Rovere, E.L., Barata, M.M.L., & Monteiro, A.G. (2001). Environmental valuation for long-term strategic planning: The case of the Brazilian power sector. *Ecological Economics*, 37, 39-51.

UNEP. (2004). *The use of economic instruments in environmental policy: Opportunities and challenges*. Geneva: UNEP.

Valêncio, N.F.L.S., & Martins, R.C. (2004). Novas institucionalidades na gestão de águas e poder local: Os limites territoriais da democracia decisória. *Interações*, 5(8), 55 – 70.

Vosti, S. A., Braz, E. M., Carpentier, C. L., d'Oliveira, M. V. N., & Witcover, J. (2003). Rights to forest products, deforestation and smallholder income: Evidence from the western Brazilian Amazon. *World Development*, 31(11), 1889-1901.

WAAP. (2006). *The second UN world water development report: 'Water, a shared responsibility'*. World Water Assessment Programme. Paris: UNESCO & New York: Berghahn Books.

Wallerstein, I. (2003). The ecology and the economy: What is rational? In *World System History and Global Environmental Change*, Conference Keynote, Lund, Sweden, 19-22 September 2003.

Wunder, S. (2007). The efficiency of payments for environmental services in tropical conservation. *Conservation Biology*, 21(1), 48–58.

Young, C.E.F. 2005. Instrumentos econômicos para o desenvolvimento sustentável: O caso brasileiro. In C. Parreira, & Alimonda, H. (Eds) *As Instituições Financeiras Públicas e o Meio Ambiente no Brasil e na América Latina* (pp. 219-248). Brasília: FLACSO.

In: Social Development
Editor: Lynda R. Elling

ISBN: 978-1-60741-612-8
© 2009 Nova Science Publishers, Inc.

Chapter 6

THE MICROCLUSTER VALUE CHAIN ANALYSIS[1]

Josep Capó-Vicedo[2]
Universitat Politècnica de València

ABSTRACT

This paper tries to study the particular workings of clusters, proposing a tool that helps with the empowerment and development of inter-organisational networks that might exist in them. It is a new tool for territorial strategic analysis focused in clustering policy based on the innovation; the microcluster value chain analysis.

Territorial competitiveness should be looked for by starting from the generation of external economies, from strategic decisions taken by those responsible for the interrelated networks, and from the identification and the empowerment of the key relationships among the agent leaders. These are the objectives that the tool proposed will try to resolve.

To achieve this, the most important thing will be to know how to locate and to diffuse the necessary knowledge to be able to identify the opportunities or key success factors that can motivate the creation of concrete inter-organisational networks in the heart of a microcluster.

Keywords: SMEs, clusters, interorganizational networks, value chain.

INTRODUCTION

In recent years, the balance between knowledge and resources has changed so dramatically in the developed economies that the former has become the most decisive factor in relation to standard of living. Knowledge has become even more important than traditional resources such as land, machinery and work.

---

[1] This research was supported financially by Polytechnic University of Valencia (PAID-06-08).

[2] Contact: Josep Capó-Vicedo; Business Management Department; Universitat Politècnica de València; Plaza Ferrándiz y Carbonell, 3 – 03801 – Alcoy (Alicante) – Spain; Phone: +34966528466 Fax: +34966528585; e-mail: pepcapo@doe.upv.es

Cooperation with others of their similar size, a larger size or a smaller size is a strategic alternative that allows enterprises to take advantage of the competitive advantages of the companies with which they have decided to associate themselves, whether these agreements are of a horizontal or vertical kind. If these agreements are carried out among a large number of companies, they can knit a lattice of relationships that create compact networks through the links established. These inter-organisational networks are usually developed in a concrete geographical environment, forming clusters.

On this subject, the new theories of growth establish a clear dependence between economic growth and the rate of accumulation of physical and human assets, this being defined as levels of knowledge, abilities and competences (OECD, 2001). The abilities and competences required nowadays are no longer only technical, but give more importance to social and organisational skills, which allow personnel to work in more fluid and interactive environments.

However, the existence of economic systems based on Small and Medium Enterprises (SMES) represents an important barrier for transition to take place from traditional economies to those based on knowledge. The European Observatory for the SMES (OES, 2003) states that, in order to develop a competitive base for these companies, on one hand it is necessary to develop human resources, and on the other, to obtain competences from outside by cooperating with external organisations, especially from those geographically close to the company.

The fact that these small and medium companies are located in a certain territory can favour greater product specialization, greater flexibility and a considerable increase in competitiveness. The grouping in function of a group of abilities, knowledge, technologies or markets, can be a catalyst that impels the innovative process in companies. In this case, the existing implicit knowledge in a territory plays a vital role, by means of the establishment of mechanisms of collaboration and participation, formal or informal, of the different public and private agents of the territory.

This paper tries to study the particular workings of these territorial clusters, proposing a new tool for territorial strategic analysis focused in clustering policy based on the innovation; the microcluster value chain analysis.

Territorial competitiveness should be looked for by starting from the generation of external economies, from strategic decisions taken by those responsible for the interrelated networks.

To achieve this, the most important thing will be to know how to locate and to diffuse the necessary knowledge to be able to identify the opportunities or key success factors that can motivate the creation of concrete inter-organisational networks in the heart of a microcluster.

Evolution of Industrial Districts and Specialised Territorial Clusters

Another important question to be kept in mind in the analysis of technological evolution processes is the fact that most of them – practically all of them in the case of manufacturing industry – are associated with a certain territory. These processes have had an influence on and, in their turn, are the results of, the historical evolutions that have occurred in these territories.

That is to say, as many authors have studied, from Marshall to Porter, Sabel, Pyke and Sengenberger, etc., when industrial processes are analysed, from the beginning of the Industrial Revolution in the 18th century up to the present day, there appear a series of phenomena of the concentration of specialised production in certain regions of advanced countries. These phenomena are the consequence of the external economies generated in the territories due to being situated close to the specific resources for a determined production chain, as Marshall correctly defined them in his study of 1919 "Industry and Trade", in which he was the first to describe the concept of industrial districts as the phenomena of the concentration of specialised production units.

When, about the year 1987, Giacomo Becattini revived Marshall's theory of industrial districts, others began to study again the phenomena of the concentration of processes of strategic change, many of them in the form of groups of local small and medium sized companies. The Italian school of the Marshall Industrial District – (Sebastiano Brusco, Roberto Cagmani, Fabio Sforzi, etc.) – have made a social and economic paradigm of industrial districts, resorting to an analysis of their evolution in their different stages of development and to the interpretation of the hierarchy of processes and production units in their network of agents, in order to justify and try to diagnose their evolutionary process.

The model, in territorial groupings, of industrial elements specialising in a determined sector of production created by Porter and known by the name of "clusters", has permitted a big advance in the understanding of the reasons why these phenomena present a high degree of geographical concentration in certain parts of advanced countries. Porter showed that the reasons for international competitive success are related to two causes: a) the geographical concentration of specialised industrial elements, and b) the presence of the appropriate determining factors of territorial competitiveness. According to this author, these are the reasons why the companies in these specialised clusters are highly successful in selling their products in international markets.

Porter's writings, referring first of all to the concept of industrial clusters (Porter 1980) and later to regional clusters (Porter, 1998 a, b) have had great influence, since they showed the importance of the close relationship existing between the economic elements that compose a cluster and the competitiveness of the companies operating within it.

The concept of a regional cluster, referring to a geographical concentration of interdependent companies (OECD, 2001; Rosenfeld, 2002), is closely related to other academic concepts utilised, such as Marshallian Industrial Districts, specialised production areas and local production systems.

The success of the networks of specialised companies in a large number of advanced countries, situated in specific territorial concentrations, has increased the interest in the study of these phenomena of geographical industrial concentration in the last two decades, both in the academic world and in organisations responsible for the creation of industrial policies and territorial development (Regional Clusters in Europe. EU, 2002). It has also increased interest both in manufactured goods (e.g. the "Terza Italia") and in the development of high-technology products (e.g. Silicon Valley). In the last decade, clusters have been recognised as areas in which conditions are very favourable either for stimulating productivity and innovation in the integrating companies or for the formation of HRs and the creation of new businesses.

The policy of clustering is giving excellent results in the most dynamic regions of the world, especially when applied to groups of small to mid-sized companies operating in a coordinated network (networking); e.g the Emilia Romana in Italy, Scotland in the UK, Arizona in the USA, Silicon Valley in California, Highway 128 in Boston USA, Valencia, Catalonia and in the Basque Country in Spain, etc.

The success of the most dynamic clusters is closely related to the way in which the leading companies and organizations in its economy manage their knowledge; that is to say, the process of creation, storing, structuring and diffusion of information and knowledge by means of pro-active policies of business and institutional co-operation. In this aspect, the development of Information and Communication Technologies (ICT) and the range of the Information Society in the territory are the determining factors.

In this sense it is important to mention that not all firms aggregate into territorial or geographical clusters. Some firms deliberately locate outside the cluster that encompasses the majority of the firms in their industry because they feel that employee retention will be higher (i.e., competitors will not be as likely to steal their employees) and their trade secrets will be easier to keep. These firms use to form "virtual" clusters, based in the use of ICT.

However, in all these processes it is obvious that there should exist a synergetic Structural Network of Relations (SNR) among the industrial entities, generating valuable external economies for most of them.

Collaboration in a Geographical Region: Clusters and Networks

The world we live in has become a global economy in which the use of ICT and advanced logistics enables relations to be established between businesses in any part of the world. Nevertheless, in order to establish successful inter-organisational relations or alliances it is important to be able to count on the so-called business ecosystems (Camarinha-Matos, 2002), i.e. on environments favourable to networks of businesses that use similar strategies and practices, where there exists mutual trust among the companies involved, as well as an atmosphere of community and stability.

The fact that businesses can be concentrated geographically in the form of clusters is a key factor for the SMES in their evolution towards the knowledge-based economy. Some companies are finding out that they can get more benefit from their organisational knowledge, even increasing their competences, within an interactive cluster that possesses informal inter-business links favourable to the creation and transfer of knowledge.

Nowadays, firms tend to stay close to one another, in search of a reserve of trained workers and specific local infrastructures. The firms that compose the cluster can obtain economies of proximity, for example, and even obtain economies of scale through the specialisation of the individual companies, joint purchase of raw materials, etc. On this aspect, as regards the range of knowledge, the proximity of institutes, universities, etc., these are proving to be more important factors than the mere fact of being in a geographical cluster.

Another important factor in clusters is the fact that, although it may sound paradoxical, the grouping of businesses is of great importance, in spite of the advances in the ICT, since the correct assimilation of tacit knowledge and innovation needs an environment of cooperation and mutual trust among people, who are more easily reachable in such circumstances. Regarding this aspect, the ICT have not yet been able to achieve better results in the exchange of knowledge (not information) than interpersonal relations.

Clusters facilitate other kinds of cooperation and association among businesses, since the continual contact and the fact of being close to one another help to establish good relations. Cooperation in networks is the norm when businesses are situated close to one another, although there are some networks of businesses separated by considerable distances. Networks can be formed among firms in a supply chain or between associated businesses.

The network organisational model involves the maximum fragmentation of the company, since it is based fundamentally on a union of companies in which each one specialises in a certain activity. This structure does not happen at random, but is an attempt to incorporate the efficiency of the functional structure, the effectiveness of divisional autonomy and the capacity to transfer skills within the group, but with no one firm exercising a strict control on the elements required to produce goods or services.

The dominant company in the value creation process of the entire system is that which will assume the responsibility of integrating the network, facilitating good relations among all the members. It must therefore reinforce its professional staff and directors in order to efficiently manage the new structure.

It should be pointed out that the fact that the different networks have the objective of providing businesses with the necessary flexibility to respond to the changing and heterogeneous demands of the market does not mean that they are intrinsically unstable or that they will not last longer than the short term and have to function merely as tactical connections. Networks may also create stable links among companies with strategic objectives, such as the so-called strategic networks. Depending on the kind of relationship, these networks may tend to be either stable or dynamic.

Necessity for a Greater Degree of Detail: Clusters and Micro-Clusters

But we understand that the aforementioned models, both the Marshallian industrial districts and Porter's cluster, although valuable and taken as a starting point, are insufficient to define pro-active clustering policies and must be added to. In the particular case of "Porter's diamond", one of the reasons for this insufficiency is that the field of analysis proposed by this author, in terms of a cluster related to a territorial technical specialisation, is too wide and it is therefore necessary to study in greater detail the specialisation of the product.

Porter's definition of a territorial cluster *("A geographically proximate group of interconnected firms and associate institutions in a particular field, linked by commonalties and complementarities"* (Porter, 1998)) does not give sufficient detail to understand how the directors of the specialised companies in a territory can take specific strategic decisions for change. Porter's conception of a cluster and his model of analysis of the diamond – based essentially on the analysis of advanced and specialised determinants of competitiveness – although it can allow the specific identification of the real concrete factors that caused development in the immediate past, is insufficient to identify the specific factors for basing future processes of strategic change, since its analytic process is essentially centred on the structural analysis of the industrial sector.

To say that one must "boost the critical specialised factors" does not tell very much to the director of a company, or even to a political administrator of a territory. The direction of the strategy must be indicated so that plans can be made for specific business strategy, competitive strategy, technological strategy, what technological research to conduct and promote, the markets to be aimed for, the emerging market sectors, the requirements of new products and processes, etc. When these are decided, the specific requirements in resources – knowledge, training, technology, machinery, infrastructure, etc. – which must be acquired, improved or developed to achieve the objectives can be decided, both in the individual company and on a territorial scale.

To achieve this degree of analytical detail, it is necessary to go beyond a SWOT analysis or the classic structural analysis of an industrial sector. One must go down to the level of in which business competition takes place: companies compete with each other with products in markets. And this brings us to the concept of the Territorial Micro-cluster; a group of specialised companies established in the same region and related to each other, not only by the technology used (industrial sector) and their geographical proximity (Marshallian Industrial District) but by the binomial (product + market), since:

- Firms that do not manufacture the same product do not compete with each other (unless they make substitutable products).
- Firms that do not sell in the same markets do not compete with each other.

It is important to remark that in the two above cases firms not compete for the same customers, but they compete on many other levels. They may compete for employees, investor dollars, community tax abatements or other forms of support, etc.

In fact, the following diversity of types of relationship could be detected among the members of a microcluster:

- **Indifference:** the members take no account whatsoever of the existence of the other member in the decision-making process. The repercussions of any action on the other member are not considered, nor is consideration given to the possible consequences to the company of the actions of the other member.
- **Competition:** two members compete with each other to obtain something that both want: markets, clients, any type of resources (human, financial, technological, physical, etc.), using different types of strategies to achieve their ends. According to the type of strategy and their attitudes to each other, the result of the competition for the microcluster may be:
    - **Negative:** The "I win-you lose" type relationship destroys value.
    - **Positive.** The "win-win" relationship creates value for the microcluster.
- **Collaboration:** The two members adopt formal or informal attitudes that help each other to achieve their objectives while each is intent on achieving his own.

The two latter attitudes, competition and cooperation, are not mutually exclusive in a relationship between two members, unlike the first (indifference), which certainly excludes any other possibility. In the particular case of the relations between two competitors, the adoption of strong reciprocal competition in the market and positive cooperation in the rest of the activities, productive or not (contact with the administration, support for universities and research centres) is beneficial for the territorial system. This is called "co-opetition", for the concepts of competition and cooperation, and is considered the relationship most likely to generate value for the microcluster.

Adopting this approach of structuring the territorial clusters in micro-clusters – composed of firms inter-related by the value chain of the production of final goods and services, or by intermediaries that perform the same function or sell in the same market – the degree of analysis can be widened and can pass from general considerations and strategies to identifying specific strategies and objectives that allow the companies in the microcluster to maintain their competitive edge in international markets, as it is remarked in table 1.

**Table 1. Strategic differences between the traditional cluster
analysis and the proposed microcluster analysis**

Traditional Cluster Analysis	Proposed Microcluster Analysis
General value and/or cost reductions To invest in R+D+I To invest in research infrastructures	To develop and control a certain Internet-based distribution channel To train a certain number of technicians in a specific technology To start up a rapid prototype production centre To make a project for holding a new specialised international commercial fair for a new type of emerging product

It is thus proposed, in this type of studies, to take the evolutive analysis down to the level of the territorial Micro-clusters, defined in terms of the binomial (product $\diamond$ market), which is the real battleground in which business-firms compete. The reasons are evident: a key factor for the competitiveness of manufacturers in a micro-cluster may not be such, or may even be negative, for companies outside it.

The Geographic Concentration of Innovation: Territorial Innovation Systems

To continue with the subject matter of the foregoing sections, recent theories of endogenous growth emphasise the fact that accumulation of knowledge and the consequent technological development are the real powers behind localised strategic changes. As certain authors have pointed out (Feldman, 1994; Sharp, 1998), the phenomena of technological cooperation directed towards strategic change – innovation in products and/or processes – are increased by geographic concentration. The flow of information and knowledge directed towards innovation is faster the smaller the physical distance between the persons responsible for taking business decisions in these fields. Innovative activity therefore presents a high degree of geographic concentration, which is even greater than that of economic activity as a whole.

This gives importance to Regional Innovation Systems (RIS) in territorial clusters (universities, technological institutes, research centres, etc.). Following Cooke et al. (2000), we understand that an RIS, in its turn, consists of two subsystems:

- The subsystem of the exploitation and application of knowledge, basically composed of the companies that form the vertical networks of supply in the value chain; and
- The subsystem of the generation and diffusion of knowledge, consisting principally of public organisations and institutions.

In this sense it is important to analyze the specific processes that have taken place in successful clusters, and therefore concentrates on the identification of the key factors in territorial competitiveness that in the past have provided powerful means to generate value and giving competitive advantages to local firms obtained from the capacities and abilities present in the elements of the local economy.

The problem, in terms of industrial and economic policies, is how to generate, distribute, manage, apply and utilise this knowledge, in order to maintain and increase the competitiveness of businesses at present in operation. The past may be unrepeatable, but it is important to achieve analogies and conclusions that permit us to control future conditions.

A CRITICAL ANALISIS OF THE MODEL OF THE VALUE CHAIN

If the existing architecture of the relationships among the elements of a microcluster is studied, the means by which value is generated internally can be studied from the network of relationships *(netchain)* existing among the firms and organisations and the influence of the quantity and quality of these relationships in the value chain of the system of production.

Lazzarini et al. (2001) correctly distinguished the difference between the concepts of "Supply Chain Analysis" (SCA) and "Network Analysis" (NA) with the aim of differentiating the sequential vertical hierarchical "customer–supplier" relationships of the supply chain (SCA) compared to the existing systemic relationships among the various typologies of the firms and organisations involved in a microcluster (NA), in which the connections or interdependencies refer to situations in which each actor makes a discrete independent contribution, formal or informal, to a given task, or in which reciprocal relationships exist where such contributions are mutually dependent.

Porter's Value Chain Model

Porter (1980, 1990) has also made an important contribution to understanding production processes by introducing the term "Value Chain". The value chain of *a firm* is a system of internal interrelated processes in which each of them – each link in the chain – adds value to the final product or service.

In Porter's proposal, the total value of the product or service created by the firm is measured by the total sum that buyers are prepared to pay to acquire this product or service. In this model, the value activities of a firm are structured in nine generic categories, divided into two groups:

a. Primary activities, which are those involved in the physical, chemical or physical-chemical transformation, marketing and distribution of the product; as well as those involved in product support and after-sales service.

b. Auxiliary activities, or those that deal with production factors and provide the infrastructure that allows the primary activities to take place (Porter and Miller, 1985).

Need for a Deeper Analysis

Based on the considerations of the preceding points, we can state that Porter's generic Model of the Value Chain, which divides the activities carried out in the production of goods and services into principal and secondary, or auxiliary, activities, is insufficient to apply a strategic analysis to a Microcluster.

Here we have another objection similar to that in the preceding section, relative to the determining factors in territorial competitiveness: it is no use talking to a business manager of principal and secondary activities, or even of essential activities - *core competences* in the line of Hamel and Prahalad (1990) – since he will not be able to use them to make strategic decisions if he cannot identify them.

More detail is needed in the analysis in order to diagnose what are the key factors for success that specifically must make him take certain decisions in his business and/or in relation to the other firms or organisations with which he is associated; customers, suppliers, related companies, public and private institutions, etc.

Also, we must not forget that Porter's model of the Value Chain was created for a specific company, and this is an additional disadvantage in its application to an analytical study of clusters and microclusters of business companies.

It is precisely the interrelations among the production phases in an industrial sector, performed by *different companies,* but geographically close to each other, that allow us to consider the concept of a Value Chain *extended* to the entire production process in a certain territory, on the basis of their relationship in terms of (product – market). This gives rise to a new concept that we consider can facilitate the strategic analysis process that we are aiming for: the *Framework of the Value Chain of a Microcluster.*

THE DESIGN OF THE FRAMEWORK OF THE VALUE CHAIN OF A MICROCLUSTER

For a Microcluster defined in terms of product and market it is possible to identify each and every one of the specific production phases involved in the transformation of the initial inputs in useful goods and services for the final consumer of the chosen objective markets. At the same time, by concentrating on a production phase, the specific technologies used or that can be used to perform this phase in the most efficient and efficacious way possible can be identified with precision.

In this way the generic concept of the production Value Chain (Porter, 1985) may be amplified towards the specific design of the Framework of the Value Chain in the

Microcluster, in the form of a graphic block diagram in which each of the "boxes" of the framework corresponds to a certain phase or link in the production chain. Each of these links is identified with a certain stage whose start and finish are perfectly defined. Such a high degree of detail even allows us to know the value generated in each phase, such as the economic cost of the resources consumed in production, and this facilitates the identification of the stage or stages in which the evolutive process is centred.

In the initial design of this framework, considering the activities defined in this way, the companies that carry out the work are not taken into account, or if they are or are not situated in the territory in question. It is a case of drawing the traditional or habitual process in which goods or services have been produced up to the present time in the territory, without considering the specific companies involved in their production.

The knowledge and the historic processes associated with a territory give a territorial microcluster its singularity and uniqueness; otherwise the Framework would be confused with another generic technological process.

Thus, by production phase (*a link* in the Value Chain) we understand the group of operations in a certain phase of the specific production process of a product, from the initial inputs of raw materials until the finished product comes into the hands of the final consumer. A phase, stage or link in the chain of value that can be unmistakeably identified from these two characteristics;

- It has perfectly defined initial and final events (markers).
- It generates value – even if at times this may be low or non-existent, in terms of the appreciation of the final consumer, as has been defined in the preceding section – and it has certain costs related to the activities carried out, which correspond to the economic cost of the resources consumed in production (materials, labour, power, information, management, etc).

From the foregoing information we can therefore design the specific Framework of the Value Chain of a Microcluster, creating a graph in the form of a flow diagram with blocks or boxes representing the links. In this diagram, each square or box must correspond to a perfectly defined phase belonging to a value-generating activity with its associated costs in proportion to the resources consumed in its performance. This degree of detail permits a critical analysis of each specific activity carried out (each box), showing the precise relationship of the value generated in the activity for the market with its associated specific costs.

Also, it must be remembered that each of the phases may be performed by internal companies or by companies from outside the territory in question, showing the opportunities for introducing value internally, in those cases in which the value/cost relationship is important and the activity is carried out outside the territory, i.e. by firms outside the Microcluster.

IDENTIFICATION OF OPPORTUNITIES FOR INNOVATION IN MICROCLUSTERS FROM THE DETERMINATION OF KEY FACTORS OF SUCCESS

The creation of value by innovation can be achieved by means of Innovation in Products and/or by Innovation in Processes.

In the preceding section we defined the differences between the basic concepts of Cost, Price and Value as the starting point to explain the importance of Innovation for businesses, since their profits depend on it.

We said that the best situation occurs with Price located between the company's Cost and the buyer's subjective Value of the product, so that, when an agreement is reached for the exchange of the product at the stipulated Price, both sides consider that they have taken an advantage from the exchange. In this way – and only in this way – wealth is created in our society. If Price is below Cost, wealth is destroyed in the form of a loss for the selling company, and if Price is above the buyer's subjective Value, wealth is destroyed when he uses his savings in exchange for nothing or for goods that will not give him the satisfaction or the service that he wanted.

So, Innovation is the basis of the creation of wealth for society and of profits for businesses. This is why it is enormously important. The difficult part is to find the right lines to follow that allow companies, by means of increasing value and/or reducing costs, to remain competitive in international markets; the determination of what we call *the key factors in competitive success.*

This is perhaps the most difficult objective to achieve in the endless search for success in business, both for individual companies and for specialised territorial clusters.

With this in mind, we propose to analyse the value chain of a microcluster, i.e. using the Framework of the Value Chain defined in the preceding section. This would mean extending Grant's analysis (1995) by amplifying it to the specialised production links of a microcluster, putting together the blocks of the different stages of production, even if they are each carried out by different firms. Grant uses the value chain of a business company for the possibilities it offers both in the formulation of strategies based on cost reduction and in differentiation.

Individual Analysis of the Links in the Chain

The detailed analysis of the production process and of the technology used in each link, relating them to the percentage of the final value estimated to be generated in this stage and to the associated costs, allows diverse alternatives to be diagnosed:

- For the phases that generate no value, from the point of view of the final consumer: they are simply eliminated.
- For the phases with high costs in relation to final value: a continual search for a greater level of efficiency through the use of new technologies, outsourcing, and if necessary contracting out the work involved in the phase, even using firms outside the geographical region if costs such as salaries, taxes, etc. are lower there.

These are the normal criteria used in the analysis of the principal links in the value chain.

Analysis of the Position of a Specific Phase in the Sequence of Links and Possibilities for Change and/or Change in Relationship with Other Links

One of the greatest successes in industrial sectors, especially in the "mature" sectors (textiles, shoe-making, etc.) has come from a reconstruction of the chain of value, designing completely new production methods, normally based on a "revolutionary" concept (Hamel y Prahalad, 1994) of the Framework of the Value Chain and achieved by a total or almost total restructuring of the technological relationships of the various links.

In the case of the mature sectors, since the products are the traditional ones (clothing, shoes, etc.), the "revolution" has taken place by the intensive use of new technologies (ICT) in the auxiliary activities of the old production chain.

At other times, when the "revolution" cannot be so radical, great innovative advances are achieved by combining antagonistic variables (dipoles), already related to the features or attributes of the product, thus alternating or changing production processes.

Key Factors of Success

The generation of value by obtaining advantages over competitors is attained by companies by utilising the differentiating characteristics (singular characteristics and strategic assets) and applying them in markets where they can be exploited to commercial advantage (Kay, 1993).

The strategic resources to obtain these advantages, as Gary Hammel describes (2000), are to be found in the area of key competences (what the company knows), strategic assets (what the company possesses) and key processes (what the company does).

A key factor in success is therefore the combination of resources and knowledge that a company must have to be used in value-generating or cost-reducing activities to give it an advantage over its competitors.

At this point the necessary question should be; How do we identify a key factor in success? How do we get together and organise the necessary resources and knowledge to beat the competition? And we must not forget that this identification must be done at the start! That is to say, before it actually gives market success.

There is only one answer, and that is by intuition. That is to say, a creative process with information sufficient both in quantity and quality, and with experienced managers responsible for making business decisions, will generate different future strategic alternatives from which the managers from experience and intuition will be able to choose the one or ones with most potential.

In their studies on creativity, Edward de Bono, 1994, and Malcolm Westcott (1968) recognise the importance of the intuitive process in creating and choosing new business ideas. However, for intuition to work well – as a mental function – it is absolutely necessary for it to be based on a long process of work and experience in which knowledge management is a fundamental process, preparing minds for the intuitive phase. This matter has little to do with luck or coincidence and a lot to do with generating relevant information and knowledge by profound analysis in order to generate viable alternatives. And it is intuition, based on the generated knowledge, that in the end impels the minds of the decision takers to choose which one or ones of the alternatives has the most potential to generate value.

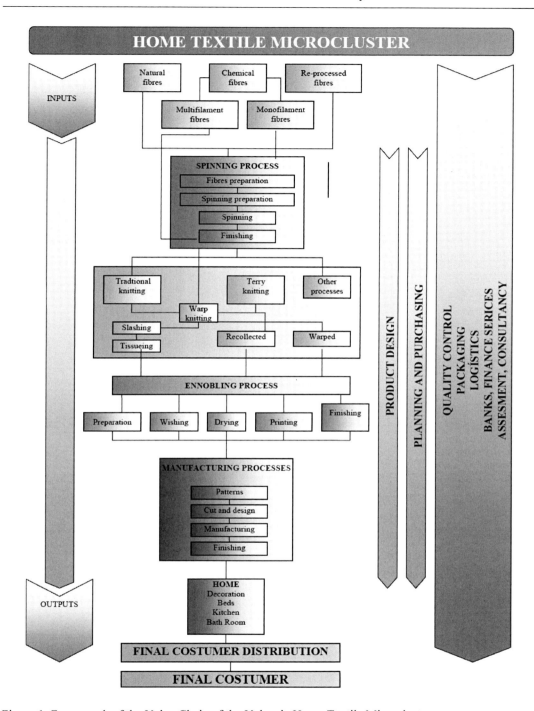

Figure 1. Framework of the Value Chain of the Valencia Home Textile Microcluster.

The information and knowledge generated both in the analytical process of the structure of microclusters in terms of (product – market) and in the process of the critical analysis of the Framework of the Value Chain must provide sufficient strategic alternatives for the managers of the companies and other bodies involved in the microcluster to be able to intuitively choose the key success factors to be included in the process of strategic change.

However, within a microcluster the alternatives generated have to be shared among the principal organisations involved. What actions must be taken to accomplish this? There are two possible ways, which are not mutually exclusive:

- By means of holding strategic *Benchmarking* sessions in which the principal managers and institutional directors of the Microcluster take part. In these sessions the results of the analysis are explained and a list is given of the most important future alternatives in the sector, discussing and approving those which appear to be the most promising.
- By correspondence, by means of a Delphi type survey, in which proposals for the best alternatives are given and other suggestions are invited, which will be discussed in a second or third round by the managers of the Microcluster.

In both cases the relevant supporting documented information ought to be available to the managers so that they have complete and up to date information on the territory.

To illustrate what we have explained, we give in the following figure a simplified map of the value Chain of the Valencia Household Textiles Microcluster. In it some of the key success factors are shown, derived from the analysis of the Microcluster.

CONCLUSIONS

From the information and knowledge gained in the analysis of the microcluster in terms of (product – market), and from the critical analysis of its Framework of the Value Chain, specific strategic alternatives are generated from which the managers involved in the microcluster can use their intuition to isolate the key success factors to be used for strategic changes, as well as the most appropriate technological and industrial policies – in a clustering approach.

In all cases, any strategic decision taken by the leaders of the microcluster must include improved cooperation among its members, making full use of the market potential for the development of new products and services to satisfy clients' new needs and propitiating the development and/or diffusion of new technologies to meet these new needs.

Therefore, it must be remembered that within the concept of the value chain, the information and knowledge that flow through it must also be taken into consideration. According to Rayport and Sviokla (1995), parallel to the physical value chain, along which the goods or services progress, a virtual value chain is generated, along which the information flows that continuously feeds the various members, including the clients, which implies a continuous process of improvement by all the members involved.

This is especially important if we consider the proposed concept of the microcluster value chain. The companies that form this microcluster value chain will have to concentrate on what they really know how to do better than their competitors, and also learn to cooperate with other companies to generate value in an atmosphere of mutual trust. For this microcluster value chain to be basically oriented towards the client, responding to his needs, desires and demands, a new organizational system becomes necessary that is capable of adapting to, and even of anticipating, changes, and of seizing whatever business opportunities are presented.

This form of organization would be that which corresponds to the process of the given value chain necessary to respond to each key factor detected, composed of the members that have the knowledge, competences and skills necessary to carry out the integrated activities through ICT, cooperating with mutual trust, in a context of minimum of hierarchical levels, continually adapting and forming an open, flexible system.

The members of this new organization should agree on a form of management in order to create a common environment of understanding, substituting the concept of obedience for that of shared decisions and negotiation. This is especially important because among the members of the organization, or virtual netchain, there are no traditional hierarchical relationships, since they are independent organizations in a situation of temporary cooperation to deal with a specific market opportunity, so that the establishing of objectives must always be by common agreement among them.

REFERENCES

Becattini, G. (1989). Sectors and/or districts: some remarks on the conceptual foundations of industrial economics. *Ed. Goodman* et alt.

Becattini, G. (1992). "El distrito industrial marshaliano como concepto socioeconómico". Cap. 4 de Los distritos industriales y las pequeñas empresas. *Min. de Trabajo y Seg. Soc.* España.

Becattini, G. (1994). El distrito marshalliano: una noción socioeconómica. *Cap. 2 de Las regiones que ganan.* Benko, G. et alt. (eds).

Becattini, G. (1996). Sistemas productivos locales y mercados globales. Rev. *Investigación Comercial,* nº 754

Benko, G. y Lipietz, A. (1994). Las regiones que ganan. Ed. *Alfons el Magnànim.* Valencia.

De Bono, Edward (1994). El pensamiento creativo. Ed. *Paidós.* Barcelona.

Feldman, M. (1994). The Geography of Innovation. Dordrecht.

Grant, Robert M. (1995). Contemporary strategy analysis: concepts, techniques, applications. Blackwell Publishers. Cambridge, Massachusetts.

Hamel, G. and Prahalad, C.K. (1994). Competing for the future. Harvard Business School Press.

Hammel, Gary (2000). Leading the Revolution. Harvard Business School Press.

Kay, John (1993). Foundations of Corporate Success. Oxford University Press.

Lazzarini, S.G., F.R. Chaddad and M.L. Cook (2001). Integrating supply chain and network analyses: the study of netchains. *Journal on Chain and Network Science,* 1 (1), 7-22.

OCDE Territorial Development Policy Committee (1999). Regional Review The Valencian Central Districts. OCDE, París, 3 de diciembre.

Porter, M.E. (1980). Competitive Strategy: Techniques for analysing industries and competitors. New York: The Free press.

Porter, M.E. and V.E. Millar (1985). How information gives you competitive advantage. Harvard Business Review, Vol. 63, July-Aug., 149-160.

Porter, M. E. (1998 a). "Clusters and Competition" y "Competing Across Locations" en "On Competition". Harvard Business School Press.

Porter, M. E. (1998 b). Clusters and the new economics competition. Rev. *Harvard Business Review,* nov – dec.

Prahalad, C.K. and G. Hamel (1990). The core competence of the corporation. *Harvard Business Review*, Vol. 68, May-June, 79-91.

Pyke, F. and Sengenberger, W. (1992). Industrial districts and Local Economic Regeneration. International Institute for Labour Studies, Geneve.

Rosenfeld, Stuart A. (2002). Just Clusters. Economic development strategies that reach more people and places. A Synthesis of Experiences. Supported by a grant from the Ford Foundation. Regional Technology Strategies, Inc. Carrboro, North Carolina. www.rtsinc.org

Sabel, Ch. (1992). Studies Trust: Building New Forms of Cooperation in a Volatile Economy. In Industrial Districts and Local Economic Regeneration. Frank Pyke and Werner Sengenberger, comp. International Institute for Labour Studies, International Labour Office. Geneve.

Scott, B. R. (1989). Competitiveness: Self Help for a Worsening Problem. Harvard Business Reviews, 67 (4). 115 - 121.

Sforzi, F. (1989): "Sistemi locali e sviluppo economico: alcune reflessioni". Rev. *Impresa & Stato,* n° 4.

Sweeney, G. (1991). Technical culture and the local dimension of entrepreneurial vitality. *Entrepreneurship and Regional Development,* vol. 3.

Westcott, Malcolm (1968). Toward a Contemporary Psychology of Intuition. Holt, Rinehard & Winston. New York.

In: Social Development
Editor: Lynda R. Elling

ISBN: 978-1-60741-612-8
© 2009 Nova Science Publishers, Inc.

Chapter 7

NEW EUROPEAN POLICY TOWARD CHRONICALLY ILL EMPLOYEES

Helen Kopnina and Joke Haafkens
Amsterdam Institute of Advanced Labour Studies
University of Amsterdam

ABSTRACT

This article provides an overview of current policies related to the chronically ill employees in the Netherlands. Different levels of policy are discussed: those formulated at the European, Dutch and organizational levels. A significantg percentage of Dutch employees suffer from longstanding diseases (classified by International Classification of Diseases - ICD), others experience impairments at work (classified by International Classification of Functioning, Disability and Health - ICF). Current policies in the European Union and in The Netherlands increasingly encourage participation of those who are impaired or disabled based on definitions of ICD and ICF formulated by World Health organization (WHO).

Recently, there has been a significant change in the Dutch policy concerning employment of chronically ill, impared or disabled people. Before 2007, employers were responsible for the management of sickness absence in order to prevent any claims for disability benefits. The new Dutch Working Conditions Act reflects the need of the government to reduce the administrative burdens on companies and eliminate superfluous rules to give companies more scope for introducing individual arrangements. According to the European Agency for Safety and Health at Work, working conditions regulations have been made simpler and easier to implement. The working conditions policy within companies became more flexible, dividing responsibility for safety, health and reintegration between both employers' and employees'. The switch to less detailed rules and more scope for individual arrangements ties in with absence and reintegration policy. In this article, we examine some of the implications of this shift.

Keywords: organizational and HRM policy, employees with chronic diseases, European employment policy, Dutch employment policy, meso-level of organizational policy, disablement process.

Introduction

The main question of our research is 'What can an organization do to enable the chronically ill to optimally function at work?' To aim this question we searched the literature for the types of organizational measures (by employers and supporting HRM) enabling employees with chronic illness to optimally perform their work. We have further inquired which measures do the professionals (employers, HRM and labor unions) find important and feasible enable the employees to optimally function at work. We have discovered that there is little known about the effectiveness of such measures since little consistent research has been done on the relationship between European and national-level policies and interventions. In this article we shall address the literature review of existing policies and interventions, which prepare the ground for further empirical inquiry. In order to achieve this, we formulated a number of assumptions. The first assumption is that chronically ill workers need to retain their jobs due to new policy pressures. Secondly, we assume that chronically ill workers want to retain their jobs if certain conditions are met. Thirdly, we assume that employers want to retain chronically ill workers if particular challenges are met. Finally, we assume that it is at the level of employers (both top management and line managers) and HRM that the policies are interpreted and changes can be implemented.

At the organizational level of policy, we make a distinction between macro- (policy), meso-(employers and HRM) and micro (employees) policy levels. We particularly focus at the meso-level (line managers, managers, HRM) because of three factors. First, while there is ample literature on both macro- and micro-levels of organizations, there is little known about the meso-level. Secondly, we hypothesize that it is precisely at the meso-level that the most relevant policy-decisions and implementation thereof occurs. Finally, we note great variation in interpretation and implementation of policies across organizations. We attribute this both to the changes in current policies and the structural differences within the organizations related to organizational culture. These differences are expressed through varied relationships and hierarchies between the stakeholders, such as employers, HRM, corporate doctors and employees.

Method

Literature study using systematic hand-search strategy involving medical, statistical, management and social science databases (Web of Science, MedLine, Pub Med, Psych Info, AMC library). We used the following types of publications: Scientific literature (peer reviewed international or Dutch publications within 'established fields or disciplines' such as social sciences, medical and management books and journals; working papers, conference papers, reports, manuscripts, unpublished papers); Handbooks, guides and articles from HRM and management professional journals; Government reports (statistics, policy, etc.); Popular media: journals, newspapers, television programs; Websites.

For the purpose of this study we shall only include physical and NOT psychological or mental disorders. We restricted literature to European cases and policies. In later phases of this research project, American and Canadian sources will be included.

The following terms in combination with each other were used: chronic, illness, disease, disability, impairment, handicap, unemployment, intervention, training, HRM, hiring, contract, policy, act, international, European, Dutch, employment, work place, employer, employee, advisor, disclosure, screening, complaints, pain, discomfort, periodic, flair-ups, sick leave, early retirement, sickness, benefits, discrimination, stigmatization, diversity, ageing, age, gender, educational level, physical, rehabilitation, reintegration, prevention, medication, consulting, advice, medical practice, corporate doctor, diabetes, multiple sclerosis, asthma, etc.

I. DEFINITIONS OF CHRONIC ILLNESS, DISABILITY AND IMPAIRMENT

Definitions of chronic illness include physical disabilities (such as multiple sclerosis or diabetes), either acquired (such as work-related and non-work-related injuries) or inherited (such as genetic disorders). Some acquired conditions such as AIDS and cancer are sometimes included. Others also include psychological or psychiatric disorders (such as depression and schizophrenia). Further, distinction can be made between manifest (or visible) and invisible (sometimes latent) disorders. The World Health Organization (WHO) developed International Statistical Classification of Diseases and Related Health Problems (ICD) (http://www.who.int/classifications/apps/icd/icd10online/). ICD distinguishes between some of the following categories of diseases: anaemia, other diseases of blood and blood-forming organs, meningitis in other specified infectious and parasitic diseases, encephalitis, myelitis and encephalomyelitis, rheumatic fever; chronic rheumatic heart diseases; other specified cerebrovascular diseases, etc.

According to the European Foundation for the Improvement of Living and Working Conditions, which draws its main resources from the European Community Household Panel (ECHP), chronically ill are defined as share of people who have any long-standing illness or disability that limits their activities in any way (http://www.eurofound.europa.eu/areas/qualityoflife/eurlife/index.php?template=6&radioindic=183&idDomain=1)[1].

WHO defines disabilities as an umbrella term, covering impairments, activity limitations, and participation restrictions. Impairment is a problem in body function or structure; an activity limitation is a difficulty encountered by an individual in executing a task or action; while a participation restriction is a problem experienced by an individual in involvement in life situations (http://www.who.int/topics/disabilities/en/). In The Netherlands, both acquired and inherited illnesses are considered as chronic, specifying that not all chronic conditions lead to disability to perform paid work. This definition does not include normal ageing and conditions that may be cured within a short time. Work disabled are defined as people who because of their chronic condition or handicap have problems finding and maintaining paid work (Bruins Slot, 2006:2).

---

[1] Certain Member States use the International Classification of Impairments, Disabilities and Handicaps (ICIDH), but frequently definitions differ. Only the European Community Household Panel (ECHP) has a common questionnaire centrally designed by Eurostat. This allows comparison across Member States that is not possible in other surveys and censuses (http://www.eurofound.europa.eu/pubdocs/2003/35/en/1/ef0335en.pdf).

In the UK, Disability Discrimination Act (1995) defines disabled as a person who has a disability if he has a physical or mental impairment which has a substantial and long-term adverse effect on his ability to carry out normal day-to-day activities. The Act also defines discrimination by the employer and duty of employer to make adjustments by listing enforcement, remedies and procedure as well as validity of certain agreements (http://www.opsi.gov.uk/acts/acts1995/ukpga_19950050_en_1).

To sum up, some of the common international definitions of chronic illness include:

- Last longer than one year
- Cause (some) limitations to what a person can do
- Require ongoing medical care
- Can occur at any age, but mostly as people get older
- Symptoms vary in severity from mild to very serious
- They do not always follow an expected pattern (flare ups)
- Vary in symptom visibility (MS – diabetes)
- Disease progression is also variable (HIV/AIDS)
- Some people experience ''flares'' or peaks of symptoms, followed by remission periods. Others experience constant symptoms.

The *International Classification of Functioning, Disability and Health* (ICF) classifies levels of functioning rather than diseases. It is a classification of health-related domains classified from body, individual and societal perspectives. Classification is possible by means of two lists: a list of body functions and structure, and a list of domains of activity and participation. In ICF, the term *functioning* refers to all body functions, activities and participation, while *disability* is similarly an umbrella term for impairments, activity limitations and participation restrictions. ICF also lists environmental factors that interact with all these components. The ICF acknowledges that the presence of disease or disorder is not causally linked to an individual's functional outcome in a linear fashion. In other words, it is recognized that two individuals may have the same diagnosis but differ in their level of functioning, or in contrast, two individuals may have the same level of functioning but differ in their diagnosis (Allan et al, 2006:238).

Related to the case of employment and illness, the following distinctions may further be made:

The *Performance qualifier* indicates the extent of participation restriction by describing the persons' actual performance of a task or action in his or her current environment.

The *Capacity qualifier* indicates the extent of Activity limitation by describing the person ability to execute a task or an action (http://www.who.int/classifications/icf/site/checklist/icf-checklist.pdf).

Aside from these technical classifications, more sociomedical approaches exist. Grounding his categorization is sociological theory, Nagi defines four central concepts: active pathology interruption of normal processes, efforts of the organism to regain normal state), impairment (anatomical, physiological, mental or emotional abnormalities or loss), functional limitation (limitation of performance at the level of the whole organism or person), and disability (limitation in performance of socially defined roles and tasks within a socio-cultural and physical environment) (Nagi, 1979:5). Building upon Nagi's theory, Verbrugge and Jette

(1994) expand on the concept of disability as a gap between personal capability and environmental demand. Within this disablement process, pathology may lead to impairments as well as to functional limitations and eventually to disability.

In their 'model of the Disablement process' Verbrugge and Jette (1994) distinguish between pathology, impairments, functional limitations and disability as forming the 'main pathway'. Pathology includes diagnoses of disease, injury, congenital or development condition. Impairment refers to dysfunctions and structural abnormalities in specific body systems (musculoskeletal, cardiovascular, neurological, etc). Functional limitations are restrictions in basic physical and mental actions (such as ambulating, reaching, stooping, etc.). Disability, finally, is defined as difficulty doing activities of daily life: job, household management, personal care, hobbies, active recreation, clubs, etc. Effecting this main pathway are several factors including risk factors, such as predisposing characteristics (demographic, social, lifestyle, etc.), intra-individual factors (lifestyle and behavioral changes, psychosocial attributes and coping and activity accommodations), and extra-individual factors (medical care and rehabilitation, medications and other regimens, external supports, built, physical and social environment) (Verbrugge and Jette, 1994: 4). Oliver (1990) criticizes the medical model of disability, which focuses on individual and his physical condition rather than society within which disability receives its label. Oliver makes a distinction between impairment and disability. While the impairment describes a body lacking part of a limb or having a defective limb; disability refers to social or cultural disadvantages imposed by society on people with physical impairments. Particularly relevant to the case of employers' and HRM's role in supporting chronically ill at work could be the extra-individual factors, playing a role at all four stages of the main pathway.

As we shall further discuss in the section on policies, the macro-level (EU and Dutch) policy focus lies on interventions during the last two elements of the main pathway (functional limitations and disabilities) rather than interventions at the two initial stages (pathology and impairment). Since this article's focus lies mainly on the meso-policies level (the employers and HRM), the disablement process and limitations in functioning conflicting with job demand rather than the disability itself, are of particular importance. This may be referred to as 'social model', defined by Stattin (2005) as 'societal/environmental construct that recognizes the importance of the interaction between the individual and the social and physical environment' (Stattin, 2005:136). Contemporary disability policies define disability according to this social model.

II. European and Dutch Statistics on Employment and Illness

European labour force is ageing, but most older workers are not working. In 2001, only 39% of 55-64 year olds were working (73% for 46-55 year olds) In 2004, this number had risen to only 41%. Only 7% of 16-24 year olds report a chronic disease. About 30% of 55-64 year olds report a chronic disease. Between 20-46% work, compared to 68% of people without a chronic disease (Wynne, 2008).

In the study using the results of Third European Survey on Working Conditions, Gimeno et al (2004) note that sickness absence percentages (including those incidentally ill rather than chronically ill) were lower in Southern European countries compared with Central and Northern European countries, and, in general, slightly higher in men than in women. Overall EU average sickness absence percentage was 14.5%, varying between 6.7% in Greece and 24% in Finland. Comparing both sexes, men generally had higher sickness absence percentages in most countries. In general, workers in Southern European countries reported less sickness absence than the EU average (Greece, 6.7%; Portugal, 8.4%; Italy, 8.5%; Spain, 11.8%; and France, 14.3%). Percentages in those countries were lower than in Central European countries, except for the United Kingdom (11.7%) and Ireland (8.3%), and Northern European countries, except Denmark (12.4%) (Gimeno et al, 2004:868).

According to the Dutch Central Bureau of Statistics (CBS), there are nearly one and a half million disabled workers per 2002 (http://statline.cbs.nl/StatWeb/table.asp?PA=70087ned). Based on the research of the Dutch Ministry of Health, Welfare and Sport, the ten most common chronic illnesses are estimated to increase by 31% within 20 years and for some illnesses by 55% due to the increase of elderly population (www.minvws.nl).

As specified in the report about disabled workers (Beckers, 2004), there were almost 11 million people in the Netherlands between the ages of 15–64 in 2002. Of these people 14,7 percent was work disabled. The proportion of disabled workers has been increasing. In 2000, 13,6 percent of all people between 15–64 years old was disabled while in 2001 this proportion has reached 14,0 percent (http://www.cbs.nl/NR/rdonlyres/51DC1C8F-1016-472A-A800 3477FB6773FD/0/2004k1v4p027art.pdf) . These statistics are based on the Survey working population, distributed among 77.5 thousand households in 2005 http://www.cbs.nl/nl-NL/menu/themas/arbeid-sociale-zekerheid/methoden/dataverzameling/korte-onderzoeksbeschrijvingen/onderzoeksbeschrijving-ebb-art.htm). According to the Dutch CBS figures in the CBS there are 974740 people on disability benefit in 2007, of which 535270 men and 439340 women (*CBS startline zoek jaaroverzicht)*

According to the figures from the CBS from November 2007 to January 2008 there are 308.000 unemployed people in the Netherlands. The number of the people diagnosed with a chronic illness in the Netherlands is between 1.5 and 4.5 million. Recent research from the Rijksinstituut voor Volksgezondheid en Milieu says this figure will greatly increase in the coming 20 years. *(www.cbs.nl)*

Based on Bruins Slot's (2006) summary of CBS statistics on the chronically ill and work disabled, around 25% of population between the ages 15-65 has a chronic illness or a handicap and around 15% is work disabled. Among the working population these percentages are 19% and around 10%, among the unemployed 28% and 17%, and among the non-working (students, house wives, etc.) the percentages are 37% and 28%. Last group of work disabled includes those who have gone through evaluation process by WAO[2], WAZ[3] and WAJONG[4], by the end of 2005 there were, respectively, 467.479, 32.889 and 143.846 people, total 644.214 work disabled on social disability benefits (Bruins Slot, 2006).

According to the report Employment and Reintegration of the Chronically Ill and Disabled, the proportion of disabled persons belonging to the labour force that is relative to the total population is not high, 44% versus 68% (Van der Velden, 2007). The employment rate has decreased in recent years, especially in the younger age groups (decrease of 13

---

[2] WAO – incapacity benefit
[3] WAZ – incapacity benefit for self-employed
[4] Incapacity Insurance (Young Disabled Persons) Act (WAJONG).

percentage points over three years). In the report 'Key social situation 2006: National Panel chronically ill and disabled', the number of chronically ill and handicapped with paid jobs has increased in the last few years, and so has the number of the partially work disabled (Brink-Muinen et al. 2007; Chronisch Ziek Tijdschrift; 2007). Still, the labor participation of the chronically ill remains lower than that of healthy workers and they work less hours a week. The income levels of the chronically ill and handicapped have risen substantially but stopped rising since 2002. In 2006 their income levels were hundreds of euro's less than the incomes of healthy workers (Brink-Muinen et al 2007).

III. European and Dutch Policies towards the Chronically Ill

European policy related to the chronically ill may be divided in disability policy, equality policy, public health policy and employment policy. While the recent shift in European policy has been towards prevention, most of these policies do not necessarily address people at risk of becoming chronically ill or disabled. Employment equity policies employ mediating mechanisms (such as employment services and vocational rehabilitation), disability management focuses on reintegration (early intervention and mediation) and job retention (human resources/equal opportunities). Incentives for both mediating and reintegration mechanisms include anti-discrimination levies such as quotas and levies (Wynne, 2008).

European Foundation for Improvement of Living and Working Conditions (2003) launched a study to examine how to drive forward the social inclusion of people with LSHPD. Published to coincide with the European Year of People with Disabilities (2003), the report aims to fuel the debate and increase policy focus on people with a chronic illness or disability, particularly those of working age (Grammenos, 2006). The report gives an overview of key issues aiming to increase policy focus on people with disabilities and chronic illness, particularly those of working age. The report reviews the nature and scale of the problems facing different groups, notably barriers to the labor market. The important findings of this study in regards to experience of people with chronic illness or disability are:

1. Physical, legal and administrative barriers for these groups persist.
2. People with chronic illness and disabilities are frequently regarded solely as objects of care.
3. Segregation starts at an early stage with children often pushed into parallel education networks or otherwise excluded from mainstream society (Illness, Disability and Social Inclusion report http://www.eurofound.europa.eu/pubdocs/2003/32/en/1/ef0332en.pdf).

According to the European Agency for Safety and Health at Work, the working conditions policy within companies became more flexible, dividing responsibility for safety, health and reintegration between both employers' and employees'. The switch to less detailed rules and more scope for individual arrangements ties in with absence and reintegration policy (http://nl.osha.europa.eu/legislation/?language=en). We may recall the classical article on psychological contact by Guest which expressed the optimistic thought that 'employees perform because they want to, or at least feel obliged to, rather than in response to financial incentives or bureaucratic requirements' (Guest, 1998:254).

Generally, European and Dutch policies overlap in areas of chronic illness and disability in relation to employment (non-discrimination act) as well as sickness absence and early retirement (which affects both chronically ill and incidentally ill employees). The Dutch government increasingly strives to better integrate European regulations, including improved working conditions on the shop floor, more support for working conditions policy and individual arrangements policy within companies, less detailed rules and fewer administrative burdens for companies (http://nl.osha.europa.eu/legislation/?language=en).

While in the past most of these policies were targeted towards reintegration rather than prevention, the shift towards preventive measures within EU legislation is apparent. Divisions of preventions are aimed at addressing factors that lead to illnesses, such as smoking. Secondary prevention means focusing on the early diagnosis of the chronic illness by early recognition of symptoms. Tertiary prevention focuses on people diagnosed as suffering from a chronic illness and aiming at preventing the illness progress (www.minvws.nl).

Kloss (2005) remarks that the movement in occupational health has since recently been towards prevention rather than treatment. Kloss traces the history of occupational law as related to illness in England. The Select Committee on Science and Technology[5] (1983) put the emphasis on preventive medicine: 'Early prevention of hazards of work and the timely adoption of preventive measures will not only alleviate individual suffering, they will lighten the financial burden that the sickness imposes upon the state. There are also sound business reasons for ensuring that a workforce remains healthy. A healthy worker is a more efficient worker' (quoted in Kloss, 2005:21).

Eurofound publishes country-based reports of case studies and examples of best practices related to various aspects of health and employment, such as Employment and labour market policies for an ageing workforce and initiatives at the workplace National overview report: The Netherlands (http://www.eurofound.europa.eu/publications/htmlfiles/ef07059.htm). In the section on Employers and HRM views, examples of best practices will be further discussed.

Employment, Social Policy, Health and Consumer Affairs (ESPHCA) Council helps to shape EU policies in employment, social, health and consumer affairs. It brings these policy areas together in order to share best practice and to develop a long term strategy for meeting EU goals. The responsibilities of the ESPHCA include: promoting employment; health and Safety in the working environment; social security and social protection; corporate social responsibility and health care (http://www.dh.gov.uk/en/Healthcare/International/EuropeanUnion/DH_4117937)

While the focus of most European-level policies is equal treatment and equal rights for the employees, chronic illness, and especially mental illness, remains very much a hidden issue. Discussion about disability tends to get stuck on the issue of rights, where there is a lack lustre consensus, but fails to move into the area of active policy implementation. As a result, the disadvantages for people with disabilities or illness do not really change: they tend to be marginalized, even stigmatized, and feel isolated from many parts of social and public policy as well as the labour market. This group also tends to experience an accumulation of problems. With less possibility of getting or keeping a job, many are deprived of adequate

---

[5] http://www.parliament.uk/parliamentary_committees/science_and_technology_committee.cfm

income. Furthermore, the public sector tends to tackle the issue from one perspective (public health) or another (social affairs) and usually not in a comprehensive way (physical illness but not mental illness; social assistance but not inclusion; benefits but not activation). There is a lack of critical assessment about how the policies work and what could be the best allocation of resources. The report makes the point that exclusion from labour market participation for health reasons is a result of many factors, demanding action in many policy areas. It also suggests that social inclusion cannot be reduced to the issue of integration into employment (http://www.eurofound.europa.eu/pubdocs/2003/35/en/1/ef0335en.pdf).

Richard Wynne of Work Research Center in Ireland notices a few paradoxes in relation to current EU policies towards the ill employees. Most services for workplace health deal only/mainly with occupational health and safety. Most services for dealing with people on incapacity benefit have weak/no links with the workplace. This may lead to a few adverse effects: healthy people becoming ill, taking absence leave and becoming long term benefit recipients with little chance of returning to work.

To provide a context for discussing Dutch policy in relation to the chronically ill, we may ponder some of the questions addressed by Van der Velden (2007) in the report Employment and Reintegration of the Chronically Ill and Disabled: What problems exist with regard to maintaining work (employment) by the chronically ill and disabled? Which bottlenecks exist regarding reintegration of the chronically ill and disabled? What are the effects at the macro-economic level of (minor) employment of the disabled and chronically ill? (Van der Velden, 2007). The first two questions can be addressed through extensive literature review of the chronically ill, identifying factors such as the fact that work load; disease related work stress and fatigue exceeding employees' capabilities of carrying the load; continuous discrimination of the chronically ill at the workplace; persistence of physical symptoms preventing the employees to function optimally, and other factors related to both personal physical limitations to job performance and to external factors related to unwillingness of employers to retain the chronically ill.

There can be a disadvantage of voluntary Disability Management where employers may focus efforts on at-risk employees they value most and there is less incentive to invest on a short term working employee and in high labour supply jobs where training costs are low. Part time jobs may be over supplied while The Netherlands has very high part-time employment rates in Europe. It is probable that employers will have less patience with such workers who have stress and depression impairments or with self-inflicted disabilities (e.g.: obesity, alcohol dependency). Therefore, it is important to have not discriminating but powerful laws that protect every employee. Disability Management project can persuade the employers that the effectiveness of the project means reduced lost time, insurance premiums and increased productivity and therefore they should be involved in the plan.

Examining Dutch reintegration program through cross-national comparison we notice that these programs were rather successful (Bloch and Prins, 2005). In 2005, 38,028 people made use of a reintegration process under the new reintegration initiative (http://www.uw.nl/). Approximately half of the number is successful and sustainable reintegration (longer than two years). Work disabled cover a very large part of the target audience for reintegration (Van der Velden, 2007). In 2005 one out of eight chronically ill applied for a paid job and a quarter of them succeeded in finding a job. Of those following the reintegration project, one out of three chronically ill got a paid job (Brink-Muinen, et al 2007). How to explain the increased participation of the chronically ill in the last few years?

Various factors contributed to the increased participation of the chronically ill and more successful return to work rates (NRC next 2008:3), including introduction of stricter medical controls targeted to stimulate labor participation in 2004; changes in implementation of insurance schemes and payment of disability benefits (The Implementation Institute Employee Insurance Schemes http://www.cbpweb.nl/indexen/ind_wsz_uwv.shtml); and retention of variety of supports that permit the returning worker to come back gradually and to draw on the supports needed including not only the typical job accommodations such as equipment, but also adapted working hours; change of workplace; job redesign and so forth (Bloch and Prins, 2002). Other factors that might have contributed to the relative success of the reintegration of the chronically ill in the workforce were the reintegration programs (Langeslag, 2007); support and prevention measures (such as Services for the Disabled Act http://www.minvws.nl/dossiers/wet_voorzieningen_gehandicapten_wvg/default.asp); increase in the quality and number of specialized care institutions, such as nursing clinics; organizations specializing in reintegration, advice and supervision; national immunization program.

The National Institute for Public Health and the Environment (RIVM http://www.rivm.nl), a government linked centre of expertise in the fields of health, nutrition and environmental protection carries out studies in the Netherlands on the prevalence of risk factors for such chronic diseases as asthma, chronic obstructive pulmonary disease (COPD), diabetes, musculoskeletal disorders, cancer and cardiovascular disorders. These studies particularly concentrate on prevention through a healthy lifestyle and/or proper attention to risk factors.

Netherlands Institute for Health Services Research organized a special National Panel for Chronically Ill and Handicapped (NIVEL http://www.nivel.nl) researching various aspects of chronic illnesses and employment of the chronically ill. Since introduction of stricter medical controls targeted at stimulating labor participation, more chronically ill started seeking paid jobs (Evaluation Law on the medical testings and the decision appointment testings occupational diseases), http://www.minvws.nl/kamerstukken/pg/2007/evaluatie-wet-op-de-medische-keuringen-en-het-besluit-aanstellingskeuringen.asp?rss)

There were also significant changes in implementation of insurance schemes and payment of disability benefits, such as The Law structure implementation work and income and Act Renewal Salary Pay (http://www.werkennaarvermogen.nl/re_loondoorbetaling.htm).

Since the introduction of this law, most of the chronically ill are still unable to work full-time, but the possibility of finding suitable part-time jobs remains limited (http://www.nivel.nl/pdf/NPCG-Kerngegevens-Maatschappelijke-situatie-2006.pdf).

Specialized care and preventive care have increased. According to Calsbeek et al (2005) approximately one in three people with chronic illness or handicap visited specialized nursing clinic in 2004. This number has increased between 1999 and 2004 from 14% to 30% in 2004 (Kerngegevens ZORG 2005). Another factor that played a role in the increase of numbers of working chronically ill was The National Immunization Program in the Netherlands. According to RIVM rapport 'The National Vaccination in the Netherlands: the incidence of the diseases' (1997-2002) the instances of infectious and chronic diseases such as meningitis, diphtheria and measles have steadily decreased (Abbink et al., 2004).

In recent years, the number of organizations specializing in reintegration, advice and supervision of the chronically ill has increased. Examples of such initiatives and organizations are Breed Platform Verzekerden & Werk [Platform for the Insured and Work] (http://corporate.bpv.nl/organisatie), Landelijke Vereniging van Arbeidsongeschikten [Rural Association for Work Disabled] (http://www.lva-nederland.nl/) and Poortwachter [The Gatekeeper], the employer forum that supports companies and institutions incorporating health management in their company culture (http://www.wetpoortwachter.nu/), Nederlandse Patiënten Consumenten Federatie (NPCF) (www.npcf.nl).

Health and Employment Related Schemes

Generally, the Dutch health policy states its aim at three objectives with regard to the chronically ill and these are: increasing life expectancy, preventing avoidable deaths, improving the quality of life. There are the following insurances:

Extension of Obligation to Pay Salary (Sickness) Act (WULBZ) obliging employers to pay up to 70% of salary to sick employees for a period of 104 weeks. This obligation applies only when there is an employment contract. Workers engaged on a different basis are insured under the Sickness Benefits Act. *Sickness Benefits Act (ZW)* entitles the insuree to sickness benefit if his/her employer is not obliged to continue paying salary under the WULBZ. The Dutch system does not distinguish among causes of illness. *Unemployment Insurance Act (WW)* insures employees against the financial consequences of unemployment. The length of time an individual receives unemployment benefit depends on his/her work history and varies from three months to three years and two months. *Invalidity Insurance Act (WAO)* provides benefit entitlements for employees who became partially or fully unfit for work before 1 January 2004 and have had that status for more than two years.

Work and Income (Capacity for Work) Act (WIA) was introduced in 2005 and replaces the WAO. The WIA provides benefit entitlements for employees who became unfit for work on 1 January 2004 or later and still have a minimum incapacity of 35% after the 104-week waiting period. The WIA comprises two schemes: IVA and WGA. The income support scheme for persons incapable of work (IVA). Under this scheme, employees who become fully and permanently incapable of work are entitled to a wage-replacing incapacity benefit, equal to 70% of monthly salary. The work resumption benefit for persons partially capable of work (WGA). Under this scheme, employees who are partially incapable of work (at least 35%) are entitled to an income supplement benefit.

All Dutch residents fall under the following schemes. *Healthcare Insurance Act (ZVW)* forms the basis of the medical insurance system in the Netherlands. Since 2006 there is a single health care insurance for everyone. The composition of the basic insurance package is laid down by law and insurance companies are obliged to accept everyone, regardless of age or health, and may not charge higher premiums for people who are sick or old. *Exceptional Medical Expenses Act (AWBZ)* provides insurance cover for major medical expenses that are not covered by healthcare insurance, such as care in a nursing home, care home or institution for disabled persons, and home care. *Incapacity Insurance Young Disabled Person Act (WAJONG)* is intended for disabled young people and students who become incapable of work during their studies.

The Law of Equal Treatment (2003)

In 2000 the directive has been determined by the European Council establishing a general framework for equal treatment in labour and profession (directive 2000/78/EG). As a result of this directive the law equal treatment has been set up on the basis of handicap and chronic sickness (WGBH/CZ) by the Dutch legislature. The WGBH/CZ (Wet gelijke behandeling op grond van handicap of chronische ziekte) became effective in 2003. This law is a component of the policy of the government whose goal is to encourage the full participation of disabled and chronically patients in the society. The WGBH/CZ is supposed to make an important contribution to the improvement of the individuals' legal right. It is the intention that in the long run this policy will become integrated in the general law for equal treatment ("Parliamentary documents" of the equal treatment bill on the basis of handicap or chronic sickness II and I, 28169).

According to the WGBH/CZ it has been prohibited to distinguish an employer on the basis of handicap or chronic sickness. A closing definition of the terms handicap or chronic sickness is not desirable since it is dependent on the context within someone experiences obstructions because of his/her handicap or sickness. In the law it is implied, however that a handicap is irreversible whereas a chronic sickness is sometimes not, but it is in any case generally long-term. The legislature has determined that short or long-term restrictions do not apply as a result of an accident in principle under the protection of this law because the possibility of convalescence is here a substantial element.

It has been prohibited for any employer to distinguish on the basis of handicap or chronic sickness at following terms:

1. The offer of a relation and the treatment at the achievement of an open relation;
2. The employment-seeking;
3. The appointment to civil servants and the termination of the service of the civil servant;
4. The labour agreements;
5. Follow up of education, education and shaping during or before a labour relation; and
6. The promotion

The employer can make distinctions, if necessary, to safeguard and secure the health of an affected employee. The legislature has indicated that changes on this exception can not be rapidly appealed: the distinction must be in any case really necessary and it does not dismiss the employer from the duty of doing effective adaptations. This may apply to the so-called high demand jobs or high-risk jobs, which include 'specific job demands'. Following the Dutch Medical Examination Act from 1998, 'specific' job demands are defined as those that exceed exposure safety levels or average human capacities to meet such demands on a daily basis, leading to increased risk of work-related health problems (Sluiter et al. 2003, Sluiter, 2006). Another exception ground is the preference policy, a distinction which aims at persons with a handicap or chronic sickness in a favoured position. A third exception ground is the social policy. Social policy includes supplies and facilities which are necessary to disabled and chronically patients and which are incorporate in the society. Social policy distinguishes itself from preference policy. The preference policy is no longer permitted if the delay has been disposed of, whereas social policy aims at compensating or raising restrictions on disabled and chronically sickness by specific terms. An extra exception ground exists at indirect distinction, the so-called objective justification ground which assesses whether there is an indication of indirect distinction of handicap or chronic sickness.

The law of equal treatment is not related to the substantial function requirements. First and foremost the ability of a person for the function is important. As long as the basis of the distinction made is not linked to the handicap, then the employer may exclude persons with a certain handicap as long as the same terms applies to others without a handicap who do not meet the function requirements. Beside the prohibition on distinction an effort obligation for the employer has also been incorporated. This means that the employer is obligated, according to the potential needs of the handicapped or chronically ill persons, to perform effective adaptations, unless these adaptations form a disproportionate tax for the employer. These obligations always apply.

Adaptations can be categorized into physical and non-physical adaptations. Therefore certain measures must be taken, which allow disabled and chronically -ill patients to comply with labour laws. A good example of that is for instance the adjustment of the working hours for a specific job. Certain adaptations need to be made in order for the disabled and chronically ill persons to be recognized as equals within our society. In this case any medical and/or labour expert's recommendations are crucial when measuring efficiency and determining whether or not the applicant is qualified. Such exceptions are only considered efficient if the adaptation required does not endanger the health and safety of the handicapped and chronically ill person or their co-workers in any way.

Obligations that must be considered specifically dependent on the situation are called "according to need". According to legislation, the responsibility lies with the disabled or chronically ill person to estimate the need for adaptation. If the employer wants to assess the necessity of an adaptation he may seek advice from the "Arbo-organization". After it has been determined which adaptation (with that also the linked cost) is effective in an attentive case, the question can be asked whether this adaptation forms a disproportionate tax. According to the legislature, with the term disproportionate tax, it is expressed that in a lawsuit the adaptation must be proportional to the impact. In the civil jurisdiction several starting points can be found, according to the memory of explaining the question how in a concrete case it has to be assessed, if provisions (on itself effective adaptation) can be reasonably desired from the employer. The employer must then make a broad assessment of the profits and charges of the adaptation concerned. Dismissal or termination of contract as a result of this breach can be considered invalid and annulled.

Medical testing (WMK) provides no violation on protection of handicapped persons. The WMK prohibits appointment testing, unless specific health requirements apply for a certain function (Popma, 2007). The employer who decides to proceed testing will have to show that he has not broken the equal treatment standard. The law stipulates that, beyond the medical testing, no questions can be raised concerning his/her medical condition and/or his/her sickness (Article 4, WMK). This states, however, that a affected person can still give information on him/herself, concerning medical issues, in order to find a way for adapting certain working conditions. On the basis of the WGBH/CZ it applies reversed the burden of proof. When a civil servant thinks that a distinction becomes a disadvantage and he founds this with facts then the employer must prove that he has not acted in contradiction with the law. This onus of proof applies also when the employer has left behind effective adaptations according to the civil servant. If an employer breaches one of the laws of employment which are applicable to a civil servant, then this termination of contract can be annulled. This protection also applies if the civil servant is within his/her right to appeal for his/her dismissal (Wet gelijke behandeling op grond van handicap of chronische ziekte).

There has been a significant change in the Dutch policy concerning employment of disabled people. Before 2007, employers were responsible for the management of sickness absence in order to prevent any claims for disability benefits. What is more, an employer had a duty to offer a suitable alternative job for the disabled employee, and adapt the work place and to finance rehabilitation programmes and pay the salaries to a maximum more than a year of those on permanent contracts.

Dutch government has recently decreased social security benefits to stimulate employees remaining at work. UWV (Institute of Implementation of Employee Insurance Schemes) has come about by 1 January 2002 as a result of aggregation of the former implementation agencies Cadans, GAK (common administration office), GUO, USZO (implementing body social security public servants), SFB (social fund construction industry) and LISV (National Social Insurance Institute) . UWV implements the employee insurance schemes such as WW, WAO incapacity benefit, WIA and the Sickness Benefits Act. Moreover UWV has a role in the implementation of the WAJONG, TW and the WAZ. UWV assesses weather an employee is entitled to a benefit according to the said regulations and laws, and stipulates the altitude and the duration of this benefit as well as supplies it (Landelijke Vereniging van Arbeidsongeschikten). The WAO incapacity benefit changes were introduced on 1 January 2004 and affected Law Work and Income to Labour capacity (WIA). Only those who received a WAO benefit by 1 January 2004, could apply for it again without strict re-evaluation procedure. A doctor of UWV in coordination with labour specialist can determine weather the employee qualifies for benefits (Lautenbach et al, 2007; Lieshout et al. 2007).

The New Working Conditions Act (2008)

The new Working Conditions Act (ArboWet) came into force on 1 January 2007, reflecting the need of the government to reduce the administrative burdens on companies and eliminate superfluous rules to give companies more scope for introducing individual arrangements. The act includes a lot of changes in relation to the previous Working Conditions Act, which dates back to 1998. Instead of general regulations imposed from above, the new act makes provisions for tailor-made rules. Employers and employees can now consult with each other before laying down agreements to ensure a safer, healthier and more pleasant workplace. The Labour Inspectorate will trust in these agreements, but will take firmer action if the rules are abused. The implication of this is the more lasses-fare state which offers less protection to the employees. For example, in organizations with up to 25 employees, the employer himself may act as a prevention officer, the role that the employer used to play in the past.

At the same time, basic regulations still need to be adhered. The law does prescribe certain target regulations, which set out the level of protection that companies must offer their employees so that they can work safely and healthily. These target regulations are described as specifically as possible in the Working Conditions Act, the Working Conditions Decree and the Working Conditions Regulation. It is then up to the employees and employers to decide how to interpret these target regulations. According to the European Agency for Safety and Health at Work, working conditions regulations have been made simpler and easier to implement. The working conditions policy within companies became more flexible, dividing responsibility for safety, health and reintegration between both employers' and employees'. The switch to less detailed rules and more scope for individual arrangements ties in with absence and reintegration policy (http://nl.osha.europa.eu/legislation/?language=en).

The new Working Conditions Act has important implications for the role of employers and employees in health and reintegration. An employer has more freedom and responsibility, allowing more scope for introducing own arrangements and superseding the health and safety rules. Interpretation of regulations is now up to individual organizations, allowing employers to consult with the labour council or employee representatives and produce a working conditions catalogue together with the employees. This catalogue will normally contain a description of the various methods and solutions employers and employees use to meet the target regulations set by the government. An employer may decide weather to produce his own working conditions catalogue, whether to use his industry's general working conditions catalogue or not use a working conditions catalogue at all and try to meet the statutory target regulations in another way (http://nl.osha.europa.eu/legislation/?language=en).

Currently, there is very little known about how these changes are being experienced by the employers and HRM within different organizations. Both employers and employees are responsible for cooperating with the return-to work plan. When there is lack of sufficient cooperation then such an employee can be dismissed and receive part or full denial of unemployment and disability benefits. An employee holding a permanent contract is normally still protected against dismissal for two years after illness occurs. Most importantly, return-to-work plan is a part of the labour contract with possible changes-proposals from the employer about the contract. Thereby, employees' rights are limited because of the limitation and they must follow directions given by their employers or else they may lose their jobs.

IV. EMPLOYERS' AND HRM'S PERSPECTIVES

Thornbory and Lewis (2006) stress the role of HRM in monitoring and maintaining not only occupational but general health of the employees through practices ranging from recruitment to health assessment procedures. Data from a series of studies in Michigan reveal that employer reports of organizational policies and practices are important in reducing the number of work-related disabilities and their consequences for the employee and the company (Amick et al., 2000). Based on the previous studies of employers and HRM, it appears that the most important factors from the medical professionals and employers' perspectives were well-informed professionals who cooperate effectively; employees' coping capacities and commitment to work; financial regulations at the workplace; adequate social security provisions, medication, and therapy; a positive attitude on the part of employers and colleagues; and suitable working conditions (Haafkens, 2008; Detaille et al, 2006; van Dijk, 2007; Meerman, 2005; Varenkamp et al: 2005). Enhancing sustainable employability for chronically ill employees can be seen as one of the tasks of HRM given their role in management: in the areas of hiring, firing and education. There is currently little evidence of successful HRM approaches aside from some examples of good practice. Yet, aside from some examples of best practices like that Kroon op het Werk (an initiative of the Dutch organizations that classifies them in terms of good practices), little consistent studies have been done examining the effect of new policies such as new Working Conditions Act upon the stakeholders in organizations.

The Poortwachter distinguishes between the 'good practice' organizations on the basis of their success in employing, supporting and re-integrating chronically ill employees. These good practices can be characterized by realization of the diversity within its own organization with the goal of increasing participation of employees. This can happen at the level of communication with employers and in particular P& O officials involved in adopting and/or replacing staff. Good practices also include planning of the organizational and structural adjustments for all employees to prevent obstructions in the workplace:

A healthy atmosphere on the work floor increases labour productivity. Moreover, employees in 'fun' companies call in sick less often. And this can save you a lot of money... Now is the time to act and set up a sound health management scheme. Many entrepreneurs are not aware of the costs involved in an employee's long-term absence through illness or in his or her (re-)integration. These costs normally remain hidden among the statistics for personnel costs. But add up all the statutory contributions, fines, and wage costs for replacement staff, and you will soon realize that sound personnel management can save you a lot of money. Smart entrepreneurs therefore act to set up sound health management schemes (http://www.kroonophetwerk.nl/plaatjes/user/File/docskohw/def%20werkgeversforum%2 0folder%20engels%20(2).pdf).

At the beginning of this article, we have inquired what the policy switch to less detailed rules and more scope for individual arrangements mean for people in organizations. While reviewed studies indicate that there are better or less successful organizations that retain or reintegrate their employees, interpretation and implementation of recent policy is still happening ad hoc. Dutch ministry of Social Affairs and Employment publishes reports containing information for employers on the subject of disability management. The latest report asserted that supervision of ill employees at the individual level, without considering the deeper causes of the problem and without consultation with other organizations about similar cases. The report mentions the fact that very little is yet known about the effects on top-down laws on not only the chronically ill but those in the position to implement policy (Ministerie van Sociale Zaken en Werkgelegenheid, 2008).

V. CONCLUSION

Elaborating a framework for the role of employers in creating a healthy work environment for chronically ill employees is a new challenge. While policies are implemented at the macro-level of European and national institutions, it is at the meso-level of the employers and HRM that the policies are interpreted and implemented. This literature study of policies towards chronically ill prepares the ground for further empirical inquiry.

The study of Bloch and Prins (2001) of different success rates of national policies aimed at reintegration of chronically ill showed the Dutch policies as comparatively successful. However, when examining the actual implementation of policies in The Netherlands, emerging pattern of differences appeared less consistent with the general policies. Introduction of new Working Conditions Act allowing for greater scope of flexibility between employer and employee has recently taken effect. The implications of this Act still need to be empirically explored.

In order to expand upon the results of this literature review, empirical study of the effects of recent changes in Dutch legislation is needed. We attempt to conduct a qualitative study to generate opinions from within the stakeholders' groups within the organizations about their experiences and suggestions about policy. These opinions are instructive for understanding how national-level policies are being interpreted and implemented in concrete contexts. We shall carry out case studies of Dutch organizations in order to establish which institutional or cultural arrangements are needed to provide 'best practice' or 'good strategy' examples.

This study prepares the ground for broader studies of organizational differences in interpretation and implementation of policy with the aim of 1). Classifying these organizations along the lines of institutional arrangements and structures in regard to chronically ill, and 2). Identifying more successful strategies for enabling the chronically ill to optimally function at work.

REFERENCES

Abbink, F., Greeff, S.C., Hof, S. van den, Melker, H.E. de (2004) Het Rijksvaccinatie programma in Nederland: het vóórkomen van de doelziekten (1997-2002). RIVM-rapport 210021001. Bilthoven: RIVM. http://www.rivm.nl/ bibliotheek/rapporten/ 210021001. html

Allan, C. M., W. N., Guptill, C. A., Stephenson, F. F. and Campbell, K. E. (2006) 'A Conceptual Model for Interprofessional Education: The international classification of functioning, disability and health (ICF)', Journal of Interprofessional Care, 20:3, 235 – 245. http://dx.doi.org/10.1080/13561820600718139

Amick, B. C. III, R. V. Habeck, Hunt, A., Fossel, A. H., Chaplin, A. Keller, R. B., Katz, J. N. (2000) Measuring the impact of organizational behaviors on Work Disability Prevention and Management. Journal of Occupational Rehabilitation, Vol. 10, No. 1.

Bloch, F.S., Prins, R. (2001), eds. *Who returns to work and why? A six-country study on work incapacity and reintegration.* London, UK: Transaction Publishers; (summary available at: http://www.issa.int/pdf/publ/2wirbooklet.pdf International Social Security Association Research Programme, Geneva).

Brink-Muinen, van den, A., P. Spreeuwenberg, P.M. Rijken (2007) Kerngegevens Maatschappelijke situatie 2006: Nationaal Panel Chronisch zieken en Gehandicapten [Key social situation 2006: National Panel chronically ill and disabled], NIVEL, Utrecht. http://www.nivel.nl/pdf/NPCG-Kerngegevens-Maatschappelijke-situatie-2006.pdf

Bruins Slot, J. H. W. (2006) 1.775.000 plus 1 arbeidsgehandicapten in de beroepsleeftijd. Chronisch zieken aan het werk. Arbo Unie 15 November 2006. http://www.arbounie.nl/ pdf/arbeidsgehandicapten_in_de_beroepsleeftijd.pdf

Calsbeek, H., Spreeuwenberg, P., van Kerkhof, M. J. W., Rijken, P. M. 9(2005) Kerngegevens ZORG 2005. Nationaal Panel Chronisch zieken en Gehandicapten. NIVEL. http://www.nivel.nl

De Croon, E.M., Sluiter, J.K., Nijssen, T.F., Kammeijer, M., Dijkmans, B.A., Lankhorst, G.J., Frings-Dresen, M.H. (2005) Work ability of Dutch employees with rheumatoid arthritis. Scandinavian Journal of Rheumatology. Jul-August, 34(4):277-83.

Detaille, S. I., Haafkens, J. A., Hoekstra, J. B. van Dijk, F. J. (2006) What employees with diabetes mellitus need to cope at work: views of employees and health professionals. Patient Education and Counseling December 2006, Vol. 64 (1-3), pp. 183-90.

Dijk, van, F. J. H. (2007) Advies SZW chronisch zieken en arbobeleid: een gericht pakket arbozorg voor chronisch zieken en gehandicapten. SZW working paper.

Dijk, van, F. J. H. (2007) Werken aan de juiste balans. Chronisch Ziek. Stichting Fonds PGO (Fonds voor patiënten-, gehandicaptenorganisaties en ouderenbonden). P. 7

Disability Discrimination Act (1995) chapter 50. Office of Public Sector Information http://www.opsi.gov.uk/acts/acts1995/ukpga_19950050_en_1

Diversity@work http://www.diversityatwork.net/EN/en_case_legal.htm

Employment and labour market policies for an ageing workforce and initiatives at the workplace National overview report: The Netherlands (http://www.eurofound. europa. eu/publications/htmlfiles/ef07059.htm

European Foundation for Improvement of Living and Working Conditions (2002). Quality of work and employment in Europe. Issues and Challenges. Foundation Paper, No. 1, February. Dublin. http://www.eurofound.europa.eu/

European Foundation for Improvement of Living and Working Conditions (2003). Illness, disability and social Inclusion. Dublin. http://www.eurofound.europa.eu/ http://www.euro found.europa.eu/pubdocs/2003/32/en/1/ef0332en.pdf Info for Indicator- chronic illness http://www.eurofound.europa.eu/areas/qualityoflife/eurlife/index.php? emplate=6&radio indic=183&idDomain=1

Gimeno, D., Banavides, F. G. Benach, J. Amick, B. C. III (2004) Distribution of sickness absence in the European Union countries. Occupational and Environmental Medicine. Vol. 61, Pages 867–869. http://eprints.ucl.ac.uk/2239/1/867.pdf

Grammenos, S. (2006) Illness, disability and Social Inclusion (report). European Foundation for Improvement of Living and Working Conditions. Centre for European Social and Economic Policy (CESEP), Brussels. 17 February http://www.eurofound.europa.eu/ publications/htmlfiles/ef0335.htm

Haafkens, J. (2008) Perspectives of HRM professionals and managers on what policies and practices are needed within an organization to enable sustained employability for chronically ill employees. Working paper 9th International Conference on Human Resource Development Research and Practice Across Europe: IÉSEG School of Management, Catholic University of Lille, 21-23 May, 2008.

Kerngegevens ZORG 2005

Kloss, D. (2005) Occupational Health Law. Blackwell Science, Oxford.

Kroon, P. (2006) Handreiking voor bedrijven: hoe het functioneren van chronisch zieken en gehandicapten te bevorderen. Meer rendement door behoud van talent. Coronel Instituut, AMC/ Doorn, March 2006.

Kroonophetwerk. Werkgeversforum. http://www.kroonophetwerk.nl http://www.kroono phetwerk.nl/Publicaties_326.html

Landelijke Vereniging van Arbeidsongeschikten (2005) Beoordeling arbeidsongeschiktheid: Informatie en tips over de WAO-, Wajong- en WAZ-keuring. Atlas, Soest.

Landelijke Vereniging van Arbeidsongeschikten (2005) Om psychische redenen. Atlas, Soest.

Landelijke Vereniging van Arbeidsongeschikten (2005) De WIA-beoordeling: Informatie en Adviezen over de Arbeidsongeschiktheidsbeoordeling. Atlas, Soest. http://www. dollekensbedrijfsarts.nl/kenniscentrum/documenten/WIA%20beoordeling.pdf

Langeslag, M. (2007) Werner helpt revalideren. Algemeen Dagblad, 7 November 2007.

Lautenbach, H., Cuijpers, M., Kosters, L. (2007) Arbeidsgehandicapten 2006. Arbeidssituatie van mensen met chronische aandoening. Report of CBS and SZW.

Lieshout, van, P. A. H. (2007) Ziek en mondig op het werk. Dilemma's bij veranderende verhoudingen. Gelling Publishing. Nieuwerkerk aan den Ijssel. http://bpv-corporate.zope.nl/organisatie/persberichten/persberichten/ziek-en-mondig-op-het-werk-dilemma2019s-bij-veranderende-verhoudingen

Meerman, M. (2005) Werken met Verschil: een pleidooi voor gedifferentieerd HRM. Openbare les. 17 March 2007. HvA Publicaties. Hogeschool van Amsterdam. http://www.hva.nl/lectoraten/documenten/ol10-050317-meerman.pdf

Meijden, van der, A. (2006) Onderzoeksverslag werknemers met een gezondheidsbeperking bij KCS. Lectoraat Gedifferentieerd HRM van de Hogeschool van Amsterdam. Juli 2006.

Mheen, van de, H., Stronks, K., Schrijvers, C.T.M., Mackenbach, J.P. (1999) The influence of adult ill health on occupational class mobility and mobility out of and into employment in the The Netherlands. Social Science and Medicine, Vol. 49, pp.509–518.

Ministerie van Sociale Zaken en Werkgelegenheid. Werken naar vermogen. Wet verlenging loondoorbetalingsverplichting bij ziekte (2004). http://www.werkennaarvermogen.nl/re_loondoorbetaling.htm

Ministerie van Sociale Zaken en Werkgelegenheid. Disability Managment: Informatie voor werkgevers (2008). http://home.szw.nl/index.cfm?menu_item_id= 13711&hoofdmenu_item_id=13825&rubriek_item=391837&rubriek_id=391817&set_id=975&doctype_id=6 &link_id=5367

Ministerie van Volksgezondheid, Welzijn en Sport www.minvws.nl

Nagi, S. Z. (1979) The concept and measurement of disability. In Disability Policies and Government Programs (Edited by Berkowitz, E. D.) pp. 1-15. Praeger, New York.

National Panel for Chronically Ill and Handicapped (NIVEL) http://www.nivel.nl

Oliver, M. (1990) The Politics of Disablement. London: Macmillan. Pp.78-94.

Parliamentary documents" of the equal treatment bill on the basis of handicap or chronic sickness II and I, 28169

Popma, J. R., Rayer, C. W. J., Westerveld, M. (2007) Tweede Evaluatie Wet op de medische keuringen. Programma Evaluatie regelgeving: deel 22. Hugo Sinzheimer Instituut, Universiteit van Amsterdam, Den Haag: ZonMw, March 2007.

Roessler, R. T., Fitzgerald, S. M., Rumrill, P. D. and Koch, L. C. (2001) Determinants of Employment Status Among People with Multiple Sclerosis. *Rehabilitation Counseling Bulletin, 10 2001; vol. 45: pp. 31 - 39.* http://rcb.sagepub.com/cgi/reprint/45/1/31

Roessler, R. T., Fitzgerald, S. M., Rumrill, P. D. (2004) Predictors of Employment Status Among People with Multiple Sclerosis. *Rehabilitation Counseling Bulletin, 1 2004; vol. 47: pp. 96 - 103.*

Sluiter, J. K. (2006) High-demand jobs: age-related diversity in work ability? Applied Ergonomics, July, 37(4):429-40.

Sluiter, J.K., de Croon, E.M., Meijman, T.F., Frings-Dresen, M.H.W. (2003) Need for recovery from work related fatigue and its role in the development and prediction of subjective health complaints. Occupational and Environmental Medicine, Vol. 60, pp. i62–i70.

Stattin, M. (2005) Retirenment on grounds of ill health. In Journal of Occupational and Environmental Medicine. Vol. 62, pp. 135-140.

Velden, van der, N. (2007) Arbeidsparticipatie en Reïntegratie van chronisch zieken en gehandicapten. July 26, 2007. iResearch, www.iresearch.nl http://www.kcco.nl/doc/spotlight/Arbeidsparticipate%20en%20reintegratie%20chronisch%20zieken%20en%20gehandicapten%20rapport.pdf

Velden, van der, N. and Terhorst, A. G. I. (2008) De zieke werknemer en privacy. Regels voor de verwerking van persoonsgegevens van zieke werknemers, College bescherming persoonsgegevens, februari 2008. http://www.cbpweb.nl/downloads_av/ AV27.pdf? refer =true&theme=blue

Verbrugge, L. M. and A. M. Jetie (1994) The Disablement Process. Social Science Medical, Vol. 38, No. 1. pp. l-14.

WGBH/CZ Recht op gelijke behandeling gehandicapten en chronisch zieken wettelijk geregeld http://www.minocw.nl/documenten/onderwijs-download-wgbh.pdf

World Health Organization http://www.who.int/topics/disabilities/en/ http://www.who.int/classifications/icf/site/checklist/icf-checklist.pdf

Wynne, R. (2008) Employment guidance services for people with disabilities/ Chronic illness and job retention http://www.introdm.be/idm/idm01.nsf/ 52b2da8b666e 069080256 aaa002ab228/995022d8285bee6fc125727300383d77/$FILE/Presentation_Wynne.pdf

In: Social Development
Editor: Lynda R. Elling

ISBN: 978-1-60741-612-8
© 2009 Nova Science Publishers, Inc.

Chapter 8

SOCIAL CAPITAL, ENTREPRENEURIAL CAPITAL AND ECONOMIC GROWTH

Inmaculada Carrasco[*] and M. Soledad Castaño[*]
University of Castilla-La Mancha, Spain

ABSTRACT

Under the framework of endogenous economic growth theory, this chapter is focused on entrepreneurial capital and its effects on economic growth. More concretely, we have centred our attention on the interactions between some proxy variables of social capital and one indicator of entrepreneurial capital.

After the two sections devoted to the literature review summary where concepts coming from economics, sociology and psychology are taken in, the empirical section of this chapter confirms firstly the positive relationship between entrepreneurial capital and economic growth. After that, we have proved that the more social capital reserve, the more entrepreneurial capital endowment. Besides that, the better institutions functioning is and the more social structure adequacy, the more social capital and entrepreneurial capital endowment. This positive connection between the social capital indicators and the entrepreneurial capital indicator, allow us to conclude that they promote economic growth not only because these variables create social capital, but also because they encourage entrepreneurial capital.

Statistical information about 28 countries collected in 2005 has been used. A GEM data set on entrepreneurial activity has been related to data from the United Nations Development Programme (UNDP), Transparency International and the Heritage Foundation. Some graphical results on the tendency among the different variables relationships are presented.

---

[*] Inmaculada.Carrasco@uclm.es
[*] MariaSoledad.Castano@uclm.es

Introduction

The theoretical framework of this chapter rests on the endogenous economic growth theory. Previous classical research had typoligized capital into three categories: physical, financial and human capital. Romer (1986, 1990) presents a model where the ensemble of productive factors (land, work and capital) is enlarged, where knowledge and technological progress is no more exogenous.

During the time, the economic growth models have been amplified to incorporate factors such as quality of institutions (North, 1990) and social capital (Putnam, 1993, 2002; Putnam & Goss 2003; Fukuyama, 1995 y 2001).

More recently, the studies try to incorporate a new dimension that evidences the importance of nascent entrepreneurs, taking into account that nascent entrepreneurs are those who first develop the new ventures' possibilities (Erikson, 2002). Holcombe (1998, 2003) suggested that entrepreneurial capital should be introduced in the production function. Entrepreneurial capital is then referred to the capacity of economic systems to create ventures and to generate knowledge spillovers. It can create value, fostering economic growth.

Some authors such as Wenners & Turik (1999), Audretsch & Turik (2000), Reynolds et al. (2002), Acs et al. (2004, 2005), Acs & Plummer (2005), Karlsson et al. (2004), Audresch & Keilbach (2004, a-b-c, 2005), Stel, Carree & Turik (2005, 2006) or Mueller, 2007 have found a positive relationship between entrepreneurship and economic performance.

It is quite common to present the different types of capital and their relationship to economic growth in an isolated form. In precedent works, we have studied the relationships between social capital and economic growth (Castaño & Carrasco, 2005; Castaño, 2007). The aim of this chapter is to study the inter-relationships between social capital and entrepreneurial capital in the promotion of economic growth. Concepts that come from economics, sociology and psychology are taken in.

The chapter is structured as follows. After the introduction, a section is devoted to collect some theoretical approaches about the relationships between social capital and entrepreneurial capital. Following, entrepreneurial capital and economic growth interactions are studied. Lastly, an empirical analysis of some relationships between social capital and entrepreneurial capital will be made. Data from 28 countries around the world have been collected, and graphical results of the different relationships are presented. The chapter finishes with a section of conclusions.

2. Social Capital and Entrepreneurial Activity: A Theoretical Approach

Following Worms (2003: 276), in a narrow sense, social capital is related to social resources creation in a social group to which individuals belong voluntarily. In a more wide sense, those resources can emerge from the relationships that an individual establishes in groups to which he or she belongs voluntarily, by hazard, because of the necessity or because of a process of social adscription.

Social capital is, then, related to social networks and to norms established to improve the functioning of those networks (Putman 1995, 2002). More concretely, Putman & Goss (2003:

14) affirm that social capital is the mix up of social networks and their associated reciprocity norms, which create value, as physical capital and human capital do. Besides that, the establishment of social norms doesn't create value by itself. Cooperation among groups and some human virtues as honesty, compromise, duties fulfilment and reciprocity are needed. Coleman (1990: 300-302) defines social capital as the ensemble of social resources inherent to social organisation, as confidence, norms and networks that can improve the efficiency of the society by fostering the coordinated action.

It is important to distinguish between including forms of social capital ("bridging") and excluding forms of social capital ("bonding"): networks founded on specific features, as race, ethnicity, religion, social status and so on, used to exclude people that don't share the specific and distinctive characteristic, while networks based on the connexion among heterogeneous groups are more inclusive (Gittell & Vidal, 1998; Barr, 1998; Kozel & Parker, 2000; Narayan, 1999; Woolcock & Narayan 2000; Alder & Kwon, 2002).

Externalities in bridging networks have more probability of being beneficial, while bonding networks (that are limited to the interior of social niches) have more probability of producing negative externalities. That doesn't mean that bonding relationships are bad, because all of us are used to obtaining more support from bonding ties than from bridging ties (Lin, 2003).

Woolcock & Narayan (2000) explain that communities are characterized for having these two dimensions of social capital. Different combinations of them produce different results associated with social capital. Economic growth is produced by a mechanism that allows individuals to take advantage of the benefits of being a more reduced community member, but it also qualifies them to acquire the skills and resources to participate in networks that overpass their own communities. So that, at the beginning, it is essential to have the bonding social capital (this one offered by family, friends or some associations), but when we want to grow and amplify our economic opportunities, we use the bridging capital more.

In another line, Flora & Flora (1993) affirmed that to facilitate a community's development, social infrastructure is necessary in order to link individual leadership to physical infrastructure (the other two key components). Social infrastructure (Swanson, 1992, cit. in Flora & Flora) has three ingredients: social institutions, human resources (technical expertise, organisational skills, educational levels or social structure—class, gender, race, ethnicity, etc.) and characteristic of social networks (innovativeness, ability to mobilize resources, ability to link up with outside expertise and information). Into this line, Flora & Flora see community as a system and define entrepreneurial social infrastructure as a mechanism for change. Entrepreneurial communities are proactive identifying problems and looking for solutions.

On the other hand, Abramowitz (1986) affirms that tenacious societal characteristics (social capability) explain a part of a country's level of productivity and consequently its potential for economic growth. The Abramowitz idea of "social capability" is referred to as the country's ability to adapt itself to changing circumstances. This ability is specially related to technological progress, so that, social structure can promote the country or region economic growth through its impact on development of technology. Social structure is essential on R&D transformation into innovation and economic growth.

3. Entrepreneurial Capital and Economic Growth

Marshall (1916) explained that the fourth productive factor is the business' organizational capacity, and Schumpeter (1934) affirmed that new combinations of knowledge are important to economic growth, because they promote new business creation by the creative destruction process. On the other hand, Porter (1990) stated that entrepreneurship is at the heart of national advantage.

Today, models of endogenous growth (Romer, 1986) have been amplified with entrepreneurial capital (Audretsch & Keilbach, 2004-a) that consider entrepreneurial capacity as a productive factor, completing the production function. They affirm that the society's capacity to create business as that of generating knowledge spillovers, can be an economic resource.

Holcombe (1998) thought that physical capital or human capital on their own can't create economic growth, because they need business creation to profit from the opportunities. The businessman is truly the economy's internal engine, because he identifies and creates new entrepreneurial opportunities.

Wennekers & Turik (1999) showed that the business creation dynamic is influenced by some psychological and sociological (cultural) facts of people. In their view, entrepreneurship is a behavioral characteristic of persons, but some geographic spaces are characterized by a culture that promotes the start-up's formation and the innovation, fostering, then, economic growth.

In their different studies, Audretsch & Keilbach (2004, a-b-c, 2005) have developed an economic growth model where they introduce entrepreneurial capital as a productive factor, demonstrating a significant positive relationship between both variables. They firstly introduced the entrepreneurial capital as a type of social capital. They also explain that knowledge on its own is not enough to generate economic growth, and that entrepreneurial capital is a good driver for knowledge. More concretely, they affirm that entrepreneurial capital promotes economic growth by fostering fast knowledge diffusion, increment competitiveness and entrepreneurial diversity.

Following Mueller (2007), Acs et. al. (2005) and Acs & Plummer (2005), new ventures are a mechanism for knowledge diffusion and knowledge exploitation. Realizing entrepreneurial opportunities by starting new firms is a mechanism for knowledge diffusion and for the exploitation of knowledge (Mueller, 2007: 356). And knowledge is an important driver of economic growth, because it increases productivity and technological progress (Romer, 1986; Lucas, 1988). But not only is the stock of knowledge important for economic growth: knowledge flows are critical, because they allow knowledge diffusion and exploitation. On the other hand, knowledge allows us to improve self-efficacy, and the increases in self-efficacy raises perceptions of opportunity, so we can state that human capital improvements benefit entrepreneurial capital.

Knowledge, or more concretely, the knowledge diffusion process, has a strong regional and spatial component, because knowledge spillovers are fostered by spatial proximity to research centers, and industrial agglomerations (Mueller, 2007). Social capital has a key role in this diffusion process, because as Mueller (2007) affirms, local, direct and interpersonal contacts allow business to access faster and easier the advances in knowledge. Local social conditions play an important role in the assimilation of innovation and consequently in its transformation into economic growth (Beugelsdijk and Noorderhaven, 2004).

Then, social capital, entrepreneurial capital and human capital are involved in the knowledge creation and diffusion process. Subsequently, social capital, human capital and entrepreneurial capital are involved in the economic growth process.

Even if as Firking (2001) states, social capital differs from human capital and entrepreneurial capital because these two last forms of capital are two types of "personal capital", as much social capital and entrepreneurial capital are conditioned by culture. Georgellis and Wall (2000) find that "entrepreneurial human capital" is a significant explanatory element of the level of entrepreneurship, distinguishing it from labor market conditions, labor force characteristics or type of industrial organization and composition.

Entrepreneurial culture fosters economic growth in different ways: (i) the start-up rate of new firms increases by valuing the social patterns conductive to entrepreneurship; (ii) intrapreneurship can encourage efficiency in existing firms; and (iii) social structure influences the capacity of countries or regions to adopt and adapt new technologies (Beugelsdijk & Noorderhaven, 2004: 202). Nevertheless, they also affirm (p. 214) that entrepreneurial attitude can both be the cause and the result of economic growth, because high growth regions attract entrepreneurs, which positively affects the general entrepreneurial attitude. All theses relationships are summarized in figure 1.

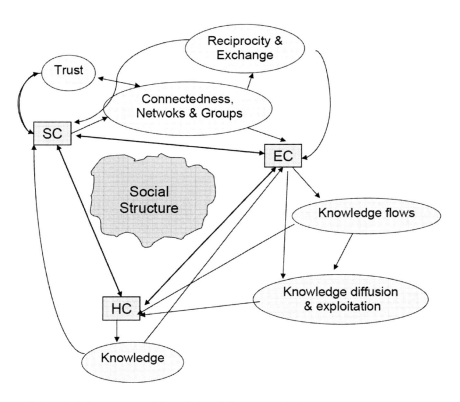

Figure 1. Social capital, Entrepreneurial capital and Human capital.

4. Some Relationships between Social Capital and Entrepreneurial Capital: An Empirical Analysis

4.1.The Concept and Measure of Entrepreneurial Capital

Following Firking (2001), the capital that an individual possesses is the sum of its economic capital (physical + financial), social capital and personal or human capital (general + specific or entrepreneurial + personal attributes). Entrepreneurial attributes are, then, an individual fact. The entrepreneurial capital approaches, consider that a region's or country's entrepreneurial capital is the addition of the entrepreneurial attributes of its people.

Two perspectives can be followed to try to define the concept of entrepreneurial capital. One defines entrepreneurial capital as the present value of an infinite series of shadow options, and the other as a multiplicative function of entrepreneurial competence and commitment.

The first perspective uses the present value idea as is used in finance. Then, entrepreneurial capital will be the present value of the future entrepreneurial behaviour (Erikson, 2002: 277):

$$\text{Entrepreneurial Capital} = (E)\ PV_{FEB} = \sum_{b=1}^{\infty} FEB$$

where (E) PV is the expected present value and FEB is the future entrepreneurial behaviour. In this sense, entrepreneurial capital is conceptualised as the present value of an infinite series of shadow options or latent potential.

The second perspective (Erikson, 2002: 278) see entrepreneurial capital as a multiplicative function of competence and commitment, following models of individual job performance that state that performance is determined by ability, motivation and opportunity, given the opportunities.

Ulrich (1998 cit. in Erikson, 2002) defines intellectual capital as a multiplicative function of competence and commitment, as an extension, entrepreneurial capital can be defined as a multiplicative function of entrepreneurial competence and entrepreneurial commitment.

Entrepreneurial capital = [Entrepreneurial Competence] × Entrepreneurial Commitment

In this sense, entrepreneurial competence is the combined capacity to identify and pursue opportunities and to obtain and coordinate the resources. This notion allows us to incorporate different entrepreneurial competence components such as feasibility, creativity, ability, conviction, behavioural control and efficacy in resource acquisition.

Nevertheless, as a measure of entrepreneurial capital, we are going to use data that Global Entrepreneurship Project offers. GEM Project considers that there are active entrepreneurs among all adult people (between 18 and 64 years old) that are involved in a venture start-up process and those who are owners-managers of a baby business (Reynolds et al. 2005). The more people involved in start-up and baby business managing process, the more entrepreneurial capital exits in this region or country.

4.2. Social Capital Measures

When studying social capital, one of the most important problems is measuring social capital reserves, hindering the determination of its effects on economic growth or its links with entrepreneurial activity. Probably it is impossible to achieve a unique and truthful social capital measure for different reasons. First, the most complete definitions are multidimensional and incorporate different levels and analysis units. Secondly, nature and social capital forms change with time according to the variation between the balance of informal organizations and formal institutions. Thirdly, since the beginning of the investigation, there have not been long-term studies on multinationals (Woolcock and Narayan 2000).

In spite of these inconveniences, there are different kinds of social capital to measure. The main ones are:

- Affiliation to associations—this presents the difficulty of obtaining the data, and an appropriate social capital measurement should also keep in mind the nature of the collective action it is capable of.
- Considering trust and values surveys—the problem with this information type is that the validity depends on how such values are determined because there is an absence of coherent data for different countries.
- To elaborate on the social capital absence indicator taking into account social indicators, such as delinquency, corruption, and others (fertility rate, divorce data, marriage data)—this kind of information supposes the absence of cooperative norms. The appearance of social deviations could indicate the lack of this capital.

Taking into account those possible measures of social capital, in this chapter we are going to use the third type of indicators: those that measure the cooperative norms. Nevertheless, we are also going to use indicators of the economic and social system stability, such as the Index of Economic Freedom or measures that pick up jointly human and social capital, such as the Human Development Index.

4.3. Some Relationships between Social Capital and Entrepreneurial Capital: An Empirical Analysis

In this section, an empirical analysis is presented. The goal is to test if there exist or not some relationships between social capital and entrepreneurial capital. The hypothesis that we want to check is that the better functioning of institutions and the more social structure adequacy the more social capital and entrepreneurial capital endowment. If we can confirm a positive connection between the social capital indicators and the entrepreneurial capital indicators, then, we could conclude that they promote economic growth not only because these variables create social capital, but also because they encourage entrepreneurial capital.

Data of 28[1] countries in 2005 have been collected. As the indicator of the entrepreneurial activity (and proxy of entrepreneurial capital), the total Entrepreneurial Activity by opportunity[2] (Opportunity-TEA) has been chosen. This variable collects the number of entrepreneurial initiatives whose main motivation to begin on is to profit an opportunity (IE, 2007). Opportunity-TEA data have been related to United Nations Development Programme (UNDP) indicators, such us GDP, Human Development, Human Capital, and Delinquency.

On the other hand, following Fukuyama (2001), to measure social capital it is necessary to use as proxy variables some indicators that quantify the absence of delinquency and crimes. North (1990) and Chhibber (2000) affirm that well running institutions foster economic growth in countries. Quality of institutions is also an indicator of social stability that a country has. In order to evaluate the quality of institutions, the Corruption Index of Transparency International and the Index of the Economic Freedom of Heritage Foundation have been chosen.

Some graphical results on the tendency among the different variables relationships are going to be presented. First of all, in figure 2, a positive relationship between Opportunity-TEA and per capita GDP growth (measured in 2005 dollars) is revealed. This indicates a positive relationship between entrepreneurial capital and economic growth, confirming the different thesis collected in section 3, particularly the theory of Audretsch and Keilbach (2004, a-b-c, 2005).

In figure 3, the relationship between Opportunity-TEA and the Human Development Index is presented. The positive slope indicates that countries with higher values of income, human capital and life expectancy at birth are also the countries with a higher entrepreneurial capital.

Then again, figure 4 shows the relationship between human capital and entrepreneurial capital. The addition of expenses in education and health[3] has been chosen as a proxy of human capital. As it occurs in the precedent figure, the slope is positive. That indicates that the more human capital reserves, the more entrepreneurial capital reserves.

The essence of social capital is trust, because it allows the collective action in its conforming networks. Trust in other people can foster new ventures creation, because it can facilitate the financial capital obtaining (Geertz, 1962; Weidenbaum & Hughes, 1996).

In turn, Alesina and La Ferrara (2000) indicate that trust can be a moral or cultural attitude. Being like this, trust should be strongly influenced by characteristics as people's type and level of education. It is easier to trust in people similar to us, such as family members or the same social, ethnical or racial group people. In addition, those authors indicate that legal institutions can affect trust: if delinquency is efficiently pursued, individuals would be more trusted, because they feel more protected against the non cooperative extreme behaviour.

---

[1] Argentina, Australia, Austria, Belgium, Brazil, Canada, Croatia, Denmark, Finland, France, Germany, Greece, Hungary, Iceland, Ireland, Italy, Japan, Latvia, Mexico, Netherlands, Norway, Slovenia, South Africa, Spain, Sweden, Switzerland, United Kingdom, United States.

[2] The GEM Project differentiates between three types of motivation: opportunity of profit a new business (Opportunity-TEA), the necessity of creating its own employment because the lack of labour opportunities (Necessity-TEA) and other intermediate situations (Other motives TEA) (IE, 2007: 46).

[3] Literature has become to consider human capital not only as the expenditure in education, but also the health expenditure, because to be a productive people one has to be in good health. (Mankiw, Romer & Weil, 1992; Benábou, 1993).

In line with those theoretical considerations, figures 5 and 6 show the relationship between social capital and entrepreneurial capital. In figure 6 a negative relationship between delinquency and Opportunity-TEA is revealed. This indicates that societies that present a higher social peace are the societies that also show a higher entrepreneurial activity.

On the other hand, figure 7 demonstrates a positive relationship between Corruption Perception Index and Opportunity-TEA[4]. The less corrupted societies present the higher trust indexes (that's to say, higher social capital -Putman, 2002-) and the higher entrepreneurial capital.

Last but not least, figure 8 relates the Index of Economic Freedom to the entrepreneurial capital. The better the institutional and legal system is, the higher the entrepreneurial activity is. Therefore institutional and legal systems encourage economic growth because they foster entrepreneurial capital.

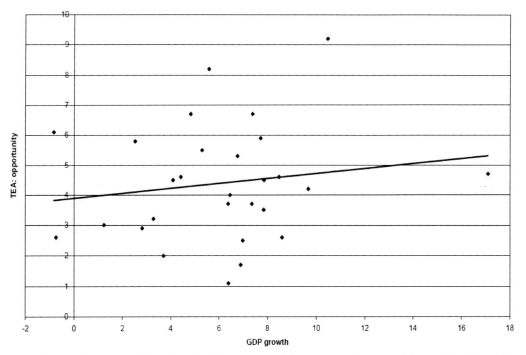

Source: Own elaboration from Global Entrepreneurship Monitor (GEM) data and Unite Nations Development Programme (UNDP) data.

Figure 2. Entrepreneurial Capital and Economic Growth.

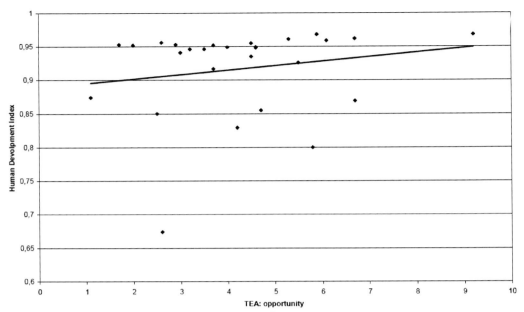

Source: Own elaboration from GEM data and UNDP data.

Figure 3. Entrepreneurial Capital and Human Development.

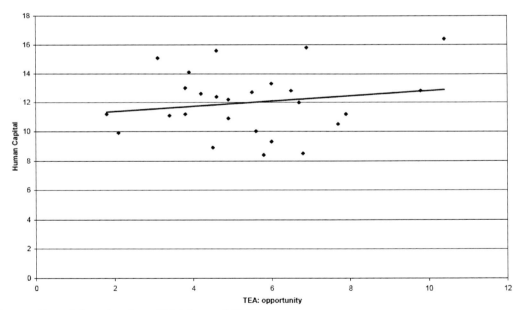

Source: Own elaboration from GEM data and UNDP data.

Figure 4. Entrepreneurial Capital and Human Capital.

---

[4] The corruption perception index ranks from 0 to 10. The higher the index, the lower is the people corruption perception in this country.

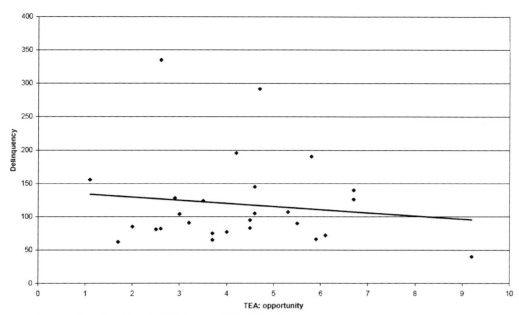

Source: Own elaboration from GEM data and UNDP data.

Figure 5. Entrepreneurial Capital and Social Capital (I).

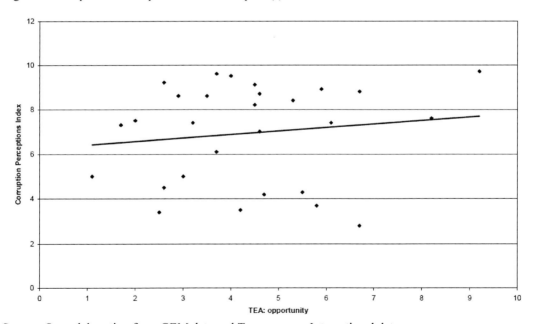

Source: Own elaboration from GEM data and Transparency International data.

Figure 6. Entrepreneurial Capital and Social Capital (II).

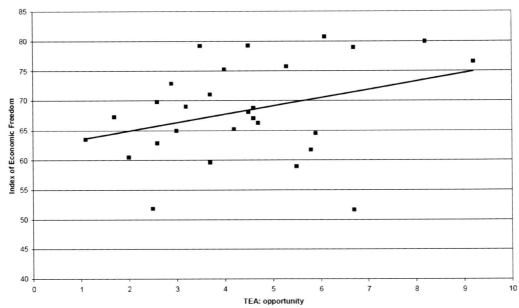

Source: Own elaboration from GEM data and Index of Economic Freedom data.

Figure 7. Entrepreneurial Capital and Institutional Framework.

5. CONCLUSIONS

Economic literature specialised in economic growth has been interested in the effects that variables such as human capital, social capital or quality of institutions have on economic growth. More recently, the attention has been focused on entrepreneurial activity, or more widely, on entrepreneurial capital and its effects on economic growth.

After the two sections devoted to the literature review summary, the empirical section of this chapter confirms firstly the positive relationship between entrepreneurial capital and economic growth.

In order to extend the knowledge on this type of interaction, we have presented the relationships between some proxy variables of social capital and one indicator of entrepreneurial capital. We have proved that the more social capital reserve, the better functioning of institutions and the more social structure adequacy, the more entrepreneurial capital endowment. Non corrupt societies, societies with low delinquency indexes and societies with a better rule of law (that guarantee the good functioning of entrepreneurial activity) are societies with a higher entrepreneurial capital endowment.

Confirming a positive connection between the social capital indicators and the entrepreneurial capital indicators, then, we can conclude that they promote economic growth not only because these variables create social capital, but also because they encourage entrepreneurial capital.

6. REFERENCES

Abramowitz, M. (1986). Catching up, forging ahead and falling behind, *Journal of Economic History* 46 (2), 385-406.

Acs, Z.; Audretsch, D. B.; Braunerhjelm, P. & Carlson, B. (2005). *Growth and entrepreneurship: an empirical assessment.* Working Paper 3205, Discussion Papers on Entrepreneurship, Growth and Public Policy. Jena, Germany: Max Plank Institute of Economics

Acs, Z. & Plummer, L.A. (2005). Penetrating the ``knowledge filter" in regional economies, *The Annals of Regional Science*, Volume 39, Number 3, 439-456

Acs, Z.; Audretsch, D. B.; Braunerhjelm, P. & Carlson, B. (2004). *The missing link the knowledge filter and entrepreneurship in endogenous growth,* Working Paper 4783, London: Center for Economic Policy Research.

Alder, P.S. & Kwon (2000). Social Capital: Prospects for a new concept, http://poverty2.forumone.com/files/11990_socialcapital_prospects.pdf

Alesina, A. & La Ferrara, E. (2000). The determinants of trust; http://www.nber.org/papers/w7621; *Working Paper* 7621.

Audretsch, D. B. & Keilbach, M. (2004-a). Does entrepreneurship capital matter? *Entrepreneurship: Theory and Practice*, 28 (5), 419-429

Audretsch, D. B. & Keilbach, M. (2004-b). Entrepreneurship and regional growth: An Evolutionary Interpretation *Journal of Evolutionary Economics*, 14 (5), 605-616

Audretsch, D. B. & Keilbach, M. (2004-c). Entrepreneurship Capital and Economic Perfomance, *Regional Studies*, 38 (8), 949-959

Audretsch, D. B. & Keilbach, M. (2005). Entrepreneurship capital and regional growth *Regional Science*, 39 (3), 457-469

Audretsch, D. B. & Turik, A. R. (2000). Capitalism and Democracy in the 21 st Century: from the Managed to the Entrepreneurial Economy, *Journal of Evolutionary Economics* 10 (1), 17-34.

Barr, A. (1998). Enterprise Performance and the Functional Diversity of Social Capital, *Working Papers 98-1*, University of Oxford, Institute of Economics and Statistics, Oxford, U.K.

Benabou, R. (1993). Heterogeneity stratification and growth, *European Summer Symposium in Macroeconomics* (CEPR), Tarragona.

Beugelsdijk, S. & Noorderhaven, N. (2004). Entrepreneurial attitude and economic growth: A cross-section of 54 regions. *Annals of Regional Science*, 38, 199-218.

Carree, M. A. & Thurik, A. R. (eds.) (2006), *Entrepreneurship and Economic Growth*, The International Library of Entrepreneurship, Vol. 6, Edward Elgar.

Carree, M. A, & Turik, A. R. (2005). *The Handbook of entrepreneurship and Economic Growth*, Cheltenham: International Library of entrepreneurship

Castaño, M.S. (2007). The Influence of Socioeconomic Factors on Economic Growth, *International Advances in Economic Research*,139-145.

Castaño, M.S. & Carrasco, I. (2005). Social Capital and Economic Growth: The Competive Advantage in Bahmani-Oskoee, M. & Galindo, M.A.: *Next Economic Growth: New Factors and New Perspectives*, New York: Nova Press.

Chhibber, A. (2000). Social Capital, the State and Development Outcomes in Dasgupta, P.; I. Serageldin (Ed), *Social Capital. A Multifaceted Perspective*, Washington: The World Bank, 2000, pp. 296-309.

Coleman, J. S. (1990). *Foundations of Social Theory*, Cambridge, Mass.: Harvard University Press

Erikson, T. (2002). Entrepreneurial capital: the emerging venture's most important asset and competitive advantage, *Journal of Business Venturing*, 17, 275-290.

Firkin, P. (2001). Entrepreneurial Capital: A Resource-Based conceptualisation of the Entrepreneurial Process. *Working Paper* N.7 Labour Market Dynamics Research Programme.

Flora, C. B. & Flora, J. L. (1993). Entrepreneurial Social Infrastructure: A Necessary Ingredient, A*nnals of American Academy of Political and Social Science*, 529, 48-58.

Fukuyama, F. (1995). *Trust: Social Virtues and the Creation of Prosperity.* NY: Free Press.

Fukuyama, F. (2001): *La gran ruptura*, Madrid: Punto de Lectura.

Geertz, C. (1962). The rotating credit association: A 'middle rung' in development. *Economic development and cultural change*, 10. 240-263.

Georgellis, Y. & Wall, H. (2000).What makes a region entrepreneurial? Evidence from Britain, *The Annals of Regional Science*, 34, 385-403.

Gittell, R. & Vidal A. (1998). *Community Organizing: Building Social Capital as a Development Strategy*, Sage Publications: Newbury Park.

Holcombe, R. (1998). Entrepreneurship and Economic Growth, *Quarterly Review of Austrian Economics* 1 (2), 45-62

Holcombe, R. (2003). The Origins of Entrepreneurial Opportunities, *The Review of Austrian Economics* 16 (1), 25-43

Instituto de Empresa (2007): *Global Entrepreneurship Monitor, Informe Ejecutivo GEM España 2007*. Madrid: Instituto de Empresa.

Karlsson,C.; Friis, C. & Paulsson, T. (2004). Relating entrepreneurship to economic growth. Working Paper. CESIS. The Royal Institute of technology

Kozel, V. & Parker V. (2000). Integrated Approaches to Poverty Assessment in India, in Bamberger M., ed*., Integrating Quantitative and Qualitative Research in Development Projects*, Washington, D.C.: World Bank.

Lin, N. (2003). *Social Capital*, Cambridge University Press, United States.

Lucas, R. E. (1988). On the Mechanics of Economic Development, *Journal of Monetary Economics*. 22 (1), 3-42.

Mankiw, N.G., Romer, D. & Weil, D.N. (1992). A contribution to the empirics of economic growth, *Quarterly Journal of Economics*, 100, February. 225-251.

Marshall, A. (1916). *Principles of Economics.* London: Macmillan.

Mueller, P. (2007). Exploiting Entrepreneurial Opportunities: The Impact of Entrepreneurship on Growth, *Small Business Economics* 28, 355-362.

Narayan, D. (1999). Bonds and Bridges: Social Capital and Poverty, *Policy Research Working Paper* N° 2167. Washington D. C.: World Bank,

North, D.C. (1990). *Institutions, Institutional Change and Economic Performance*; Cambridge (UK), Cambridge University Press.

Porter, M. (1990). *The competitive advantage of nations*. London: Macmillan.

Putnam, R (2002). *Solo en la Bolera*, Barcelona: Galaxia Gutenberg,

Putnam, R. (1995). Tuning In, Tuning Out: The Strange Disappearance of Social Capital in America, *Political Science and Politics* (december), 664-683.

Putnam, R. D. (1993) *Making Democracy Work. Civic traditions in modern Italy*, Princeton, NJ: Princeton University Press.

Putnam, R. D & Goss (2003) Introducción, in Putnam, R. D (ed): *El declive del capital social*. Barcelona: Galaxia Gutenberg, 7-34.

Reynolds, P., Bosma, N., Autio, E., Hunt, S., De Bono, N., Servais, I., López-García, P. & Chin, N. (2005). Global Entrepreneurship Monitor: Data Collection, Design and Implementation 1998-2003, *Small Business Economics* 24, 205-231.

Reynolds, P.; Hay, M.; & Camp, R.M. (2002). *Global Entrepreneurship Monitor. 2002 Executive Report*. Babson College; London Business School.

Romer, P. (1986). Increasing returns and long-run growth, *The Journal of Political Economy*, 95, (5) 1002-1037

Romer, P. (1990). Endogenous Technological Change, *The Journal of Political Economy*, 98(5) 71-102

Schumpeter, J. (1934). *The Theory of Economic Development*. Cambridge: Harvard University Press.

Stel, A.;Carree, M.; & Thurik, R. (2005). The Effect of Entrepreneurial Activity on National Economic Growth, *Small Business Economics*, Vol. 24, N. 3, 311-321.

Weidenbaum, M. & Hughes, S. (1996). *Bamboo Network: How Expatriate Chinese Entrepreneurs Are Creating a New Economic Superpower in Asia*. New York: The Free Press

Wennekers, S. & Turik, A. R. (1999). Linking entrepreneurship and economic growth, *Small Business Economics*, 13, 27-55.

Woolcock, M. & Narayan, D. (2000). Social capital: implications for development theory, research and policy, *World Bank Research Observer*, 15 (2), 225-249.

Worms, J. P. (2003). Viejos y nuevos vínculos en Francia, in Putnam, R. D (ed): *El declive del capital social*. Barcelona: Galaxia Gutenberg,. 273-344.

In: Social Development
Editor: Lynda R. Elling

ISBN: 978-1-60741-612-8
© 2009 Nova Science Publishers, Inc.

Chapter 9

HOW GENERAL MANAGERS INFLUENCE ORGANIZATIONAL SOCIAL CAPITAL: THE NEED OF NEW THEORETICAL PERSPECTIVES

David Pastoriza
HEC Montreal, Canada

ABSTRACT

The incapacity of theories like Transaction Cost Economics or Agency Theory to explain how management may influence social capital should induce scholars to advance in new conceptual developments that allow a better understanding of the managerial processes that allow social capital to flourish. This paper revisits and reconsiders whether the classic management functions that portrait the executive as a strategist, resource allocator, and structure and systems designer, are really contributing to the creation of social capital in the firm. The aim of the paper is not to propose specific mechanisms of managerial influence, but to reflect on the necessity of new theoretical perspectives that profound on the general management roles that truly lead to social capital creation.

1. INTRODUCTION

The concept of social capital has become increasingly popular in a wide range of social science disciplines. Despite the similarities researchers have taken to study social capital, there are differences and sometimes contradictory treatments to this concept. According to the level of analysis, it has been studied as an attribute of nations (Fukuyama, 1995), communities (Putnam, 1993), organizations (Tsai and Ghoshal, 1998) or individuals (Portes and Sensenbrenner, 1993). While the concept of social capital has received considerable attention at the community and individual level of analysis, there is comparatively less research focused on social capital as an attribute of organizations (Leana and Van Buren, 1999). The level of analysis of this paper will be, precisely, the organization. Studies on social capital can vary not only on the level of analysis, but also on the focus of analysis.

Authors study social capital focusing in the social network tying an individual or community to other external actors –bridging view- or in the collectivity internal characteristics –bonding view- (Nahapiet and Ghoshal, 1998; Baker and Obstfeld, 1999; Adler and Kwon, 2002). The focus of this chapter will be both the bridging and bonding view. According to these parameters of analysis, we base our study in the definition of Nahapiet and Ghoshal (1998), who state that social capital is "the sum of actual and potential resources embedded within, available through, and derived from the network of relationships possessed by a social unit" (1998: 243).

Organizational social capital is proving to be a powerful factor explaining several organizational concerns (Adler and Kwon, 2002) like strengthening stakeholder's relations, information sharing, solidarity benefits, fomenting entrepreneurship, or diminishes the probability of opportunism (e.g., Edelman et al., 2004; Sanderfur and Haumann, 1998; or Tsai and Ghoshal, 1998). It is a resource tightly bounded to the organization, it cannot be traded on an open market and it cannot be easily exchanged from one social system to another (Nahapiet and Ghoshal, 1998). These features make of social capital one of the most enduring sources of competitive advantage for the firm if management can influence its development and appropriate its value (Nahapiet and Ghoshal, 1998). Several authors have pointed out the necessity of further research to understand the factors that influence individuals for activating social capital (e.g., Adler and Kwon, 2002). While there are studies that focus on the importance of human resource practices (e.g., Leana and Van Buren, 1999; Leenders and Gabbay, 1999; Cohen and Prusak, 2001), or the impact of manager's behaviors on social capital (e.g., Bolino et al., 2002; Hodson, 2005; Pastoriza et al., 2008), research has paid less attention to understand the specific role that general managers can play to develop an organization context that facilitates social capital to flourish. The aim of this paper is, precisely, to explore the management functions conducive to a positive organizational context that favours social capital. It exposes the need to rethink the traditional managers' roles of strategy designers, resource allocators, and structures and systems architects.

After this brief introduction, the second section of the paper revises the most influential theories of managerial action over the last years –Porter's theory of competitive strategy, Agency Theory and Transaction Cost Economics-. It underlines the main flaws of those theories and stresses their incapability to explain how management may influence the creation of organizational social capital. The section argues about the necessity of building up a model of managerial influence that overcomes the shortcomings of managerial prescriptions derived from Agency Theory or Transaction Cost Economics (Nahapiet et al., 2005). The third section of the paper proposes the creation of a supportive organizational context as an alternative to the management theories based on industrial and organizational economics. The concept of organizational context, which derives from the strategy process literature (Bower, 1970; Burgleman, 1983a and 1983b; Bartlett and Ghoshal, 1994; Birkinshaw, 1999), suggests that the main goal of general managers should be that of creating a positive and moral institutional environment that instils in the organizational members a level of identification and implication beyond that justified by administrative systems alone. The fourth section details the implications that creating such an organizational context has for the top managers' roles and responsibilities. In a nutshell, this last section revisits Ghoshal and Bartlett's thoughts on how top management roles should move beyond the mere design of systems, structures and strategy, towards a focus in purpose, people and process.

2. BEYOND ORGANIZATIONAL ECONOMICS MANAGEMENT THEORIES

Management ability to influence social capital is constrained by prevailing assumptions of human intentionality such as self-interest and opportunism (see, e.g., Williamson, 1975). Those assumptions, which derive from industrial and organizational economics literature, suggest a rather restrictive form of social exchange (Moran and Ghoshal, 1996; Ghoshal et al., 1999; Ghoshal, 2005). From this under-socialized perspective, relationships between persons are seen as primarily instrumental, being the achievement of own self-interest the dominant intention (Rocha and Ghoshal, 2006). Agency theory or transaction cost economics, which have influenced the practice of management, have presented a view of individual-organization relationship that is grounded in the assumption that human motivation and intentionality are passive and pathological (Ghoshal, Bartlett and Moran, 1999). According to Ghoshal and Bartlett (1997), much of modern management is based on research and theories of corporate behavior that were often framed by economist who disliked and distrusted companies. Their theories have collectively created an amoral philosophy of management premised on a highly instrumental relationship between the company and society on the one hand, and between the company and its employees on the other. This amoral philosophy of management is reflected in the daily choices and actions of most managers, who conform to the established norms rather than to any conscious understanding of their underlying assumptions and logic. Ghoshal, Bartlett and Moran (1999) argue that it is not that management is inherently harmful or evil, but that the current problem lies in the deeply narrow and pessimistic assumptions of academics and practitioners about both the role of the organization in society and the nature of individuals and their motivations. Several authors (i.e., Ghoshal, 2005; Pfeffer and Fong, 2002; or Clegg and Ross-Smith, 2003) argue that practice is just a reflection of the tyranny of theory; this is, that academic prescriptions, instead of providing remedies, have tightened the squeeze on managers and companies. Three strands of economic perspectives have dominated this managerial discourse: Porter's theory of strategy, Agency Theory, and Williamson's Transaction Cost Economics.

The first highly influential strand of theory is Michael Porter's strategic theory. According to this author, the essence of strategy is competing with surrounding forces –i.e., employees, customers, suppliers, etc- to appropriate as much value as possible. Strategy is positioning to grab all you can, while preventing anyone else from appropriating that value (Ghoshal, Bartlett and Moran, 1999). In this value-appropriation scenario, it is somehow difficult to find compatibilities between the interests of the company and those of society; employees become a source of value to achieve economic objectives. Contrary to this view, Moran and Ghoshal (1996) propose organizations as powerful levers that enable people to productively defy the market's institutional forces. In their conceptual framework, economic development as a result of an iterative process of creating and realizing value through resource combinations and exchanges.

The second theoretical strand is Agency Theory –AT- (Jensen and Meckling, 1976). This theory assumes that the firm is conceived as a nexus of contracts. A crucial relationship is that between the principal and the agent. A party –the principal- determines the work that another party –the agent- undertakes (Eisenhardt, 1985). The design of contracts motivates rewards and supervises the agent's efforts. The role of the manager –agent- is serving to shareholders

–principal- and maximizing their returns. This logic leads to introduce practices to reduce a CEO's power on the board -e.g. by expanding the number of independent members on corporate boards- (Ghoshal, 2005) or to align the manager's interests with those of the shareholders -e.g., paying managers by bonus, stock options, etc-. These views stand in contrast to Barnard's ideas, who stated that "it is utterly contrary to the nature of men to be sufficiently induced by material or monetary considerations to contribute enough effort to a cooperative system to enable it to be productively efficient to the degree necessary for persistence over an extended period" (1938: 93; quoted in Ghoshal and Bartlett, 1994).

The third influential strand of theory is Transaction Cost Economics –TCE-. According to Williamson, one of top management main roles is that "preventing" the organization from those who want to do harm: "some people are opportunistic, not just self interested, but worse. They make promises knowing well that, should the benefits from breaking them exceed the costs, they would do so in an instant. They lie and cheat. While most people may not be like that, some are, and it is not possible to separate, ex-ante, those who are from those who are not" (1975: quoted in Ghoshal, 2005). Being more specific, Williamson (quoted in Ghoshal and Moran, 1996) roots his theory in some human assumptions: First, the individual is unable of developing interpersonal trust -not based on safeguards-; second, it is unaffected by socialization considerations; and finally, it is unable to interiorize the motives of a counterpart in a transaction, even in a transaction of indefinite interactions. As a result from these behavioral assumptions, Williamson assigns to the manager the use of hierarchical authority to prevent that opportunistic employees benefit from the organization. It does so by controlling in every single moment what everyone is doing, tailored instructions and use of hierarchical position to monitor, vigilance, reward or punish every single individual to ensure that everybody does what is expected to do (Ghoshal, 2005).

These managerial theories developed from economic models have received much criticism. The first is that their assumptions about the human being are incomplete and harmful; besides they can legitimize organizations as institutions (Donaldson and Davis, 1991; Donaldson, 2002; Milgrom and Roberts, 1992; Moran and Ghoshal, 1996; and Pfeffer, 1997 and 2005). Second, its logic distorts more than illuminates what an organization actually is, and introduces disfunctionalities among the managers, employees and shareholders (Hirsch et al., 1990; Perrow, 1986; Ghoshal and Moran, 1996). Third, it is divorced from reality, because it ignores the complexities of organizational life, such as authority or identification. (Simon, 1991; Donaldson, 1995; Davis and Schoorman, 1997; Kanter, 2005). Fourth, it considers that individuals are not influenced by their social environment to produce cooperative behavior (Perrow, 1972; Granovetter, 1985; Donaldson, 1990 and 1995; Pfeffer, 1997). Fifth, its logic leads to a self-fulfilling prophecy (Gergen, 1973; Ferraro et al., 2005); that is, managerial surveillance on employees generates negative attitudes and behaviors on employees, such as free-riding (Lepper and Greene, 1975; Marwell and Ames, 1981; Baker, Jensen and Murphy, 1988; Enzle and Anderson, 1993; Frank and Schulze, 2000). In other words, the management's distrust of employees leads to an increased need for more surveillance and control –known as the "dilemma of the supervisor"- (Ghoshal and Moran, 1996). Sixth, it contradicts current managerial practices which decrease hierarchy, incentives and control and emphasize a more people-oriented management (Deci, 1975; Lepper and Greene, 1975; Pfeffer, 1997). Seventh, it causes harm to employee moral (Perrow, 1972; Moran and Ghoshal, 1996; Clegg and Ross-Smith, 2003). And finally, it shows a lack of empirical success, as its predictions have yet to be validated (Hirsch et al., 1987; Green and

Shapiro, 1994; Pfeffer, 1997). The findings from economic models cannot be generalized to every situation (Donaldson, 2002; Davis, Schoorman, Donaldson, 1997).

3. THE NEED OF A NEW THEORETICAL PERSPECTIVE.

According to Ghoshal, Bartlett and Moran (1999), it is time to expose the old, disabling assumptions and replace them with a different, more realistic set that can release the vast potential still trapped in the economic models. It would certainly help to move away from the convergent pessimistic view of human nature and the role of companies in society. Ghoshal (2005) states that moving towards a more humanistic perspective may not readily yield sharp, testable propositions, but on the other hand it would not provide reductionist managerial prescriptions. A new management philosophy should posit a very different moral contract between the company on the one hand, and the individual and society on the other. With this purpose in mind, several authors –i.e., Bartlett and Ghoshal (1994), Ghoshal, Bartlett and Moran (1999), Birkinshaw (1999); Gibson and Birnkinshaw (2004)- have started to work on a model of management influence based on the idea of creating a positive organizational context that influences employees to exchange information and knowledge, orient towards common goals, and contribute with their behavior to a generalized form of trust in the organization. To set the origins of the term organizational context we have to go back to Bower's (1970) and Doz and Prahalad's (1990) work on resource allocation process in a large diversified corporations. These authors originally defined context as the set of direct mechanisms –i.e., degree of formalization of positions and relations, information systems, measurement and rewarding systems- that foster certain behaviors in employees, but its emphasis is on relatively tangible systems and processes such as incentive or career management systems, rather than on more intangible or social attributes such as a system's capability to stretch employees. This way, top management would have in its hands the administrative mechanisms that serve as levers that influence behavior of managers and employees bellow the top of the hierarchical organization Burgelman (1983a and 1983b). That is, the corporate managers in large diversified firms, through the purposeful shaping of the context induce the desired strategic behavior (Haspelagh, 1986).

With the work of Bartlett and Ghoshal (1994) and Birkinshaw (1999), the concept of organizational context has evolved beyond the pure focus on direct mechanisms of influence, towards more indirect and social mechanisms. The organizational context, as proposed by these authors, appears to encourage employees' involvement at an emotional level. The new conceptualization of organizational context can be defined as "the set of administrative and social mechanisms that shape the behaviors of actors in the organization, over which top management have some control" (Birkinshaw, 1999: 10). A key part of the definition of organizational context is the recognition that it is composed by two sets of mechanisms: "administrative" and "social" mechanisms. The administrative mechanisms of influence –i.e., compensation systems, report relationships, hierarchical relationships- are oriented to shape individuals´ behavior and can be changed rapidly. The social mechanisms of influence, on the contrary, are a set of tangible and concrete managerial actions taken over a long period of time that cannot be achieved overnight. The managerial actions and processes that constitute the social mechanisms –i.e., help and guidance to employees, equity in decision making processes, involvement of individuals in collective decisions affecting them, create a shared ambition, involvement of lower hierarchical levels, transparency in the access to resources, etc- are oriented to instil in their members a level of identification and implication beyond that justified by administrative systems alone. The organizational context is very much aligned with the humanizing culture approach proposed by Mele (2003) as an antecedent of organizational social capital.

A positive organizational context results as a function of the sum of tangible and concrete managerial actions over a long period of time. It is the interaction between managerial decisions and the resulting organizational context what lies at the core of a company's management process (Bartlett and Ghoshal, 1994). Doz and Prahalad (1988) and Ghoshal and Bartlett (1994) argued that the creation of a supportive organizational context must be the first priority of general managers, and reflects a good measure of an organization's quality of management. This organizational context would be very aligned with Barnard's idea about the important role that managers should play in creating an institutional context that inspires faith on employees. The idea of organizational context reflects somehow what Hamel and Prahalad (1993) have described as a paradox of management: that leadership cannot be planned for, but neither can it happen without a well-founded aspiration. Thus, the paper argues that the main role of general managers to create social capital is, beyond that of designing the employment stability practices, to create an appropriate organizational context through ongoing managerial processes (Ghoshal and Bartlett, 1994). Yet, the ability of top management to shape this appropriate organizational context has tremendous implications for top-management roles and responsibilities. Management must shift attention towards the creation and management of processes more directly related to adding value than on facilitating internal administrative activities (Bartlett and Ghoshal, 1997).

4. MOVING TOWARDS PEOPLE, PURPOSE AND PROCESS

Creating a supportive organizational context implies focusing in a set of managerial roles that are distant of those created when large corporations focused in growing, during the seventies and eighties. By that time, when financial capital was the scarce resource, top management primary role was to determine strategy as well as to create structures and systems to shape employees' behavior in ways that would support the capital allocation decisions (Bartlett and Ghoshal, 1994). As firms grow larger and complex, top managers needed sophisticated systems to ensure that headquarters could monitor and influence the plans of specific business units. To manage growth, managers created diversified organization that required a divisional structure with tight designed planning and control systems. This increasingly complex organization forms enabled companies to grow, but at the expense of fragmenting companies' resources, creating vertical communication channels that isolated business units and prevented information flows. The power of systems and structures in large complex organizations minimized the idiosyncrasies of human behavior. Employee's activities would be increasingly fragmented and systematized. Under this paradigm, most large companies become highly standardized and efficient in terms of operations, and its employees are managed like inputs in a depersonalized system (Ghoshal and Bartlett, 1995a & 1995b).

These complex structures and systems allowed general managers to manage growth, but this control transforms in rigidity when the purpose of the firm is to capitalize on the knowledge of organizational members. Practitioners and researchers have recognized over the last years the limitations of the classic hierarchical organizations. As the knowledge era evolved, the scarce resources shifts from capital to knowledge. Firm's competitive advantage, in a knowledge economy, is increasingly dependent on the development of social capital. Quite often, the scarcest corporate resource is the expertise of the people on the front lines, and less and less the financial funds that top management controls. The knowledge and expertise of firm tends to reside at the operating level, rather than at the top of the hierarchy. Firm's competitive advantage in a knowledge economy is increasingly dependent on its ability to develop a social capital that is conducive of intellectual capital (Tsai and Ghoshal, 1999). This shift from a capital-intensive economy towards a knowledge-intensive economy poses the necessity of challenging the conventional management roles. Nevertheless, existing literature on social capital does not distinguish between the roles and responsibilities that managers should play at different organizational levels, like if manager's role at higher levels of the hierarchy were similar but bigger than the manager at a level below.

Top-level managers should not simply manage the organization as an economic entity whose activities could be directed through strategic plans, resource allocation processes, and management control systems. Instead of monitoring the employees to conform to the firm's systems, rules and policies, the overall objective should be to leverage and capitalize on their knowledge and expertise of each organizational member. Somehow, there must be a movement from corporate engineering to employee empowerment (Bartlett and Ghoshal, 1995c). It is important that managers see the firm as a social institution that captures the energy and commitment of organizational members, not considering employees as individuals who are contractually bonded to the firm. Bartlett and Ghoshal reflected the necessity of moving beyond the existing approach of managing the organization as an economic entity with tools such as systems and structure design, towards a more dynamic activities based on purpose, people and processes. Their main ideas could be synthesized as follows: First, as opposed to being formulators of corporate strategy, top managers should become shapers of a corporate purpose with which employees can identify and feel a sense of personal commitment (Bartlett and Ghoshal, 1994). They establish a sense of purpose that defines how the company will create value for society. Second, instead of focusing on formal structures that control resources, top managers should put efforts in building processes of competence building, entrepreneurship and corporate renewal (Bartlett and Ghoshal, 1995a). In a nutshell, they should build organizational processes that add value by having the organization working more effectively together. And third, from builders of systems that isolate management from the organization and makes them treat organizational members as production factors, managers must transform into the developers of people, helping individuals to become the best they can be (Bartlett and Ghoshal, 1997). Rather than monitoring the performance of business units through abstract systems, they should focus their attention in the motivation of people within those business units (Bartlett and Ghoshal, 1995b).

In sum, the nature social capital makes of it a resource that can hardly arise from mere organizational design. It represents the organic growth of variables –i.e., generalized trust, associability- that need time to be developed. I have argued that this development results from the deliberate, consistent and ongoing managerial processes oriented to create a positive organizational context. It has been argued that the creation of such an organizational context presents a challenge to the top management of the firm, who must reconsider old traditional management roles and managerial economic theories like Transaction Cost Economics or Agency Theory. Those theories, which have dominated the management literature over the last decades, have presented an overly pessimistic view of what happens in organizations. To develop a sound conceptual model of social capital development it is necessary to overcome the restrictive and under-socialized prescriptions of those economic models (Rocha and Ghoshal, 2006). Moving towards this humanistic managerial perspective may not readily yield sharp and testable propositions (Ghoshal, 2005), but on the other hand, it would not provide simple and reductionist managerial propositions. This paper, by building a bridge between social capital and general management literatures, has stressed the importance of advancing in theoretical and empirical developments that deepen on the management roles that are conducive of social capital in the firm.

REFERENCES

Adler, P. S., & Kwon, S. 2002. Social capital: Prospects for a new concept. *Academy of Management Review*, 27: 17-40.

Baker, G. P., Jensen, M. C., & Murphy, K. J. 1988. Compensation and incentives: Practice vs. theory. *Journal of Finance*, 43: 593-616.

Baker, W. E., & Obstfeld, D. 1999. Social capital by designing structures, strategies, and institutional context. In R. A. J. Leenders, & S. M. Gabbay (Eds.), *Corporate social capital and liability*: 89-117. Norwell, MA: Cambridge University Press.

Barnard, C. 1968. *The functions of the executive*. Cambridge: Harvard University Press.

Bartlett, C. A. and Ghoshal, S. 1995c. Rebuilding behavior context: Turn process reengineering into people rejuvenation, *Sloan Management Review,* 37 (1): 11-24.

Bartlett, C. A., & Ghoshal, S. 1994. Changing the role of top management: Beyond strategy to purpose. *Harvard Business Review*, 72: 79-88.

Bartlett, C. A., & Ghoshal, S. 1995b. Changing the role of top management: Beyond structure to processes. *Harvard Business Review*, 73: 86-96.

Bartlett, C. A., & Ghoshal, S. 1997. The myth of the generic manager: New personal competencies for new management roles. *California Management Review*, 40: 92-116.

Bartlett, C., & Ghoshal, S. 1995a. Changing the role of top management: Beyond systems to people. *Harvard Business Review*, 73: 132-142.

Birkinshaw, J. 1999. The determinants and consequences of subsidiary initiative in multinational corporations. *Entrepreneurship Theory and Practice*, 12: 9-36.

Bolino, M. C., Turnley, W. H., & Bloodgood, J. M. 2002. Citizenship behavior and the creation of social capital in organizations. *Academy of Management Review*, 27: 505-522.

Bower, J. L. 1970. *Managing the resource allocation process*. Boston: Harvard Business School Press.

Burgelman, R. A. 1983a. A process model of internal corporate venturing in the diversified major firm. *Administrative Science Quarterly*, 28: 223-244.

Burgelman, R. A. 1983b. A model of the interaction of strategic behavior, corporate context and the concept of strategy. *Academy of Management Review*, 8: 61-70.

Clegg, S. R., & Ross-Smith, A. 2003. Revising the boundaries: Management education and learning in a postpositivist world. *Academy of Management Learning & Education*, 2: 85-98.

Cohen, D., & Prusak, L. 2001. In good company: How social capital makes organizations work. *Harvard Business Review*, 80: 107-107.

Davis, J. H., & Schoorman, F. D. 1997. Toward a stewardship theory of management. *Academy of Management Review*, 22(1): 20-47.

Deci, E. 1975. *Intrinsic motivation.* New York: Plenum.

Donaldson, L. 2002. Damned by our own theories: Contradictions between theories and management education. *Academy of Management Learning & Education*, 1: 96-106.

Donaldson, L., & Davis, J.H. 1991. Stewardship theory or agency theory: CEO governance and shareholder returns. *Australian Journal of Management*, 16: 49-66.

Doz, Y., & Prahalad, C. K. 1981. Headquarters influence and strategic control in MNCs. *Sloan Management Review*, 23: 15-29.

Eisenhardt, M., K. 1989. Agency theory: An assessment and review. *Academy of Management Review*, 14(1): 57-74.

Enzle, M. E., & Anderson, S. C. 1993. Surveillant intentions and intrinsic motivation. *Journal of Personality & Social Psychology*, 64: 257-266.

Ferraro, F., Pfeffer, J., & Sutton, R. L. 2005. Economics language and assumptions: How theories can become self-fulfilling. *Academy of Management Review*, 30: 8-24.

Frank, B., & Schulze, G. G. 2000. Does economics make citizens corrupt? *Journal of Economic Behavior & Organization*, 43: 101-113.

Fukuyama, F. 1995. *Trust: the social virtues and the creation of prosperity.* New York: The Free Press.

Gergen, K. J. 1973. Social psychology as history. *Journal of personality and social psychology*, 26(2): 309-320.

Ghoshal, S. 2005. Bad management theories are destroying good management practices. *Academy of Management Learning & Education*, 4: 75-91.

Ghoshal, S., & Bartlett, C. A. 1994. Linking organizational context and managerial action: The dimensions of quality of management. *Strategic Management Journal*, 15: 91-112.

Ghoshal, S., & Bartlett, C. A. 2000. *The individualized corporation: a fundamentally new approach to management.* Chantam, Kent: Random House.

Ghoshal, S., & Moran, P. 1996. Bad for practice: A critique of the transaction cost theory. *Academy of Management Review*, 21: 13-47.

Ghoshal, S., Bartlett, C. A., & Moran, P. 1999. A new manifesto for management. *Sloan Management Review*, 40: 9-20.

Gibson, C., & Birkinshaw, J. 2004. The antecedents, consequences, and mediating role of organizational ambidexterity. *Academy of Management Journal*, 47: 209-227.

Granovetter, M. 1985. Economic action and social structure: The problem of embeddedness. *American Journal of Sociology*, 91: 481-510.

Green, D. P., & Shapiro, I. 1994. *Pathologies of rational choice theory: A critique of applications in political science.* New Haven: Yale University Press.

Hamel. G. & Prahalad, C.K. 1993. Strategy as stretch and leverage. *Harvard Business Review*, 71: 75-84.

Haspelagh, P. 1986. Conceptualising the strategic process in diversified firms: The role and nature of the corporate influence process: INSEAD working chapter 86/09.

Hirsch, P.M., & Friedman, R., & Koza, M.P. 1990. Collaboration or paradigm shift? Caveat emptor and the risk of romance with economic models for strategy and policy research. Organization Science, 1: 87-97.

Hodson, R. 2005. Management behavior as social capital: A systematic analysis of organizational ethnographies. *British Journal of Industrial Relations*, 43: 41-65.

Jensen, M. C., & Meckling, W. H. 1976. Theory of the firm: Managerial behavior, agency costs and ownership structure. *Journal of Financial Economics*, 3: 305-360.

Kanter, R. M. 2005. What theories do audiences want? Exploring the demand side. *Academy of Management Learning & Education*, 4: 93-95.

Leana, C. R., & Buren, V. 1999. Organizational social capital and employment practices. *Academy of Management Review*, 24: 538-555.

Leenders, R. A. J., & Gabbay, S. M. 1999. *Corporate social capital and liability*. Norwell, MA: Kluwer Academic Publishers.

Lepper, M. R., & Greene, D. 1975. Turning play into work: Effects of adult surveillance and extrinsic rewards on children´s intrinsic motivation. *Journal of Personality and Social Psychology*, 28: 479-486.

Marwell. G., & Ames, R.E. 1981. Economists free ride. Does anyone else? Journal of Public Economics, 15: 295-311.

Mele, D. 2003. Organizational humanizing cultures: Do they generate social capital? *Journal of Business Ethics*, 45: 3-14.

Milgrom, P., & Roberts, J. 1992. *Economics, organization and management*. Englewood Cliffs: Prentice Hall.

Moran, P. 2005. Structural vs. relational embeddedness: Social capital and managerial performance. *Strategic Management Journal*, 26: 1129-1151.

Moran, P., & Ghoshal, S. 1996. Theories of economic organization: The case for realism and balance. *Academy of Management Review*, 21: 58-72.

Nahapiet, J., & Ghoshal, S. 1998. Social capital, intellectual capital, and the organizational advantage. *Academy of Management Review*, 23: 242-266.

Nahapiet, J., Gratton, L., & Rocha, H. O. 2005. Knowledge and relationships: When cooperation is the norm. *European Management Review*, 45: 1-12.

Pastoriza, D., Ariño, M. A., & Ricart, J. E. 2008. Ethical managerial behavior as antecedent of organizational social capital. *Journal of Business Ethics*, 78: 329-341.

Perrow, C. 1972. *Complex organizations: A critical essay*. Glenview, Ill: Scott, Foresman and Company.

Pfeffer, J. 1997. *New directions for organization theory, problems and prospects*. New York: Oxford University Press.

Pfeffer, J. 2005. Why do bad management theories persist? A comment on Ghoshal. *Academy of Management Learning & Education*, 4: 96-100.

Pfeffer, J., & Fong, C. T. 2002. The end of business schools? Less success than meets the eye. *Academy of Management Learning & Education*, 1: 78-95.

Portes, A. and Sensenbrenner, J. 1993. Embeddedness and immigration: Notes on the social determinants of economic action, *American Journal of Sociology*, 98(2): 1320-1350.

Putnam, R. D. 1993. *Making democracy work: Civic traditions in modern Italy*. Princeton, NJ: Princeton University Press.

Rocha, H. O., & Ghoshal, S. 2006. Beyond self-interest revisited. *Journal of Management Studies*, 43(3): 585-619.

Sandefur, R. L., & Laumann, E.O. 1998. A paradigm for social capital. *Rationality and Society*, 10(4): 481-501.

Simon, H. A. 1991. Organizations and markets. *Journal of Economic Perspectives*, 5: 25-44.

Tsai, W., & Ghoshal, S. 1998. Social capital and value creation: The role of intrafirm networks. *Academy of Management Journal*, 41: 464-476.

Williamson, O. E. 1975. *Markets and hierarchies, analysis and antitrust implications: a study in the economics of internal organization.* New York: Free Press.

In: Social Development
Editor: Lynda R. Elling

ISBN: 978-1-60741-612-8
© 2009 Nova Science Publishers, Inc.

Chapter 10

HOW DOES PERSONALITY DEVELOP OVER THE LIFE-COURSE: RESULTS OF THE BRNO LONGITUDINAL STUDY ON LIFE-SPAN DEVELOPMENT

Marek Blatný, Martin Jelínek and Terezie Osecká*

Institute of Psychology, Academy of Sciences of the Czech Republic
Veveri 97, 602 00 Brno, Czech Republic

ABSTRACT

The chapter gives an overview of the main results of the Brno Longitudinal Study on Life-span Development. This builds upon the longitudinal study of children carried in the Institute of Psychology at Brno, Czech Republic, in the sixties and seventies. The paper starts with information about the original project and how we have searched for participants and built on current sample from the original cohort. A great deal of attention is paid also to methodology which combines quantitative and qualitative approaches.

Results from five studies concerning personality development are presented. First of them deals with the prediction of adult personality from behaviors observed in the nursling and toddler stages, the second with stability and developmental trends of intelligence in childhood and adolescence, the third with stability and change of personality in adolescence, the fourth with longitudinal stability of personality traits and self-concept between adolescence and middle adulthood, and the fifth with subjective perception of personal change in life-long perspective.

Keywords: life-span development, personality stability and change, longitudinal study.

---

[*] E-mail: blatny@psu.cas.cz

INTRODUCTION

The psychological research has not systematically dealt with the issue of personality development in adulthood for a relatively long time. Although the number of outstanding theorists formulated their concept of development in adulthood - including its periodization and psychological characterization of individual stages (C. G. Jung, E. H. Erikson, R. Havighurst) - still in 1983 Josef Langmeier, leading Czech child psychologist, said in his Developmental Psychology that the psychology of adulthood and old age was much less elaborate than the psychology of childhood and adolescence. He stated that there was a small number of empirical studies which dealt with development in adulthood.

This flaw was sufficiently removed during the 1980s and 90s. Developmental psychology of the adults established itself as an independent psychological discipline (Demick, Andreoletti, 2003; Lemme, 1999), canonical (normative) life course of an adult (also regarding the gender) was described in terms of both transitions (changes in state or role) and goals or/and tasks (Settersten, 2003; Wapner, Demick, 2003). The wider theoretic and methodological frameworks (often on the inter-disciplinary base) were formulated for the research of human development. Among them there are mainly the theory of life course (Elder, Kirpatrick Johnson, Crosnoe, 2003; Giele, Elder, 1998), lifespan psychology (Baltes 1997/2003), holistic interactionism (Magnusson, 1999), holistic, developmental, systems-oriented perspective (Wapner, Demick, 2003), and developmental systems theory (Ford, Lerner, 1992; Lerner, 2002).

The key issue of development in adulthood remains the longitudinal stability of personality and conditions of its changes. It is generally accepted that personality is a multifaced construct that must be examined through numerous and diverse methods. Personality as the system of stable components - traits (e.g. personality dispositions both inborn or gained during the early stages of development) and personality as self which is formed in the social context (stable system of self-perceptions and concepts of other people and world as whole) belong to basic conceptualizations of personality (Helson, 1996; Cloninger, 2003). While the high stability is found namely in traits, the area which is more vulnerable to changes is a socially anchored part of personality (self, character) - interpersonal characteristics, attitudes, values, etc.

The issue of lifespan development was included in the research plan of the Institute of Psychology of the Academy of Sciences of the Czech Republic in 2000. A decision was made that the research on adult development would capitalize on the potential of the longitudinal study of children undertaken by the Institute in the 1960s and 1970s. The objective was to activate the sample from the longitudinal research of mental development of children and use its participants again within a new longitudinal study of adults.

This paper gives an overview of the main results of the Brno Longitudinal Study on Life-span Development. The paper starts with information about the original project and how we have searched for participants and built on current sample from the original cohort. In the second part results from five studies concerning personality stability and change are presented.

Brno Longitudinal Study on Life-Span Development

The Past: "The Psychological Development of School Children Coming from Different Social Environments" (1961 -1980)

The original longitudinal study titled "The psychological development of school children coming from different social environments" was solved by The Institute of Psychology of the Academy of Sciences of the Czech Republic between 1961 and 1980. The original methodology was based on the recommendations of the international organization "Centre International de l'Enfance", residing in Paris from 1952, whose aim was to monitor somatic and psychological development of children in the long term. The methodology was used also by other centers established e.g. in London, Zurich, Geneva, Stockholm, Oslo and Brussels. Within the former Czechoslovakia, Prague (1956-86) and Brno (1961-80) centers participated in the research in Czech Republic, and Bratislava and Košice in Slovakia. Brno sample consisted of 557 children born between 1961 and 1964; the gender distribution was even (50.1% of girls). The sample was designed to represent the general population. The first diagnostic session took place at age 6 months. Follow-ups have been carried out at ages 9, 12, 18, 24, 30, and 36 months. After 36 months, the sessions were carried out once a year (from 4 to 18 years of age of participants). Children were tested on their birthday, or as close to this date as possible.

The missing value pattern analysis (Blatný, Jelínek, Osecká, 2001) revealed the anticipated regularity – the data concerning the subjects involved are usually complete until their leaving the research for different reasons. Thus, if there is a data missing concerning an individual at a certain age level, there is a high probability that there are no further details available regarding this individual. Out of the former number of 557 subjects, less than 350 were examined at the age of 16; at the age of 18, it was already only about 150 people. The decrease of subjects at age of 16 years was caused by the transition from primary school to secondary school and the decrease between 16 and 18 years of age was caused by the termination of the original project; the subjects born earlier were yet participating in the examination at the age of 18, whereas the subjects born later didn't.

The Present: "Stability, Variability and Prediction of Psychological Characteristics in Adulthood: Taking up the Longitudinal Research of Children"(2000 – 2004)

Goals of the Project

The main goal of the project was to find the participants in the children's mental development research and solicit their renewed cooperation. In a letter, we sent to the former collaborators, we asked them to meet us at least once. In the end, all of the people that visited us at the institute also agreed to continue with further cooperation.

At a scientific level, the project was aimed at:

1. personality stability and changes in a long-term perspective,
2. subjective perception of one's own person's changes, as compared to objective data,

3. predictive value of personality and behavioral characteristics from childhood and adolescence in order to predict psychological characteristics in adulthood.

In the course of the project, the research part was expanded to re-analyses of the former data. We took this measure especially because at the time of children's longitudinal research, advanced statistical methods were not available, and these methods permitted analyses leading to new original results. Beside the scientific goals, it was our purpose to ensure the conservation of the original data by converting them to an electronic version.

Sample

Between 2001 and 2005, we asked part of the original sample – 332 persons – to co-operate in the follow-up study focused on the life-span human development. With the request to find out the current addresses of the children's longitudinal research participants we appealed to the Czech Republic Police Force However, due to the Personal Data Protection Act from 2000, they could find only 245 participants out of 557. Letters were sent to last known addresses of additional 158 participants of original study but 71 returned as "not known at this address". There were no addresses available for the rest of the participants.

Our request letter was answered by 142 persons: 138 persons agreed to participate (54 men and 84 women), whereas 3 women and 1 man declined explicitly to co-operate. We contacted the people who reacted positively to our request by phone. At last, the meeting in the Institute of Psychology was attended by 83 persons: 33 of them were university graduates, 39 completed secondary education and 11 finished professional school; 52 persons were married for the first time, 6 were unmarried, 12 were divorced, 8 married again after divorce, 4 in another form of cohabitation after divorce, 1 woman married again after becoming a widow; 7 persons remained childless, 21 had 1 child, 39 had 2 children, 14 had three children, one participant had 4 children, and one participant had 5 children (average = 1.81).

Analysis of differences between people who agreed to co-operate and those who did not answered our letter did not show any differences in psychological characteristics between these two groups (Blatný, Jelínek, Osecká, 2001, 2005). The only difference found was the time spent participating in the original longitudinal research – the people agreeing to cooperate spent longer period of time in the original research; this fact could have been the cause of a stronger motivation to continue while adult.

However, we found differences concerning psychological variables between people who agreed to participate and people who actually did participate in the research – as regards the people who visited the Institute for real, a slightly higher level of intelligence was ascertained during their childhood and adolescence, than was the case with people who didn't come to the survey despite their initial agreement.

These findings correspond to the fact that there is a larger participations of university graduates (45 %) in the sample then it is typical for this age group in the general population in the Czech Republic, where the university graduates are represented only by 14 % (Czech Statistical Office, 2007).

Instruments

Owing to a relatively low number of subjects, we decided to use more extensively the qualitative methodology; thus, the project has a quantitative and a qualitative part.

In the quantitative part of the project, we tackled questions of long-term stability and changes in personality and predictive values of childhood and adolescence characteristics for predicting psychological characteristics in adulthood. For the purpose of observing the personality stability and changes, questionnaires and self-report scales were replicated, i.e. their version for adults: Eysenck Personality Inventory (Eysenck, Eysenck, 1964), Wechsler's Intelligence Test WAIS-III (Wechsler, 1999), Rokeach´s Test of Values (Rokeach, 1973) and 15 self-report scales from the Semantical differential of different terms (next to the term I for instance mother, soldier, tractor). In predicting the psychological characteristics in adulthood, we targeted a larger complex of personality traits in the framework of a five-factor personality model, self-concept variables (self-esteem, self-concept clarity, self-efficacy, 53 self-report scales beyond the fifteen replicated), and life satisfaction. We used Czech versions of following questionnaires and scales: NEO-FFI (Costa, McCrae, 1992), Rosenberg's self-Esteem Scale (Rosenberg, 1965), Self-Concept Clarity Scale (Campbell, Trapnell, Heine, Katz, Lavalle, Lehman, 1996), General Self-Efficacy Scale (Křivohlavý, Schwarzer, Jerusalem, 1993) Satisfaction With Life Scale (Pavot, Diener, 1993).

In the qualitative part of the research we were concerned especially with questions of treatment and organization of life experience, evaluation of one's own life, comparison of the childhood and adolescence ideas about life with the current real situation and subjective perception of the change of one's own self. As a technique, we chose an interview focused on lifeline concept. The approach is inspired by the lifeline technique of Jiří Tyl (Tyl, 1986; also Říčan, Ženatý, 1988), completed by principles of conducting a narrative interview according to McAdams (1993). In Tyl´s conception, the lifeline serves the primary purpose of a projective diagnostic technique; in our research, we used it above all as a means of structuring the narration about life; in a partial interpretation however, the projective component of the lifeline was also used – i.e. its shape (Čermák, 2004).

The interview focused on lifeline concept is semi-structured. The informant is at first asked to draw a line expressing his/her life a then he/she is asked in successive steps to mark the point of present on the line, to speak about (and perhaps even mark on the line) important events in his/her life, about important persons, about future perspectives. The last task of the informant is to draw an ideal lifeline, or a line that would express the course of life in general.

For the needs of taking up the past research and of present research aims, other topics were included in the interview – relationship to parents and siblings, interests and hobbies and fulfilling of professional schemes of the adolescence period. We explicitly asked also about the perceived change of personality (if the informant did not mention this spontaneously by him/herself).

The Future: "The Integration of Life Experience in Adulthood: Emotional Dispositions, Personal History, and Life Perspectives" (Since 2006)

At present, the second phase of longitudinal research in adulthood, which is concerned with the theme of personal coherence, is already under way.

The primary objective of the project is to contribute to the knowledge reflecting how people integrate their life experience. The attention is focused both on conscious strategies and implicit processes, as well as on mechanisms which maintain personality coherence.

Simultaneously we continue with the research of the longitudinal stability of personality, as well as with the prediction value of antecedent data about personality.

In this phase, we also target other goals beyond the scientific issues. Above all, we continue efforts in order to find other participants in the original longitudinal study. A second important goal is to develop a closer cooperation with the Prague research group. Both teams are in mutual contact since 2002; now we should above all unify our methodology for further observation and temporal coordination of other phases of research.

MAIN RESULTS

In the next part of the chapter results from five studies concerning personality development are presented. First of them deals with the prediction of adult personality from behaviors observed in the nursling and toddler stages, the second with stability and developmental trends of intelligence in childhood and adolescence, the third with stability and change of personality in adolescence, the fourth with longitudinal stability of personality traits and self-concept between adolescence and middle adulthood, and the fifth with subjective perception of personal change in life-long perspective.

Study 1: Relationship between Child Temperament and Adult Personality

One of the main aims of the first phase of the newly established research of lifespan human development was the examination of the predictive value of childhood and adolescence data for predicting psychological characteristics in adulthood. One of the first studies was therefore devoted to the relationship between early child temperament and adult personality (Blatný, Jelínek, Osecká, 2007).

For the time being there is probably no research that would prove empirically a relationship between early child temperament and adult personality. Longitudinal projects, which are the only ones that could bring forward such a proof, are focused either on the development of psychological functions and personality during childhood and adolescence (e. g. Block, 1996; Goldsmith, Lemery, Nazan, & Buss, 2000; Halverson & Deal, 2001), or they study adult personality stability in people over 18 years of age (e. g. Morizot, Le Blanc; 2003, Roberts, Helson, Klohnen; 2002, Viken, Rose, Kaprio, Koskenvuo; 1994). Studies tracking personality stability and changes over the life span development are rather rare (Costa, McCrae, 2001) and if they exist at all, they start most frequently from the age of 8 to 12 years of children (Hampson, Goldberg, Vogt, Dubanoski, 2006; Pulkkinen, 1996; Shiner, Masten, Tellegen, 2002). In doing this, they do not prove sufficiently that the personality traits are innate and continuous over the life span.

The strongest evidence to date of the continuity of personality from childhood to adulthood was offered by Caspi and his colleagues (Caspi, 2000; Caspi, Moffitt, Newman, Silva, 1996; Caspi, Harrington, Milne, Amell, Theodore, Moffitt, 2003) who studied the relationship between children's behavioral styles at age 3 and their personality traits in adolescence and young adulthood. Caspi found out significant links of child temperament and adult personality traits: for example, adult personality of children who were initially diagnosed as Undercontrolled was characterized by impulsivity, unreliability and antisocial behaviors; the inhibited children tended to be unassertive and depressive in adulthood.

Although the research of Caspi and his colleagues is the strongest evidence to date that child's behavioral styles can predict adult personality traits, it does not focus on the early developmental stages: children at age 3 has been usually influenced by the effects of socialization, environment and upbringing. The present study therefore focuses on the prediction of adult personality traits from behaviors observed before the age of 3, i.e. in the nursling and toddler stages, when real innate, temperamental dispositions are supposed to be manifested in child behavior.

According to some authors there are doubts about the feasibility of prediction of later personality differences prior to the second year of life due to the intercorrelated cognitive emotional changes (e.g. self-conscious emotions like shame) that take place during this period; furthermore, transient conditions (e.g., temporary illnesses) and subsequent experiences with environment might modify early psychological characteristics (Caspi, 2000). However temperamental characteristics are defined as innate or emerging during the first year of life and then forming the main personality traits in adulthood (Buss, 1991; Cloninger, 1994; Kagan, 1994). It is therefore justifiable to search for relationship between child temperament and adult personality.

Besides the link of child temperament and adult personality traits, we also focused on the possibility in adults to predict self-variables representing emotional experiences and evaluative inferences. According to some authors, various aspects of self-concept such as self-esteem, self-control and generalized self-efficacy combined with neuroticism form a broad personality trait termed core self-evaluations (Erez, Judge, 2001). Similarly Watson, Suls, and Haig (2002) suggest that global self-esteem measures define one end of a bipolar continuum, with trait indicators of depression defining the other. Many other cross-sectional studies have found that temperament and personality dimensions such as neuroticism/negative affectivity and extraversion/positive affectivity are powerful determinants of self-esteem (Blatny, Jelinek, Blizkovska, Klimusova, 2004; Klein, 1992; Tarlow, Haaga, 1996; Watson, Suls, Haig, 2002).

Standard method of assessing child temperament was not included in the research; therefore, for the operationalization of temperament we used the rating scales on which experimenters were evaluating the child's behavior during the examination.

The set of 34 rating scales in 5-point Likert format for description of child behavior was used for children from age 6 months to 10 years. The more structured the behavior of children, the more rating scales were used. Only scales relevant for behaviour description of children of all age groups (from the age of 6 months) were used and those not relevant for children under 3 years old were excluded (e.g. self-criticality, self-confidence in performing the. examination). Formal criterion also played a role in scale selection. Rating scales used in the study were both unipolar (e.g. frequency of positive social responses) and bipolar (difficult vs. easy initial adaptation) but only unipolar scales, predominant in the set, were selected. Twelve selected scales focused on the following aspects of behavior: Interest in examination, Nervousness (neuroticism), Positive emotional expressions, Negative emotional expressions, Frequency of positive social responses, Intensity of positive social responses, Frequency of negative social responses, Intensity of negative social responses, General reactivity, General activity, Aggression against things/objects, Conformity (obedience).

In the present study, we included the scales for 4 age brackets in the analysis (12, 18, 24 and 30 months of age). These scales cover nursling and toddler stages of development (Langmeier, Langmeier, Krejcirova, 1998). We did not use data from age 6 and 9 months due to a lot of missing values in some of the rating scales (e.g. Conformity). Theoretically based selection was validated also empirically: we performed series of factor analyses for selected age bracket (12 to 30 months). The analysis showed that factor structure of child behavior is almost identical in all age levels in terms of sufficient number of factors and factor loadings of individual items.

We calculated mean values for each temperament characteristic of the period being monitored (i.e. 12 to 30 months). For each rating scale, a minimum of 3 measurements had to be performed. Data obtained in this way were analyzed by factor analysis (maximum likelihood method, direct oblimin rotation, delta = 0). Effective sample size in childhood depended on age bracket and on concrete methods. Data of 386 children (51% of girls) were analyzed by factor analysis with mean scores. The results are included in table 1.

Table 1. Dimensions of child temperament: Factor analysis results (pattern matrix)

	Factor 1	Factor 2	Factor 3
Positive social responses (frequency)	,926		
Positive social responses (intensity)	,917		
Positive emotional expressions	,768		
Interest in examination	,585		
Aggression against things/objects		,802	
General activity	,421	,598	
Conformity (obedience)		-,497	
General reactivity		,432	
Negative social responses (frequency)			,925
Negative social responses (intensity)			,919
Negative emotional expressions			,768
Nervousness (neuroticism)	-,447		,560

Note. Factor loadings with absolute values < 0.4 are not mentioned in the table.

Factor analysis yielded 3 factors with eigenvalues > 1. This solution seemed to be suitable also with respect to scree plot; a total percentage of explained variance was 67%. Correlations of individual factors are the following: : r = .144 for the first and second factor, r = -.342 for the first and third factor and r = .450 for the second and third factor. Identified factors were interpreted as positive affectivity (factor 1), disinhibition vs. inhibition (factor 2) and negative affectivity (factor 3). This result corresponded with e.g. Clark's (2005) general structure of temperament based on the review of temperament and personality psychopathology researches.

The obtained factor scores representing dimensions of child temperament were correlated to adult personality traits. Adult personality was measured with the Eysenck Personality Inventory (Eysenck, Eysenck, 1964) and the NEO-FFI questionnaire (Costa, McCrae, 1992). As to the self-variables we dealt with self-esteem and self-efficacy on the basis of the following scales: Rosenberg Scale of Self-Esteem (Rosenberg, 1965) and General Self-

Efficacy Scale (Křivohlavý, Schwarzer, Jerusalem, 1993). Data of 72 persons (43 females) were assessed to identify the relationship between behavior in childhood and adult personality, some data from childhood were missing in remaining 11 persons (ie. they didn't participate at more than one examination during the studied period from 12 to 30 months). Table 2 presents respective Pearson's correlation coefficients.

Table 2. Relationships between dimensions of child temperament and adult personality: Correlation analysis results

		Positive affectivity	Disnhibition	Negative affectivity
EPI	Neuroticism	-,098	-,067	,043
	Extraversion	,199	,246*	,073
NEO-FFI	Neuroticism	,016	-,090	-,066
	Extraversion	,134	,213	,002
	Openness to experience	,087	,001	-,050
	Agreeableness	,193	,002	-,214
	Conscientiousness	,100	,058	-,028
SELF	Self-esteem	,027	,091	,075
	Self-efficacy	,043	,341**	,209

* Correlation is significant at the 0.05 level, ** Correlation is significant at the 0.01 level.

No significant correlations were found between child positive affectivity and child negative affectivity and personality characteristics in adulthood. Child disinhibition correlates positively with adult extraversion measured by EPI and with self-efficacy. Correlation between disinhibition and extraversion was significant at the 0.05 level and correlation between disinhibition and self-efficacy was significant at the 0.01 level.

Since the correlations between the factors are of similar magnitude of the significant correlation coefficients found among children temperament and adult traits, significant associations may only reflect spurious effects and correlation among predictors may over-estimate true associations. Therefore, we decide to perform multiple regression analysis to test for unique associations. Only the relationship between child disinhibition and generalized self-efficacy has shown as significant (table 3).

Table 3. Predicting self-efficacy in adulthood from dimensions of child temperament: Regression analysis results

	β	t	Sig.
Positive affectivity	-,048	-,357	,722
Disinhibition	,329	2,464	,016
Negative affectivity	,095	,727	,470

$R^2=0,13$; F=3,54; p=0,019.

Although, relationships between dimensions of child temperament and personality characteristics in adulthood have the expected direction (e.g. child negative affectivity is connected to adult hostility), they are rather weak. We identified only two significant correlations: between child disinhibition and adult extraversion and between child disinhibition and generalized self-efficacy. Using regression analyses with factor scores as predictors, only the relationship between child disinhibition and generalized self-efficacy has shown as significant.

We are convinced that a weak connection between child emotional dimensions (positive affectivity, negative affectivity) and adult traits containing emotional component (neuroticism - negative affectivity, agreeableness and extraversion – positive affectivity) is due to the fact that emotional behaviors are mostly controlled and influenced during the socialization. Positive emotional and social responses are generally desirable and, as such, reinforced from early childhood. And in the same way negative emotional and social responses are constricted or at least corrected. This finding was highlighted by Diener et al. (1999) who even believe that positive emotions are - especially in Euro-American culture - "socialized".

The child disinhibition holds – as the only one – a certain connection with personality traits in adulthood. This can be explained by the fact that this dimension is most purely temperamental trait, activity being its substantial component. For example Buss and Plomin (1984; Buss 1991) who distinguish in their EAS theory of temperament three dimension – emotionality (understood as distress), activity and sociability – consider activity as the main temperamental trait since this is the only formal or "stylistic" personality trait.

As far as the relationship between child disinhibition and adult extraversion is concerned it is just the activity and assertiveness which we see as the connecting link. Activity and assertiveness form the disinhibition factor in childhood and they are also important defining features of extraversion trait in adulthood.

On the basis of child disinhibition we can most reliably predict high adult self-efficacy. This fact, above all, significantly supports assumption about temperamental nature of core self-evaluations (Erez, Judge, 2001) and provokes some theoretical and methodological questions. According to Bandura (1977, 1999), the construct of self-efficacy is based on personal experience (particularly on the mastery experience) that develops during the life span through repeating similar experiences. Our results indicate that people are primarily disposed to have qualities associated with self-efficacy. These qualities include resilience, self-determination, flexibility and feelings of control. At least we can say that innate qualities provide the appropriate matrix for formation of social cognitive components of personality.

Modest relationship between child's temperament and adult personality also might be due to dimesions of child's temperament and personality traits in adulthood representing different psychological constructs. The fact was emphasized by Asendorpf (1992) who showed the necessity to differentiate between stability of individual differences and continuity of psychological constructs.

Study 2: Stability and Development Trends of Intelligence in Children Aged 3-15

Intelligence is not considered a constant ability, and a substantial amount of attention has always been given to the study of its development and stability (Ruisel, 2000). Although it is possible to achieve some level of reliability in predicting IQ based on measurements undertook at an early age, the notion of stability of intelligence measured in children cannot be mentioned until after their third year of age (Krohn, Lamp, 1999) or, according to some authors, until the age of five (Cohen, Swerdlik, 1999). The two variables of the greatest relevance to the stability of the scores reached in intelligence tests, are the child' age at the time of the first measurement, and the interval between the test administrations. It applies generally that the older the child at the time of the first testing and the shorter the interval between the measurements, the greater the stability reached. This regularity was formulated by Honzik as early as 1948 (Honzik, Macfarlane, Allen, 1948, quote according to Gustafsson, Undheim, 1992) who herself calls it a ⎕truism of longitudinal studies of children" (Honzik, 1976). The studies of stability of intelligence measured show that following the tenth year of age stability can be considered as very high (Gustafsson, Undheim, 1992). For example Humphreys (1989) identified a correlation of 0.56 between the measurements using Wechsler's intelligence test between 2 and 9 years of age, whereas those taken between 9 and 15 years already reached 0.78. He inferred that the actual correlation value in older children between the abilities at two age levels equals approximately a number of 0.96, raised to the power by the number of years passed between the measurements.

The stability of the individual differences in intelligence further increases during adolescence and remains during adulthood. For example Arbuckle et al. (1998) found a high level of stability even with a 45-year interval between measurements; Owens (1966) identified a 0.79 correlation between the measurements using the Army Alfa test at 19 and 50 years of age etc. A remarkably high stability was also proved for an age interval of 11 - 77 – the correlation value when applying the Moray House Test method equalled 0.73 (Deary et al., 2000).

In the study presented (Jelínek, Klimusová, Blatný, 2003) we have focused on the stability of intelligence levels in different age groups during adolescence. Although the research up to now testifies to a very high stability of intelligence, its long-term levels are not constant. The changes between individual measurements may be caused by accidental deviations e.g. as a result of situation factors at the time of testing, they may, however, reflect long-range tendencies in intelligence development. Therefore we have tried to identify whether different trends in intellectual development exist, and have also taken into account gender differences.

At the beginning, 557 children born in Brno between the years 1961 and 1964 were included in the longitudinal research ⎕Mental development of school-age children in different social environments". After third year of age 453 individuals were followed (224 boys and 229 girls). The first measurement of intelligence took place at the age of 3, the last at the age of 15 of the research participants. Intelligence was measured using the Terman-Merrill test (T-M), the 2nd. Stanford revision of the Binet-Simon test, form L, at the ages of 3, 5, 7 and 10. The Wechsler intelligence test, WISC, was administered at the children's 8 and 12 years of age. At 14 the children were examined by the Meili Analytical Intelligence Test (AIT), form 1, and at 15 by the Amthauer I-S-T test, form A. At the time of data collection, an officially published handbook had only been available for the AIT (Smékal, 1970) and IST (Hrabal, 1973) tests. The other tests used were experimental versions.

As one of our goals was to study the course of intelligence development, we only used the data gathered from 364 individuals (of them 181 boys and 183 girls), which was available from at least three out of the four initial measurements. This group of 364 individuals was not different from the group of those eliminated as for the boys and girls proportion or the average level of intelligence measured by the Terman-Merrill test at three years.

The stability of the measured intelligence was determined by means of Pearson's coefficient of correlation between the data from the individual measurements (IQ scores). The coefficient was always adjusted to reliability levels of the different tools. The data on reliability levels had been obtained from the handbooks and other sources (e.g. Svoboda, 1999; Svoboda, Krejčířová, Vágnerová, 2001). For T-M, the value of 0.90 was used to correct the correlation coefficients, 0.85 for WISC, 0.70 for AIT and 0.90 for I-S-T. Table 4 presents the overview of the corrected correlation coefficients. It follows from the analysis of the measured intelligence stability that the higher the child's age and the shorter the interval between measurements, the higher is the measured intelligence stability (the interpretation is somewhat complicated by using different methods at older age levels).

Table 4. Correlation coefficients adjusted to reliability levels

	T-M3	T-M5	T-M7	WISC8	T-M10	WISC12	AIT14
T-M5	*0,676*						
T-M7	*0,648*	*0,784*					
WISC8	0,519	0,707	0,843				
T-M10	*0,466*	*0,610*	*0,761*	0,796			
WISC12	0,443	0,599	0,741	*0,896*	0,803		
AIT14	0,510	0,619	0,697	0,741	0,744	0,837	
I-S-T15	0,459	0,558	0,720	0,810	0,784	0,868	0,878

Note.: The numbers behind the abbreviated method names specify age at the time of the method administration. The numbers in italics are the correlation coefficients between the same method measurements at different ages.

Besides the examination of intelligence stability we have also analyzed the development trends of this characteristic, using a cluster analysis (non-hierarchical method, k-means) and an exploration factor analysis (Principal components analysis). We have standardized the values measured for each test with regard to the results reached by all the research participants in the given test at the relevant age levels, as they were mostly experimental test versions without corresponding standards available. As a result, values transformed to z-scores were included in the analysis.

Considering the fact that the results might have been distorted through the use of different methods of measurement, we have created a typology of intelligence development in two ways: one based only on the measurement results reached by the T-M test (at 3, 5, 7 and 10 years of age), and the other based on the measurements with all the tools (from 3 to 15 years of age). In both cases we have in gradual steps found the solutions for 3, 4, 5 and 6 individuals clusters. The solutions for types 3 to 5 rather reflected the differences in the levels of intelligence measured, therefore only the solutions for 6 types were interpreted, where the types are differentiated based on levels of intelligence as well as course of development. The centres of 6 types identified using the values from the T-M test are shown in diagram 1.

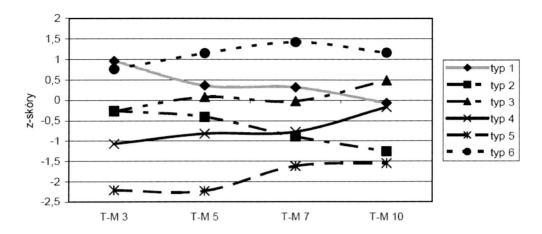

Graph 1. Course of intelligence development measured by T-M – solutions for 6 types.

Types 3, 4 and 5 are characterized by the increasing tendency of development, however, they differ mainly in the general level of performance. The most common type represented (27% of the group) is type 3 – with an average performance slightly increasing with age. Another type with a mildly ascending course of development is marked by number 4 (10%) in the graph; at the beginning the performance is by one standard deviation below the average and at the age of 10 years it reaches the average level of the whole group. The two aforementioned types are similar in profile shape and only differ in general levels. The early-stage ascending tendency is also observed in type 6 (18%), reaching its peak at the age of 7; this type involves generally above-average performances. Generally below-average performances, on the other hand, are characteristic for type 5 (6%) where a more pronounced increase occurs between the measurements at ages of 5 and 7 years.

Further we identified two types with the descending course of development and different levels of performance (types 1 and 2). The course of development for type 1 (21%) can be viewed as inverse to the course of type 4, beginning at a slightly above-average level, and at ten years this type ends up at the same average level as type 4. Type 2 (18%) is characterized by a continuously descending tendency toward below-average levels.

The types identified through the analysis based on all the measurements with the different methods are to a considerable degree identical to the types established based on the T-M test measured values, and it was found in this connection that the greatest dynamic of development takes place within the first 8 to 10 years of age of the child; this finding is consistent with the above results relating to intelligence development stability, which indicate a greater stability of the intelligence measured in the older children.

By means of factor analysis we have further extracted two non-rotated factors from 4 measurements using T-M test, from 3 to 10 years of age (see table 5), which together accounted for a large part of the variance (84.4%). The first factor is consistent with the performance levels, while the other reflects the linear trend in the course of development. If it gets positive values, the level gradually increases, while it decreases with negative values. Based on the factor scores we can describe trends of development for individuals in this way.

Table 5. Factor Analysis Results – non-rotated factors

	F1	F2
T-M 3 years of age	0.769	-0.551
T-M 5 years	0.859	-0.141
T-M 7 years	0.897	0.154
T-M 10 years	0.797	0.510
% of clarified dispersion	69.2%	15.2%

We wanted to know whether these trends reflect the typologies of individuals identified through the cluster analysis. Graph 2 shows that types 1-5 are well differentiated both in terms of level and increase or decrease (both factors are represented in unit of standard deviations), while the distinctive feature of type 6 is rather the level – as it includes both individuals with the decrease and increase tendencies.

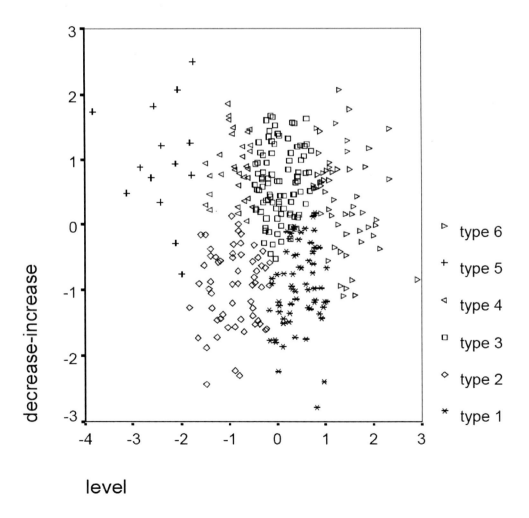

Graph 2. Relation between decrease-increase and level factors and types of individuals identified based on T-M test measurements.

In relation to the typology of intelligence development we focused on the proportions of boys and girls within the types identified. The greatest differences were found in type 1 and type 4. The number of girls is larger in type 1, characterized by the initial above-average level gradually descending to the average. On the other hand, a larger number of boys in relation to girls was included in type 4, with below-average performance at a younger age and its gradual increase reaching the average level. The results are consistent with the correlations between gender and the scores of the level (r=0.04, p=0.44) and decrease-increase (r=-0.15, p<0.01) factors. To conclude, girls and boys' average levels between 3 and 10 years of age do not differ, though in girls we have rather observed a slight decrease in performance while in boys the performance tends to increase as they grow older.

Study 3: Stability and Changes of Personality in Adolescence: Analysis at the Level of Personality Types

Personality stability is predominantly studied in adults – the lower limit in these researches is around twenty years of age. The focus on adult population is a logical one – according to many authors, the personality is fully formed only between 20th and 30th year of age and it is connected with the performing of social roles, especially in marriage and at work (e.g. Haan, Millsap, Hartka, 1986). Correlation coefficients found in adolescents are thus always lower than in adults (Costa, McCrae, 1997, Roberts, DelVicchio, 2000). Helson and Moane (1987) who studied personality changes of women between college and mid-adulthood indicate the age of 27 as an important divide.

In regard of a lower number of studies concerned with personality continuity during adolescence as compared with research on adult population, we focused our attention on the period of adolescence. We were interested to see whether the lower personality stability during this period would be confirmed, compared to coefficients discovered in adults, as indicated by above mentioned survey and meta-analytical studies (Costa, McCrae, 1997, Roberts, DelVicchio, 2000).

Second goal of our research was to assess the advantages of a typological approach to longitudinal data, which lately appears to be a suitable complement to the traditional correlative approach (Blatný, Urbánek, 2004). The study is at the same time an example of effective use of archival data, the gathering of which is, especially in cases of longitudinal research, particularly time-consuming (James, Paul, 1993).

The personality stability is usually ascertained in the framework of separate personality traits and its level is expressed by the value of correlation coefficient. However, the problem of correlation analysis is that it uses standardized variables and this means that it does not take into account the raw values of these variables but only their deviation from group average. Naturally, this brings useful information about the rate of prevalence of subjects in the selected group that are at the same time above (or below) the average in both surveys. If the correlation is lower that one (and this is the case for all of them in empirical data), there are nonetheless always subjects who are above average regarding one trait at a given age level, and below average at another age level (and vice-versa). This means that their relative position at an imaginary scale of the trait measured is unstable. Synchronous observation of an individual's position on the scales of several variables is enabled by some of the more advanced methods of correlation or regression analysis, e.g. analyses of canonical correlations (Cohen, Cohen, 1983), or procedures of cluster analysis.

Cluster analysis compared to the correlation analysis stems from the factual averages of items and enables the process of independent classification of informants into typological clusters acquired separately at individual age levels. The typological approach thus permits to observe not only the stability in light of personality types to which the subject belongs, but also the transfers between different types, i.e. the orientation of ongoing changes. This procedure is known also as Configural Frequency Analysis (Von Eye, 2002).

We decided to use the typological approach not only because of some of the above-described advantages, which it can offer as compared with the classical correlation analysis, but also because the question of convenience of using particular procedures in order to assess the level of stability of certain psychological variables must always be considered in the given theory's context. In our case, the relevant theory is Eysenck's approach of temperament, which connects the dimensional and the typological approach of temperament: the basic temperamental dimensions of extraversion and neuroticism are forming two orthogonal axes, into the constellation of which the classical temperamental types can be placed according to Eysenck: a stable introvert is phlegmatic, an unstable introvert is melancholic, a stable extravert is sanguineous and an unstable extravert is choleric. For this reason, the most suitable procedure for the personality stability observation appears to be one of the cluster analysis methods, whose result would be an empirical typology.

The sample was composed of 126 subjects (59 boys and 67 girls) with data available from personality measurement both at the age of 16 and 18. The personality typology (see below), however, was created on the basis of data coming from participants on given age levels (for the age of 16: N = 333, 168 boys and 165 girls, for the age of 18: N = 158, 81 boys and 77 girls – these numbers became even slightly lower during the analysis because of the existence of missing values).

The personality was measured three times in all, and by two instruments: at the age of 16 and 18 years by the Maudsley Personality Inventory (MPI, Eysenck 1959), at 17 years of age by Catell's 16 PF. For the purpose of our study, we used only the data obtained by the same method, i.e. Eysenck's MPI.

We observed the stability in the framework of individual personality traits by the correlation analysis. The level of personality traits' stability expressed by correlation coefficient is for the extraversion equal to 0.63 and for the neuroticism 0.71.

We created the personality typology by using a non-hierarchical method of cluster analysis (K-means cluster in software SPSS 10.0) on the MPI items. We obtained a solution for 2 to 6 types for the age of both 16 and 18 years. We decided to use four clusters since these clusters correspond relatively closely to the distribution into four temperamental types: sanguineous, phlegmatic, melancholic and choleric. Clusters denomination criterion was the average level of extraversion and of neuroticism in a given cluster. With regard to the distribution of trait introversion-extraversion, which is shifted towards the pole of extraversion, clusters of subjects were labeled as introverts although their level of introversion is close to the boundary and approaches the theoretical average of the scale (values from 23.0 to 24.3 with the scale range of 0 to 48). The results can be found in table 6.

How Does Personality Develop over the Life-Course

Table 6. Results of cluster analysis

		Extraversion		Neuroticism		
		m	SD	m	SD	N
16 years	Sang.	34.27	4.66	10.39	5.65	113
	Phlegm.	24.33	5.19	17.22	6.27	63
	Melan.	23.40	5.78	34.39	5.72	57
	Choler.	34.03	4.22	25.26	6.07	74
	Total	30.15	7.01	19.83	6.86	307
18 years	Sang.1	30.51	6.06	9.16	4.33	57
	Sang.2	32.39	6.28	17.72	3.95	36
	Melan.	23.00	5.87	32.36	6.52	25
	Choler.	34.26	3.52	29.63	5.62	27
	Total	30.38	6.72	19.10	10.71	145

At the age level of 16 and 18 years the results were – except for the order in which particular clusters were identified – very similar. The only one – but serious – difference is the fact that for the eighteen year old no cluster was identified corresponding to phlegmatic i.e. subjects characterized by a low level of both extraversion and neuroticism. On the contrary, two clusters of subjects with high extraversion and low neuroticism were identified, their only difference being the level of emotional stability. We labeled them as sanguineous 1 and sanguineous 2.

We analyzed the type stability on the basis of contingency tables, we checked statistical significance by χ^2 test. We checked whether individual subjects were included as regards analyses at both age levels into the same cluster. We created a contingence table containing the classification of subjects at the level of 16 years in lines and the classification at the level of 18 years in columns (table 3). Because of the missing data in samples of both age levels the scope of the select sample was considerably reduced – table 7 contains only subjects who were classified at both age levels.

Table 7. Analysis of the type stability: contingency table

		18 years				
		S1	S2	M	Ch	Total
16 years	Sang.	**29**	7	2	2	40
	Phleg.	16	7	3	2	28
	Melan.	2	5	**13**	4	24
	Chol.	2	11	6	**15**	34
	Total	49	30	24	23	126

Although the equivalence between mutually corresponding clusters is far from perfect, the relationship between lines and columns of this table is statistically significant ($\chi2$ = 70.099, df = 9; p < 0.001): number of subjects keeping their cluster membership is therefore statistically significant. Number of subjects who were at both age levels included into the cluster identified in the same way are highlighted in the table by bold print. In all 64 subjects are concerned which, out of the overall number of 126 subjects in this table, corresponds to 50.8%. For a visual view, we also present the results in a diagrammatized version (pictures no. 1 to 4).

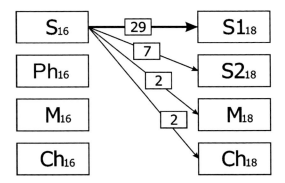

Picture 1. Results of of the type stability analysis: Sanguinics.

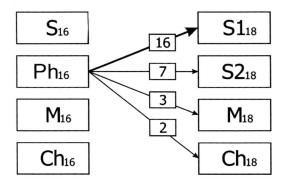

Picture 2. Results of of the type stability analysis: Phlegmatics.

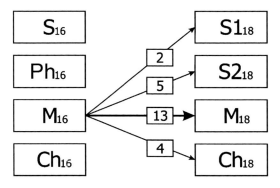

Picture 3. Results of of the type stability analysis: Melancholics.

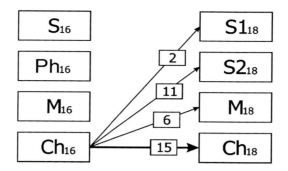

Picture 4. Results of of the type stability analysis: Cholerics.

Analysis of stability at the level of personality types corresponds to the results of correlation analysis: 51% of respondents keep their belonging to the type at the age of 16 and 18 years, whereas the proportion of subjects with persistent personality to subjects for whom a change occurred is statistically significant. As regards the personality changes, for 40% of subjects they are caused by a change of level of only one personality dimension: we identified this change as ⊏passage into related type". For instance, phlegmatic – stable introverts – become sanguineous – stable extraverts. The change in both dimensions is a very sporadic one, it happened in only 9% of cases; we identified this change as ⊏passage into opposite type". Thus, out of total number of changes 82% happen in only one of the dimensions and only 18% happen in both dimensions at the same time.

Our findings support observations concerning high personality stability, even in the adolescence period when the personality is still taking shape. We account for the high stability by biological bases of extraversion and neuroticism that express basic personality dispositions in the domain of emotionality and overall directivity. Changes found can thus be interpreted rather as developmental changes in which it is above all the change in adolescents´ social position that is reflected: in both personality traits changes happen predominantly towards socially desirable poles, i.e. towards extraversion and emotional stability, whereas this trend is stronger in case of extraversion. We account for this trend by social factors, be it higher need and frequency of social contacts, or self-presentation in accordance with social acceptability.

The study's results above all bring about the question of what, from the psychological point of view, can be considered as personality ⊏change". Analysis of stability at the level of personality types demonstrates that only less than one fifth of changes are occurring at the same time in both of personality dimensions observed (called passage into opposite type). The question remains whether the increase or decrease in one personality trait while the other's level remains stable can be considered as a "personality change".

Study 4: Personality Stability between Adolescence and Mid-Adulthood

The fact, that personality is highly stable in time, was supported with broad empirical evidence (Costa, McCrae, 1997, Roberts, DelVecchio, 2000). Current research therefore deals with more specific subjects of personality stability. One of these questions is stability and changes of individual components of personality. While the high stability is found namely in traits (i.e. personality dispositions both inborn or gained during the early stages of development), the area which is more vulnerable to changes is a socially anchored part of personality conceptualized within different theoretical approaches as self (self-concept), ego, or character. In the next study, we therefore focused on examining long-term stability of personality traits and of self-evaluations between adolescence and mid-adulthood (Blatný, Jelínek, Osecká, 2004).

We expected a higher stability of basic personality traits such as extraversion and neuroticism; however, we also expected certain continuity of self-concept. The bases of self-evaluation criteria are established in childhood and external standards for the evaluation of one's own behavior are internalized between 9 and 11 years of age into the personal self-regulating system (Higgins, 1991). General standards for self-appraisal and the evaluation it implies (negative vs. positive self-concept) are therefore anchored on a long-term basis in the image of one's own self. For them too a considerable stability can thus be supposed, even throughout such a turbulent period as adolescence.

We completed this study in those days when we were still searching for participants from the original study therefore the sample consists only 56 people (34 women and 22 men).

Personality characteristics of extraversion and neuroticism were assessed at the age of 16 by means of Maudsley Personality Inventory (Eysenck, 1959), and in adulthood by means of Eysenck Personality Inventory (Eysenck, Eysenck, 1964). Self-evaluation in adolescence was observed at the age of 14 by means of a research version of Coppersmith's Self-Esteem Inventory C.S.E.I. (Coopersmith, 1967). C.S.E.I. measures four elements of self-esteem – global self-esteem, academic self-esteem, social self-esteem (on the part of one's peers) and family self-esteem. The sum of all of these elements expresses total self-esteem. Varying self-concept in adulthood – self-esteem, self-efficacy, self-concept clarity – was determined by the following self-concept scales: Rosenberg Self-Esteem Scale (Rosenberg, 1965), Self-Concept Clarity Scale (Campbell, Trapnell, Heine, Katz, Lavalle, Lehman, 1996) and General Self-Efficacy Scale (Křivohlavý, Schwarzer, Jerusalem, 1993). Relationships between variables were observed by means of correlation analysis.

Table 8. Stability of personality traits: correlation analysis

| | | Adulthood | |
		Extraversion	Neuroticism
16 years	Extraversion	0,536**	-0,239
	Neuroticism	-0,255	0,414**

* Correlation is significant at the 0.05 level.
** Correlation is significant at the 0.01 level.

In table 8 are given the results of the personality traits´ stability analysis and table 9 contains results of the self-esteem's stability analysis. A relatively high stability was found as regards personality traits – correlation of 0.54 for extraversion and 0.41 for neuroticism. Correlations by their size correspond to correlation coefficients usually found at this age level, i.e. in the course of repeated measurement between adolescence and mid-adulthood: e.g. Roberts and DelVecchio (2000) allege on the basis of meta-analysis of 152 studies median correlation of personality stability at the age of 12 to 29 years r = 0,5.

Table 9. Stability of self-concept: correlation analysis

		Adulthood		
		Self-esteem	Self-efficacy	Self-concept clarity
14 years Self-esteem	Global	0,049	0,071	0,261
	Peer	0,190	0,162	0,201
	Family	0,194	-0,132	0,018
	Academic	0,072	0,166	0,280*
	Total	0,150	0,110	0,287*

* Correlation is significant at the 0.05 level.
** Correlation is significant at the 0.01 level.

There is a relatively little connection between self-concept in adolescence and in mid-adulthood. Evaluation of one's own self is apparently subject to external influences to a much higher degree than personality traits. Self-esteem in adolescence is moreover not related to global self-esteem in adulthood, but to self-concept clarity. Campbell (1990, Campbell, Trapnell, Heine, Katz, Lavalle, Lehman, 1996) defines self-concept clarity as the extent up to which the self-concept contents are clearly and convincingly defined, up to which they are internally consistent and temporarily stable. Self-concept clarity is, according to her, supported by a fair self-knowledge and it results in a higher self-esteem and an overall positive emotional approach to oneself. It is thus likely that a well-anchored identity is a unifying factor of the emotional relationship to oneself during the lifespan development.

Study 5: Subjective Perception of Personal Change

Although we were able to prove not only continuity between the child temperament and the adult personality, but also a considerable personality characteristics´ stability between adolescence and mid-adulthood, it also results from previous studies that people are changing: the highest observed correlations (around the value of 0.5) explain at most only one third of the variance in the first and the second measurement.

The general purpose of our study was to investigate, how the people themselves perceive whether and in which way they change, or whether or to which extent they remain the same (Blatný, Osecká, 2005). With the help of a narrative interview and free telling about the change of their own person, we tried to capture what objective methods are not able to reflect: sources, circumstances, and character of the change of personality, and personal conception and interpretation of these changes (i.e. what people consider as a change and how they understand it). This study was done only with part of the sample (56 subjects, 34 women and 22 men) as well as the previous one.

We used the lifeline technique (Čermák, 2004, Tyl, 1985). Respondents were asked to draw a line representing their lives and then were invited to tell a story about their lives. The interview is semi-structured. Respondents are gradually asked to speak about important events in their lives, about people who they considered important, and about their future prospects (they may also be asked to draw important points on the line). Their last task is to draw an ideal lifeline.

During the interview, we also asked a question about the change of personality. It was as follows: ⌐Do you have a feeling that you have changed (during your life)?" By asking the question about the change of their own person during the interview, we had the possibility to take into consideration the statements about the change in the context of the whole life story.

We decided to analyze only the interviews where the question about the change was raised explicitly. The final number of analyzed interviews was 41 (17 men and 24 women). The remaining fifteen interviews were excluded for the following two reasons: the first reason was technical problems such as a bad quality of the recording; the second, more frequent reason was the fact that the question about the change was not explicitly raised. Despite the fixed structure of the interview, we did not follow it rigidly. The development of the interview was guided by the nature of communication with participants. For example, in one case it was necessary to provide the respondent with a therapeutic intervention.

We assumed that most people would consider themselves stable, that they would perceive their life as coherent, and that they would feel the changes of their person only in some aspects of their personality. Our assumption may be expressed with the following statement: ⌐Yes, I have changed, but it depends..." Therefore, we expected the following development: Apart from the answer to the question about the change of personality (WHETHER they had changed), respondents would also speak about IN WHICH DOMAIN they had changed (i.e. ⌐domain" of the change).

During the analysis, it emerged that the statements contained another two categories of the description of the change. The first category was related to the source or cause of the change, i.e. WHY respondents had changed. We labeled this category ⌐causal agent" of the change. The second category was related to the process of the change, i.e. HOW the change had happened. This category was labeled ⌐mode" of the change. In table 10 the numbers of statements in individual categories are given. The question WHETHER the respondent had changed was of course answered by all participants, therefore it is not included in the table. According to our assumption, the majority of respondents said in which domain they had changed, the number of twenty-six respondents stated the cause of the change and twenty respondents stated the process of the change.

Table 10. Categories of telling about the change

	Categories of statements about personal change	Number of answers
Assumed	Domain of change	36
Revealed during analyzing	Causal agent of change	26
	Mode of change	20

Results of analysis of the category WHETHER are given in table 11. Thirty-four people said they had changed - their answer was YES. However, nobody said they had become somebody else or had been completely changed (including, for example, the change of a life style, break-up with some milieu etc.). They always referred to a partial change, saying: ⌐Yes, I have changed, but only partly." Six people said they had not changed, but they always added some specification. (⌐No..., but you know, it changes you, some kind of event, when a relative dies...now, when I have a child, I have a different view..."). These answers were labeled NO, BUT... and we consider them more or less subcategories of the answer YES. Only one person said he/she had not changed.

Table 11. Perception of personal stability and change

WHETHER Change had occurred	N	(%)
YES	34	83
NO, BUT...	6	15
NO	1	2

The number of 36 people said IN WHICH DOMAIN they had changed. The identified areas of changes correspond to psychological characteristics of an adult person (Říčan, 1990, Vágnerová, 2000). Individual areas of changes are given in table 12. The ‚plus" and ‚minus" indicate the direction of normative change - for example the change towards higher self-confidence, greater rationality etc. We have created only the category ‚activity" which contains not only physical activity (which might be subordinated to ‚physical changes"), but also social and overall activity (‚Now I am not as active as I used to be."). All changes are also interpretable in the terms of five-factor model of personality where the decreases in neuroticism (increase of calm, rationality, and self-confidence) and extraversion (activity), and increases in conscientiousness (responsibility, autonomy) and agreeableness (responsiveness) are suggested (Costa, McCrae, 1989).

Table 12. Domains of the change

In WHICH domain change had occurred		Trend	Number of statements		
			F	M	Total
Autonomy		(+)	4	2	6
Responsibility		(+)	1	3	4
Self –confidence		(+)	4	0	4
Calm		(+)	4	3	7
Rationality		(+)	4	1	5
Responsiveness		(+)	1	2	3
Values	Women	Towards family	4		7
	Men	Towards profession		3	
Bodily changes		(-)	1	2	3
Activity		(-)	1	1	2
Others			2	1	3

The causal agent of the change (WHY respondents had changed) was given by 26 respondents. Their reasons were either general (‚Life taught me a lesson" – 11 cases) or specific (childbirth, parenthood, partner's influence, divorce – 15 cases). Similarly, as the mentioned areas of changes correspond to psychological characteristics of an adult person, the causes of changes are represented by events that normally appear in the life of an adult person. The mentioned causes of changes correspond to life transitions, as showed for example by Settersten (2003) – e.g. leave home, marry, enter parenthood, exit full-time schooling, enter full-time work, settle on career/job.

The last category is the mode of the change (the answer to the question HOW). Again, there were two basic kinds of answers - the change as a turning point or a leap, and the change as a movement or development. The answer describing the change as developmental was more frequent (14 developmental interpretations vs. 6 turn interpretations) and in several cases was directly described as ⌐maturity" or ⌐growing up".

The fact that we asked about the feeling of change within the narrative interview enabled us to consider the change and its subjective perception in the context of the whole life story. This method revealed another important factor which influences the subjective perception of not only things which are generally common (such as getting married, having children, etc.), but also the things which they themselves *expected* to happen. For this conclusion we do not have as much quantifiable evidence as in the previous case, because this connection is mostly included in the statements implicitly. One of the respondents, whose statement was classified in the category *no, but* ..., expressed it explicitly in the following way: "I think that I am what I have expected from myself to be ...".

Moreover, the methodology used enabled us mainly to identify and describe also the particular cases of personality changes. Considering the small number of respondents, there were not many of them. Only in three cases the description or feeling of change markedly differed from the prevailing answers. Among these cases we also included the mentioned case of so-called "non-change" (the only one). Although we assumed a high stability of personality, this answer was really exceptional in the context of all other answers. Two other persons referred to an important personal change.

Despite the uniqueness of their personal stories, all three respondents had one thing in common: something unusual happened in their lives, or their whole life had an untypical, non-normative course. Of course, radical conclusions cannot be drawn from three cases but it is a support of the previous findings about the connection between life course and perceived personal change.

The case of the "non-change" is represented by a woman who – as the only one – has not got married yet, has not had a partner and still lives with her parents. However, the conclusion "no life changes, no personality changes" would be too simplistic. It follows from her story that she is quite satisfied with her lifestyle – her distinct characteristics are expressed by passivity and certain general immaturity. Therefore it is very likely that the cause of her lifestyle, along with her personal stability (or rather non-development), consist in personality resources or personality predispositions.

In the second case, the connections between life course and personal change are much clearer. This case was about a woman who – in her opinion – had changed a lot: "... I have a feeling that I have changed a lot, and not only once. When I was thinking about it, I had a feeling as if I had been experiencing a number of totally independent existences ...". She relates these individual existences to individual stages of her life: happy childhood, crises in adolescence, a relatively long period of loneliness after graduation which she bore with difficulties because she longed for a family, a period of happiness when she succeeded in finding a partner and starting a family, break-up of the marriage – divorce and current lawsuit about the custody of her children. The described changes correspond to characteristic changes of an adult in its direction, but they are more intensive and deeper. The woman herself says she has changed for the worse – she says she has become rougher and hardened. She sees the cause of changes not only in her life but also in her personality: "… I used to be a sort of person, … sort of non-assertive, sort of submissive … maybe these events made me level off with the majority of people". However, it is generally valid that non-normative life course is connected with non-normative personal change.

The last case is the story of a father whose seven-year-old son died. It is an event which is obviously not common (normative) and which is not normally expected. In the interview, the man called the son's death, "the most important event in his life". In this context he himself started to speak about how this event had changed him. We ourselves have not asked him any question about it. He sees his change in the revaluation of his priorities: he devotes himself to his family much more than in the past, he consciously lives "at present", and he does not "dramatise" troubles and difficulties as much as in the past. However, in general, middle-aged men are more focused on their profession and they are concerned with performance and achievement.

We can conclude that people reflect (perceive) that they change. In our sample, all people gave this answer – with the exception of one person. The majority of people perceive the change of their own person as normative, ie. corresponding to their age and life experience. *They are not somebody else*, they have only changed in certain aspects of their person. These normative changes of their own persons are linked with normative life events, or with life course. People consider as normal also those changes which they themselves expected to happen. Unusual personality change is connected with disrupting the principles of normativeness and expectability.

CONCLUSION

The longitudinal study of lifelong human development carried out in Brno is valuable for its duration in particular – almost fifty years have passed since its initiation. Moreover, children were observed since 3 months of age, which gives us unique possibility to connect information about early child's development with data on psychological characteristics in adult age.

Unfortunately, the study was negatively influenced by certain circumstances in time of its origination and process. Above all, it was not planned as prospective longitudinal study of human life-span development at the beginning. The original project, whose potential is utilised and further developed by the Brno Longitudinal Study of Life-Span Development, was dedicated to psychological development in childhood and adolescence and was terminated after the respondents have reached adulthood. Whereas the upper age limit had been originally set to 21 years, the research was stopped on the basis of an administrative decision three years earlier – this does not change the fact that termination of the study was pre-planned. Therefore, methods asking for ideas of their future, aims in life, personal and social perspectives were not included in the research.

A certain disadvantage lies in the fact that only limited range of psychological variables was monitored in the original longitudinal research of children. The research focused especially on cognitive development – intelligence was tested by various methods on different age levels ten times in total – less attention was paid to other variables which means they were assessed only once in some cases such as self-esteem in 14 years of age or they were not assessed at all such as conduct problems.

The methodological part of the project was influenced by two facts above all. First, it was an interdisciplinary study which was concerned not only with psychological, but especially paediatric, anthropological and social aspects of child's development; a number of psychological methods must have been necessarily limited. Second, the study originated in unfavourable historical context. Former Czechoslovakia (a state which split into the Czech Republic and Slovakia in 1992) became totalitarian state and Soviet satellite after the communist coup in 1948 for a long time. Academic activity, in humanitarian and social sciences especially, was dictated by Marxist-Leninist ideology, free competition of ideas was virtually liquidated and communication with colleagues from the "West" (which means the democratic countries) was drastically limited. Ideas from the Western world including scientific projects and cooperation were penetrating the rigid Stalinist country just slowly. Therefore it must be said that in the 1960s the project had somewhat obsolete research design, which followed the basis of findings of the turn of the 1940s and the 1950s. For comparison, the Jyväskylä Longitudinal Study of Personality and Social Development led by Lea Pulkkinen originates in the second half of the 1960s, which included much broader spectrum of variables from the beginning.

Also the last of the handicaps of the Brno longitudinal study of life-span development is influenced by historical circumstances. It is the fact that participants of the original study were addressed as late as twenty years after its termination, so we don't have data from the period of their early adulthood, quite crucial period in terms of lifelong development, at disposal. Even though authors of the study dealt with the idea of its renewal at the beginning of the 1990s, the extensive transformation of Czech economy after the fall of the "Iron Curtain" was in progress at that time and there was lack of finances for such projects. Not until the establishment of scientific foundations in the second half of the 1990s it was possible to put the project into life.

Considering the circumstances mentioned above, the study does not provide us with detailed image of nature and conditions of personality development and above all it does not record the continuum of these changes. However, albeit the Brno longitudinal study of life-span development is rather a series of partial substudies, its indisputable quality lies in studying the human development on the basis of data acquired by repeated assessment of the same individuals. In other words, the conclusions about human development provided by the study do not represent deduction from entirely separate studies with various research samples, but rigorous approximation derived from life paths of longitudinally observed individuals.

What conclusions can we draw from the presented studies?

People are developing and changing and they are aware of these changes (Study 5). At the same time, they see continuity in their life stories - they are not becoming somebody else, they are only changing in certain aspects of their person. The changes reported by our participants are represented rather by shifts and alterations than by turns and transformations. Moreover, the majority of people perceive the change of their own person as normative, ie. corresponding to their age and life experience. In case unusual personality changes do occur, they are connected with non-normative and/or unexpectable life course.

Innate characteristics and capabilities – temperament traits and intelligence – preserve great stability in time (Study 2, 3). We also confirmed a pattern observed earlier showing that the shorter the interval between individual assessments, the higher the stability of a trait or capability. Nevertheless, even between adolescence and mid-adulthood, in spite of twenty-year interval, personality traits of extraversion and neuroticism preserve high stability expressed by 0.54 or 0.41 correlation coefficients (Study 4). Moreover, different versions of the Eysenck's Personality Inventory were used to assess the traits (Maudsley Personality Inventory in adolescence and Eysenck Personality Inventory in adulthood) and thus it is possible that relations between personality in adolescence and personality in adulthood are still underestimated.

Adult personality can be predicated even on the basis of early child temperament over forty years (Study 1). This partial study was first to give empirical evidence of continuity between child temperament and adult personality that was only supposed so far.

Socially constructed part of personality is subject to changes to a much larger extent. Study 4 shows that there is a relatively little connection between self-concept in adolescence and in mid-adulthood. Nature of these changes is approached in Study 5. Regarding question about perceived change of their own personality, our participants mentioned mostly changes in the sphere of interpersonal relations, attitudes, values and self-regard: these statements constituted seven of ten identified categories in total, the remaining three statements were concerned with physical changes and temperament (decrease of neuroticism – "calming down" – and activity).

We encounter two approaches explaining normative changes of personality traits in adulthood at present. According to Five Factor Theory (McCrae, Costa, 1999; McCrae, Costa, Ostendorf, Angleitner, Hrebickova, Avia, Sanz, Sánchez-Bernardos, Kusdil, Woodfield, Saunders, Smith, 2000), people are genetically predisposed to change. Authors based their theory on the fact that people across cultures show normative developmental changes during the life course, such as the tendency to become more agreeable, conscientious, and emotionally stable. On the contrary, the Social Investment theory proposes that personality development is largely the result of experiences in universal social roles in young adulthood (Helson, Kwan, John, Jones, 2002; Roberts, Wood, Smith 2005).

Personality changes that we identified in our research are indeed interpretable in the terms of five-factor model of personality and they correspond with anticipated trends: the decreases in neuroticism (increase of calm, rationality, and self-confidence) and extraversion (activity), and increases in conscientiousness (responsibility, autonomy) and agreeableness (responsiveness) (Costa, McCrae, 1989; McCrae, Costa, 1999). However, our participants explain these changes by normative life-course and canonical events - childbirth, parenthood, partner's influence, divorce. Thus it seems that our result rather supports the Social Investment Theory.

In general, our findings indicate – in accordance with Funder et al. (1996) – that the essence of human development does not lie in consistency, but coherency. This coherence is the result of a process by which early experiences form a template for the interpretation of later experiences in life, and by which aspects of personality which develop early can affect how people select and change their social environments. Hence, the issue of personality coherence represents dominant topic of current psychology across individual disciplines and theoretical approaches.

ACKNOWLEDGMENTS

The study is a part of Research project of Institute of Psychology, Academy of Sciences of the Czech Republic (identification code: AV0Z70250504) and was supported by the Czech Science Foundation (Grant No. 406/06/1408).

REFERENCES

Arbuckle, T. Y., Maag, U., Pushkar, D., & Chaikelson, J. (1998). Individual Differences in Trajectory of Individual Development Over 45 Years of Adulthood. *Psychology and Aging, 13,* 663-675.

Asendorpf, J. B. (1992). Beyond stability: Predicting inter-individual differences in intra-individual change. *Europen Journal of Personality, 6,* 103-117.

Baltes, P.B. (1997/2003). On the incomplete architecture of human ontogeny: Selection, optimization, and compensation as foundation of developmental theory. In U.M. Staudinger, U. Lindenberger (Eds.), *Understanding human development: Dialogues with life span psychology* (pp. 17-43). Boston: Kluwer Academic Publishers.

Bandura, A. (1977). Self-efficacy: Toward a unified theory of behavioral change. *Psychological Review, 84,* 191-215.

Bandura, A. (1999). Social cognitive theory of personality. In D. Cervone, & Y. Shoda (Eds), *The coherence of personality* (pp. 185-241). New York/London: The Guilford Press.

Blatný, M., Jelínek, M., Blížkovská, J.. & Klimusová, H. (2004). Personality correlates of self-esteem and life satisfaction. *Studia Psychologica, 46,* 97–104.

Blatný, M., Jelínek, M., & Osecká, T. (2001). Present and perspectives of the project ⌐Stability, variability and prediction of psychological characteristics in adulthood: Taking up the longitudinal research of children" (article in Czech). In D. Vobořil, & H. Klimusová (Eds.), *Konference Sociální procesy a osobnost: sborník abstrakt.* Zprávy – Psychologický ústav, Vol. 7, No. 2. Brno: Psychologický ústav.

Blatný, M., Jelínek, M., & Osecká, T. (2004). The stability of personality between adolescence and middle adulthood: Personality traits and self-concept (article in Czech). In I. Ruisel, D. Lupták, & M. Falat (Eds.), *Sociálne procesy a osobnosť 2004.* Bratislava: Ústav experimentálnej psychológie SAV (CD-ROM).

Blatný, M., Jelínek, M., & Osecká, T. (2005). The possibilities of the prediction of adult personality from data from childhood and adolescence: Main Results of Brno Longitudinal Study on Life-Span Development (article in Czech). In I.Sarmány-Schuller, & M.Bratská (Eds.), *Psychológia pre život - alebo ako je potrebná metanoia* (pp. 50-62). Dunajská Streda: SPS pri SAV / Pelikán.

Blatný, M., Jelínek, M., & Osecká, T. (2007), Assertive toddler, self-efficacious adult: Child temperament predicts personality over 40 years. *Personality and Individual Differences, 43,* 2127-2136.

Blatný, M., & Osecká, T. (2005). Subjective perception of personal change. In N. Kelly, C. Horrocks, K. Milnes, B. Roberts, & D. Robinson (Eds.), *Narrative, Memory & Everyday Life* (pp. 59-67). Huddersfield, University of Huddersfield Press.

Blatný, M., & Urbánek, T. (2004). Personality stability and change in adolescence: The analysis on the level of personality types (article in Czech). *Československá psychologie, 48,* 289-297.

Buss, A. H. (1991). The EAS theory of temperament. In J. Strelau, & A. Angleitner (Eds.), *Explorations in temperament: International perspectives on theory and measurement* (pp. 43-60). New York: Plenum Press.

Buss, A. H., & Plomin, R. (1984). *Temperament: Early developing personality traits.* Hillsdale, NJ: Erlbaum.

Block, J. (1996). Studying personality the long way. In D.C.Funder, R. D. Parke, C. Tomlinson-Keasey, & K. Widaman (Eds), *Studying lives through time* (second printing, pp. 9-41). Washington, DC: American Psychological Association.

Campbell, J.D. (1990). Self-esteem and clarity of self-concept. *Journal of Personality and Social Psychology, 59,* 538-549.

Campbell, J. D., Trapnell, P. D., Heine, S. J., Katz, I. M., Lavalle, L. F., & Lehman, D. R. (1996). Self-concept clarity: Measurement, personality correlates, and cultural boundaries. *Journal of Personality and Social Psychology, 70,* 141-156.

Caspi, A, (2000). The child is father of the man: Personality continuities from childhood to adulthood. *Journal of Personality and Social Psychology, 78,* 158-172.

Caspi, A., Harrington, H., Milne, B., Amell, J.W., Theodore, R.F., & Moffitt, T.E. (2003). Children's behavioral styles at age 3 are linked to their adult personality traits at age 26. *Journal of Personality, 71,* 495-513.

Caspi, A., Moffitt, T. E., Newman, D. L., & Silva, P. A. (1996). Behavioral observations at age 3 predict adult psychiatric disorders: Longitudinal evidence from a birth cohort. *Archive of General Psychiatry, 53,* 1033-1039.

Cloninger, C.R. (2003). Completing the psychobiological architecture of human personality development: Temperament, character, and coherence. In U.M. Staudinger, & U. Lindenberger (Eds.), *Understanding human development: Dialogues with life span psychology* (pp. 159-181). Boston: Kluwer Academic Publishers.

Cohen, J., & Cohen, P. (1983). *Applied multiple regression/correlation analysis for the behavioral sciences* (Second edition). Hillsdale, NJ: Lawrene Erlbaum.

Cohen, R. J., & Swerdlik, M. E. (1999). *Psychological assessment and testing* (4th ed.). Mountain View, CA: Mayfield.

Coopersmith, S. (1967). *The Antecedents of Self-Esteem.* San Francisco, CA: W.H. Freeman & Company.

Costa, P.T.Jr., & McCrae, R.R. (1989). *The NEO-PI/NEO-FFI manual supplement.* Odessa (FL): Psychological Assessment Resources.

Costa, P. T., Jr., & McCrae, R. R. (1992). *Revised NEO Personality Inventory (NEO PI-R) and the NEO Five-Factor Inventory (NEO-FFI) professional manual.* Odessa, FL: Psychological Assessment Resources.

Costa, P.T.Jr., & McCrae, R.R. (1997). Longitudinal stability of adult personality. In R. Hogan, J. Johnson, & S. Briggs (Eds.), *Handbook of personality psychology* (pp. 269-290). New York: Academic Press.

Costa, P. T., Jr., & McCrae, R. R. (2001). A theoretical kontext for adult temperament. In T. D. Wachs, & G. A. Kohnstamm (Eds), *Temperament in context* (pp. 1-21). Mahwah, NJ: Lawrence Erlbaum Associates.

Czech Statistical Office (2007). *Population and Housing Census March 1, 2001.* http://www.czso.cz/eng/redakce.nsf/i/population_and_housing_census

Čermák, I. (2004). "Genres" of life -stories. In D. Robinson, Ch. Horrocks, N. Kelly, & B. Roberts (Eds.), *Narrative, memory, and identity: Theoretical and methodological issues* (pp.211-221). Huddersfield, University of Huddersfield Press.

Deary, I. J., Whalley, L. J., Lemmon, H., Crawford, J. R., & Starr, J. M. (2000). The stability of individual differences in mental ability from childhood to old age: Follow-up of the 1932 Scottish Mental Survey. *Intelligence 28,* 49-55.

Demick, J., & Andreoletti, C. (2003). *Handbook of adult development.* New York: Kluwer Academic/Plenum Publishers.

Diener, E., Suh, E. M., Lucas, R. E., & Smith, H. L. (1999). Subjective well-being: Three decades of progress. *Psychological Bulletin, 125,* 276-302.

Elder, G.H.Jr., Kirpatrick Johnson, M., & Crosnoe, R. (2003). The emergence and development of life course theory. In J.T. Mortimer, M.J. Shanahan (Eds.), *Handbook of the life course* (pp. 3-19). New York: Kluwer Academic/Plenum Publishers.

Erez, A., & Judge, T. A. (2001). Relationship of core self-evaluations to goal setting, motivation, and performance. *Journal of Applied Psychology, 86,* 1270-1279.

Eysenck, H.J. (1959). *Manual of the Maudsley personality inventory.* London, University Press.

Ford, D.H., & Lerner, R.M. (1992). *Developmental systems theory: An integrative approach.* Newbury Park: Sage Publications.

Funder, D.C., Parke, R.D., Tomlinson-Keasey, C., & Widaman, K. (1996). Preface. In D.C. Funder, R.D. Parke, C. Tomlinson-Keasey, & K. Widaman (Eds.), *Studying lives through time: Personality and development* (pp. XIII-XV). Washington, DC: American Psychological Association.

Giele, J.Z., & Elder, G.H.Jr. (1998). Life course research: Development of a field. In J.Z. Giele, & G.H.Jr. Elder (Eds.), *Methods of life course research: Qualitative and quantitative approaches* (pp. 5-27). London: Sage Publications.

Goldsmith, H. H., Lemery, K. S., Nazan, A., & Buss, K. A. (2000). Temperamental substrates of personality development. In V. J. Molfese, & D. L. Molfese (Eds), *Temperament and personality development across the life span* (pp. 1-32). Mahwah, NJ: Lawrence Erlbaum Associates.

Gustafsson, J. E., & Undheim, J. O. (1992). Stability and change in broad and narrow factors of intelligence from ages 12 to 15 years. *Journal of Educational Psychology, 84,* 141-149.

Halverson, C. F., & Deal, J. E. (2001). Temperamental change, parenting, and the family context. In T. D. Wachs, & G. A. Kohnstamm, (Eds), *Temperament in context* (pp. 61-79). Mahwah, NJ: Lawrence Erlbaum Associates.

Haan, N., Millsap, R., Hartka, E. (1986). As time goes by: Change and stability in personality over fifty years. *Psychology and Aging, 1,* 220-232.

Hampson, S. E., Goldberg, L. R., Vogt, T. M., & Dubanoski, J. P. (2006). Forty years on: Teachers' assessments of children's personality traits predict self-reported health behaviors and outcomes at midlife. *Health Psychology, 25,* 57-64.

Helson, R. (1996). Comparing longitudinal studies of adult development: Toward a paradigm of tension between stability and change. In D.C. Funder, R.D. Parke, C. Tomlinson-

Keasey, & K. Widaman (Eds.), *Studying lives through time: Personality and development* (pp. 93-119). Washington, DC: American Psychological Association.

Helson, R., Kwan, V. S. Y., John, O. P., & Jones, C. (2002). The growing evidence for personality change in adulthood: Findings from research with personality inventories. *Journal of Research in Personality, 36,* 287–306.

Helson, R., & Moane, G. (1987). Personality change in women from college to midlife. *Journal of Personality and Social Psychology, 53,* 176-186.

Higgins, E.T. (1991). Development of self-regulatory and self-evaluative processes: Costs, benefits, and trade-offs. In M.R. Gunnar, & L.A. Sroufe, (Eds.), *Self-processes in development: The Minnesota Symposium on Child Development* (vol. 23). Hillsdale, NJ: Erlbaum.

Honzik, M. P. (1976). Value and limitations of infant tests: An overview. In M. Lewis (Ed.), *Origins of intelligence: Infancy and early childhood.* New York: Plenum Press.

Honzik, M. P., Macfarlane, J. W., & Allen, L. (1948). The stability of mental test performance between two and eighteen years. *Journal of Experimental Education, 17,* 309-324.

Hrabal, V. (1973). *TSI (R. Amthauer) Manual* (in Czech). Bratislava, Psychodiagnostické a didaktické testy.

Humphreys, L. G. (1989). Intelligence: Three kinds of instability and their consequences for policy. In R. L. Linn (Ed.), *Intelligence: Measurement theory and public policy.* Urbana: University of Illinois Press.

James, J.B., & Paul, E.L. (1993). The value of archival data for new perspectives on personality. In D.C. Funder, R.D. Parke, C. Tomlinson-Keasey, K. Widaman, (Eds.), *Studiing lives through time: Personality and development* (pp. 45-64). Washington DC: American Psychological Association.

Jelínek, M., Klimusová, H., & Blatný, M. (2003). Stability and development trends of intelligence in children aged 3-15 (in Czech). *Československá psychologie, 47,* 392-404.

Klein, H. A. (1992). Temperament and self-esteem in late adolescence. *Adolescence, 27,* 689-694.

Křivohlavý, J., Schwarzer, R., & Jerusalem, M. (1993). General Self-Efficacy Scale (in Czech). http://www.yorku.ca/faculty/academic/schwarze/czec.htm, last accessed in Apr 2002.

Krohn, E. J., & Lamp, R. E. (1999). Stability of the SB:FE and K-ABC for young children from low-income families: A 5-year longitudinal study. *Journal of School Psychology 37,* 315-332.

Langmeier, J., Langmeier, M., & Krejčířová, D. (1998). *Developmental psychology* (book in Czech). Prague: H&H.

Lemme, B.H. (1999). *Development in adulthood* (2nd edit). Boston: Allyn and Bacon.

Lerner, R.M. (2002). *Concepts and theories of human development* (3rd edit). London: Erlbaum.

Magnusson, D. (1999). Holistic interactionism: A perspective for research on personality development. In L.A. Pervin, & O.P. John, (Eds.), *Handbook of personality: Theory and research* (2nd ed., 219-247). New York: Guilford Press.

McAdams, D. (1993). *The stories we live by. Personal myths and the making of the self.* New York: The Guildford Press.

McCrae, R. R., & Costa, P. T., Jr. (1999). A Five-Factor theory of personality. In L.A. Pervin, & O.P. John, (Eds.), *Handbook of personality: Theory and research* (2nd ed., pp. 139-153). New York: Guilford Press.

McCrae, R. R., Costa, P. T., Jr., Ostendorf, F., Angleitner, A., Hrebickova, M., Avia, M. D., Sanz, J., Sánchez-Bernardos, M. L., Kusdil, M. E., Woodfield, R., Saunders, P. R., & Smith, P. B. (2000). Nature over nurture: Temperament, personality, and life span development. *Journal of Personality and Social Psychology, 78,* 173-186.

Morizot, J., & Le Blanc, M. (2003). Continuity and change in personality traits from adolescence to midlife: A 25-year longitudinal study comparing representative and adjudicated men. *Journal of Personality, 71,* 705-755.´

Owens, W. A. (1966). Age and mental abilities: A second adult follow-up. *Journal of Educational Psychology, 57,* 311-325.

Pavot, W., & Diener, E. (1993). Review of the SatisfactionWith Life Scale. *Psychological Assessment, 5,* 164-172.

Pulkkinen, L. (1996). Female and male personality styles: A typological and developmental analysis. *Journal of Personality and Social Psychology, 70,* 1288-1306.

Roberts, B. W., & DelVecchio, W. F. (2000). The rank-order consistency of personality from childhood to old age: A quantitative review of longitudinal studies. *Psychological Bulletin, 126,* 3-25.

Roberts, B.W., Helson, R., & Klohnen, E. C. (2002). Personality development and growth in women across 30 years: Three perspectives. *Journal of Personality, 70,* 79-102.

Roberts, B. W., Wood, D., & Smith, J. L. (2005). Evaluating Five Factor Theory and social investment perspectives on personality trait development. *Journal of Research in Personality, 39,* 166-184.

Rokeach, M. (1973). *The Nature of Human Values.* New York: Free Press.

Rosenberg, M. (1965). *Society and the adolescent self-image.* Princeton: Princeton University Press.

Ruisel, I. (2000). *Basics of psychology of intelligence.* (book in Czech). Praha: Portál.

Říčan, P. (1990). *The Way through Life* (book in Czech). Praha: Panorama.

Říčan, P., & Ženatý, J. (1988). *Theory and practice of projective techniques* (book in Czech). Bratislava: Psychodiagnostické a didaktické testy.

Settersten, R.A.Jr. (2003). Age structuring and the rhytm of the life course. In J.T. Mortimer, & M.J. Shanahan (Eds.), *Handbook of the life course* (pp. 81-98). New York: Kluwer Academic/Plenum Publishers.

Shiner, R. L., Masten, A. S., & Tellegen, A. (2002). A developmental perspective on personality in emerging adulthood: Childhood antecedents and concurrent adaptation. *Journal of Personality and Social Psychology, 83,* 1165-1177.

Smékal, V. (1970). *Analytical Intelligence Test* (manual in Czech). Bratislava: Psychodiagnostické a didaktické testy.

Svoboda, M. (1999). *Psychodiagnostics of adults* (book in Czech). Praha: Portál.

Svoboda, M., Krejčířová, D., & Vágnerová, M. (2001). *Child and adolescent psychodiagnostics* (book in Czech). Praha: Portál.

Tarlow, E. M., & Haaga, D. A. F. (1996). Negative self-concept: Specifity to depressive symptoms and relation to positive and negative affectivity. *Journal of Research in Personality, 30,* 120-127.

Tyl, J. (1985). *Time horizons: Contribution to the concept of life-time and methods of its research* (Thesis in Czech). Praha, Filozofická fakulta.

Vágnerová, M. (2000). *Developmental psychology* (book in Czech). Praha: Portál.

Viken, R. J., Rose, R. J., Kaprio, J., & Koskenvuo, M. (1994). A developmental genetic analysis of adult personality: Extraversion and neuroticism from 18 to 59 years of age. *Journal of Personality and Social Psychology, 66,* 722-730.

Von Eye, A. (2002). *Configural Frequency Analysis.* Hillsdale, NJ: Lawrence Erlbaum Assoc Inc.

Wapner, S., & Demick, J. (2003). Adult development: The holistic, developmental, and systems-oriented perspective. In J.Demick, & C. Andreoletti, (Eds.), *Handbook of adult development* (pp. 63-84). New York: Kluwer Academic/Plenum Publishers.

Watson, D., Suls, J., & Haig, J. (2002). Global self-esteem in relation to structural models of personality and affectivity. *Journal of Personality and Social Psychology, 83,* 185-197.

Wechsler, D. (1999). *WAIS III – experimentální verze.* Brno: Psychodiagnostika.

In: Social Development
Editor: Lynda R. Elling

ISBN: 978-1-60741-612-8
© 2009 Nova Science Publishers, Inc.

Chapter 11

DISRUPTION OF SOCIAL DEVELOPMENT IN CHILDREN WITH AUTISM SPECTRUM DISORDERS

Gianluca Esposito[1] and Sergiu P. Paşca[2]

[1] Department of Cognitive Science, University of Trento, Italy
[2] Center for Cognitive and Neural Studies (Coneural), Cluj-Napoca, Romania

ABSTRACT

During the last few decades, a number of studies have emphasized that children who exhibit signs of developmental delay often display abnormal trajectories in their social development. Among these conditions, Autism Spectrum Disorders (ASD) stand as a special case. ASD is a complex neuropsychiatric group of disorders that affects the brain's typical development of social and communication skills to varying degrees. Common features of ASD include impairment in social interaction, communication (both verbal and nonverbal), information processing, and patterns of behavior that are restricted and repetitive. One of the signature aspects of ASD points to the social-skills deficit. Most children with ASD have tremendous difficulty engaging in everyday social interaction and seem unable to form emotional bonds with others. Research has suggested that, although children with ASD are attached to their caregivers, their expressions of attachment are unusual and difficult to interpret. Furthermore, children with ASD have difficulty in understanding unspoken social cues, which are fundamental for social interaction (e.g. a smile or a grimace). Children with ASD also have difficulties with regulating their emotions and lack the ability to attribute mental states to themselves and others, making them unable to comprehend or predict other people's responses to their own actions. The aim of this article is to review several watershed studies that have investigated the disruption of social development in ASD, and to close with a presentation of current knowledge about the underlying neurobiology of social abnormalities that characterize this spectrum of disorders.

Keywords: Social Development, Autism Spectrum Disorders, Neurobiology.

INTRODUCTION

Autism Spectrum Disorders (ASD) is a complex neuropsychiatric group of disorders that affects the brain's typical development of social and communication skills to varying degrees. Common features of ASD include impairment in social interaction, communication (both verbal and nonverbal), information processing, and patterns of behavior that are restricted and repetitive. The social-skills deficit is a signature characteristic of ASD that stands prominent. Most children with ASD have tremendous difficulty engaging in everyday social interaction and seem unable to form emotional bonds with others. Research has suggested that, although children with ASD are attached to their caregivers, their expression of attachment is unusual and difficult to interpret. Furthermore, children with ASD generally do not respond to unspoken social cues, which are fundamental for social interaction (e.g., a smile or a grimace). Children with ASD show an inability to regulate their emotions and lack the capacity to attribute mental states to themselves and others, making them unable to comprehend or predict other people's responses to their own actions. These traits are more than likely present since birth, but become more evident towards the end of the first year of life as the expectations for certain social interaction become more complex and nuanced over time. These children seem incapable of sharing their attention with others and are inept at reacting in a congruent fashion to others' emotions (Gallese, 2006). They have also great difficulties in recognizing human facial expressions or in displaying imitative behaviors. All of these early manifestations of autism share a common root: the cognitive skills required to establish social relationships (the primary purpose of social development) are seriously impaired.

Starting from these considerations, the aim of this chapter is to review studies that have investigated the disruption of social development evidenced in ASD. In the next pages, we will describe different hypotheses, which in the last two decades have been employed in approaching the social deficit in children with ASD; in particular we will discuss:

1. The Deficit of Theory of Mind Hypothesis
2. The Weak Central Coherence Hypothesis
3. The Mirror Neurons Hypothesis
4. The Neurobiological Bases of Social Dysfunction in ASD.

1. THE DEFICIT OF THEORY OF MIND HYPOTHESIS

The capacity to predict the behavior of others provides considerable benefits to individuals. This skill also allows individuals to influence and manipulate the behavior of their conspecifics (Whiten & Byrne, 1997; Gallese, 2006) or to achieve higher levels of social exchange. In order to predict others' behaviors, individuals need a capacity for attributing mental states—intentions, beliefs, and desires—to others. This capacity has been defined as Theory of Mind (ToM, Premack & Woodruff, 1978), and it is central to typical social development. To attribute mental states to others and consider these mental states as causes of behavior means also to represent the mind as a "generator of representations" (Perner & Leekman, 2008). In turn, to attribute this capacity to the mind implies an understanding that others' mental representations of the world do not necessarily reflect reality and can differ from individual to individual. This also means that such a "mind" is able to maintain, simultaneously, different representations of the world (Leslie, 1987; Leslie et al, 2004). In this view, one of the staple achievements of social development is acquiring the ability to attribute false belief. This implies the recognition that others can have beliefs about the world that are wrong.

Several studies have shown that reasoning associated with beliefs and desires begins very early during child development. The early belief–desire reasoning has been largely researched through experimental setup, usually requiring subjects to perform a false-belief task and/or its variants. The initial false-belief task (used to test ToM ability) was developed by Wimmer and Perner (1983). Numerous versions have been proposed, but the Sally-Anne task is probably the most common version of the false-belief task (Baron-Cohen & Belmonte, 2005). In this task, an experimenter uses two dolls, "Sally" and "Anne." Sally has a basket and Anne has a box. Experimenters show to the child a simple skit in which Sally puts a marble in her basket and then leaves the scene. While Sally is away and cannot watch, Anne takes the marble out of Sally's basket and puts it into her box. At that point, Sally returns and the subjects are asked where they think Sally will look for her marble. Children are considered to pass the test if they understand that Sally will most likely look inside her basket before realizing that her marble isn't there. This means that, in order to pass the task, children must be able to understand that another's mental representation of the situation is different from their own, and subjects must be able to predict behavior based on that understanding. In this case, they would know that Sally has a false belief. The false-belief task has also been modified so as to be sure that children who fail the tasks do so because they lack the ToM ability required, and not because the tasks are too cognitively demanding for them. The inability to pass the false-belief task at four years of age is usually considered as an indicator of developmental delay.

Research about ToM in a number of different populations (human and animal, adults and children, typically and atypically-developing) have been conducted since the first paper by Premack and Woodruff: "Does the chimpanzee possess theory of mind?" These studies emphasize ToM to be an innate, genetically determined ability in humans. Yet this ability requires stimulus in the way of social experiences over the years in order to be honed. However, some studies also consider ToM as a continuum, meaning that, in the whole population, different individuals may present more or less competences in ToM. This spectrum ranges from very complete and accurate to minimally functional competences in ToM, and people with ASD may be placed in the lower part of this continuum.

Individuals with ASD have been sometimes referred to as mind-blinded because of the difficulties they encounter with perspective taking (i.e., the ability to understand scenarios from another's perspective). The first paper which suggested that children with ASD have problems in employing ToM adequately was published in 1985 (Baron-Cohen, Leslie & Frith). Since 1985, studies have highlighted several times that children with ASD exhibit particular difficulties with tasks that require the child to understand another person's beliefs (Leslie et al, 2004). Subsequently, some functional neuroimaging studies, investigating the putative brain regions active during Theory-of-mind tasks, found that the medial prefrontal cortex and the temporoparietal junction may play a crucial role (Adolph, 2009). Nonetheless, a number of studies that aimed at investigating the neural substrates of ToM in autism have confirmed the deficits in the medial prefrontal and cingulate cortex, but other studies failed to do so.

In summary, recent empirical findings suggest this hypothesis as being inadequate to fully address the all the core ASD deficits. Furthermore, reports of high-functioning individuals with ASD pose as another objection to the hypothesis of ASD as being a mere deficit of Theory of Mind (e.g. Grandin, 2006; see Gallese, 2001). More studies are needed in order to clearly delineate the brain regions that process the ToM abilities, and the degree to which these neural pathways are affected in children with ASD.

2. THE WEAK CENTRAL COHERENCE HYPOTHESIS

The Weak Central Coherence theory (WCC) suggests that a specific cognitive style, related to specific perceptual skills, leads to a limited ability of understanding scenarios and behavior in relation to their context. In short, the WCC theory suggests a compromised capacity "to see the big picture." This impairment has often been described as the core disruption in ASD. By means of this theory, qualifying how children with ASD can show high abilities in subjects like math and at the same time have trouble with language and social skills becomes possible. For this reason, the WCC theory has been placed among the more prominent models for attempting to explain the core deficits particular to ASD. Two different neural models have been proposed with relation to WCC processing in subjects having ASD. The first model postulates the existence of a specific pathway or region in the brain that is damaged. The second proposed model suggests a more diffused change in the level of neuronal connectivity.

A 'persistent preoccupation with parts of objects' is one of the criteria for autistic disorder in the current diagnostic procedures (DSM-IV, APA, 1994). This behavior was also described by Leo Kanner in his pioneering work (1944). Indeed, Kanner described his first 11 cases as predominantly interested in details and highlighted their incapacity to experience the whole. This tendency is specific to those with ASD; in typically developing subjects, their inclination is to process incoming information in terms of totality (Frith, 1989), avoiding special attention for details and surface structure.

The WCC theory, often referred to also as "detail-focused processing style," has been received with great enthusiasm because its approach addresses aspects of ASD that other theories have neglected (e.g. areas of talent, super-acute perception, and lack of generalization, Happè 1999). Additionally, the idea of a fragmented perception in spite of a more gestalitic perception has often been described in autobiographical accounts of autism (Grandin, 2006). Indeed, perceptual abnormalities (e.g. hypersensitivity), often reported by clinicians but less often investigated, may be related to context-free processing (Happè & Frith, 2006). Hence, if ASD subjects show deficits in extracting prototypes (Klinger & Dawson, 2001), they would also have problems in recognizing similar situations as "alike," and this phenomena would necessarily generate problems in generalization skills (Happè & Frith, 2006).

Over the years, the role played by WCC in qualifying the deficit in social understanding has been discussed. Initially, a causal role was attributed to the WCC in integrating information for high-level meaning underlying the deficits in social understanding (Frith,

1989). However, the fact that detail-focused processing can be found across the ASD, regardless of the social competences (Happè & Frith, 2006), suggests that the problems in WCC and the social deficit may be not directly related. As proposed by Happè (1999), considering autism as related to a number of different cognitive processes, including global–local processing, social cognition and other functions, is more plausible. Within this framework, the WCC theory does not attempt to explain all aspects of ASD, although the suggestion that an exaggerate focus on details might play a role in ensuring abnormal social function poses as likely. For example, featural processing might interfere with facial emotion's recognition and influence interpretation of social behavior that is context-sensitive.

In general, while the WCC deficit is a fascinating hypothesis, whether or not its bias relates specifically to ASD, as compared to other clinical groups, is unclear. Some recent evidence has highlighted that this deficit may form part of the broader autism phenotype (Happè & Frith, 2006).

3. THE "MIRROR NEURONS" HYPOTHESIS

One hypothesis that has been highly investigated in recent years with relation to the social development in ASD is the "mirror neurons" hypothesis, proposed by the Italian group at the University of Parma (Rizzolatti et al, 1996; Gallese, 2001, Fogassi et al, 2005). This hypothesis postulates that social development is not merely rooted "social meta-cognition"; instead, social cognition involves accompanying processes, which involve physical and tangible sensations. Indeed, Gallese (2006) goes so far as to assert that this additional dimension of social cognition is "embodied," allowing individuals to feel a corporeal reaction, which mediates between the multimodal experiential knowledge we retain in our own bodies and the experience we imagine others to have. Gallese has also proposed that the capacity to share experiences with others is the basis for the development of a shared interpersonal space (called *shared manifold*). This "shared manifold" (Gallese, 2001, 2005) can be characterized at the functional level as an embodied simulation (Gallese, 2005), a specific mechanism whereby our brain/body system models its interactions with the world. The presumably empirical base for this system is considered to be a class of premotor neurons, discovered in the ventral premotor cortex of the macaque monkey brain and called "mirror neurons" (Gallese et al., 1996; Rizzolatti et al., 1996). These neurons do not only discharge electrical impulses when the monkey executes goal-related hand actions, like grasping objects, but also fire in the same manner when observing other individuals (monkeys or humans) executing similar actions (Rizzolatti et al., 1996). Since this discovery, many studies have demonstrated the existence of a "mirror neuron" system, matching action-perception and execution in the human brain as well (Rizzolatti & Craighero, 2004; Rizzolatti et al., 2001; Gallese et al., 2004).

More recently, studies have also described the existence of a mechanism for mirroring emotions and sensations. As described by Gallese (2006), when individuals see the facial expression of someone else, this perception leads them to experience a particular affective state; this affective state reflects the other's emotion and can be experienced, and therefore is directly understood by means of an "embodied" simulation. This process foresees a mutual activation of a neural mechanism both in the observer and the observed. Research has proven that this mutual activation is present during several emotional experiences, such as disgust or pain. These studies, for instance, have poignantly illustrated the phenomenon of mutual activation readily apparent in the subjective experience of pain and the direct observation or symbolically mediated knowledge of someone else experiencing a painful sensation (Singer et al., 2004). Other studies have shown that when individuals face the intentional behavior of others (mirroring the other's emotional state), they also experiences a specific phenomenal state defined as "intentional attunement" (Gallese, 2006). These "embodied" simulations serve as paramount in understanding the many mechanisms involved in social cognition, and said processes can be neurobiologically characterized though the "mirror neuron" system.

Starting from this background, Gallese hypothesized that the deficits of social behavior observed in those with ASD might be ascribed to a malfunctioning "mirror neuron" system, which would impede "embodied-simulation" mechanisms. Accordingly, any capacity for experiencing "intentional attunement" would be severely compromised. In turn, these underdeveloped neurobiological pathways all point to the anticipatory mechanism as null and void. Several findings support this idea (Oberman et al, 2005; Cattaneo et al. 2007). Cattaneo and colleagues, for example, using electromyographic recordings, have shown that in children with ASD there is an impairment of the actions chains representation and they propose that, as a consequence of this functional impairment, children with ASD may understand the intentions of others cognitively, but do not possess the mechanism for understanding them experientially (or empirically). In particular, the study suggests that children with ASD cannot fully comprehend the intention of others and, unlike typically developing children, they are unable to organize their action using a forward mechanism. The absence of a forward mechanism was also investigated by Schmitz and colleagues (2003). Specifically, the study analyzed postural adjustments in children with ASD, demonstrating how they use motor strategies which basically take their cues from feedback stimuli, rather than acting on feed-forward modes of control; in doing so, the children with ASD lacked the anticipatory postural adjustments. Although these anticipatory deficits are not intrinsically social, however, they could stem from a disruption from within the executive control domain of a functional mechanism—"embodied" simulation—which can be considered the base of social sharing.

Studies on imitation provide evidence, which focus more on the social aspects of "embodied" simulation deficits as expressed in ASD. Children with ASD show problems in imitative behaviors and these problems seem to be ASD specific since they are not present in children with developmental delay but not having ASD (Rogers, 1999). Is it conceivable that such deficits of imitation are due to a malfunctioning of the "mirror neuron" system and lead to the incapacity to create a motor equivalence between observed and observer? Also, studies on emotional-affective deficits in ASD highlight how a dysfunctional "mirror neuron" system may trigger the social and emotional deficits observed in the disorder (e.g. Dapretto et al., 2006).

Although the "mirror neurons" hypothesis has been strongly supported by many researchers worldwide, there are some critical issues that need to be addressed. A major issue is related to the fact that the "mirror neuron" hypothesis is primarily a *motor theory*. When someone starts a movement aimed to attain a goal, the final goal of the whole action is present in the agent's mind and is somehow reflected in each motor act of the sequence and the intention of the action is set before the beginning of the movement. Using the "mirror neuron" system, an observer can "mirror" the actions chain of another person. Moreover, it is arguable the possibility to predict the intention of the action using only the "mirror neurons" system (since a given action can be originated by very different intentions). This consideration has led Jacob and Jeannerod (2005) to argue against the relevance of "mirror neurons" for social cognition and, in particular, for determining the intentions of others (Gallese, 2006).

4. THE NEUROBIOLOGICAL BASES OF SOCIAL DYSFUNCTION IN ASD

ASD is a clinically and etiologically heterogeneous group of systemic disorders, with a strong genetic component and, most likely, considerable environmental influences (Persico & Bourgeron, 2006; Abrahams & Geschwind, 2008). Although the neurobiological bases of autism(s) are still far from being understood, in this subchapter, we review some of the studies that tried to uncover the molecular mechanisms behind or neurofunctional correlates of social development disruptions in autism.

In 1990, Brothers proposed, in light of the animal lesion studies, electrophysiology and clinical evidence, that the "social brain" in primates consists of three key regions: amygdala, orbitofrontal cortex, and the superior temporal sulcus (STS; Brothers, 1990). In almost two decades since this model was put forward, evidence accumulated in favor of other key regions to social cognition processing in humans: parietal cortex with its "mirror neurons," medial prefrontal cortex, insula, fusiform gyrus, and inferior frontal gyrus. Many of these regions have been feverishly investigated in people with ASD (mostly in small cohorts of high functioning individuals with ASD or subjects with Asperger's syndrome) and have been proven to show various levels of abnormalities in social-skills related tasks (Amaral, 2008). For example, several studies investigated STS, a region processing the actions and intentions of others through visual analysis of biological-motion cues; indeed, this region displays numerous abnormalities in autistic individuals: anatomical (i.e., decreased concentration of gray matter, delayed/incomplete sulcal development, decreased cortical thickness, postmortem abnormalities, bilateral hypoperfusion) and functional (e.g., reduced activity to faces, lack of modulation in a gaze shift task that conveys different intentions, etc.) (Zilbovicius et al., 2006; Pelphrey & Carter, 2008; Redcay, 2008). In addition, a significant negative correlation was observed between the ADI-R score and the cerebral blood flow in the left superior temporal gyrus (Gendry Meresse et al., 2005). Similarly, a considerable number of studies, both anatomical and functional, have been conducted in relation to the putative role of the amygdaloid region of the brain (i.e. the amygdala) in autism; at the moment, many consider that this region, crucial in many aspects of emotional processing, plays a central role in the development of the autistic phenotype, especially in the social-communication domain (Schulkin, 2007). In a recent and comprehensive meta-analysis of 24 studies, Di Martino and colleagues looked for the brain correlates of social functioning (e.g., mentalizing, emotional processes, face perception) in ASD, and found greater likelihood of hypoactivation in regions classically associated with social impairments in previous neurobiological models (perigenual anterior cingulate cortex, medical prefrontal cortex, and amygdala), but also pointed to regions of recent interest in the social cognition literature (i.e., right anterior insula) (Di Martino et al., 2009). This study also highlights that, despite considerable clinical and task heterogeneity, the functional imaging studies indicate ASD-related patterns of aberrant activation in social versus nonsocial cognitive domains. Nonetheless, following the identification of specific brain regions *correlated* to various aspects of social and communication impairments in autism, studies that employ an "interacting, developing brain systems" perspective are required (Pelphrey & Carter, 2008), in order to dissect the real contributions of each region and, accordingly, to tailor effective therapeutic interventions.

Another interesting hypothesis for the dysfunction of social cognition in autism is that related to the von Economo cells (or spindle neurons); these neural cells, located in the anterior cingulate and frontoinsular cortex, may be involved in the fast intuitive assessment of complex situations (Allman et al. 2005). Although a recent study did not find, as expected, a decrease in the number of these cells in the frontoinsular cortex from people with ASD (Kennedy et al., 2007), other studies bring evidence that the regions harboring these special group of neurons display abnormalities in children with autism (Allman et al., 2005). Further studies, employing more subtle and specific methods of investigation will certainly decide on this issue.

The use of endophenotypes or intermediary phenotypes has been proposed to assist in reducing the heterogeneity and identify with greater reliability the potential genetic regions of susceptibility to neuropsychiatric conditions (Gottesman & Gould, 2003). This approach, employed with success recently to developmental language disorders (Vernes, Newbury et al. 2008), is now starting to be utilized in revealing the molecular underpinnings of social disruption in ASD. For instance, Duvall and colleagues pursued the first genome-wide scan for social endophenotype in autism using a quantitative measure of social impairments (i.e., Social Responsiveness Scale) in 190 autistic probands and 57 unaffected siblings (Duvall et al., 2007). The authors identified two loci carrying potential genetic risk variants on chromosomes 11 and 17, with the highest score on chromosome 11 (z= 3.22). Nonetheless, a more recent genome-wide study performed on 976 multiplex families from the Autism Genome Project Consortium failed to find significant linkage for the social subphenotype, despite a reasonable heritability for this trait (Liu et al., 2008).

Murphy and collaborators, in an *in vivo* SPECT study, investigated the serotonergic system (5-HT) in eight adults with Asperger's syndrome and found a significant reduction in cortical 5-HT_{2A} receptor binding in cortical regions crucial to human social communication (Murphy et al., 2006); most interesting is the significant correlation (r = -0.837, $p < 0.02$) between abnormalities in the reciprocal social interaction (domain A of the Autistic Diagnostic Interview-Revised) and the estimated binding potential in the anterior and posterior cingulate and the right frontal cortex.

In the last decade, the two neuropeptides oxytocin (OXT) and arginine vasopressin (AVP) emerged as key mediators in a wide range of social behaviors and social cognition in mammals (e.g., social recognition, communication, parental care, territorial aggression and social bonding) (Israel et al. 2008). Several studies indicated, in both non-clinical and clinical subjects, that disturbances in the pathways related to these two neurohypophyseal hormones can lead to deficits in social behavior. Lerer and collaborators undertook an extensive genetic study in 152 subjects with ASD, in which they genotyped 18 tagged single nucleotide polymorphisms (SNPs) across the entire oxytocin receptor (OXTR) gene (Lerer et al., 2008).

Their analysis revealed two SNPs, one in intron 3 and the other in exon 4, to be associated with total scores on the Vineland Adaptive Behavior Scales (VABS); moreover, five SNPs showed significant association with VABS communication subdomains and one SNP with socialization. The same group reported a significant association between three microsatellites in the arginine vasopressin 1a receptor gene (AVPR1a) and the VABS scores ($p = 0.009$) in children with autism (Yirmiya et al., 2006). More recently, Yrigollen et al. confirmed the involvement in autism of allelic variants in genes regulating the development of affiliate behaviors (PRL- prolactin, PRLR- prolactin receptor, and OXTR), while for the two loci related to PRL an association for the combined ADI and communication skills multivariate phenotype was observed (Yrigollen et al., 2008). Plasma levels of OXT have also been shown to be reduced in autism and, more interestingly, the diminished levels of this plasma circulating octapeptide proved to be correlated to social skills (Modahl et al., 1998). Administration of intranasal OXT in healthy subjects improves "mind-reading" (Domes et al., 2007), increases the number of fixations and total gaze time toward the eye region (Guastella et al., 2008), enhances positive communication behavior (Ditzen et al., 2008), while intravenous administration of OXT in people with ASD improves affective speech comprehension, suggesting that it might facilitate social information processing in those with autism (Hollander et al., 2007). Furthermore, it has even been hypothesized that OXT administration during labor could down regulate the OXTR and hereby contribute to the social deficits that characterize autism and related behavioral disorders (Wahl, 2004). The abovementioned studies, connecting the pathways of these "social behavior" neuropeptides (i.e., OXT, AVPR, PRL) with the autistic phenotype, not only have significant implications for understanding the molecular neurobiology of the core social deficits in autism, but also generate potential therapeutic targets.

CONCLUSION

This chapter aimed at reviewing studies that have investigated the disruption of social development evidenced in ASD. We have described different hypotheses, which in the last decades have been employed in approaching the social deficit in children with ASD; in particular we have discussed: (i) the deficit of Theory of Mind hypothesis, (ii) the Weak Central Coherence hypothesis, (iii) the Mirror Neurons hypothesis; then we have briefly presented some of the recent studies on the neurobiological bases of social dysfunction in ASD. In general, at this stage, there is a lack of empirical evidence, doubled frequently by a lack of agreement, on the most fundamental neurobiological and psychological mechanisms of ASD. Future studies should not only reveal the etiological factors, but also help us understand "how" and "why" different domains of impairment cluster together as the "autistic phenotype". We believe that vigorous effort should be put in the following years in studying the different aspects of the disorder at multiple levels and with a plethora of methodological approaches.

REFERENCES

Abrahams, B. S. and D. H. Geschwind (2008). Advances in autism genetics: on the threshold of a new neurobiology. Nat Rev Genet 9(5): 341-55.

Adolfh, R. (2009) The Social Brain: Neural Basis of Social Knowledge. *Annual Review of Psychology* 60:18.1–18.24.

Allman, J. M., K. K. Watson, et al. (2005). Intuition and autism: a possible role for Von Economo neurons. *Trends Cogn Sci* 9(8): 367-73.

Amaral, D. G., Schumann, C.M. (2008). Neuroanatomy of autism. *Trends Neurosci* 31(3): 137-45.

APA (1994). *Diagnostic and Statistical Manual of Mental Disorders DSM-IV-TR Fourth Edition (Text Revision).* American Psychiatric Publishing.

Baron-Cohen, S. & Belmonte, M. K. (2005). Autism: A Window Onto the Development of the Social and the Analytic Brain, *Annual Review of Neuroscience.* 28, 109-126.

Baron-Cohen, S. (1998). Does the study of autism justify minimalist innate modularity?, *Learning and Individual Differences.* 10(3):179-191.

Baron-Cohen, S.; Leslie, A. M. & Frith, U. (1985). Does the autistic child have a theory of mind?, *Cognition.* 21(1):37-46.

Brothers, L. (1990). The social brain: a project for integrating primate behavior and neurophysiology in a new domain. Concepts in Neuroscience 1: 27-51.

Cattaneo, L.; Fabbri-Destro, M.; Boria, S.; Pieraccini, C.; Monti, A.; Cossu, G. & Rizzolatti, G. (2007). Impairment of actions chains in autism and its possible role in intention understanding, *Proc Natl Acad Sci U S A.* 104(45): 17825–17830.

Colle, L.; Baron-Cohen, S. & Hill, J. (2007). Do children with autism have a theory of mind? A non-verbal test of autism vs. specific language impairment, *Journal of Autism and Developmental Disorders.* 37(4):716-723.

Dapretto, M.; Davies, M. S.; Pfeifer, J. H.; Scott, A. A.; Sigman, M.; Bookheimer, S. Y. & Iacoboni, M. (2005). Understanding emotions in others: mirror neuron dysfunction in children with autism spectrum disorders, *Nature Neuroscience.* 9(1):28-30.

Di Martino, A., K. Ross, et al. (2009). Functional brain correlates of social and nonsocial processes in autism spectrum disorders: an activation likelihood estimation meta-analysis. Biol Psychiatry 65(1): 63-74.

Ditzen, B., M. Schaer, et al. (2008). Intranasal Oxytocin Increases Positive Communication and Reduces Cortisol Levels During Couple Conflict. Biol Psychiatry.

Domes, G., M. Heinrichs, et al. (2007). Oxytocin improves mind-reading in humans. Biol Psychiatry 61(6): 731-3.

Duvall, J. A., A. Lu, et al. (2007). A quantitative trait locus analysis of social responsiveness in multiplex autism families. Am J Psychiatry 164(4): 656-62.

Fogassi, L.; Ferrari, P. F.; Gesierich, B.; Rozzi, S.; Chersi, F. & Rizzolatti, G. (2005). Parietal lobe: from action organization to intention understanding, *Science.* 308(5722):662-667.

Frith, U. (1989). *Autism: explaining the Enigma*, Blackwell.

Gallese, V. (2001). The shared manifold hypothesis. From mirror neurons to empathy, .

Gallese, V. (2005). Embodied simulation: From neurons to phenomenal experience, *Phenomenology and the Cognitive Sciences.* 4(1): 23-48.

Gallese, V. (2006). Intentional attunement: A neurophysiological perspective on social cognition and its disruption in autism, *Brain Research.* 1079(1):15-24.

Gallese, V.; Fadiga, L.; Fogassi, L. & Rizzolatti, G. (1996). Action recognition in the premotor cortex, *Brain.* 119(2):593-609.

Gallese, V.; Keysers, C. & Rizzolatti, G. (2004). A unifying view of the basis of social cognition, *Trends in Cognitive Sciences.* 8(9):396-403.

Gendry Meresse, I., M. Zilbovicius, et al. (2005). Autism severity and temporal lobe functional abnormalities. Ann Neurol 58(3): 466-9.

Gottesman, II and T. D. Gould (2003). The endophenotype concept in psychiatry: etymology and strategic intentions. Am J Psychiatry 160(4): 636-45.

Grandin, T. (2006). *Thinking in Pictures, Expanded Edition: My Life with Autism*, Vintage.

Guastella, A. J., P. B. Mitchell, et al. (2008). Oxytocin increases gaze to the eye region of human faces. Biol Psychiatry 63(1): 3-5.

Happè, F. & Frith, U. (2006). The Weak Coherence Account: Detail-focused Cognitive Style in Autism Spectrum Disorders, *Journal of Autism and Developmental Disorders.* 36(1):5-25.

Happè, F. (1999). Autism: cognitive deficit or cognitive style?, *Trends in Cognitive Sciences.* 3(6):216-222.

Hollander, E., J. Bartz, et al. (2007). Oxytocin increases retention of social cognition in autism. Biol Psychiatry 61(4): 498-503.

Israel, S., E. Lerer, et al. (2008). Molecular genetic studies of the arginine vasopressin 1a receptor (AVPR1a) and the oxytocin receptor (OXTR) in human behaviour: from autism to altruism with some notes in between. Prog Brain Res 170: 435-49.

Jacob, P. & Jeannerod, M. (2005). The motor theory of social cognition: a critique, *Trends in Cognitive Sciences.* 9(1):21-25.

Kanner, L. (1944). Early infantile autism, *The Journal of Pediatrics.* 25(3):211-217.

Kennedy, D. P., K. Semendeferi, et al. (2007). No reduction of spindle neuron number in frontoinsular cortex in autism. Brain Cogn 64(2): 124-9.

Klinger, L. G. & Dawson, G. (2001). Prototype formation in autism, *Development and Psychopathology.* 13, 111-124.

Lerer, E., S. Levi, et al. (2008). Association between the oxytocin receptor (OXTR) gene and autism: relationship to Vineland Adaptive Behavior Scales and cognition. Mol Psychiatry 13(10): 980-8.

Leslie, A. M. (1987). Pretense and representation: The origins of theory of mind, *Psychological Review.* 94(4):412-426.

Leslie, A. M.; Friedman, O. & German, T. P. (2004). Core mechanisms in theory of mind, *Trends in Cognitive Sciences.* 8(12):529-533.

Liu, X. Q., A. D. Paterson, et al. (2008). Genome-wide linkage analyses of quantitative and categorical autism subphenotypes. Biol Psychiatry 64(7): 561-70.

Modahl, C., L. Green, et al. (1998). Plasma oxytocin levels in autistic children. Biol Psychiatry 43(4): 270-7.

Murphy, D. G., E. Daly, et al. (2006). Cortical serotonin 5-HT2A receptor binding and social communication in adults with Asperger's syndrome: an in vivo SPECT study. Am J Psychiatry 163(5): 934-6.

Oberman, L. M.; Hubbard, E. M.; McCleery, J. P.; Altschuler, E. L.; Ramachandran, V. & Pineda, J. A. (2005). EEG evidence for mirror neuron dysfunction in autism spectrum disorders, *Cognitive Brain Research.* 24(2):190-198.

Pelphrey, K. A. and E. J. Carter (2008). Brain mechanisms for social perception: lessons from autism and typical development. Ann N Y Acad Sci 1145: 283-99.

Pelphrey, K. A. and E. J. Carter (2008). Charting the typical and atypical development of the social brain. Dev Psychopathol 20(4): 1081-102.

Perner, J. & Leekam, S. (2008). The curious incident of the photo that was accused of being false: Issues of domain specificity in development, autism, and brain imaging, *The Quarterly Journal of Experimental Psychology.* 61(1):76-89.

Perner, J.; Frith, U.; Leslie, A. M. & Leekam, S. R. (1989). Exploration of the autistic childs theory of mind: Knowledge, belief, and communication, *Child Development.* 60(3). 689-700.

Persico, A. M. and T. Bourgeron (2006). Searching for ways out of the autism maze: genetic, epigenetic and environmental clues. Trends Neurosci 29(7): 349-58.

Premack, D. & Woodruff, G. (1978). Does the Chimpanzee have a Theory of Mind?, *Behavioural and Brain Sciences.* 1, 515-526.

Redcay, E. (2008). The superior temporal sulcus performs a common function for social and speech perception: implications for the emergence of autism. Neurosci Biobehav Rev 32(1): 123-42.

Rizzolatti, G. & Craighero, L. (2004). The mirror-neuron system, *Annu Rev Neurosci.* 27, 169-192.

Rizzolatti, G.; Fadiga, L.; Gallese, V. & Fogassi, L. (1996). Premotor cortex and the recognition of motor actions, *Cognitive Brain Research.* 3(2):131-141.

Rizzolatti, G.; Fogassi, L. & Gallese, V. (2001). Neurophysiological mechanisms underlying the understanding and imitation of action, *Nature Review Neuroscience.* 2(9):661-670.

Rogers, S. (1999). *An examination of the imitation deficit in autism*, In: Nadel, J, Butterworth, G. (Eds.). *Imitation in Infancy.* Cambridge Univ. Press, Cambridge, pp. 254–279.

Schulkin, J. (2007). Autism and the amygdala: an endocrine hypothesis. Brain Cogn 65(1): 87-99.

Singer, T.; Seymour, B.; ODoherty, J.; Kaube, H.; Dolan, R. J. & Frith, C. D. (2004). Empathy for pain involves the affective but not sensory components of pain, *Science.* 303(5661):1157-1162.

Vernes, S. C., D. F. Newbury, et al. (2008). A functional genetic link between distinct developmental language disorders. N Engl J Med 359(22): 2337-45.

Wahl, R. U. (2004). Could oxytocin administration during labor contribute to autism and related behavioral disorders?--A look at the literature. Med Hypotheses 63(3): 456-60.

Whiten, A. & Byrne, R. W. (1997). *Machiavellian Intelligence II : Extensions and Evaluations*, Cambridge University Press.

Yirmiya, N., C. Rosenberg, et al. (2006). Association between the arginine vasopressin 1a receptor (AVPR1a) gene and autism in a family-based study: mediation by socialization skills. Mol Psychiatry 11(5): 488-94.

Yrigollen, C. M., S. S. Han, et al. (2008). Genes controlling affiliative behavior as candidate genes for autism. Biol Psychiatry 63(10): 911-6.

Zilbovicius, M., I. Meresse, et al. (2006). Autism, the superior temporal sulcus and social perception. Trends Neurosci 29(7): 359-66.

In: Social Development
Editor: Lynda R. Elling

ISBN: 978-1-60741-612-8
© 2009 Nova Science Publishers, Inc.

Chapter 12

CHILDREN'S SOCIAL INTERACTIONS
IN CULTURAL CONTEXT

Rachel Lechcier-Kimel, Janet Chung,
Celia Hsiao and Xinyin Chen[*]
The University of Western Ontario, Canada

Over the past 20 years increased attention has been given to the study of cultural influence on socialization, social interactions and relationships, and individual socioemotional and cognitive development (Chen & French, 2008; Cole, Tamang, & Shrestha, 2006; Edwards, 2000). Findings from a variety of research projects have indicated that culture plays a vital role in determining the experiences of children with different characteristics. Social interactions serve as a major context that mediates the links between cultural forces and individual development.

Culture is often defined as a system of shared beliefs, values, and customs that people within a group, community, or society endorse and use to guide their social interactions and to cope with their world (Ji, Peng, & Nisbett, 2000). The cultural system is transmitted and develops from generation to generation through learning as well as continuous construction and innovation (Best & Ruther, 1994). Cultural norms and values provide guidelines for understanding and interpreting social behaviors and thus influence the manifestations of the behaviors (Chen, Wang, & DeSouza, 2006). Cultural norms and values play a role in child development largely through children's interaction with their environment (Greenfield, Suzuki & Rothstein-Fisch, 2006). Culture not only shapes and organizes the environments in which children's social interactions occur, but also affects the ways in which children interact with others.

---

[*] Contact Information: Xinyin Chen, Ph.D. Professor; Department of Psychology; University of Western Ontario; Westminster Hall, Windermere Road; London, Ontario, Canada; N6A 3K7; Email: xchen@uwo.ca; Office phone: 519-661-2111, ext. 84596; Fax: 519-850-2554

CULTURE AND DEVELOPMENT

Developmental theorists have explored cultural influence on human development from several major perspectives. Among them, Bronfenbrenner's ecological systems theory (Bronfenbrenner & Morris, 2006) views culture broadly as a part of the environmental context for human development. Bronfenbrenner's theory delineates four types of interrelated systems. The first, known as the microsystem, includes immediate environments such as the family, classroom, peer group, and neighbourhood. A person's biological characteristics are also considered part of the microsystem. Second, the mesosystem refers to interactions among microsystems, focusing on connections between immediate environments (such as home and school). Next, the exosystem consists of external environments such as parental workplaces that indirectly influence development. Finally, the macrosystem is the larger social context and includes factors such as political systems and national economy. In the earlier versions of the theory, cultural beliefs, norms, and values are included mainly in the macrosystem (Bronfenbrenner, 1979). However, Bronfenbrenner's recent works (Bronfenbrenner & Morris, 2006) have emphasized that culture may impact all systems at the micro- to macro-levels. In addition to its direct effects, culture may regulate child development through organizing social settings such as community services and school and daycare conditions.

The sociocultural theory is another major perspective concerned with the effects of culture on human development (Vygotsky, 1978). Generally, this theory suggests that children learn through social interactions with other people and that learning occurs first at the social level and only afterwards at the individual level (Vygotsky, 1978). The process of guided learning is a key component of the sociocultural theory; experienced peers and adults, as skilled instructors, teach new skills to children. Vygotsky emphasizes the importance of social interaction with adults and more capable peers as primary influences on learning, and learning is thus viewed as a socially mediated process. Children interact and communicate with others through dialogues in order to learn the cultural values of their society. Because all human activities inevitably take place in cultural settings, they cannot be understood apart from these settings (Woolfolk, 2004).

CULTURAL VALUES OF SOCIAL INITIATIVE AND BEHAVIORAL CONTROL

In the study of children's social functioning, most researchers emphasize initiative in social situations or active participation and demonstration of appropriate behaviours (Rubin & Rose-Krasnor 1992). As the tendency to prompt and maintain social interactions, initiative requires a high interest in social activities. Behavioural control, on the other hand, reflects the ability to self-regulate behaviors and emotions and is thus connected to the demonstration of appropriate behaviours (Chen & French, 2008). The maintenance of appropriate behaviours is seen as another crucial component of social competence since it encompasses aspects of social responsibility and concern for others (Eisenberg, Fabes, & Spinrad, 2006; Kochanska & Aksan 1995).

Recent research has shown that the value placed on the dimensions of social initiative and norm-based behavioral control in children and adolescents depends on the specific cultural context (Chen & French, 2008). Western cultures that place high value on assertive behaviours and the achievement of autonomy tend to view social initiative as an important developmental goal. In these cultures, social initiative is seen as an index of maturity and accomplishment (Chen & French, 2008). On the other hand, cultures that do not strongly emphasize self-oriented or individualistic goals tend to place higher value on self-regulation and control. In these cultures, group cohesion is seen as critical and it is the duty of socialization agents to teach children to suppress and control their own individual desires in order to achieve group wellbeing (Triandis, Bontempo, Villareal, Asai & Lucca, 1988).

For example, some Asian cultures such as Chinese and Korean cultures highly appreciate and encourage discipline and perseverance. As a result, children must demonstrate behavioral control and an understanding of the general social expectations that serve to facilitate the development of control. Free play is often limited to short periods of outdoor gross motor activity (Farver, Kim & Lee, 1995). In these cultures, a sense of group identity and a concern for others are the core values that direct children's social interaction; disputes with peers are often solved by children without teacher intervention. Lack of behavioral control is viewed as a serious problem in children and adolescents (Zhou, Eisenberg, Wang & Reiser, 2004).

In Western cultures where individualistic goals are emphasized, social initiative is seen as necessary and important for achieving personal accomplishment and success (Chen & French, 2008). As a result, children in Western societies experience a variety of activities as well as free play opportunities in which they can learn independence, self-expression, and self-confidence (Farver et al., 1995). In contrast to Western cultures, since children from group-oriented cultures such as China, Japan, and Korea are expected to comply with external demands, social initiative may not be seen as an important social skill. Moreover, social initiative needs to be directed by prosocial orientations; without adequate control, it is likely to be manifested as externalizing behavior that may threaten the benefits of others and group functioning (Chen & French, 2008; Chen Li, Li, Li, & Liu, 2000).

CULTURE AND SOCIAL INTERACTIONS

Peer interactions, as the social exchange involving one participant's elicitation of another participant's social response, provide a rich and complex context for children to communicate with and influence each other (Rubin, Bukowski, & Parker, 2006). During children's social interactions, one child's initiation may influence another child's response, and the quality of response to an initiation may also influence the pattern of future interactions.

Cultural differences in the extent to which children make social initiations and in the quality of social initiations have been documented. Farver et al. (1995), for example, found that Korean American children displayed more unoccupied and shy behaviors and made fewer active initiations than European American children in a naturalistic peer interaction setting. Relatively lower levels of social initiations were also found in Chinese and Indonesian children, compared with their North American counterparts (Chen, DeSouza, Chen, & Wang, 2006; Farver & Howes, 1988).

The nature of social initiations that children make towards those with particular social-behavioral characteristics may differ across cultures as well. Farver et al. (1995), for example, found that Korean-American children initiated play in different ways than their Anglo-

American counterparts. Korean-American children tended to make initiations by offering objects or engaging in parallel activities, whereas Anglo-American children engaged in more direct social contact, particularly in the form of pretend play. Cultural differences in social initiations may also be illustrated in the experiences of shy children in peer interactions in China and North America. Shyness, a behavioral manifestation of internal anxiety in challenging social situations, is regarded as incompetent and immature in Western cultures (e.g., Coplan & Armer, 2007). However, shy-restrained behaviour is regarded an indication of mastery and accomplishment and is thus endorsed in traditional Chinese culture (Liang, 1987). The different cultural values lead to different peer attitudes toward children who display shy, wary, and inhibited behaviors.

Chen, DeSouza et al. (2006) investigated how shy children engaged in peer interactions in samples of Chinese and Canadian children. Four same-sex children at 4 years of age were observed in free play sessions in the laboratory. Shyness was assessed based on children's onlooker (watching the activities of others but not entering the activity) and unoccupied (an absence of focus or intent, wandering aimlessly or staring blankly into space) behaviors. The results first indicated that shy Chinese and Canadian children were less likely than their non-shy counterparts to make active initiations. Thus, in both cultures, shy children's internal anxiety, vigilance, and wariness may prevent them from initiating social contact in an assertive manner (e.g., Asendorpf, 1991; Rubin, Burgess, & Coplan, 2002).

There were differences between the samples in the voluntary initiations that peers made to shy children. When peers voluntarily made initiations, the initiations were more likely to be coercive (e.g., a direct demand such as "Gimme that," or verbal teasing) and less likely to be cooperative (e.g., "Can I play with you?") in Canada. This was not the case in China; peer voluntary initiations to shy and non-shy children did not differ. Thus, compared with their counterparts in Canada, when initiating their social interactions with shy children, peers in China were clearly more supportive and less antagonistic and forceful.

Cross-cultural variations may be more evident in children's responses to social initiations. According to Dodge, Pettit, McClaskey and Brown (1986), children display their behaviors in social situations on the basis of the processing of a set of social environmental cues including several steps such as the encoding of social cues, the mental representation of those cues, accessing potential behavioral responses, the evaluation and selection of an optimal response, and finally the enactment of the optimal response. This social information processing model indicates that social interactions begin with the exposure to a set of social cues. These social cues are seen as the criterion from which the child judges the social situation or task. Therefore, a child's behavior in a social situation may occur as a function of the way that child processes social cues in that particular situation (Dodge et al., 1986). The manner in which social cues are processed is likely to be culture-specific. First, a child must engage in encoding which involves classifying the social event in terms of event types that are recognized by the culture (Mesquita & Frijda, 1992). Then, the child must apply a set of interpretation rules to the encoded cues in order to derive meaning. These rules of interpretation are often highly complex and culturally defined. For example, if a child has acquired a rule in the culture that calls for the interpretation of peer hostility when a scowl is observed on a peer's face, then the child will interpret the situation as a manifestation of peer hostility.

Moreover, culture-specific social responses may result from the behavioral repertories that are developed based on culturally defined expectations of actions that are considered appropriate under certain situations (Mesquita & Frijda, 1992). Culture may provide guidance for how children judge response styles and strategies as "optimal" and how they select and use the response styles and strategies. For example, Farver et al. (1995), found that Korean-American children tended to respond cooperatively to peers' initiations. In contrast, Anglo-American children were more aggressive and negative in their responses to peer initiations, which according to the authors, suggests a higher tolerance for aggressive and competitive behaviors in American culture. In Chen, DeSouza et al.'s study (2006), peers in Canada and China responded differently to social initiations made by shy children. When shy Canadian children initiated a social interaction, peers were more likely to make negative responses such as overt refusal, disagreement, and intentional ignoring of an initiation (e.g., "No!", "I won't do it."). However, peers responded in a more positive manner in China by controlling their negative actions and by showing approval, cooperation, and support (e.g., "I really like your drawing!"). Moreover, shy children also made different responses to peer initiations. When peers made social initiations, shy children in Canada were more likely to respond negatively than their counterparts in China. Therefore, different experiences of shy children may result in their different attitudes and behaviors toward others. Social support that shy children in China receive may help them engage in positive peer interactions. However, the difficulties and frustrations that Canadian shy children experience may facilitate the formation of negative attitudes toward others and the development of maladaptive behavioral styles.

Cultural influence on children's social interactions may be reflected in their responses to peer conflict situations. Markus and Linn (1999) have argued that persons with an independent worldview tend to address interpersonal conflicts through assertive engagement. In contrast, persons with an interdependent worldview typically attempt to minimize the disturbance and maintain relationships than to find solutions to resolve it. Cross-cultural research has yielded evidence supporting this argument. For example, Medina, Lozano and Goudena (2001) found that preschool children in the Netherlands more often than children in Andalusia, a more collectivistic society, focused on maintaining individual perspectives and displayed assertiveness and imposition of personal views during conflicts. Moreover, whereas conflicts in Dutch children often resulted in further negative interactions, Andalusian children tended to resolve conflicts and reach agreement by compromise or submission. Schneider Fonzi, Tomada, and Tani (2000) found that children in Central Italy were more likely than Canadian children to respond to conflicts between friends by maintaining respect for rules. Finally, French, Pidada, and Victor (2005) found that Indonesian children more frequently reported exhibiting disengagement and submission during conflict than did U.S. children.

SOCIAL INTERACTIONS BETWEEN FRIENDS AND NON-FRIENDS: A CROSS-CULTURAL STUDY IN CHINESE AND CANADIAN CHILDREN

We recently conducted a study of social interactions with peers in Chinese and Canadian children. The participants were 200 Chinese and 168 Canadian 11-year-old children. The study aimed to test several hypotheses. First, we expected that given the cultural encouragement of sociability in North America, Canadian children would make more initiations to peers. Second, based on the argument that cooperation is highly encouraged in Chinese culture, we expected that Chinese children would demonstrate higher levels of positive response such as approval and lower levels of negative responses such as rejection during interactions.

Participants visited the University laboratories in quartets to take part in a video-taped peer interaction session which lasted for approximately 60 minutes. Each group consisted of two pairs of friends; each child had one friend in their group and two non-friends. All groups were of the same-sex. The observational paradigm consisted of free play, group discussion, and a series of cooperative, problem-solving and competitive tasks. The data for this study were based on the two free play sessions (each lasting 15 minutes).

Fifteen specific types of initiation (e.g. prosocial behaviour, direct demand and nonverbal play behaviour) and thirteen types of response (e.g. reaction with positive affect, answer question/offer explanation and intentional non-response) were coded. The initiation codes were aggregated into three broad categories: Low Power (LP), High Power (HP), and Passive. The response codes were aggregated into the following three types: Positive, Information Exchange, and Rejection.

Repeated multivariate analysis of variances revealed overall effects of gender, culture, and friend vs. non-friend status, $F(1, 364) = 4.37$, 43.43 and 2.07, $p < .05$, .001, and .05, respectively, for social initiations, and overall effects of culture and friendship status, $F(1, 358) = 17.98$ and 38.07, $p < .001$, and .001, respectively, for social responses. Follow up univariate analyses indicated that, in general, boys had higher scores than girls on high power initiations. Chinese children had higher scores on passive initiations and low power initiations and lower scores on high power initiations than Canadian children. Moreover, Chinese children had higher scores on positive responses and lower scores on negative responses than Canadian children. The cultural differences were more evident in social interactions between friends than non-friends. The means, standard deviations, and F tests are presented in table 1.

The results clearly indicated that during social interactions, especially between friends, Chinese children were more likely to use passive and low power strategies, such as prosocial behaviors and indirect requests, whereas Canadian children tended to use more high power strategies such as direct commands and prohibitions in making initiations. Moreover, Chinese made more positive responses such as approval and agreement to peer initiations. In contrast, Canadian children were responded to peer initiations more negatively. The cross-cultural results were consistent with our expectations and the literature (e.g., Chen, Chung, & Hsiao, 2008), and indicated that children's social interactions are guided by general cultural beliefs and values such as Chinese values of cooperation, self-control, and group harmony.

Table 1. Means and Standard Deviations of Social Initiations and Responses in Chinese and Canadian Children

	China			Canada			F value	
	Boys	Girls	Total	Boys	Girls	Total	Gender	Culture
Social Interactions with Friends								
Passive initiations	.40	.43	.42	.18	.05	.11	.72	23.08
	(.65)	(.76)	(.72)	(.50)	(.21)	(.39)		
Low power initiations	9.13	9.60	9.41	6.19	4.31	5.25	1.65	56.29***
	(5.41)	(6.46)	(6.05)	(4.76)	(2.78)	(4.00)		
High power initiations	.29	.38	.34	.99	.45	.72	4.26*	12.84***
	(.60)	(.84)	(.75)	(1.60)	(.84)	(1.30)		
Positive responses	5.89	5.43	5.62	3.61	2.41	3.01	6.37*	29.71***
	(3.88)	(3.76)	(3.80)	(3.14)	(2.08)	(2.72)		
Information exchange	3.45	4.40	4.02	2.92	2.10	2.51	.00	5.20*
	(2.38)	(3.93)	(3.42)	(2.83)	(2.09)	(2.52)		
Negative responses	1.09	1.06	1.07	1.61	1.20	1.41	.20	4.44*
	(1.36)	(1.31)	(1.323)	(2.03)	(1.60)	(1.84)		
Social Interactions with Non-Friends								
Passive initiations	.15	.08	.11	.02	.00	.01	3.16	18.98***
	(.36)	(.27)	(.31)	(.11)	(.00)	(.08)		
Low power initiations	3.94	2.31	2.96	2.20	3.64	2.92	.10	.47
	(2.94)	(2.87)	(3.00)	(2.03)	(3.11)	(2.71)		
High power initiations	.45	.13	.26	.38	.18	.28	13.58***	.03
	(.84)	(.41)	(.64)	(.86)	(.54)	(.73)		
Positive responses	2.06	1.22	1.56	.92	1.17	1.04	3.56	22.38***
	(1.72)	(1.48)	(1.63)	(1.24)	(1.19)	(1.22)		
Information exchange	2.10	1.33	1.64	1.64	3.06	2.35	3.06	1.50
	(2.33)	(1.89)	(2.11)	(2.14)	(2.83)	(2.60)		
Negative responses	.96	.35	.60	.66	.33	.49	13.97***	3.05
	(1.32)	(.77)	(1.07)	(.94)	(.72)	(.85)		

*Note. SD*s are in parentheses under *M* scores.

* *p* < .05 ** *p* < .01 *** *p* < .001

CONCLUDING REMARKS

Cross-cultural research has demonstrated the importance of cultural factors in children's social development. Culture affects the patterns of social interactions and relationships. Through organizing interactions and relationships, culture constructs distinct social contexts for children and adolescents to develop their socioemotional characteristics and cognitive abilities according to socialization goals.

In this chapter, we have focused on two major aspects of social interactions: initiations and responses. We argue that the tendency and the nature of initiations that children make to others are culturally bound. For example, children across cultures may differ significantly in how they initiate social interactions with other children (Chen, DeSouza at al., 2006). Cultural norms may affect ways in which people respond to social initiations (Markus & Kitayama, 1991). These arguments have been supported by the findings from projects conducted by our team as well as others. Cultural influence may occur in multiple ways. We focus particularly in this chapter on the socialization processes in which children learn how to interpret, evaluate, and handle the information received from others in interactions.

There is only limited research on children's social interactions from a cultural perspective. Moreover, the existing research relies mostly on cross-cultural comparisons, especially between children in Western and non-Western societies. Although the findings are important in revealing cultural differences, they provide limited information about how culture guides children to engage in peer interactions. In addition, it is important to note that cultural exchanges and interactions during globalization may lead to the merging, co-existence, and integration of diverse value systems (Tamis-LeMonda et al., 2008). For example, individualistic ideologies and values such as assertiveness and autonomy have been introduced into many non-Western societies and exerted influence on social behaviors and interaction styles of children in these societies. However, Western values are likely to be integrated with the cultural traditions. It will be interesting to investigate how children interact with others in culturally integrated and sophisticated settings. In today's multicultural society, such research will have remarkable implications for education and professional work since the findings are likely to help us better understand the social functioning of children with different backgrounds.

REFERENCES

Asendorpf, J. B. (1991). Development of inhibited children's coping with unfamiliarity. *Child Development, 62,* 1460-1474.

Best, D. L., & Ruther, N.M. (1994). Cross-cultural themes in developmental psychology. An examination of texts, handbooks and reviews. *Journal of Cross-Cultural Psychology, 25,* 54-77.

Bronfenbrenner, U. (1979). *The Ecology of Human Development.* Cambridge, MA: Harvard, University Press.

Bronfenbrenner, U., & Morris, P. A. (2006). The bioecological model of human development. In W. Damon (Series Ed.) & R. M. Lerner (Vol. Ed.), *Handbook of child psychology: Vol 1. Theoretical models of human development* (pp. 793-828). New York: Wiley.

Chen, X., Chung, J., & Hsiao, C. (2008). Peer interactions, relationships and groups from a cross-cultural perspective. In K. H. Rubin, W. Bukowski, & B. Laursen (Eds.), *Handbook of Peer Interactions, Relationships, and Groups* (pp. 432-451). New York, NY: Guilford.

Chen, X., DeSouza, A., Chen, H., & Wang, L. (2006). Reticent behavior and experiences in peer interactions in Canadian and Chinese children. *Developmental Psychology, 42,* 656-665.

Chen, X., & French, D.C. (2008). Children's social competence in cultural context. *Annual Review of Psychology, 59,* 591-616.

Chen, X., Li, D., Li, Z., Li, B., & Liu, M. (2000). Sociable and prosocial dimensions of social competence in Chinese children: Common and unique contributions to social, academic and psychological adjustment. *Developmental Psychology, 36,* 302-314.

Chen, X., Wang, L., & DeSouza, A. (2006). Temperament and socio-emotional functioning in Chinese and North American children. In X. Chen, D. French, & B. Schneider (Eds.), *Peer relationships in cultural context* (pp.123-147). New York: Cambridge University Press.

Cole, P.M., Tamang, B.L., & Shrestha, S. (2006). Cultural variations in the socialization of young children's anger and shame. *Child Development, 77,* 1237-1251.

Coplan, R.J. & Armer, M. (2007). A "multitude" of solitude: A closer look at social withdrawal and nonsocial play in early childhood. *Child Development Perspectives, 1,* 26-32.

Dodge, K.A., Petit, G.S., McClaskey, C.L., & Brown, M. (1986). Social competence in children. *Monographs of the Society for Research in Child Development, 51* (2, Serial No. 213).

Edwards, C.P. (2000). Children's play in cross-cultural perspective: A new look at the Six Culture Study. *Cross-Cultural Research, 34,* 318-338.

Eisenberg, N., Fabes, R.A., & Spinrad, T.L. (2006). Prosocial development. In N. Eisenberg (Ed.), *Handbook of child psychology: Vol. 3. Social, emotional, and personality development* (pp. 646-718). New York: Wiley.

Farver, J.M., & Howes, C. (1988). Cultural differences in social interaction: A comparison of American and Indonesian children. *Journal of Cross-Cultural Psychology, 19,* 203–315.

Farver, J.M., Kim, Y.K., & Lee, Y. (1995). Cultural Differences in Korean- and Anglo-American Preschoolers' Social Interaction and Play Behaviors. *Child Development, 66(4),* 1088-1099.

French, D.C., Pidada, S., & Victor, A. (2005). Friendships of Indonesian and United States youth. *International Journal of Behavioral Development, 29,* 304-313.

Greenfield, P.M., Suzuki, L.K., Rothstein-Fisch, C. (2006). Cultural pathways through human development. In K.A. Renninger & I.E. Sigel. (Eds.) *Handbook of child psychology: Vol. 4. Child Psychology in practice* (pp. 655–699). New York: Wiley.

Ji, L., Peng, K., & Nisbett, R. E. (2000). Culture, control, and perception of relationships in the environment. *Journal of Personality and Social Psychology, 78,* 943-955.

Kochanska, G., & Aksan, N. (1995). Mother-child mutually positive affect, the quality of child compliance to requests and prohibitions, and maternal control as correlates of early internalization. *Child Development, 66,* 236-254.

Liang, S. (1987). *The outline of Chinese culture.* Shanghai Teachers' University Press, Shanghai, China: Xue Lin.

Markus, H.R., & Kitayama, S. (1991). Culture and the self: Implications for cognition, emotion, and motivation. *Psychological Review, 9,* 224-253.

Markus, H.R., & Lin, L.R. (1999). Conflictways: Cultural diversity in the meanings and practices of conflict. In D.A. Prentice & D.T. Miller (Eds.), *Cultural Divides: Understanding and Overcoming Group Conflict* (pp. 302-333). New York: Russell Sage Foundation.

Medina, J.A.M., Lozano, V.M., & Goudena, P.P. (2001). Conflict management in preschoolers: A cross-cultural perspective. *International Journal of Early Years Education, 9,*153-60.

Mesquita, B., & Frijda, N.H. (1992). Cultural variations in emotions: A review. *Psychological Bulletin, 112,* 179-204.

Rubin K.H, Rose-Krasnor L. (1992). Interpersonal problem-solving and social competence in children. In V.B. van Hasselt & M. Hersen (Eds.), *Handbook of social development: A lifespan perspective* (pp. 283–323). New York: Plenum.

Rubin, K. H., Bukowski, W., & Parker, J. G. (2006). Peer interactions, relationships, and groups. In N. Eisenberg (Ed.), *Handbook of child psychology: Vol 3. Social, emotional, and personality development* (pp. 571-645). New York: Wiley.

Rubin, K. H., Burgess, K. B., & Coplan, R. J. (2002). Social withdrawal and shyness. In: P. K. Smith & C.H. Hart.(Eds.), *Blackwell handbook of childhood social development* (pp. 330-352). Malden, MA: Blackwell Publishers.

Schneider, B.H., Fonzi, A., Tomada, G., & Tani, F. (2000). A cross-national comparison of children's behavior with their friends in situations of potential conflict. *Journal of Cross-Cultural Psychology, 31,* 259-266.

Tamis-LeMonda, C. S., Way, N., Hughes, D., Yoshikawa, H., Kalman, R. K., & Niwa, E. (2008). Parents' goals for children: The dynamic co-existence of collectivism and individualism in cultures and individuals. *Social Development, 17,* 183-209.

Triandis H.C, Bontempo R., Villareal M.J., Asai M., Lucca N. (1988). Individualism and collectivism: Cross-cultural perspectives on self-ingroup relationships. *Journal of Personality and Social Psychology, 54,* 323–33.

Vygotsky, L. S. (1978). M. Cole, V. John-Steiner, S. Scribner & E. Souberman (Eds.), *Mind in society: The development of higher psychological processes.* Cambridge, MA: Harvard University Press.

Woolfolk, Anita. (2004). *Educational Psychology* (9th ed). Boston: Allyn and Bacon.

Zhou Q., Eisenberg N.,Wang, Y., Reiser, M. (2004). Chinese children's effortful control and dispositional anger/frustration: Relations to parenting styles and children's social functioning. *Developmental Psychology, 40,* 352–66.

In: Social Development
Editor: Lynda R. Elling

ISBN: 978-1-60741-612-8
© 2009 Nova Science Publishers, Inc.

Chapter 13

"WHY SHOULD I BEHAVE IN THIS WAY?" RULE DISCRIMINATION WITHIN THE SCHOOL CONTEXT RELATED TO CHILDREN'S BULLYING

Simona C. S. Caravita[*]*, *Sarah Miragoli* *and Paola Di Blasio*

Center of Research in Developmental and Educational Dynamics (C.R.*I.d.e.e.*),
Department of Psychology, Catholic University of the Sacred Heart, Milano (Italy)

ABSTRACT

Social domain model states that by interacting with the social contexts, children organize their moral knowledge in distinct domains, mainly related to (1) moral obligations, aimed at granting persons' well-being and rights and non-dependent on social expectations, (2) social-conventional rules, aimed at preserving the social orders and dependent on authorities' dictates [Turiel, 1983], and (3) personal choices. A more social-conventional perception of moral obligations may express a less mature morality, and make easier rule breaking actions, such as aggressive behavior.

This chapter aims to explore the relationships between morality and aggressive behaviors, in particular bullying. First, research and theorizations on morality and social behaviors are presented, mainly focusing on the social domain model of morality. Then, bullying is analyzed as a group-phenomenon in which children participate in different ways, that is as bullies, victims, defenders of the victimized peer(s), and bystanders. The associations between moral processes, bullying behavior and the other forms of participation in bullying situations are discussed.

A study is described, investigating children's perceptions of moral and social-conventional rules, related to roles of involvement in bullying episodes. 129 children (aged 7–10 years), and 182 early adolescents (aged 11–15 years) filled in the Participant Role Questionnaire, assessing forms of participation in bullying, and a self-report measure, assessing the discrimination of moral and social-conventional rules in the school context. Children perceive moral and social-conventional rules as distinct kinds of obligations. Bullies do attribute more characteristics of the social-conventional domain to

---

[*] simona.caravita@unicatt.it

all the rules, and in adolescence judge the breaking of social-conventional rules more acceptable than peers, especially defenders, do. The age-level (mid-childhood vs. early adolescence) has some moderation effects. Practical implications for the anti-bullying intervention are discussed.

Keywords: morality, bullying, mid-childhood, early adolescence.

INTRODUCTION

Morality can be conceived as the ability to decide on wrong and right issues within the social relationships, and to behave accordingly, mostly with reference to the system of rules regulating the social interactions within communities. There is some evidence that from an early age children spontaneously recognize as non acceptable behaviors infringing norms aimed at protecting people from harm [e.g., Helwig, Zelazo, & Wilson, 2001]. These research data suggest that morality is based on "an act's harmful consequences" [Turiel, 1998; p. 904], since even children judge the moral transgressions as wrong in reason of their intrinsic consequences of harm [Turiel, 1983]: an act is wrong when it is hurting others, or violates individual rights.

Assuming this definition of morality and a conceptualization of aggressions as behaviors aimed at injuring or damaging another person [Coie & Dodge, 1998], a clear overlap exists between morality and aggressive acts: all the intentional aggressions are moral transgressions and many moral transgressions involve physical or verbal attacks against others [Arsenio & Lemerise, 2004].

Scholars have broadly presumed the existence of a strong link between morality, and social behaviors, in particular delinquent or aggressive ones. However, at least in the area of developmental psychology, the two lines of research on morality and aggressiveness have mostly been proceeding independent of each other, and only few models have tried to provide a comprehensive explanation of the relationships existing between these two dimensions [e.g., Arsenio & Lemerise, 2004].

This chapter aimed at investigating the associations between morality and aggressive behaviors, by presenting the debate on morality components and social actions, and reporting a study on the comprehension of moral and social-conventional rules among children involved in bullying situations. A group view of bullying is assumed as a phenomenon in which children participate in different ways, as bullies, victims, defenders of victims, and bystanders [Salmivalli, Lagerspetz, Bjorkqvist, Österman, & Kaukiainen, 1996].

MORALITY AND SOCIAL BEHAVIORS

For centuries, philosophers and psychologists have attempted to understand the complex nature of moral development from childhood to adulthood, and the relation existing between morality and social behaviors. Human moral functioning involves different psychological dimensions: reasoning, and knowledge of right and wrong in social relationships, emotions, such as guilt and shame, and the empathic concern of the other's pain,. However, particular attention has been devoted by developmental scholars to the cognitive components of morality, that is moral reasoning processes and knowledge.

Classic stadial theories, such as Piaget [1932] and Kohlberg's conceptualizations [1981], conceive moral development as proceeding through a set of invariant stages that build cognitive and social skills. Each stage is characterized by different conceptions about the nature of norms, the origins of their value, and by different evaluation criteria of actions (e.g., the magnitude of the damage that the act produces, and the intentionality and the purpose of the action). Thus, moral reasoning skills develop from a more immature conception of norms as founded and guaranteed by adults' authority to an understanding of rules as valid for themselves in reason of their purposes (preserving individual rights and welfare, or maintaining the social order). Based on their rule comprehension, in the early stages of development children also consider the rule transgression as more acceptable, if non discovered by the authorities.

In stadial models social thinking and action are thought as closely related to each other, so that behaving in the right way should spontaneously follow the comprehension of what is the right action. However, some empirical research and clinical observations in adults and children have revealed that a gap exists between knowledge of norms and actual behaviors: knowing rules and understanding what should be the right action do not coincide to behaving in accordance to norms and values [Ross & Nisbett, 1991; Turiel & Smetana, 1984].

More recent theorizations [Bandura, 1986] state that the association between moral thinking and moral action is complex and bidirectional. The moral judgement influences how the person behaves in social situations, in turn the action,ì and the following feedbacks and interpretations of the social interaction play a role in building individual values, criteria and patterns of moral reasoning.

Bandura [1986] proposed that moral action can be understood through the interactions between the individual characteristics, the social environment, and the behavior, along with the self-perception within the social setting. He argued that moral behavior, and knowledge are learnt and formed within the relationships with others, by obtaining reinforcements or punishments, and by observing other people being rewarded or punished for their behaviors. By interacting with the social environment the person also constructs his or her own personal moral criteria and conduct standards, on the basis of which he/she evaluates both the own and the another's action as right or wrong. Further, self control processes are formed by the person, so that he/she feels a self-esteem decrease and negative emotions when the own behavior violates the own values and conduct standard,.

However, also *disengagement* mechanisms able to deactivate the self-control processes, and avoid the self-sanctions, may be acquired through social interactions. For instance, people can morally justify their negative actions or compares them with others of greater magnitude, in order to make and perceive own behaviors as acceptable. Aggressive behaviors may stem from these moral disengagement mechanisms, so that, even if a moral principle is understood and believed to be universally valid, these thinking processes allow the person to behave contradicting it and without feeling guilty.

A DOMAIN THEORY OF MORALITY

Children develop their judgements and concepts of justice and right by interacting with others within the social environment, as a result of their understanding and interpreting the events and the social interactions associated to different areas of experience. This process leads to construct distinct domains of moral knowledge and judgement about right and wrong, domains that strongly influence the behavior [Turiel, 1983].

Based on early social experiences [Helwig & Turiel, 2004], children organize their moral knowledge by distinguishing among behaviors and events falling into three different areas of social interactions and social reasoning: the *moral domain*, pertaining to the person's rights and welfare (i.e., issues of intentional harm, fairness, deliberate harm and right); the *social-conventional domain*, pertaining to arbitrary rules aimed at favouring the social order (i.e., rules that promote smooth social interactions); the *personal domain*, concerning issues related to the individual area of choice (e.g., the choice of friends, or preferences about dresses) [Much & Shweder, 1978; Nucci & Nucci, 1982a; 1982b; Nucci & Turiel, 1978, 2000].

The distinction between the domains of morality and social conventions is particularly emphasized by Turiel [1983]. Judgements about moral obligations (moral rules) are universally valid and non-dependent on social expectations, context and/or authorities' dictates. On the contrary, conventional rules are set by authorities to better coordinate social relationships in social systems. Consequently, judgements related to conventional norms are relative, and dependent on the context and authorities' statements. When children are asked questions about the rule alterability, moral rules are more likely than social-conventional ones to be considered as unalterable across contexts, since they entail acts with intrinsic consequences of harm or unfairness. When faced with a moral transgression, children may consider its direct harming consequences, and conclude that this behavior is wrong [Turiel, 1983; Smetana, 1988; Smetana & Braeges, 1990]. For this reason, children judge the moral transgression non rule-contingent and non-acceptable, and non-dependent on the context in which it happens and the authorities' willingness.

In contrast, for social conventions the connections between rules and acts are more arbitrary and less easy to understand from the intrinsic properties of the social interaction. Judgements about social-conventional transgressions are more context-specific, since these acts infringe norms that can be changed by the group agreement or authorities' commands, and whose value derives from social systems and hierarchies. Consequently, the children's interpretations of events pertaining to the social-conventional domain are influenced by the context [Catron & Masters, 1993; Siegal & Storey, 1985; Smetana, Schlagman, & Adams, 1993], and children may even judge the transgression as acceptable when the context changes. On the other hand, when children deal with social-conventional transgression, with no intrinsic consequences of harm or unfairness, they interpret the rule-breaking action as based on extrinsic features of the event (on context and on authorities), so that they are likely to evaluate social-conventional transgressions as less wrong than moral ones.

There is evidence that children make judgements and classify actions in terms of the moral or social-conventional domains from a very young age [Nucci & Turiel, 1978; Smetana, 1984; Smetana & Braeges, 1990; Smetana, Schlagman, & Adams, 1993; Tisak & Turiel, 1988; Zelazo, Helwig, & Lau, 1996]. Studies [for reviews, see Tisak, 1995; Turiel, 1998; Helwig & Turiel, 2004] have shown that starting from an early age (three years) children are aware of the consequences of moral actions, including injury and the emotions felt by the others, possess moral concepts that are independent of authority, and view situations such as stealing or hitting without provocation as wrong because of their intrinsic unfairness [Helwig, Zelazo, & Wilson, 2001]. Children are also able to distinguish basic moral and social-conventional events by about 4 years [Smetana, 1981; Smetana & Braeges, 1990].

On summary, when children are asked questions about the alterability and other properties of norms, moral rules are more likely to be judged as unalterable and generalizable across contexts than social-conventional ones, and the moral transgression to be evaluated as less acceptable than the social-conventional one.

Anyway, also a moral event, implying harming others, can be evaluated as depending on a social-conventional rule or a personal choice [Tisak & Jankowski, 1996]. Attributing social–conventional features to moral norms is likely to be linked with the aggressive behavior. There is some evidence that in provoked situations violent youngsters judge moral transgressions as more acceptable than non-violent peers, and behavioral disorder children tend to focus more on social-conventional aspects of moral transgressions, such as leading to a punishment [Astor, 1994, Nucci & Herman, 1982]. In turn, the belief that transgression is acceptable predicts the aggressiveness [Crane-Ross, Tisak & Tisak, 1998].

BULLYING: AN INDIVIDUAL BEHAVIOR AND A GROUP-PHENOMENON

Among the aggressive conducts, bullying is a more proactive than reactive type of aggression [Camodeca; Goossens, Meerum Terwogt, & Schuengel, 2002], characterized by the intentionality and the reiteration of aggressions, and by an imbalance of the power between the bully and his/her victim [Olweus, 1993]. At a group level, bullying is also a phenomenon largely influenced by features and processes internal to the formal and informal peer-networks [Rodkin, 2004; Garandeou & Cillessen, 2006]. D. Olweus [1993] states that within the peer-group the attitudes toward the victimized class-mates are likely to change negatively, increasing the victims' risk to continue to be harassed. Furthermore, 88 % of bullying episodes happen when other peers are present [Hawkins, Pepler, & Craig, 2001].

In addition to bullying others, as the ringleaders or their active assistants, children can participate in bullying situations by taking the side of the victims and comforting them, that is defending the victimized peer(s), or by being more passive bystanders, that is giving a non-active support to bullies, or witnessing the episodes and trying to stay out of them [Salmivalli et al., 1996]. Even if scholars have mostly investigated factors related to the main roles of bully and victim, recently an increasing attention has been devoted to the other forms of participation in bullying, by examining the characteristics of children active in defending their peers or witnessing bullying situations [e.g., Caravita, Di Blasio, & Salmivalli, 2009; Gini, 2006].

BULLYING AND MORALITY

The bullying behavior is associated with emotional and cognitive features and processes which either contribute to or determine the assumption of the bully role. With reference to this pattern of characteristics typical of bullies, already in 1993 Olweus talked about a bully's "aggressive personality". In particular, in addition to evaluating the violence positively, when compared to their peers children bullying others show higher levels of moral disengagement, even in the form of a lack in moral commitment and a expression of higher disengagement emotions (i.e., indifference or pride) related to bullying [Gini, 2006; Menesini, Sanchez, Fonzi, Ortega, Costabile, & Lo Feudo, 2003]. Lower levels of empathic skills are also associated with bullying behavior [e.g., Espelage, Mebane, & Adams, 2004; Gini, Albiero, Benelli, & Altoè, 2007; Warden & MacKinnon, 2003].

Overall, these outcomes suggest a lack of morality of children and adolescents that bully their peers. At a cognitive level, youngsters harassing others seem to have a tendency to self-justify their violent acts that break moral norms [Gini, 2006], whilst at an emotional level they show difficulties in both the affective empathic responsiveness to other's pain [Espelage et al., 2004], and the expression of moral emotions, such as guilt and shame [Menesini et al., 2003].

In contrast, when compared to their peers children that actively take the side of the victimized class-mates are characterized by a lower tendency to self-justify [Gini, 2006]. In general, moral disengagement processes are negatively related to defending the victims when the effects of age are controlled for ($r = -.22$, $p < .001$) [Gini, 2006]. Furthermore, higher empathic abilities are positively linked to this prosocial behavior [Gini et al., 2007], and among males the affective component of empathy can promote defending behaviors when the child has a high status as socially preferred within the peer-group [Caravita et al., 2009]. In summary, children helping and supporting their bullied class-mates seem to be distinguished by higher levels of cognitive and affective morality than their peers with different roles of participation in bullying.

INVOLVEMENT IN BULLYING AND MORAL DOMAINS: AN EMPIRICAL STUDY

Overall, the literature suggests the value of considering the associations between the morality components and the involvement in bullying. Anyway, at our knowledge scholars have not studied the bullying behavior, along with the other forms of participation in bullying, in relationship to the different domains of moral judgment [Turiel, 1983].

A study was carried out in order to investigate the associations between roles of involvement in bullying, and the discrimination of moral and social-conventional rules in the school context. The attention was focused on school, since bullying usually happens in the school environment, and differences between moral and social-conventional rules are present even in this context [Buchanan-Barrow & Barrett, 1998]. Some school rules have a clear moral value, since they aim at preserving children's safety and well-being (e.g., "do not hit class-mates"), whilst other rules mainly aim at conserving the proper functioning of the context (e.g., "do not leave school library books scattered on the floor"). These latter norms are social-conventional, since they depend on the dictates of the context-authorities (i.e., teachers and head-teachers), and their content is more closely related to the features of the school-context.

AIMS AND HYPOTHESES OF THE STUDY

Based on Turiel's assumptions and the literature on moral domain reasoning of violent and delinquent children [e.g., Astor, 1994], a study was realized, mainly aimed at exploring differences in school rule perception of children differently participating in bullying situations. Bullies, both ringleaders and their assistants (active agents of bullying), were hypothesized to attribute to all the school rules, including moral rules, more social-conventional characteristics. In particular in comparison to their peers, bullies were thought to perceive all the norms as more dependent on school authorities, changeable, and having a higher context-related validity. Consequently, bullies might also evaluate school-rule breaking as more acceptable (i.e., less wrong) than their class-mates involved in bullying with other roles. In contrast, defenders of victims were believed to have a higher morality than their peers, that is to be able to better understand the intrinsic value of rules, and to perceive the violation of the rules, above all moral rules, as more wrong.

As a secondary purpose of the study, we tried to further confirm that children understand moral and social-conventional norms as distinct and different kinds of rules. Besides differing in the degree to which their value is perceived to depend on authorities' dictates, moral and social-conventional rules are presumably distinguished in the children's perception by further characteristics, such as the extent to which their transgression is judged to be wrong. The norms aimed at forbidding harmful actions, that is the moral rules, are likely to be conceived by children to be valid also out of the school context, and to be less alterable than rules with social-conventional purposes. Further, actions infringing moral rules may be evaluated as more wrong than behaviors violating social-conventional norms.

Lastly, we investigated possible age-related differences in the understanding of moral and social-conventional rules, by comparing mid-children and early adolescents. Although children discriminate between moral and social-conventional rules from an early age [e.g., Smetana & Braeges, 1990], by growing youngsters may be more able to recognize the specificity of moral rules, and to attribute fewer social-conventional features to this kind of rule. Early-adolescents should also perceive at a higher extent the unacceptability of moral transgressions in comparison to violations of social-conventional rules.

METHOD

Sample

311 Italian youngsters (range of age: 7 to 15 years; average age: 11.12, s.d.: 2.06), 159 males and 146 females participated in this study[1]. At the time of the data collection, 129 participants (middle-childhood-group; 7-10 years, average age: 9.00, s.d.: 0.89) were third-, fourth- and fifth graders, attending the last three years of primary school in the Italian system, whilst 182 early adolescents (11-15 years, average age: 12.7, s.d.: 1.02) attended sixth-seventh- and eight-grades, the three grades of middle school in Italy.

47.9% of the participants had a middle-low Socio-Economic Status (SES), 31.8% came from middle SES families, and 14.5% belonged to middle-high SES families. The SES level of the participants' families was assessed by asking the children to report their parents' or main caregivers' occupations and the educational qualifications of both.

INSTRUMENTS

Participation in Bullying Episodes

Forms of participation in bullying episodes were assessed by administering the Italian version of the *Participant Role Questionnaire* (PRQ) [Menesini & Gini, 2000; Salmivalli et al., 1996]. The measure includes 20 items describing different behavior scenarios, organized into five scales assessing different participant roles associated with bullying: *ringleader bully* (4 items, alpha = .93; e.g., "Starts bullying"); *assistant of bully,* who helps the bully in bullying (2 items, alpha = .81; e.g., "Joins in the bullying"); *reinforcer of the bully,* who sustains the bullying (5 items, alpha = .86; e.g., "Laughs at bullying"); *defender of the victim,* who defends the child bullied (5 items, alpha = .86; e.g., "Tries to stop bullying"); *outsider,* who tries not to be involved in bullying (4 items, alpha = .73; e.g., "Stays away from bullying"). A twenty-first item of the measure assesses victimization (i.e., "Is victimized").

Each item requests limited (5 class-mates) same- and cross-gender peer-nominations: each child indicates the school-mates that most often behave in the way described by the item, and then evaluates how often each of the nominated classmates behaves in that way, using a 2-point scale (1=sometimes, 2=often). Each item score is the sum of received nominations for each child, ponderated by the frequency of the behavior, whilst the sum of the scale items, divided by the number of evaluators, is the scale score, ranging from 0.00 to 2.00. The scale scores are then standardized by class, and a role is assigned to each child, taking the highest scale score and considering whether it is higher than 0 (i.e., the class-average).

---

[1] Six children did not report their gender.

Rule Understanding

In order to investigate the children's ability to discriminate between moral and social-conventional rules and the children's understanding of different aspects of the rules in the school context, a self-report questionnaire was developed based on the interview schedule by Buchanan-Barrow and Barrett [1998].

The measure includes four hypothetical scenarios, in which school rules of two different domains, that is moral rules vs. arbitrary social-conventional rules, were transgressed by a child. Each of the two kinds of rules is assessed through two scenarios, in order to ensure that possible differences between the rule types emerging from the questionnaire were not solely due to specific features of the particular scenarios presented for each category. Therefore, two scenarios are about moral rules, that is rules forbidding actions inflicting - physical or psychological - harm on another child (i.e., *pushing a child off a climbing frame*, and *taking a child's book*), and two scenarios are about social-conventional rules, that is norms not directly related to avoiding harming others, and whose purposes may be less understandable to children (i.e., *running in the corridor*, and *leaving school library books scattered on the floor*). In each scenario the school rule and its transgression are described very briefly, giving little indication on to the purpose of the child's action. An example of a moral-rule scenario is as follows (see the Appendix for all the four scenarios):

> In Davide's school, there is a rule that you must never push anyone off the climbing frame. One day at school, when Davide is playing on the climbing frame, he pushes Stefano so hard that he falls to the ground.

Then, for each scenario five questions are proposed to the respondent, each evaluating one dimension of the child's rule comprehension, and testing whether the rule is perceived as depending on school authorities (i.e., the teacher and the head-teacher), changeable, and specific to the school context, and whether the rule breaking is perceived as acceptable or non-acceptable:

1. *rule dependence on the teacher's authority* (e.g., "Would it be OK for Davide to push someone off the school climbing frame if a teacher told him he could do that?");
2. *rule dependence on the head-teacher's authority* (e.g., "Supposing the Head told Davide he could push someone off the school climbing frame, would it be all right then?");
3. *acceptability of the rule breaking*, (e.g., "Do you think what Davide did was right or wrong?");
4. *rule changeability* (e.g, "Do you think this rule may be changed?");
5. *rule dependence on the context/rule generalizability*, that is the perception of the acceptability of the rule breaking behavior, and consequently of the rule value, in contexts different from school (e.g., "Do you think Davide's behavior would have been right or wrong, if he pushed somebody off the climbing frame outside of the school?").

According to Buchanan-Barrow and Barrett's interview schema, each item is scored on a dichotomous scale. For *rule dependence on teacher/head-teacher's authority*, and *rule changeability* items NO answers are scored as 0, and YES answers as 1, so that score 1 indicates that the scenario obligation is perceived as dependent on school authorities or alterable. For *acceptability of the rule breaking*, and *rule dependence on the context*, WRONG answers are scored as 0, and RIGHT answers as 1; for these dimensions score 1 indicates that the rule-breaking action is judged as acceptable, in each context (*acceptability of the rule-breaking*) or in contexts other than school (*rule dependence on the context*), so that the norm is violable or non-generalizable (context-dependent).

Each dimension of the two categories of rules (moral vs. social-conventional) is assessed by 2 items. For each dimension a 3 level total score is obtained by summing the item scores of the two scenarios: 0 (two "NO/WRONG" responses), 1 (one "YES/RIGHT" response, and one "NO/WRONG" response), 2 (two "YES/RIGHT" responses). For the moral-rule scenarios, dimensions' alpha indexes went from .72 (*rule dependence on the context*) to .96 (*acceptability of the rule breaking*), with exception of *rule changeability* (alpha = .47); for the social-conventional scenarios dimensions' alpha indexes were included from .64 (*rule changeability*) to .92 (*acceptability of the rule breaking*), with exception of *rule dependence on the context* (alpha = .49). Overall, per each dimension a higher score indicates that higher social-conventional characteristics are attributed to that kind of obligation (moral vs. social-conventional)

PROCEDURE

The questionnaires were group-administered in a single session to each class, with the participants sitting at their desks. During the administration a researchers' assistant was present, reading the children written instructions in order to explain the procedure for filling in each questionnaire, and answering the children's questions. The administrator also underlined the anonymity of the answers. For PRQ, on the basis of the measure authors' norms, the children were introduced to the following definition of bullying:

> Bullying is when one child is repeatedly exposed to harassment and attacks from one or several other children. Harassment and attacks may be, for example, shoving or hitting someone, calling him/her names or making jokes about him/her, leaving him/her out of the group, taking his/her things, or any other behavior meant to hurt someone. It is not bullying when two students with equal strength or equal power have a fight, or when someone is occasionally teased, but it is bullying, when the feelings of one and the same student are intentionally and repeatedly hurt.

The definition of bullying was read by the research assistant, and children were requested to report some examples of bullying episodes, in order to be sure they had understood the difference between bullying acts and generic aggressions. Then, the subjects were asked to think about situations in which someone has been bullied and to answer the questionnaire.

The order of administering the two questionnaires was counterbalanced over classes. No time-limit was set for completion, but the average time of filling in was about one hour. At the end of every session the research assistant put the questionnaires in a big envelope and closed it with the children watching.

RESULTS

Before exploring whether children differently involved in bullying have a different understanding of school norms and their transgressions, we examined children and early adolescents' perception of moral and social-conventional rules as distinct kinds of norms, and possible moderation effect by the age-level (mid-childhood vs. early adolescence).

Moral and Social-Conventional Rules as Distinct Kinds of Rules

Along with the association with avoiding harming others, the feature mostly defining the difference between moral and social-conventional rules is the higher dependency of the latter on the authority establishing the norm. Based on this assumption, and focussing on *rule dependence on the teacher's authority* and *rule dependence on the head-teacher's authority*, an exploratory factor analysis (EFA) was performed [MPlus 5, Muthèn & Muthèn 1998–2004], by including the 8 items assessing these two dimensions for both the moral and the social-conventional scenarios. Two factors with a eigenvalue higher than 1.00 appeared, and the two-factor solution obtained better fit indexes than the one-factor solution (Estimator WLSMV; one-factor solution: $\chi2(20) = 239.16$, p = .00; CFI = .97, SRMR = .15; two-factor solution: $\chi2(13) = 87.32$, p = .00; CFI = .99, SRMR = .07). Looking at the factor loadings of the single items, the four items of the two moral scenarios loaded the first factor (Quartimin rotated factor loadings from .89 to .97) better than the second one (Quartimin rotated factor loadings from -.03 to .07). In contrast, the 4 items related to social-conventional rule scenarios loaded the second factor (Quartimin rotated factor loadings from .77 to .98) better than the first one (Quartimin rotated factor loadings from -.11 to .17).

Then, a confirmatory factor analysis (CFA) was performed, in order to compare the one-factor solution, specifying all the eight items as indicators of only one factor (a only one kind of rule), with the two-factor solution, in which the four items related to the two moral rule scenarios were specified as indicators of the same factor (named Moral Rule Factor) and the other four as indicators of the second factor (named Social-Conventional Rule Factor).

The two-factor model obtained slightly better fit indexes than the one-factor model (Estimator WLSMV; one-factor solution: $\chi2(6) = 20.88$, p = .002; CFI = .99, WRMR = .73, $\chi2/df = 3.48$; two-factor solution: $\chi2(6) = 19.37$, p = .004; CFI = .99, WRMR = .60, $\chi2/df = 3.23$).

Overall, the outcomes from both the EFA and the CFA gave some evidence that two different kinds of rule exist in the perception of children: the moral norms, conceived to be less dependent on the teacher's and head-teacher's authority (proportion of responses in the category YES of the four items on *rule dependence on teacher/head-teacher's authority*, related to the moral scenarios: between 17% and 24%), than the social-conventional ones (proportion of responses in the category YES of the four items on *rule dependence on teacher/head-teacher's authority*, related to the social-conventional scenarios: between 37% and 48%).

Perceived Characteristics
of Moral and Social-Conventional Rules

In order to explore the different characteristics of moral and social-conventional rules, for each of the five assessed rule dimensions (i.e., *rule dependence on teacher's* or *head-teacher's authority, acceptability of the rule breaking, rule changeability, and rule dependence on the context*) a Multivariate Analyses of Variance was performed, in which the kind of scenario/rule (moral vs. social-conventional) was specified as within-subject factor. For each rule dimension, the total scores of both moral and social-conventional scenarios were first transformed in arc-sine.

The kind of rule had a significant effect on all the five dimensions explored (table 1). MANOVAs again confirmed that moral rules were perceived as less dependent on teacher/head's authority than social-conventional rules ($F(1, 303) = 45.93$, $p < .001$, and $F(1, 303) = 74.09$, $p < .001$ respectively). Furthermore, moral norms were reported to be less changeable, and less dependent on context, that is more generalizable, than social-conventional rules. The transgression of moral norms was also considered more wrong ($F(1, 303) = 217.41$, $p < .001$).

**Table 1. Means (Standard Deviations) of the rule dimensions
by the kind of rule (moral vs. social-conventional)**

	Moral rules	Social-conv. rules	Df	F	η^2
Rule dependence on teacher's authority	.28 (.53)	.52 (.66)	1, 303	45.93***	.13
Rule dependence on head-teacher's authority	.31 (.57)	.63 (.69)	1, 303	74.09***	.20
Acceptability of the rule-breaking	.03 (.16)	.66 (.75)	1, 303	217.41***	.42
Rule changeability	.23 (.49)	.35 (.56)	1, 302	19.09***	.06
Rule dependence on the context	.01 (.34)	.36 (.51)	1, 303	74.27***	.20

Note. * $p < .05$; ** $p < .01$; *** $p < .001$.

Age-Related Differences in the Perception of Rules

When the age-level (mid-childhood vs. early adolescence) was included in the MANOVA model as between-subject independent variable, the significant main effect of the kind of rule continued to be present for all the five dimensions investigated ($ps < 001$), and significant main effects of age on *rule dependence on teacher's* and *head-teacher's authority*, and *acceptability of the rule breaking* appeared (table 2).

The age-level also moderated the effects of the kind of rule on *rule dependence on head-teacher's authority* (kind of rule X age-level: $F(1, 302) = 11.56$, $p = .001$), and on the *acceptability of rule-breaking* (kind of rule X age-level: $F(1, 302) = 1022.31$, $p = .001$). Follow-up MANOVAs were performed separately among children and early adolescents, for these two dimensions. Main effects of the kind of rule on *rule dependence on head-teacher's authority* and *acceptability of rule breaking* were significant (*ps* < .01) in both the age-level. However, children scored higher than early-adolescents on all the dependent variable scores, showing to perceive both the moral and the social-conventional rules as more highly dependent on head-teacher's authority, and more breakable than older youth do. These differences were stronger for the social-conventional rules (table 2).

Involvement in Bullying and Perception of Moral and Social-Conventional Rules

On the basis of peer-nominations (PRQ), four groups of youngsters with different forms of participation in bullying episodes were identified: 82 children bullying peers as ringleaders or ringleader assistants, named *bullies* (26.4 % of the sample, 92.7 % were boys; 43 children and 39 early adolescents); 87 *defenders of the victim(s)* (28 % of participants, 75,9 % were girls; 38 children and 49 early adolescents); 54 *victims* (17.4 % of the sample, 54,9 % were boys; 22 children and 32 early adolescents) 88 *bystanders*, that is youngsters non actively involved in bullying situations (28.3 % of participants, 60 % were girls; 26 children and 62 early adolescents). Chi Square tests showed that bullying groups significantly differed for both gender ($\chi^2(3) = 86.53$, $p < .001$), and age ($\chi^2(3) = 9.46$, $p < .05$).

A MANOVA was performed on each of the examined rule dimensions, by specifying bullying groups (4-level between subject factor) and the kind of rule (2-level within subjects factor) as independent variables. In addition to the confirmed significant main effects of the kind of rule on all the rule dimensions considered, forms of participation in bullying were shown to have significant main effects (*ps* < .05) on all the investigated characteristics of the rule, with the exception of *rule changeability* (table 3). Student-Newman-Keuls post-hoc tests revealed that bullies perceived the rules as more dependent on teacher/head-teacher's authority, and more context-related, that is less generalizable, than peers with other roles. Furthermore, victims and defenders scored higher than bystanders on the *rule dependence on teacher's* and *head-teacher's authorities* (*rule dependence on teacher's authority* mean scores: Bullies = .57; Victims = .48; Defenders .34; Bystanders = .25; *rule dependence on head-teacher's authority* mean scores: Bullies = .69; Victims = .51; Defenders .42; Bystanders = .30; *rule dependence on the context*: Bullies = .20; Bystanders .09; Victims = .06; Defenders = .02).

With reference to the perception of the *acceptability of the rule-breaking*, a interactive effect of bullying groups by kind of rules appeared ($F(3, 300) = .3.49$, $p < .05$, $\eta^2 = .03$). Follow-up ANOVAs were performed to test bullying groups' differences on the perceived *acceptability of rule-breaking* of moral-rules and social-conventional rules separately. The bullying groups significantly differed only for the social-conventional rules (moral rules: $F(3, 303) = .89$, *ns*; social-conventional rules: $F(3, 303) = 4.22$, $p = .01$, $\eta^2 = .04$). Student-Newman-Keuls post-hoc tests revealed that bullies scored significantly higher than victims and bystanders on the acceptability of the social-conventional rule-breaking behaviors (table 3).

Table 2. Means (Standard Deviations) of the rule dimensions by the kind of rule (moral vs. social-conventional) and the age-level (mid-childhood vs. early adolescence)

	Moral rules		Social-conventional rules		F		
	Mid-child. (n = 129)	Early ad. (n = 175)	Mid-child (n = 129)	Early ad. (n = 175)	Rule Kind	Age-level	Rule kind X Age-level
Rule dependence on teacher's authority	.35 (.57)	.23 (.50)	.64 (.69)	.43 (.63)	47.39***	7.91**	1.41
Rule dependence on head-teacher's authority	.40 (.62)	.25 (.52)	.86 (.71)	.46 (.63)	84.08***	20.04***	11.56***
Acceptability of the rule-breaking	.04 (.14)	.02 (.17)	1.43 (.39)	.09 (.32)	1246.73***	1022.31***	797.51***
Rule changeability	.18 (.45)	.26 (.52)	.29 (.52)	.39 (.59)	18.17***	2.67	.13
Rule dependence on the context	.09 (.32)	.11 (.35)	.37 (.53)	.36 (.50)	73.55***	.01	.21

Note. $* p < .05; ** p < .01; *** p < .001$.

Table 3. Means (Standard Deviations) of the rule dimensions by the kind of rule (moral vs. social-conventional) and the bullying groups (Bullies vs. Defenders vs. Victims vs. Bystanders)

	Moral rules				Social-conventional rules				F		
	Bullies (n = 81)	*Defenders (n = 87)*	*Victims (n = 51)*	*Bystanders (n = 85)*	*Bullies (n = 81)*	*Defenders (n = 87)*	*Victims (n = 51)*	*Bystanders (n = 85)*	*Rule Kind*	*Bullying gr.*	*Rule kind X Bull. gr.*
Rule dependence on teacher's authority	.44 (.62)	.21 (.45)	.37 (.62)	.15 (.42)	.70 (.75)	.48 (.63)	.59 (.68)	.34 (.55)	42.78***	6,38***	.39
Rule dependence on head-teacher's authority	.51 (.68)	.21 (.47)	.40 (.62)	.18 (.45)	.87 (.74)	.63 (.70)	.62 (.68)	.42 (.58)	66.51***	8.04***	1.68
Acceptability of the rule-breaking	.05 (.26)	.02 (.11)	.03 (.12)	.01 (.08)	.89 (.75)	.65 (.77)	.60 (.74)	.49 (.70)	209.68***	4.58**	3.49*
Rule changeability	.33 (.58)	.16 (.42)	.24 (.52)	.20 (.45)	.44 (.62)	.29 (.53)	.33 (.55)	.34 (.55)	16.81***	1,76	.18
Rule dependence on the context	.20(.48)	.04 (.19)	.15 (.44)	.04 (.13)	.40 (.56)	.28 (.47)	.38 (.47)	.39 (.52)	68.81***	2,69*	1,29

Note. * $p < .05$; ** $p < .01$; *** $p < .001$.

Possible age-level moderations on the main and interactive effects of bullying groups were explored by adding the age-level as between-subject factor to the MANOVA models. The age-level moderated the main effects of bullying groups on *rule dependence on the context* (age-level X bullying group: $F(3, 296) = 3.10$, $p < .05$, $\eta^2 = .03$), and *on the acceptability of the rule-breaking* (age-level X bullying groups: $F(3, 296) = 6.14$, $p < .001$, $\eta^2 = .06$). With reference to the perceived *acceptability of rule-breaking*, the age-level also significantly moderated the interactive effect of kind of rule by bullying groups (age-level X kind of rule X bullying groups: $F(3, 296) = 3.50$, $p < .05$, $\eta^2 = .03$).

In order to make clearer the moderation effects by the age-level, for both the *rule dependence on the context* and the *acceptability of the rule-breaking*, follow-up MANOVAs specifying the kind of rule and bullying groups as independent factors were performed among children and early adolescents separately. The main effect of bullying groups on *rule dependence on the context* was significant only among early adolescents (children: $F(3, 125) = .21$, *ns*; early adolescents: $F(3, 171) = 5.51$, $p = .001$, $\eta^2 = .09$), with bullies scoring significantly higher than bystanders and defenders (early adolescents' *rule-dependence on the context* mean scores: Bullies = .41; Victims = .26; Bystanders .20; Defenders = .11).

With reference to the perceived *acceptability of the rule-breaking*, the main effect of bullying groups and the interactive effect of kind of rule by bullying groups were again significant only among early adolescents (main effect of bullying groups: $F(3, 171) = 7.42$, $p = .001$, $\eta^2 = .12$; interactive effect of kind of rule X bullying groups: $F(3, 171) = 5.14$, $p = .01$, $\eta^2 = .08$). Since the main effects of the interacting variables are not interpretable when the interactive effects are significant, follow-up one-way ANOVAs of bullying groups effects on the perceived *acceptability of rule-breaking* were performed separately for the moral and the social-conventional rules among early adolescents. In adolescence, bullying groups significantly differed only for the *acceptability of social-conventional rule-breaking*, with bullies scoring significantly higher (Student-Newman-Keuls post-hoc tests) than victims, bystanders and defenders (Social-conventional rule *acceptability of the rule-breaking* mean scores: Bullies = .30; Victims = .05; bystanders .04; Defenders = .00).

CONCLUSION

Rule Domains and Age-Related Differences

In accordance with Turiel's assumptions [1983], also in our data children show to discriminate between different kinds of rules, that is moral and social-conventional obligations. Both the Exploratory and the Confirmatory Factor Analysis confirmed that moral rules, aimed at protecting others from harm, and social-conventional norms, having the purpose to preserve the appropriate functioning of the context, are distinct kinds of obligations in the perception of children, and the social-conventional rules are believed to be more dependent on the context-authorities' dictates.

Further, youth correctly attribute more social-conventional characteristic to obligations that are more aimed at preserving the social order in school, than preserving well-being of persons. Thus, besides being believed to depend on authorities, these norms are understood to be more alterable, and context-related than moral rules, and their transgressions is judged to be more acceptable. Mid-children, in particular, appear to perceive a higher difference between moral rules and social-conventional obligations, evaluating the former as less dependent on authorities, and less breakable than the latter.

This picture of the children comprehension of rules is coherent with the literature showing that children are able to discriminate among moral and social-conventional obligations from a early age [e.g., Smetana & Braeges, 1990; for a review see also Helwig & Turiel, 2004]. Nevertheless, our outcomes also suggest that the ability of distinguishing different kinds of rule changes with the age, and a more complex understanding of the nature of norms probably appears in adolescence.

In the present study two close levels of age were compared, that is mid-childhood vs. early-adolescence, however adolescents (11-15 year) showed to believe that the value of rules granting people from harm does not stem from authorities' willingness at a higher extent than a little younger children (7-10 years) do. On the other hand, in comparison to children, adolescents attribute a higher intrinsic validity to the social-conventional rules, that they consider to depend on authorities' dictates more than moral rules but in a smaller measure than children believe.

Altogether, and considering that early-adolescents judge the transgression of all the types of norms more wrong than children do, a conception of all the rules as intrinsically valid and non-violable seem to characterize the early adolescence age. By growing, children develop more complex and articulate concepts of rights, justice, and democracy, and become increasingly able to drew distinctions between social contexts, and to understand for what situations and decisions adult authorities is more appropriate. They also learn to discriminate and consider in their judgments moral and social-conventional aspects of the same situation [Helwig & Kim, 1999; Helwig & Turiel, 2004]. For all these reasons, in early adolescence youth may be more able to understand the purposes of social-conventional norms, and better recognize their intrinsic value.

RULE COMPREHENSION AND ACTUAL BEHAVIOR

Children's understanding of rules has been found to be only partially related with the youth's forms of participation in bullying. Compared to their peers, above all bystanders, bullies perceive the validity of rules as more dependent on the context-authorities, and in early adolescence they judge the norms to be more related to the context and less generalizable than bystanders and defenders do. Overall, youngsters bullying others seem to attribute to the norms a higher conventionality, revealing a less-mature conception of the roots of norms.

However, bullies evaluate transgressions as more acceptable than peers only when they are adolescents and the obligation is social-conventional. Even if bullies' more social-conventional comprehension of rules suggests some their difficulties in recognizing the intrinsic values of norms, children bullying peers do understand that the transgression of moral rules is wrong. Therefore, a gap seems to exists between the evaluation of non-acceptability of the moral transgressions, and the actual action breaking moral rules (the bullying behavior).

Other studies [Tisak & Jankowski, 1996] found that young offenders consider moral transgressions more wrong than breaking-actions of social-conventional norms, but they report both moral and conventional reasons when asked to support their judgments. Similarly, children with behavioral disorders focus more on the conventional components of actions when considering moral transgressions [Nucci & Herman, 1982]. These research data are coherent with the overall pattern of our outcomes, showing bullies to be more concerned about social-conventional facets of norms than their peers, but also to be able to understand the moral transgression as wrong. This outcome could be explained by the hypothesis that youngsters, used to behaving aggressively, start to conceive aggressive behaviors as normal and conventional [Harvey, Fletcher, & French, 2001], therefore as actions related to the social-conventional domain of decision and, for this reason, less wrong. In accordance with this supposition in the present study early-adolescent bullies already show a tendency to consider social-conventional rules as more breakable than their peers do.

However, it is also conceivable that other psychological mechanisms and processes intervene, and explain the separation emerged in bullies between the judgments on moral transgressions and their actual behavior. Even if children are able to understand and evaluate the moral transgressions as wrong, the moral disengagement processes may allow them to behave aggressively and to self-justify their violation actions. On the other hand, a lack in the emotional empathic skill of sharing the other's pain, may make the moral transgression easier, even if it is comprehended as wrong. Research data on higher moral disengagement mechanisms and emotions, and lower empathic skills typical of bullies [e.g., Menesini et al., 2003; Espelage et al., 2004; Gini, 2006] give some support to this hypothesis.

In the present study we explored neither the justifications children can report for their judgements, nor the possible components of morality able to moderate the associations between moral reasoning and knowledge, and the actual behavior. Future research projects may follow these two lines of research, trying to better understand the morality of bullying.

From the Research to the Intervention

The bullies' social-conventional understanding of rules appeared in this study, along with bullies' higher tendency to moral disengaging [Gini, 2006], underline the value that anti-bullying intervention programs also aim to enhance children's morality. Children should be taught to comprehend the roots of the norms and their intrinsic value as foundations of the social system, and to discriminate and consider the moral, conventional, and personal components of the social actions. Enhancing children's moral reasoning skills of recognizing the situation aspects pertaining to different domains of moral reasoning and decisions may also help the child to correctly interpret the social interactions, by improving the on-line social information processes from which aggressions may originate [Arsenio & Lemerise, 2004].

Recent intervention programs also extend the attention from bullies and victims to the bystanders, trying to mobilize them to support the victimized peers [Salmivalli, Kärnä, & Poskiparta, in press]. As hypothesized, in the present study defenders of the victims appear to understand the rules as less dependent on authorities and context than bullies do, and to perceive the rule transgressions as more unacceptable. However, bystanders have been found to have even a better understanding of the values of obligations, and to view rule-breaking actions as more wrong then all their peers. Bystanders' moral reasoning and knowledge are not lacking but do not seem to promote actual pro-social behaviors. These last data suggest that effective intervention programs should focus on all the components of the morality, also including empathic skills and moral emotions, that may be able to lead from the moral understanding to the moral actual action.

ACKNOWLEDGMENTS

The authors are grateful to the students, teachers, and school administrators who participated in this study. A particular acknowledgment is due to Elena Rivolta for her help in the data collection. Correspondence regarding this article should be sent to Simona C. S. Caravita, C.R.*I.d.e.e.*, Dipartimento di Psicologia, Università Cattolica del Sacro Cuore, L.go Gemelli, 1, 20123, Milano, Italy. Electronic mail may be sent to simona.caravita@unicatt.it.

REFERENCES

Arsenio, W. F., & Lemerise, E. A. (2004). Aggression and moral development: Integrating social information processing and moral domain model. *Child Development,* 75, 4, 987-1002.

Astor, R. A. (1994). Children's moral reasoning about family and peer violence: the role of provocation and retribution. *Child Development,* 65, 1054-1067.

Bandura, A. (1986). *Social Foundations of Thoughts and Action.* Englewood Cliffs, NJ: Prentice Hall.

Buchanan-Barrow, E., & Barrett, M. (1998). Children's rule discrimination within the context of the school. *British Journal of Developmental Psychology,* 16, 539-551.

Caravita, S., Di Blasio, P., & Salmivalli, C. (2009). Unique and interactive effects of empathy and social status on involvement in bullying *Social Development*, 18, 140-163.

Camodeca, M., Goossens, F.A., Meerum Terwogt, M., & Schuengel, C. (2002). Bullying and victimization among school-age children: Stability and link to proactive and reactive aggression. *Social Development,* 11, 332–345.

Catron, T. F., & Masters, J. C. (1993). Mothers' and children's conceptualizations of corporal punishment. *Child Development,* 64, 1815-1828.

Coie, J. D., & Dodge, K. A. (1998). Aggression and antisocial behavior. In W. Damon, & N. Eisenberg (Eds.), *Handbook of child psychology,* Vol. *3: Social, emotional, and personality development* (pp. 779-862). New York: Wiley.

Crane-Ross, D. A., Tisak, M. S., & Tisak, J. (1998). Aggression and conventional rule violation among adolescents: social reasoning predictors of social behavior. *Aggressive Behavior,* 24, 347-365.

Espelage, D. L., Mebane, S. E., & Adams, R. S. (2004). Empathy, caring, and bullying: Toward an understanding of complex associations. In D. L. Espelage, & S. M. Swearer (Eds.), *Bullying in American schools: A social-ecological perspective on prevention and intervention* (pp. 37-61). Mahwah NJ, London: Lawrence Erlbaum Associates Publishers.

Garandeau, C. F., & Cillessen, A. H. N. (2006). From indirect aggression to invisible aggression: A conceptual view on bullying and peer group manipulation. *Aggression and Violent Behavior,* 11, 612–625.

Gini, G. (2006). Social Cognition and Moral Cognition in Bullying: What's Wrong?. *Aggressive Behavior,* 32, 528–539.

Gini, G., Albiero, P., Benelli, B., & Altoè, G. (2007). Does empathy predict adolescents' bullying and defending behavior? *Aggressive Behavior,* 33, 467–476.

Harvey, R. J., Fletcher, J., & French, D. J. (2001). Social reasoning: A source of influence on aggression. *Clinical Psychology Review,* 21, 447-469.

Hawkins, D. L., Pepler, D. J., & Craig, W. M. (2001). Naturalistic observations of peer interventions in bullying. *Social Development,* 10, 512-527.

Helwig, C. C., & Kim, S. (1999). Children's evaluations of decision-making procedures in peer, family and school context. *Child Development,* 70, 502-512.

Helwig, C. C., & Turiel, E. (2004). Children's social and moral reasoning. In P. K. Smith, & C. H. Hart (Eds.), *Blackwell Handbook of Childhood Social Development.* (pp. 475-490). Malden: Blackwell Publishing Ltd.

Helwig, C. C., Zelazo, P., & Wilson, M. (2001). Children's judgements of psychological harm in normal and noncanonical situations. *Child Development,* 72, 66-81.

Kohlberg, L. (1981). *Essays on moral development: The philosophy of moral development.* San Francisco: Harper & Row.

Much, N., & Shweder, R. A. (1978). Speaking of rules: The analysis of culture in breach. In W. Damon (Ed.), *New directions for child development: Moral development.* (pp. 19-39). San Francisco: Jossey-Bass.

Menesini, E., & Gini, G. (2000). Il bullismo come processo di gruppo. Adattamento e validazione del Questionario Ruoli dei Partecipanti alla popolazione italiana (En. tr., Bullying as a group process. Adaptation and validation of the Participant Role Questionnaire to the Italian population). *Età Evolutiva,* 66, 18–32.

Menesini, E., Sanchez, V., Fonzi, A., Ortega, R., Costabile, A., & Lo Feudo, G. (2003). Moral emotions and bullying: A cross-national comparison of differences between bullies, victims and outsiders. *Aggressive Behavior,* 29, 515-530.

Muthén, L., & Muthén, B. (1998–2004). *Mplus user's guide* (3rd ed.). Los Angeles, CA: Muthén & Muthén.

Nucci, L. P., & Herman, S. (1982). Behavioral disordered children's conceptions of moral, conventional, and personal issues. *Journal of Abnormal Child Psychology,* 10, 411-426.

Nucci, L. P., & Nucci, M. S. (1982a). Children's responses to moral and social conventional transgression in free-play settings. *Child Development,* 53, 1337-1342.

Nucci, L. P., & Nucci, M. S. (1982b). Children's social interactions in the context of moral and conventional transgressions. *Child Development,* 53, 403-412.

Nucci, L. P., & Turiel, E. (1978). Social interactions and the development of social concepts in preschool children. *Child Development,* 49, 400-407.

Nucci, L. P., & Turiel, E. (2000). The moral and the personal: Sources of conflicts. In L. Nucci, G. Saxe, & E. Turiel (Eds.), *Culture, thought, and development.* (pp. 115-140). Mahwah, NJ: Lawrence Erlbaum Associates.

Olweus, D. (1993). *Bullying at school. What we know and what we can do.* Oxford, UK: Blackwell Publishing Ltd.

Piaget, J. (1932). *The moral judgement of the child.* London: Routledge and Kegan Paul.

Rodkin, P. C. (2004). Peer ecologies of aggression and bullying. In D. L. Espelage, & S. M. Swearer (Eds.), *Bullying in American schools: A social-ecological perspective on prevention and intervention* (pp. 87-106). Mahwah NJ, London: Lawrence Erlbaum Associates Publishers.

Ross, L., & Nisbett, R. M. (1991). *The person and the situation: Perspectives on social psychology*. Philadelphia: Temple University Press.

Salmivalli, C., Kärnä, A., & Poskiparta, E. (in press). From peer putdowns to peer support: A theoretical model and how it translated into a national anti-bullying program. In S. Shimerson, S. Swearer & D. Espelage (Eds.), *International handbook of school bullying*.

Salmivalli, C., Lagerspetz, K. M. J., Bjorkqvist, K., Österman, K., & Kaukiainen, A. (1996). Bullying as a group process: Participant Roles and Their Relations to Social Status Within the Group. *Aggressive Behavior*, 22, 1-15.

Siegal, M., & Storey, R. M. (1985). Day care and children's conceptions of moral and social rules. *Child Development,* 56, 1001-1008.

Smetana, J. G. (1981). Preschool children's conceptions of moral and social rules. *Child Development,* 52, 1333-1336.

Smetana, J. G. (1984). Toddlers' social interactions regarding moral and conventional transgressions. *Child Development,* 55, 1767-1776.

Smetana, J. G. (1988). Adolescents' and parents' conceptions of parental authority. *Child Development,* 59, 321-335.

Smetana, J. G., & Braeges, J. (1990). The development of toddlers' moral and conventional judgements. *Merrill-Palmer Quarterly,* 36, 329-346.

Smetana, J. G., Schlagman, N., & Adams, P. W. (1993). Preschool children's judgements about hypothetical and actual transgressions. *Child Development,* 64, 202-214.

Tisak, M. S. (1995). Domains of social reasoning and beyond. In R. Vasta (Ed.), *Annals of child development* (V. 11, pp. 95-130). London: Jessica Kingsley.

Tisak, M. S., & Jankowski, A. M. (1996). Societal rule evaluations: Adolescent offenders' reasoning about moral, conventional, and personal rules. *Aggressive Behavior,* 22, 195-207.

Tisak, M. S., & Turiel, E. (1988). Variation of seriousness of transgressions and children's moral and conventional concepts. *Developmental Psychology,* 24, 352-357.

Turiel, E. (1983). The development of social knowledge: *Morality and convention.* San Francisco: Jossey-Bass.

Turiel, E. (1998). The development of morality. In W. Damon, & N. Eisenberg (Eds.), *Handbook of child psychology, Vol. 3: Social, emotional, and personality development* (pp. 863-932). New York: Wiley.

Turiel, E., & Smetana, J. G. (1984). Social knowledge and social action. The coordination of domains. In W. M. Kurtines & J. L. Gewirtz (Eds.), *Morality, moral behavior, and moral development: Basic issues in theory and research* (pp. 261-282). New York: Wiley.

Warden, D., & MacKinnon, S. (2003). Prosocial children, bullies and victims: An investigation of their sociometric status, empathy and social problem-solving strategies. *British Journal of Developmental Psychology,* 21, 367–385.

Zelazo, P. D., Helwig, C. C., & Lau, A. (1996). Intention, act, and outcome in behavioral prediction and moral judgment. *Child Development,* 67, 2478-2492.

APPENDIX

The four scenarios included in the measure assessing rule understanding.

Scenarios assessing the child's understanding of moral (school) rules
1. In Davide's school, there is a rule that you must never push anyone off the climbing frame. One day at school, when Davide is playing on the climbing frame, he pushes Stefano so hard that he falls to the ground.
2. In Lucia's school there is a rule that you must not take other children's things. One day, Lucia takes Andrea's book when he's not looking and puts it in her bag.

Scenarios assessing the child's understanding of social-conventional (school) rules
1. In the school of Guglielmo a rule is in force so that to run inside the scholastic building is never allowed. One day, when the lessons of the morning are finished, William very quickly races along the corridor because he wants to be the first one to go out into the courtyard.
2. In the school of Rachel there is a rule according to which one must always rearrange in the special spaces the scholastic materials (i.e., the books methodically in the shelves of the bookstore after finishing reading them, the notebooks in order of colour in the closet…). One day, after Rachel has skimmed through many books, she has simply abandoned them all on the floor of the bookstore and she has gone out for lunch.

In: Social Development
Editor: Lynda R. Elling

ISBN: 978-1-60741-612-8
© 2009 Nova Science Publishers, Inc.

Chapter 14

EVERYDAY THEORIZING AND THE CONSTRUCTION OF KNOWLEDGE

Sherrie Bade

Thompson Rivers University, Kamloops, BC, Canada

In modern societies non-academic citizens are rarely recognized for their ability to construct knowledge. Engagement with theory that contributes to knowledge development is considered the mandate of professionals or those who are situated within academic circles. It is apparent to many individuals, including academics, that through day-to-day decision making the average person, although not associated with traditional research bodies, actively theorizes and constructs knowledge. A general acknowledgement of these abilities encourages collaboration among all citizens and prevents the unhealthy marginalization of a large segment of the population. As well, theory development and knowledge construction become demystified and result in communities of learning, collaboration and civility.

Diverse worldviews directly shape ontological and epistemological understandings related to what counts as valid theory and credible knowledge. The empiricist believes that true knowledge exists objectively outside of the person and is waiting to be discovered; those with a constructivist perspective believe that knowledge is relative, subjective and dependent on context (Crotty, 2007). The empirical world view values objectivity whereas more relative worldviews "reconnect what empiricism [has] separated–the dualism of the knowing subject and the object of knowing" thereby valuing subjectivity and lived experience (Smith & Hodkinson, 2005, p. 917). Kirby, Greaves and Reid (2006) discuss knowledge construction as a political process which has traditionally been conducted by universities and institutes of research. Those who drive the political process also have the power to control knowledge generation. A common yet little understood phrase is that "knowledge is power." One wonders if this is true. Are not professionals and academics who define what constitutes knowledge more powerful than knowledge itself? "Whoever is in a position of power is able to create knowledge supporting that power relationship. Whatever a society accepts as knowledge or truth inevitably ends up strengthening the power of some and limiting the power of others" (Brookfield, 2005, p. 136). To interrupt the power brokering of this political process, academic and non-academics alike can choose to work together to construct knowledge that retains power within the community by remaining responsive to identified community goals.

Partnerships between professionals, particularly those working within the system, and citizens that are developed in a respectful and thoughtful manner encourage mutual empowerment (Vanderplaat, 2002). Mutual empowerment is a relational endeavour that involves all who are involved in the community development process. "One can never be just an empowerer or a person in need of empowerment. In a mutual approach to empowerment, everyone involved, regardless of position of power and privilege, recognizes that she or he is both agent and subject … in a truly empowering process everyone changes" (Vanderplaat, 2002, pp. 93-94). Community Based Research (CBR) is one form of inquiry which includes both academic and experiential citizens working in collaboration to seek mutual empowerment. This occurs as local knowledge is valued as an alternative to mainstream research/knowledge production. Participatory research supports each person as they make meaning of their life experiences and supports them as these experiences are then expanded into useful knowledge. In this way the experiential knowledge of community members constructively critiques social inequities and may also address social issues more effectively at the local level.

The *Moving Women Beyond Bars: Building Community* initiative is one example of how those from academic circles are able to partner with vulnerable and experiential women in the community (Warnell, Bade & Carriere, 2008). The starting place for this initiative is bringing women having past conflict with the law and their mentors/allies into safe and communicative spaces where relationships may form and community develop. As trust builds it is anticipated that a participatory research team will evolve to identify the issues criminalized women experience as well as to generate useful grass roots knowledge. Foundations for this kind of research with women are currently being structured at the local level through other innovative initiatives some of which include *Linking Women to Health and Wellness* (Carriere, 2008) and *Voice: Challenging the Stigma of Addiction* (Paivinen & Bade, 2008). Initiatives such as *Moving Women Beyond Bars: Building Community* demonstrate that those who are experiential or have lived experiences outside of the mainstream may resist a system that silences them and respond by organizing into visible, knowledgeable and influential communities (Jurgens, 2005; Kerr, Small, Peeace, Douglas, Pierre & Wood, 2006; Rabinovitch & Lewis, 2001; Rans, 2005). Researching with people, rather than on them, produces healthy empowered communities and contributes to egalitarian relationships within a civil society.

Civil society is essentially comprised of "all those forms of collective human association not directly controlled by the state or corporations" (Brookfield, 2005, pp. 234-235). People come together and stand outside of the complex bureaucracies that control people's lives through the mechanisms of money and power (Habermas, 1984). Integral to civil society is the development of community spaces or what Habermas calls the public sphere which "is the civic space or 'commons' in which adults come together to debate and decide their response to shared issues and problems" (Brookfield, 2005, p. 230). Power is shared, not reluctantly but generously so that community is built and lives are open to common purposes. Civil society is a place where connections are made and relationships established. It does not require a formal gathering but occurs wherever people meet. Relationships that form in the public sphere are based on mutual respect and understanding as well as a valuing of the knowledge that comes from a range of lived experiences. Each brings what they can offer to mutually explore and theorize about what works and what does not work in everyday worlds. Grassroots knowledge is then constructed to determine avenues toward egalitarian communities in which civility and health are promoted at both the individual and community level.

If valid knowledge development is believed to rest within the purview of professionals in the academy then the everyday theorizing capabilities of individuals within the community remain unrecognized or if recognized, discounted. However, if theory generation is viewed as a product of ordinary people's discovery of personal meaning within the experiential world then theory and knowledge generation become different in content but not in kind to that of the professional or academic. With this understanding, partnerships between academic and non-academic citizens may be developed in a respectful and thoughtful manner to build a strong and healthy civil society.

REFERENCES

Brookfield, S. D. (2005). *The power of critical theory.* USA: Jossey-Bass.

Carriere, G. (2008). Linking women to health and wellness: Street ourtreach takes a population health approach. *International Journal of Drug Policy, 19,* 205-210.

Crotty, M. (2007). *The foundations of social research.* Thousand Oaks, CA: Sage Publications, Inc.

Habermas, J. (1984). *The theory of communicative action* (T. McCarthy, Trans. Vol. 2). Boston: Beacon Press.

Jurgens, R. (2005). *"Nothing about us without us" greater, meaningful involvement of people who use illegal drugs: A public health, ethical, and human rights imperative.* Toronto, Ont., Canada: Canadian HIV/AIDS Legal Network.

Kerr, T., Small, W., Peeace, W., Douglas, D., Pierre, A., & Wood, E. (2006). Harm reduction by a "user-run" organization: A case study of the Vancouver area network of drug users (VANDU). *The International Journal of Drug Policy, 17*(2), 61-69.

Kirby, S. L., Greaves, L., & Reid, C. (2006). *Experience research social change: Methods beyond the mainstream.* Peterborough, Ont., Canada: Broadview Press.

Paivinen, H., & Bade, S. (2008). Voice: Challenging the stigma of addiction; a nursing perspective. *International Journal of Drug Policy, 19,* 214-219.

Rabinovitch, J., & Lewis, M. (2001). *Impossible, eh? The story of peers.* Vancouver, BC: Save the Children Canada.

Rans, S. A. (2005). Hidden treasures: Building community connections by engaging thegifts of *people on welfare, people with disabilities, people with mental illness, older adults, young people. Evanston, IL: ABCD Institute.

Smith, J. K., & Hodkinson, P. (2005). Relativism, criteria, and politics. In N. K. Denzin & Y. S. Lincoln (Eds.), *The sage handbook of qualitative research* (3rd ed., pp. 915-932). Thousand Oaks, CA: Sage Publications, Inc.

Vanderplaat, M. (2002). Emancipatory politics and health promotion practice: The health professional as social activist. In E. Young & V. Hayes (Eds.), *Transforminghealth promotion practice* (pp. 87-98). Philadelphia, PA: F. A. Davis Company.

Warnell, R., Bade, S., & Carriere, G. (2008). *Moving women beyond bars: Building community*. Vancouver, BC: Women's Health Research Network: Team Community-based Research Funds.

Acknowledgment: The author would like to acknowledge and thank Star Mahara, a colleague at Thompson Rivers University, for her editorial support and conversations regarding this commentary.

In: Social Development
Editor: Lynda R. Elling

ISBN: 978-1-60741-612-8
© 2009 Nova Science Publishers, Inc.

Chapter 15

ON SNIPS AND SNAILS: PERCEPTIONS OF THE ORIGINS OF GENDER DIFFERENCES

Jessica W. Giles[1], Christa G. Ice[2] and Talia C. Gursky[3]
[1] University of Colorado/Naropa University, U.S.A.
[2] University of West Virginia, U.S.A.
[3] Tufts University, U.S.A.

ABSTRACT

The present study examines children's tendency to engage in stereotyping and essentialist reasoning about gender-related preferences. Across 2 studies, 132 3-8-year-olds engaged in individual interviews where they were asked to make predictions about hypothetical 5-year-olds' toy, color, and occupation preferences, and then asked to make a series of inferences about the nature and causal origins of those preferences. Several patterns of results emerged. There was a curvilinear relationship between the tendency to suggest gender stereotypical preferences and participant age, with stereotype-consistent responses peaking at age 5 and then declining afterwards. Children's tendency to engage in essentialist reasoning showed a similar age-related pattern. In addition, although children provided more stereotype-consistent responses when reasoning about boys than girls, they showed an increased tendency to essentialize the preferences of girls. These results contribute to growing evidence that although essentialist reasoning is accessible in a wide range of domains, it is differentially instantiated across contexts.

ACKNOWLEDGMENTS

The authors wish to thank Brian Compton for assistance with computer programming, and Ashley Beaufort, Missy Grahn, Matt Groebe, Ann Rice, Jen Samson, and Corey Sullivan for assistance with data collection and coding. The authors would especially like to thank the administrators, teachers, parents, and children at Children's House Montessori, Christ the King School, David Lipscomb Elementary, and Ezell Harding School. Address requests for further information to Jessica W. Giles, 2130 Arapahoe Ave. Boulder, CO 80302. Email: gilesj@colorado.edu.

INTRODUCTION

Gender is a highly salient category, one that children and adults use to make a wide range of nonobvious inductive inferences (Maccoby, 1988; Martin, 1989; Rothbart & Taylor, 1992). Indeed, from an early age, children learn that gender information is a very useful tool for making sense of the social world (Bussey & Bandura, 1992; see Huston, 1985, and Ruble & Martin, 1998). As early as preschool, children show systematic tendencies to use gender to make predictions about a wide range of behavioral outcomes (Miller, Tautner & Ruble, 2007), including behaviors as diverse as aggression, helping, sports, and shopping (Giles & Heyman, 2005; Ruble & Dweck, 1995; Serbin, Powlishta & Gulko, 1993; see also Signorella, Bigler, & Liben, 1993, for a review and meta-analysis).

In addition to examining children's reasoning about the relationship between gender and behavior, recent research has examined how beliefs about gender might figure into children's reasoning about *mental states*, such as emotional reactions to events, dispositions, and preferences (Ruble & Martin, 1998). For example, even 2-year-olds systematically distinguish male from female with regard to traits, emotions, and trait-relevant behavior (Cowan & Hoffman, 1986; Kuhn, Nash, & Brucken, 1978; Serbin, Powlishta, & Gulko, 1993). Additionally, children as young as preschool age realize that gender categories go beyond perceptual appearances and capture important similarities and differences between people (Gelman, Collman, & Maccoby, 1986).

Of interest in the present research is children's tendency to use gender information to reason about *preferences*. In particular, we are interested in the extent to which children of different ages might make use of gender stereotypes when making inferences about the kinds of preferences that males and females have. Conversely, we are also interested in the circumstances under which children predict preferences that are decidedly inconsistent with gender stereotypes. In other words, when are children most likely to hold flexible beliefs about gender-related preferences? This investigation contributes to a growing effort to better understand the broader sociocognitive context of resistance to stereotyping (Bem, 1983; Brown & Gilligan, 1992; hooks, 1992; Liben & Bigler, 2002; Ward, 1996).

Although many different kinds of preferences have been examined in the literature (see Ruble & Martin, 1998, for an overview), we have chosen for investigation a common set of three: color preference, toy preference, and preference for a future occupation. These kinds of preference-related stereotypes have indeed been examined previously in the literature (e.g. Aubry, Ruble, & Silverman, 1999; Bailey & Nihlen, 1990; Picariello, Greenberg, & Pillemer, 1990), but what sets the present study apart is that we are interested not only in the kinds of preferences children report for boys versus girls, but also in the kinds of explanations children give for *why* these preferences exist. Gelman and Kalish (1993) have suggested that if children's social categories are indeed theory-based, then causes should be crucial to their category representations. In fact, Gelman (2003) has gone so far as to suggest that children are *causal determinists*, that is, that they are highly motivated to seek out the causes for what they observe in the world.

In particular, we are interested in the tendency for children to provide internal, biological, or nativist explanations for behavior (see also Choi, Nisbett, & Norenzayan, 1999, Hofstede, 1980, and Miller, 1984). Indeed, there is increasing evidence that in many contexts, young children's causal inferences about the social world are driven by what Gelman (2003) has referred to as an *innards principle*. In other words, children tend to believe that a person's biological *stuff* determines or at least largely constrains outward behavior. Although this phenomenon is by no means limited to children (see Haslam, 200x), there is substantial evidence that such tendencies towards *essentialist reasoning* may be especially marked in childhood (Gelman, 2003).

Indeed, the circumstances under which people engage in *psychological essentialism* has been a major focus of several converging research traditions, including those investigating the development of biological understanding, achievement motivation, and person perception (see Gelman, 2003). Psychological essentialism is the tendency to conceive of entities as having deep underlying natures that make them what they are, and that constrain potentially observable properties and behaviors (Medin, 1989; Medin & Heit, 1999; see also Gelman, Coley, & Gottfried, 1994, concerning essentialist reasoning in young children). When a characteristic is viewed in an essentialist way, it is thought to be a fundamental aspect of the entity that possesses it, and highly resistant to change (see Martin & Parker, 1995).

Recent research has examined people's essentialist beliefs about a wide variety of constructs, including social categories (Giles & Heyman, 2005; Haslam & Levy, 2006; Hirschfeld, 1996; Rothbart & Taylor, 1992), traits (Gelman, Heyman, & Legare, 2005), intelligence (Dweck, 1999), and sociomoral behavior (Giles, 2009; Giles & Heyman, 2003; Maas, Marecek, & Travers, 1978). An important conclusion to emerge from this research is that essentialist beliefs are more than a mere set of ontological abstractions (Haslam & Levy, 2006); on the contrary, they have important real-world implications, notably for social decision-making. For example, essentialist beliefs about aggression have been receiving increasing attention because they are associated with a tendency to exhibit motivational helplessness in the face of social challenge (Giles & Heyman, 2003; see also Dweck, 1999) and a tendency to make punitive judgments across a range of domains, including judgments of other people's guilt or innocence (Gervey et al., 1999; Giles, in press A; see Giles, 2003).

In light of substantial evidence that essentialist reasoning has important implications for social decision making, and in light of longstanding theoretical debates across the social sciences regarding the relationship between essentialist reasoning and the maintenance of hegemonic power structures, the present study seek to examine children's early emerging beliefs about gender differences in social behavior, and their tendency to essentialize these differences.

The present study had three interrelated goals. The first was to examine age-related patterns in children's tendency to make stereotype-consistent predictions about the preferences of boys versus girls. Based on an examination of literature reviews regarding the preferences that children view as gendered (Ruble & Martin, 1998), we included three of the most salient preference categories for children to consider for both male and female story characters: color preferences, occupational preferences, and toy preferences. Along these same lines, we were also interested in examining age-related patterns in the tendency to make stereotype-inconsistent inferences about preferences.

A second goal was to examine children's tendency to essentialize the preferences that they espoused. Specifically, to what extent do children view preferences as innately driven, stable over time, fixed, and persistent? What is the relationship between providing stereotype-consistent responses and making essentialist inferences about preferences? This goal speaks to the suggestion of Haslam (1998) that more research be undertaken to examine the relationship between stereotyping and causal attribution (see also Haslam & Levy, 2006; and Haslam, Rothschild, & Ernst, 2000).

A third goal was to examine the possibility that children might invoke essentialist frameworks differentially as a function of the gender of children they are reasoning about. This possibility is reasonable in light of evidence that even young children do not hold and utilize a general, undifferentiated set of causal attributions for social behavior, but rather have access to a range of causal explanations that they can invoke differentially depending on the particulars of the situation they are reasoning about (Giles & Heyman, 2004a, 2004b).

The present study engaged a broad range of children, from preschoolers to third graders. Although this presents some additional complexity in terms of examining age-related patterns, we included such a broad range in order to gain a more complete picture of the shape of age-related change in stereotyping and in essentialist reasoning.

STUDY 1

Method

Participants

Eighty-two participants (43 boys and 39 girls; M = 5ym, range 3y6m to 8y11m) were recruited from four ethnically diverse private schools in a large urban city in the mid-South of the United States.

Of the children who participated in this study, 73% were of Caucasian descent, 20% were of African-American or African descent, 5% were of Asian-American or Asian descent, and 1% was of Hispanic-American or Hispanic descent.

Procedure

Participants were interviewed individually at their schools during the school day, by one of 4 trained female experimenters. Interviews lasted roughly 20 minutes, and were presented in random order as part of a larger battery of measures. At the beginning of the interview, children were told, "I'm talking to kids today about what people are like. I am going to tell you about some kids I know and then I am going to ask you some questions about how you think those kids might feel and act. There are no right or wrong answers, just tell me what you think."

Design

Overview

Each participant received a total of 30 questions. These questions were grouped into 6 scenarios that varied in a 2 x 3 design. The manipulated variables were *character gender* (male, female) and *domain* (toy preference, color preference, and occupational preference). Character gender appeared in random order, and domain was nested in character gender, such that the three possible domains appeared in random order within each block of character gender. Within each of the 6 permutations, participants were asked a series of five questions.

Open-Ended Prediction Question

To introduce a character gender block, the script read, "Imagine a 5-year old [boy/girl]." Then, within a given character gender block, the script presented the domain manipulation via the following randomly ordered open-ended prediction questions:

What color do you think this [girl/boy] likes best?
What toy do you think this [girl/boy] likes to play with the most?
What do you think this [girl/boy] wants to be when [s/he] grows up?

Coding Open-Ended Prediction Questions

Responses were coded according to typically gender consistent (C), gender neutral (N), or typically gender inconsistent (I) responses. Coding for gender consistent and gender inconsistent responses consisted of a conservative, exclusive and exhaustive list of responses. Based on a close reading of the extent literature on gender stereotypes in early childhood (Ruble & Martin, 1998, provides a thorough overview), we prepared a conservative and exclusive list of stereotype-consistent responses as well as a conservative and exclusive list of stereotype-inconsistent, with most responses falling into a neutral category. By deliberately being very conservative in terms of what we were willing to call stereotype-consistent or – inconsistent behavior, we attempted to err on the specificity rather than the sensitivity side. Responses were coded by three independent coders who were blind to study hypotheses. Cohen's kappa was .95 or greater for all questions, and discrepancies were resolved through discussion.

Color Preference

Responses were coded as stereotype-consistent (C), neutral (N), or stereotype-inconsistent (I) responses (these were mutually exclusive categories). The following responses were considered stereotype-consistent for the female character: *pink, purple, lavender, hot pink, peach, and glitter*. The following actual responses were considered stereotype-consistent for the boy vignette: *blue, black, navy, and camo*. Stereotype-inconsistent responses were simply those responses that would be considered stereotype-consistent if they were given in regards to the other gender. For example, *pink* was a stereotype-inconsistent response regarding male characters, and *blue* was a stereotype-inconsistent response for female characters. All responses not coded as gender consistent or gender inconsistent were coded as gender neutral.

Toy Preference

Responses were coded as either stereotype-consistent (C), neutral (N), or stereotype-inconsistent (I) responses. The following responses were considered stereotype-consistent for the female characters: *doll (including Barbie, Bratz, Strawberry Shortcake, Polly Pockets, etc.), jewelry, makeup, bunnies, ponies, princess toys, ballerina toys, Hello Kitty, and Carebears*. The following responses were considered stereotype-consistent for male characters: *cars/trucks, trains, construction/building equipment, dinosaurs, balls (baseballs, footballs) superheroes (Superman, Batman, etc.), and videogames*. As in the color preference scenario, stereotype-inconsistent responses were defined as responses that would have been classified as stereotype-consistent if they were given in regards to the opposite gender (e.g.

pairing a male character with *tiara*). Neutral responses included responses such as *puzzles, crayons,* and *construction paper.*

Occupational Preference

Responses were coded as either stereotype-consistent (C), neutral (N), or stereotype-inconsistent (I) responses. The following responses were considered stereotype-consistent for female story characters: *mommy, teacher, nurse, model, cheerleader, princess, ballerina,* and *gymnast.* The following responses were considered stereotype-consistent for male story characters: *firefighter, police officer, doctor, ninja, construction worker, football/baseball player, mailman, racecar driver, pilot, astronaut,* and *soldier.* As in the other scenarios, stereotype-inconsistent responses were defined as responses that would have been classified as stereotype-consistent if they were given in regards to the opposite gender (e.g. pairing a female character with *knight*). Examples of neutral responses included *zookeeper, writer,* and *singer.*

Inference Questions

Following presentation of the open-ended prediction question in any given one of the 6 possible character gender/domain combinations, participants were asked a series of four inference questions in random order. These questions asked children to reason about nature of the particular preferences that they themselves suggested in the open-ended questions. Thus, their responses to the open-ended prediction questions were actually embedded into the verbiage of each inference question (denoted by blanks in the examples below)[1].

Origins. Children were asked, "Was s/he born to like _____, or did s/he learn to like _____,?" 'Born' responses were coded a 1, and 'learn' responses were coded a 0.

Temporal stability. Children were asked, "Some kids would say that s/he will still like _____ when s/he is 10 years old. Do you think this is right or wrong?" The response options "right" or "wrong" were presented in random order. Responses were coded 1 for 'right' and 0 for 'wrong.'

Malleability. Children were asked, "Could s/he stop liking _____ if s/he tried? If yes, would it be easy or hard for her/him to stop?" The response options 'easy' and 'hard' were presented in random order. Responses were coded 1 for 'no,' 0.5 for 'hard,' and 0 for 'easy.'

Unsupported persistence. Children were asked, "Do you think s/he would still like _____, if no other [girls/boys] liked _____?" Responses were coded 1 for 'yes' and 0 for 'no.'

---

[1] Note that the wording in inference question examples listed here pertains to the color and toy preference conditions. The wording is slightly different in the occupational preference conditions. In those conditions the word "like" is simply replaced with the words "want to be a _____"

Responses to these questions were coded 1 for an essentialist response and 0 for not an essentialist response. These questions were summed for a total score that ranges from 0 – 4, where 4 consists of essentialist responses on all questions.

Essentialist Reasoning

Responses to the four inference questions were summed for each scenario to create an essentialist reasoning score for each scenario (see Giles, 2003, and Giles, in press, for a discussion of the interrelatedness of these indices). Essentialist responses were those responses that indicated innate origins, stability, lack of malleability, and persistence (see Heyman & Giles, 2004), and were always denoted by a 1 in the scoring for each individual question. Essentialist reasoning scores per scenario could thus range from 0-4, with 0 denoting no essentialist responses, and 4 denoting essentialist responses on all 4 questions.

In addition to calculating an essentialist reasoning score for each scenario, we also calculated a total essentialist reasoning score for each participant, created by summing essentialist reasoning scores over all 6 scenarios. Any given participant could thus have a Total Essentialist Reasoning score that could range from 0 to 24. Actual Total Essentialist Reasoning scores ranged from 6 to 22, with a mean score of 14.

RESULTS

Preliminary Analyses

Initial stepwise analyses revealed no significant effect of participant ethnicity, participant gender, school, or experimenter, so these variables were excluded from the analyses.

Open-Ended Prediction Measure

Age-Related Patterns

An examination of stereotype-consistent responses to the as a function of participant age revealed an inverse U-shaped quadratic function, such that stereotype-consistent responses were lowest among 3-year-olds and 8-year-olds and higher among children between these ages, $F(2, 79) = 5.21, p < .05$ (see Appendix A).

Stereotype-inconsistent responses also varied quadratically as a function of participant age, $F(2, 79) = 4.10, p < . 05$. In this case however, the function was U-shaped the other way, such that stereotype-inconsistent responses were highest among 3-year-olds and 8-year-olds, and lowest among children between these ages (see Appendix B).

Stereotype-Consistent Responses

Participants provided more stereotype-consistent responses when asked about boys than when asked about girls, $M = 2.13$ versus 1.85 out of 3, $F(1, 81) = 4.07, p < .05$. Participants were more likely to give stereotype consistent responses in the color and toy conditions than they were in the occupation condition, 54% (averaged over color and toy) versus 37% of the time, a difference that significantly departs from chance, $p < .001$.

Stereotype-Inconsistent Responses

Participants provided more stereotype-inconsistent responses when asked about girls than when asked about boys, $M = .67$ versus .13 out of 3, $F(1, 81) = 33.20$, $p < .0001$. Participants were more likely to give stereotype-inconsistent responses in the occupation condition than in the other two conditions, 14% (averaged over color and toy) versus 5.5% of the time, a different that significantly departs from chance, $p < .05$.

Essentialist Reasoning Measure

Age-Related Patterns

An examination of the relationship between age and the tendency to give essentialist responses revealed a significant quadratic curvilinear relationship, $F(2, 79) = 4.86$, $p < . 05$, such that the 3- and 8-year-olds were less likely to essentialize than the other age groups (see Appendix C).

There was no significant relationship between the tendency to essentialize and the tendency to provide stereotype-consistent or stereotype-inconsistent responses.

Manipulation Effects

A 2 (*character gender*: male, female) x 3 (*domain*: color, occupation, toy) analysis of variance on participants' essentialist reasoning scores revealed no significant effects. However, when considering each type of question separately, the following effect emerged: Participants were more likely to say that female characters' preferences were inborn than they were to make the corresponding inference about boys, $M = 1.59$ versus 1.24 out of 3, $F(1, 81) = 5.51$, $p < .03$. No other manipulation effects emerged with regard to the inference questions.

Intercorrelations

The tendency to essentialize when reasoning about color preferences was correlated with essentializing when reasoning about toy preferences, $r(81) = .41$, $p < .0001$, and occupational preferences, $r(81)= .25$, $p < .05$. Essentializing toy preferences was correlated with essentializing occupational preferences, $r(81)= .25$, $p < .05$. In addition, the tendency to essentialize when reasoning about male characters was correlated with the tendency to essentialize when reasoning about female characters, $r(81)= .49$, $p < .0001$. These findings suggest that although contextual information provides children as a whole with a set of tools for differentially invoking essentialist attributions, there are nonetheless significant individual differences such that some children are more likely than others to essentialize preferences across contexts (see Giles & Heyman, 2004a, 2004b, for related results).

Linking Essentialist Reasoning and Stereotyping

In light of Haslam's (1998) articulation of the connection between stereotyping and essentialist reasoning among adults, one question of interest in the present study was the extent to which essentialist reasoning might be associated with the tendency to engage in stereotyping. Overall, there was no correlation between the tendency to give stereotype consistent responses and scores on the essentialist reasoning measure when taken as a whole, but when questions in the essentialist reasoning measure were considered separately, the following pattern emerged: The tendency to infer innate origins was associated with an increased tendency to give stereotype-consistent responses, $r(81) = .40$, $p < .01$. In addition, the tendency to infer innate origins was associated with a decreased tendency to give stereotype-inconsistent responses, $r(81) = -.26$, $p < .05$.

DISCUSSION

Study 1 yielded three main findings. First, age was a significant but nonlinear predictor of a tendency to provide stereotype-consistent responses, stereotype-inconsistent responses, and essentialist responses. In particular, the youngest and oldest children seemed less likely to stereotype and less likely to essentialize preference than children in the middle age ranges. Second, participants were more likely to stereotype regarding the preferences of boys than regarding the preferences of girls, although they viewed girls preferences as more innately driven. Third, participants who engaged in stereotyping seemed more likely than other participants to attribute preference to innate causation.

STUDY 2

In Study 1, participants showed increased levels of essentialist reasoning about girls than about boys, but only on questions concerning innate causation. Participants did not show any tendency to use character gender as a tool for making inferences about the stability, malleability, or unsupported persistence of preferences. This differential use of gender information is consistent with previous evidence suggesting that beliefs about causal origins constitute a particularly important aspect of reasoning about gender (Gelman, 2003; Heyman & Giles, 2006). The conclusion from Study 1 that children may attribute the preferences of girls especially to innate origins could be strengthened if we would demonstrate that the results would obtain using diverse assessment tools. A major goal of Study 2 is therefore to replicate these findings from Study 1 using a simplified format, in which information about preferences is provided *to* children rather than provided by them. In addition, Study 2 sought to replicate the finding that children may be more likely to essentialize stereotype-consistent than stereotype-inconsistent preferences.

METHOD

Participants

Participants were 50 3-8-year-olds (25 boys and 25 girls; M = 5y10m, range 3y11m to 8y10m), recruited from four ethnically diverse private schools in a large urban city in the mid-South of the United States. None of the participants in Study 2 had participated in Study 1.

Of the children who participated in Study 2, 80% were of Caucasian descent 16% were of African-American or African descent, and 5% were of Asian-American or Asian descent, a pattern that did not differ significantly from the sample obtained in Study 1.

Procedure

Participants were interviewed individually at their schools as in Study 1, and heard the same introductory statement.

Design

Overview

Each participant received a total of 8 questions. A single question followed each of 8 randomly ordered scenarios that varied in a 2 x 2 x 2 within-subjects design. The manipulated variables were *character gender* (male, female), *domain* (toy preference, color preference[2]) and *stereotype-consistency* (consistent, inconsistent).

The stereotype-consistent and stereotype-inconsistent toys and colors used in Study 2 were selected by determining the modal stereotype-consistent responses to the toy preference and color preference questions in Study 1. "Pink" and "dolls" were the stereotype-consistent color- and toy- preferences for female characters, respectively, and thus were also used as the stereotype-inconsistent responses for male characters. "Blue" and "trucks" were the modal stereotype-consistent color- and toy- preferences for male characters, respectively, and thus were also used as the stereotype-inconsistent responses for female characters.

Scenarios Had the Following Format

Color preference. "I know a [girl/boy] whose favorite color is the color [pink/blue]."
Toy preference. "I know a [girl/boy] who likes to play with [dolls/trucks] best."

Origin Question

Following hearing any given scenario, participants were asked whether the character learned to have the favorite color/toy, or whether s/he was born to have that favorite color/toy. These options were presented in random order. 'Learned' responses were coded as 0, and 'born that way' responses were coded as 1.

RESULTS

Preliminary Analyses

Preliminary stepwise analyses revealed no significant effects of participant gender, participant ethnicity, school, or experimenter, so these variables were not included in the analyses.

---

[2] Occupation preference was not included in Study 2 in the interest of creating a shorter measure.

Age-Related Patterns

A significant quadratic function emerged when examining the relationship between age and the tendency to impute innate causation, $F(2, 47) = 8.38$, $p < .01$, such that the tendency to infer that a character was "born that way" increased from 3 to 5 and then declined subsequently.

Manipulation Effects

Loglinear analyses (see Landis and Koch, 1979, for justification) revealed a significant effect of *character gender*, such that participants were more likely to impute innate origins to female compared to male characters, 57% versus 44% of the time, $G^2(1)= 6.77$, $p < .01$. There was also a significant effect of *domain*, such that participants were more likely to impute innate origins to color preference than to toy preference, 55% versus 46% of the time, $G^2(1)= 3.89$, $p < .01$, a finding that also emerged in Study 1. In addition, as in Study 1, analyses revealed a significant effect of *consistency*, such that participants were more likely to impute innate causation to stereotype-consistent information than to stereotype-inconsistent information, 57% versus 44% of the time, $G^2(1)= 6.78$, $p < .01$. No other significant effects emerged.

DISCUSSION

The present study replicates the main findings of Study 1. Specifically, Study 2 also suggests that age predicts essentialist reasoning in a significant nonlinear way, increasing from 3 to 5 and then declining subsequently, a finding that is consistent with Gelman's (2003) discussion of preschoolers as especially prone to essentialist reasoning. In addition, as in Study 1, Study 2 suggests that children may be more likely to impute innate causation to the preferences of girls than to the preferences of boys. In addition, Study 2 reinforces the conclusion that children are more likely to impute innate causation to preferences that are stereotype-consistent.

GENERAL DISCUSSION

The present study suggests three main conclusions. First, the tendency to stereotype preferences, and the tendency to provide stereotype-inconsistent predictions, and the tendency to essentialize preferences are all related to participant age in a curvilinear fashion, with stereotyping and essentialist reasoning peaking around the age of 5. Second, children showed an increased tendency to stereotype the preferences of boys compared to the preferences of girls, but were more likely to essentialize the preferences of girls. Third, the tendency to stereotype preference was predictive of an increased tendency to essentialize preference. Each of these conclusions will be considered in turn.

Age-Related Patterns

One of the most interesting things to come out of the present study is a window into the notion that across development, conceptual development might not proceed in a continuous, linear fashion. In the present study, many significant quadratic functions emerged when mapping the relationship between age and children's response patterns when asked to make open-ended predictions about preferences. Whether mapping the frequency of stereotype-consistent or stereotype-inconsistent responding, the tendency to apply gender stereotypes appeared to increase until around 5 years old and then decrease afterward.

The curvilinear age-related patterns that emerged in the present study may the reflect developmental change that Signorella et al. (1993) and Trautner et al (2005) have articulated; namely, that the shape of the curve stems from an early lack of stereotype-consistent knowledge, followed by a period of increased rigidity in the application of stereotypes, followed by a period of increased cognitive flexibility.

When simply looking at the shape of the functions obtained in the present study, it appears that the youngest and the oldest children responded similarly, whereas children in the middle showed a different pattern of responding. But are the 3- and 8-year-olds necessarily responding similarly for the same underlying reasons? A careful reading of the stereotyping literature delivers a dose of caution regarding moving from an observation of similar scores to the conclusion that there are similar *explanations* for these similar scores (see Signorella et al., 1993). That is, different underlying cognitive mechanisms might explain older versus younger children's responding.

For example, one possible explanation for this pattern of results may be that 3-year-olds might provide relatively few stereotype consistent responses because they simply don't yet have as firm a grasp on what the stereotypes are (see Blakemore, 2003, and Miller et al., 2007, for discussions), whereas 8-year-olds, although cognitively aware of stereotypes, may be less likely to rely on them when making inferences, or less likely than younger children to buy into them (see Trautner et al., 2005). Such a possibility should be examined systematically in future research.

On a related note, the present study revealed a similar curvilinear pattern in children's tendency to engage in essentialist reasoning, with the youngest and oldest children giving fewer essentialist responses than children in the 4-6 age range. This finding is interesting in light of the fact that some studies have supported the conclusion that essentialist reasoning increases with age (Giles, 2009) and others have supported the opposite conclusion, that essentialist reasoning in fact decreases with age (Lockhart, Chang, & Story, 2002.) The present study suggests that it is possible that both are true. Although as Giles (2003) has noted, it is difficult to directly compare across studies due to the use of diverse assessment tools and divergent age ranges, the present results at least begin to reconcile these seemingly discrepant findings in the literature.

Caveat

Despite the consistent pretty curves demonstrated in the present study, as with any cross-sectional design, one must be careful not to impute developmental change. It is entirely possible that cohort effects may play a role in the present findings (e.g. perhaps the 4-6-year-olds share increased stereotyping and essentialist reasoning for reasons entirely unrelated to their developmental age). For this reason, firm conclusions about the nature of these curvilinear patterns await the results of longitudinal investigations.

Gender Stereotypes About Preferences

A second main set of findings to emerge from the present study suggests that children show differential patterns of reasoning about the preferences of males versus females. For example, participants were more likely to provide stereotypical responses when predicting the preferences of boys, compared to girls. One question that has appeared consistently in the literature on children's gender stereotypes is the extent to which stereotypes are reflective of actual gender differences in behavior (e.g. Heyman, 2001). This issue highlights an broader debate about the extent to which concepts are actually tethered to reality (see Giles & Heyman, 2005, for a discussion), and is anchored a rich constructivist frame of inquiry that runs through a wide range of scholarly traditions, from Buddhist psychology (e.g. Rosch, 1988) to clinical psychology (Rosenhan, 1973), to linguistics (e.g. Whorf, 1956), to the study of episodic memory (e.g. Ceci & Bruck, 1993).

One important question of interest is whether children hold these differential stereotypes about preferences at least in part because boys' preferences actually *are* more stereotype-consistent. This possibility is reasonable in light of Pollack's (1998) notion of the Boy Code, which suggests that oppressive social and cultural structures, which are often referred to as *gender straightjackets,* constrain and shape the behavior and mental life of boys. According to Pollack, such constraints compel boys to behave in stereotypical ways to avoid the social repercussions of norm violations. Indeed, there is evidence that boys in our culture face especially harsh sanctions in the peer group for gender norm violation (see Bailey, Bechtold, & Berenbaum, 2002; Pollack, 1998; and Thorne, 1988, for related).

There are other possible explanations for the present findings, however. For example, perhaps boys are no more likely than girls to hold stereotype-consistent preferences, but it is simply that the stereotypes regarding boys are broader, or better articulated, or more widely understood. Future research should attempt to tease apart these alternative explanations.

Gender Stereotyping

Another interesting finding to emerge from the present study is that although participants were more likely to provide stereotype-consistent responses when reasoning about the preferences of boys, they were more likely to attribute the preferences of girls to innate causation than they were to make the corresponding inference regarding boys. These nativist views of female preferences to a certain extent make sense in light of popular ideology about gender roles (e.g. the notion that women are by nature gentle and nurturing and thus drawn to play with dolls and seek out helping professions; see Heyman & Giles, 2006). However, one could just as easily make the same argument regarding boys being "naturally" more drawn to things with wheels, to building things, etc. This finding emerged across both studies, but it is as of yet unclear why this tendency might exist, or whether it will continue to emerge in subsequent investigation. Indeed, it seems to run counter to the results of Giles and Heyman

(2004b), who have demonstrated that preschool-aged children are more likely to essentialize the behavior of boys than girls when the outcomes of behavior are negative but the underlying intentions are ambiguous (e.g. a character was described as "spilling your milk", or "tearing your art project.") However, given that the behaviors children were asked to reason about in the present investigation versus Giles and Heyman's (2004b) study are so different, it is not clear why this apparent discrepancy in essentialist tendencies has emerged. Perhaps children essentialize certain things more in girls, and other things more in boys (see Giles, 2003, for related arguments).

Linking Essentialist Reasoning to Stereotyping

Another key finding to emerge from the present study is a correlation between the tendency to make nativist inferences and a tendency to engage in gender stereotyping about preferences. This finding is consistent with evidence that children who essentialize behavior are more likely than other children to readily place others into evaluative categories, seek out diagnostic information, and engage in correspondent inference (see Giles, 2003, and Heyman & Gelman, 1999, 2000). In addition, this connection is not surprising in light of Giles' (in press B) suggestion that both essentialist reasoning and stereotyping might be mediated by a need for cognitive closure.

This finding is moreover consistent with the cultural notion that gender constitutes a "natural kind," (Rothbart & Taylor, 1992) that is, that gender categories are conceived of as real rather than imagined, biologically mediated, and found in nature rather than created (Gelman, 2003). Although this conceptualization of gender has received innumerable criticisms across the developmental, sociological, anthropological, and feminist literatures, which provide weighty evidence for the notion of gender as a socially constructed category (see Rothbart & Taylor, 1992), essentialist frameworks continue to receive their fair share of attention in popular culture (see Heyman & Giles, 2006, for a discussion). Moreover, their presence in popular culture may serve a powerful reifying function, perpetuating and even magnifying gender difference (Fredericks & Eccles, 2002; see Hacking, 1995)

Future Directions

The present project has several methodological limitations that should be addressed in future research. First, because this was a cross-sectional study, we were only able to make inferences about age-related patterns, and not about developmental change per se. Future research should attempt to follow children longitudinally, to examine the ways in which their reasoning about gender-related preferences might change over time.

Second, future research should expand size and the cultural diversity of the sample, so that we can amass sufficient power to examine the ways in which different cultural worldviews might relate to children's reasoning about gender-related preferences. For example, across the world cultures have very different ideas about gender-typical colors, toys, and occupational choices, and even in the United States, there are broad cultural, religious, and even regional differences in the kinds of preferences that are deemed as appropriate for males versus females (Bailey & Nihlen, 1990; Lobel et al., 2001; Maccoby & Jacklin, 1987; Zammuner, 1987).

Third, future research should make use of a more detailed instrument to measure children's beliefs about innate causation, in order to gain a greater understanding of the dimensions and the depths of their inferences. A good place to start would be Gelman, Heyman, and Legare's (2005) 14 item measure of essentialism; Giles (2005) has condensed this scale to 5 items and has demonstrated reasonable measurements fidelity.

Aside from the need for these methodological extensions, there are several interesting theoretical questions that remain unanswered. For example, how might children's predictions about stereotype-inconsistent behaviors map onto their own tendencies to hold stereotype-inconsistent preferences? Do they predict what is true for themselves, as standpoint theory might suggest? In light of substantial evidence of the egocentrism of preoperational children, who are known to project their own mental states onto others (see Piaget, 1954), one possibility is that children who hold who stereotype-inconsistent preferences for others may also be more likely to predict such preferences for others, as would be consistent with simulation theory (Davies & Stone, 1995; Harris, 1995; Kahneman & Tversky, 1982; see Ruble & Dweck, 1995, for related discussions).

Second, important questions remain about the tendency to provide stereotype-inconsistent responses. To what extent does the holding of stereotype-inconsistent preferences actually relate or not relate to the expression of such preferences? Are there certain contexts in which children are more or less willing to express the preferences that they do have? Evidence from Thorne (1998) suggest that children may be more likely to express stereotype-inconsistent preferences around opposite-sex peers, in contexts where androgyny and/or free expression are valued, and least likely to express them around same gender peers (see Pollack, 1998, for related discussion). Future research might endeavor to combine interviews with careful observation of children in different social settings, and perhaps with peer-, teacher- and parent- report, to get a much clearer understanding of these relationships.

CONCLUSION

The present studies, taken together, contribute to a growing body of evidence suggesting that young children's generalized beliefs affect their psychological interpretations of specific situations (Dweck, 1999; Giles & Heyman, 2004b; Harris, 1989; Heyman & Gelman, 1999, 2000; Lagattuta & Wellman, 2001). Moreover, they also inform growing debates about the domain-specificity of essentialist reasoning. Children in the present study were more likely to essentialize some preferences than others, and were also more likely to essentialize the preferences of girls rather than boys. These data reinforce the notion that whereas essentialist frameworks may be accessible in a wide range of domains, they are differentially instantiated across contexts (Gelman, 2003; Giles & Heyman, 2004a, 2004b). That this is true lends credence to the idea that children do not universally apply one undifferentiated notion of psychological causation in a one-size-fits-all kind of a way, but rather have a variety of explanatory tools at their disposal when making inferences about social behavior (Giles & Heyman, 2004b, Hickling & Wellman, 2001).

APPENDIX A. FREQUENCY OF STEREOTYPE-CONSISTENT RESPONSES AS A FUNCTION OF PARTICIPANT AGE

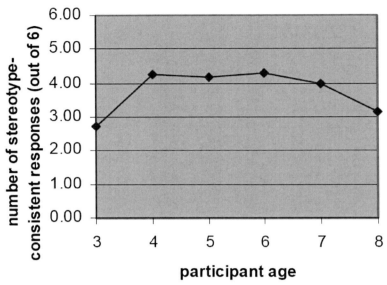

$F(2, 79) = 5.21, p < .05.$

APPENDIX B. FREQUENCY OF STEREOTYPE-INCONSISTENT RESPONSES AS A FUNCTION OF PARTICIPANT AGE

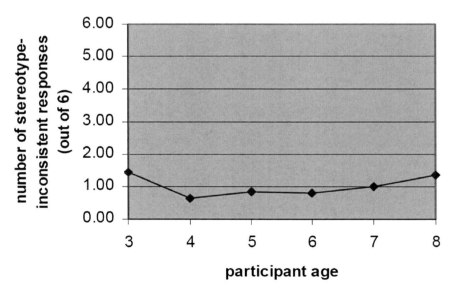

$F(2, 79) = 4.10, p < .05.$

APPENDIX C. FREQUENCY OF ESSENTIALIST RESPONSES AS A FUNCTION OF PARTICIPANT AGE

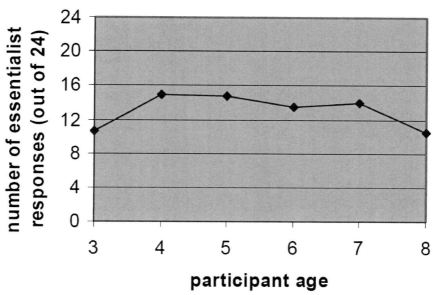

$F(2, 79) = 4.24, p < .05$.

REFERENCES

Aubry, S., Ruble, D.N., & Silverman, L.B. (1999). The role of gender knowledge in children's gender-typed preferences. In L. Balter & C.S. Tamis-LeMonda (Eds.), *Child psychology: A handbook of contemporary issues* (pp. 363-390). New York: Psychology Press.

Bailey, B.A., Nihlen, A.S. (1990). Effect of experience with nontraditional workers on psychological and social dimensions of occupational sex-role stereotyping by elementary school children. *Psychological Reports, 66,* 1273-1282.

Bailey, J.M., Bechtold, K.T., & Berenbaum, S.A. (2002). Who are tomboys and why should we study them? *Archives of Sexual Behavior, 31,* 333-341.

Bem, S. (1983). Gender schema theory and its implications for child development: Raising gender-aschematic children in a gender schematic society. *Signs, 8,* 598-616.

Blakemore, J.E.O. (2003). Children's beliefs about violating gender norms: Boys shouldn't look like girls and girls shouldn't act like boys. *Sex Roles, 48,* 411-419.

Brown, L.M., & Gilligan, C. (1992). *Meeting at the crossroads: Women's psychology and girls' development.* Cambridge, MA: Harvard University Press.

Bussey, K., & Bandura, A. (1992). Self-regulatory mechanisms governing gender development. *Child Development, 63,* 1236-1250.

Ceci, S.J., & Bruck, M. (1993). The suggestibility of the child eyewitness: A historical review and synthesis. *Psychological Bulletin, 113,* 403-439.

Choi, I., Nisbett, R.E., & Norenzayan, A. (1999). Causal attribution across cultures: Variation and universality. *Psychological Bulletin, 125,* 47-63.

Cowan, G., & Hoffman, C. D. (1986). Gender stereotyping in young children: Evidence to support a concept-learning approach. *Sex Roles, 14,* 211–224.

Davies, M., & Stone, T. (1995). Introduction. In M. Davies & T. Stone (Eds.), *Folk Psychology* (pp. 1-43). Oxford: Blackwell.

Dweck, C. S. (1999). *Self-theories: Their role in motivation, personality, and development.* Ann Arbor, MI: Edwards Brothers.

Fredericks, J.A., & Eccles, J.S. (2002). Children's competence and value beliefs from childhood through adolescence: Growth trajectories in two male-sex-typed domains. *Developmental Psychology, 38,* 519-533.

Gelman, S. A. (2003). *The essential child: Origins of essentialism in everyday thought.* New York: Oxford University Press.

Gelman, S. A., Coley, J. D., & Gottfried, G. M. (1994). Essentialist beliefs in children: The acquisition of concepts and theories. In L. A. Hirschfeld, & S. A. Gelman (Eds.), *Mapping the mind: Domain specificity in cognition and culture* (pp. 341–365). New York: Cambridge University Press.

Gelman, S.A., Collman, P., & Maccoby, E.E. (1986). Inferring properties from categories versus inferring categories from properties: The case of gender. *Child Development, 57,* 396-404.

Gelman, S.A., Heyman, G.D., & Legare, C.H. (2005). *Developmental changes in the coherence of essentialist beliefs.* Paper presented at the biennial meeting of the Society for Research in Child Development, Atlanta, GA.

Gelman, S.A., & Kalish, C.W. (1993). Categories and causality. In R. Pasnak & M.L. Howe (Eds.), *Emerging themes in cognitive development (Vol. 2): Competencies* (pp. 3-32). New York: Springer-Verlag.

Gervey, B. M., Chiu, C., Hong, Y., & Dweck, C. S. (1999). Differential use of person information in decisions about guilt versus innocence: The role of implicit theories. *Personality and Social Psychology, 25,* 17–27.

Giles, J.W. (2003). Children's essentialist beliefs about aggression. *Developmental Review, 23,* 413-443.

Giles, J.W. (2005). On murderers and sex offenders: The sociocognitive consequences of using noun labels to refer to people who perpetrate violence. Unpublished manuscript.

Giles, J.W. (2009). Differentiation and coherence in patterns of reasoning about aggression. In F. Columbus (Ed.), *Aggressive Behavior.* New York: Nova Science Publishers.

Giles, J.W. (in press A). On murderers and sex offenders: The sociocognitive consequences of using noun labels to refer to people who perpetrate violence.

Giles, J.W. (in press B). Psychological essentialism and legal decision-making: Police investigators', prosecutors', and defense attorneys' reasoning about future dangerousness and amenability to treatment.

Giles, J.W., & Heyman, G.D. (2003). Preschoolers' beliefs about the stability of antisocial behavior: Implications for navigating social challenges. *Social Development, 12,* 182-197.

Giles, J.W., & Heyman, G.D. (2004a). Conceptions of aggression and withdrawal in early childhood. *Infant and Child Development, 13,* 407-421.

Giles, J.W., & Heyman, G.D. (2004b). When to cry over spilled milk: Preschoolers' use of category information to guide inferences about ambiguous behavior. *Journal of Cognition and Development, 5*, 359-382.

Giles, J.W., & Heyman, G.D. (2005). Children's beliefs about the relationship between gender and aggressive behavior. *Child Development, 76,* 107-121.

Hacking, I. (1995). The looping effects of human kinds. In D. Sperber, D. Premack, & A.J. Premack (Eds.), *Causal cognition: A multidisciplinary debate* (pp. 351-394). New York: Clarendon Press/Oxford University Press.

Harris, P. L. (1989). *Children and emotion: The development of psychological understanding.* Malden, MA: Blackwell.

Harris, P. L. (1995). From simulation to folk psychology: The case for development. In M. Davies & T. Stone (Eds.), *Folk Psychology* (pp. 207-331). Oxford: Blackwell.

Haslam, N.O, Rothschild, L., & Ernst, D. (2000). Essentialist beliefs about social categories. *British Journal of Social Psychology, 39,* 113-127.

Haslam, N.O. (1998). Natural kinds, human kinds, and essentialism. *Social Research, 65,* 291-314.

Haslam, N.O., & Levy, S.R. (2006). Essentialist beliefs about homosexuality: Structure and implications for prejudice. *Personality and Social Psychology Bulletin, 32,* 471-485.

Heyman, G. D. (2001). Children's interpretation of ambiguous behavior: Evidence for a ''boys are bad'' bias. *Social Development, 10,* 230 – 247.

Heyman, G. D., & Gelman, S. A. (1999). The use of trait labels in making psychological inferences. *Child Development, 70,* 604–619.

Heyman, G.D., & Gelman, S.A. (2000). Beliefs about the origins of human psychological traits. *Developmental Psychology, 36,* 663–678.

Heyman, G.D., & Giles, J.W. (2004). Valence effects in reasoning about evaluative traits. *Merrill-Palmer Quarterly, 50,* 84-109.

Heyman, G.D., & Giles, J.W. (2006). Gender and psychological essentialism. *Enfance, 58,* 293-310.

Hickling, A. K., &Wellman, H. M. (2001). The emergence of children's causal explanations and theories: Evidence from everyday conversation. *Developmental Psychology, 37,* 668–683.

Hirschfeld, L.A. (1996). *Race in the making: Cognition, culture, and the child's construction of human kinds.* Cambridge, MA: MIT Press.

Hofstede, G. (1980). *Culture's consequences: International differences in work-related values.* Beverly Hills, CA: Sage. hooks, b. (1992). *Black looks: Race and representation.* Boston: South End Press.

Huston, A. C. (1985). The development of sex typing: Themes from recent research. *Developmental Review, 5,* 1–17.

Kahneman, D., Tversky, A. (1982). The simulation heuristic. In D. Kahneman, P. Slovic, & A. Tversky (Eds.), *Judgment under uncertainty* (pp. 201-208). Cambridge: Cambridge University Press.

Kuhn, D., Nash, S. C., & Brucken, L. (1978). Sex-role concepts of two- and three-year-old children. *Child Development, 49,* 445–451.

Lagattuta, K. H., & Wellman, H. M. (2001). Thinking about the past: Early knowledge about links between prior experience, thinking, and emotion. *Child Development, 72,* 82–102.

Landis, J. R., & Koch, G. G. (1979). The analysis of categorical data in longitudinal studies of behavioral development. In J. R. Nesselroade & P. B. Baltes (Eds.), *Longitudinal research in the study of behavior and development* (pp. 233–261). New York: Academic.

Liben, L., & Signorella, M. (1993). Gender-schematic processing in children: The role of initial interpretations of stimuli. *Developmental Psychology, 29*, 141–149.

Lobel, T.E., Gruber, R., Govrin, N., & Mashraki-Pedhatzur, S. (2001). Children's gender-related inferences and judgments: A cross-cultural study. *Developmental Psychology, 37*, 837-846.

Lockhart, K. L., Chang, B., & Story, T. (2002). Young children's beliefs about the stability of traits: Protective optimism? *Child Development, 73*, 1408–1430.

Maas, E., Marecek, J., & Travers, J. R. (1978). Children's conceptions of disordered behavior. *Child Development, 49*, 146–154.

Maccoby, E. E. (1988). Gender as a social category. *Developmental Psychology, 24*, 755–765.

Martin, C. L., & Parker, S. (1995). Folk theories about sex and race differences. *Personality and Social Psychology Bulletin, 21*, 45–57.

Martin, C.L. (1989). Children's use of gender-related information in making social judgments. *Developmental Psychology, 25*, 80-88.

Medin, D. L., & Heit, E. (1999). Categorization. In B. J. Bly, & D. E. Rumelhart (Eds.), *Cognitive Science* (pp. 99–143). San Diego: Academic Press.

Medin, D.L. (1989). Concepts and conceptual structure. *American Psychologist, 44*, 1469-1481.

Miller, J. G. (1984). Culture and the development of everyday social explanation. *Journal of Personality and Social Psychology, 46*, 961–978.

Miller, C.F., Trautner, H.M., & Ruble, D.N. (2006). The role of gender stereotypes in children's preferences and behavior. In C. Tamis-LeMonda & L. Balter (Eds.), *Child psychology: A handbook of contemporary issues* (2nd ed.) (pp. 292-323). Philadelphia: Psychology Press.

Piaget, J. (1954). *The construction of reality in the child.* Oxford, England: Basic Books.

Picariello, M.L., Greenberg, D.N., & Pillemer, D.B. (1990). Children's sex-related stereotyping of colors. *Child Development, 61*, 1453-1460.

Rosch, E. (1988). Principles of categorization. In E.E. Smith, & A.M. Collins (Eds.), *Readings in cognitive science: A perspective from psychology and artificial intelligence* (pp. 312-322). San Mateo, CA: Morgan Kaufmann, Inc.

Rosenhan, D.L. (1973). On being sane in insane places. *Science, 179*, 250-258.

Rothbart, M., & Taylor, M. (1992). Category labels and social reality: Do we view social categories as natural kinds? In G.R. Semin & K. Fiedler (Eds.), *Language, interaction and social cognition* (pp. 11-36). London: Sage Publications.

Ruble, D. N., & Dweck, C. S. (1995). Self conceptions, person conceptions, and their development. In N. Eisenberg (Ed.), *Review of personality and social psychology: Social development, Vol. 15* (pp. 109–139). Thousand Oaks, CA: Sage.

Ruble, D. N., & Martin, C. L. (1998). Gender development. In N. Eisenberg (Ed.), *Handbook of child psychology: Social, emotional, and personality development* (pp. 933–1016). New York: Wiley.

Signorella, M.L., Bigler, R.S., & Liben, L.S. (1993). Developmental differences in children's gender schemata about others. *Developmental Review, 13*, 147-183.

Thorne, B. (1993). *Gender play: Girls and boys at school.* New Brunswick, NJ: Rutgers University Press.

Trautner, H.M., et al. (2005). Rigidity and flexibility of gender stereotypes in children: Developmental or differential? *Infant and Child Development, 14,* 365-380.

Ward, J.V. (1996). Raising resisters: The role of truth telling in the psychological development of African-American girls. In B. Leadbetter & N. Way (Eds.), *Urban girls: Resisting stereotypes, creating identities* (pp. 85-99). New York: New York University Press.

Whorf, B.L. (1956). *Language, thought, and reality: Selected writings.* Cambridge, MA: MIT Press.

Zammuner, V.L. (1987). Children's sex role stereotypes: A cross-cultural analysis. In P. Shaver & C. Hendrick (Eds.), *Review of personality and social psychology: Sex and gender* (pp. 272-293). Newbury Park, CA: Sage Publishers.

INDEX

A

ABC, 243
abnormalities, xi, 168, 169, 247, 250, 253, 254, 257
absorption, 62
academics, xii, 41, 42, 43, 135, 141, 203, 291
accidental, 223
accountability, 21
accuracy, 52
achievement, 176, 203, 237, 261, 297
action research, 4
activation, 173, 251, 254, 256
activism, 72
acute, 250
Adams, 73, 82, 272, 274, 287, 289
adaptation, 4, 28, 177, 219, 244
addiction, 293
adjustment, 177, 267
administration, viii, 34, 88, 90, 92, 99, 104, 105, 107, 108, 109, 110, 119, 127, 135, 138, 154, 178, 224, 255, 258, 278
administrative, ix, 89, 90, 106, 108, 137, 165, 171, 172, 178, 202, 205, 206, 237
administrators, 12, 138, 287, 295
adolescence, x, xii, 213, 214, 216, 217, 218, 223, 227, 231, 232, 233, 236, 237, 239, 240, 241, 243, 244, 270, 279, 280, 282, 284, 285, 312
adolescents, xii, 227, 231, 260, 261, 266, 269, 274, 275, 276, 280, 281, 284, 285, 287
adult, x, 3, 5, 31, 46, 47, 73, 98, 183, 190, 210, 213, 214, 216, 218, 219, 220, 221, 222, 227, 233, 235, 236, 237, 239, 240, 241, 242, 244, 245, 285
adult education, 3, 73
adult learning, 3, 31, 47
adult population, 98, 227
adulthood, x, 45, 47, 81, 213, 214, 216, 217, 218, 219, 221, 222, 223, 227, 232, 233, 237, 238, 239, 240, 241, 243, 244, 270

adults, 64, 67, 68, 70, 75, 98, 214, 217, 219, 227, 244, 249, 254, 257, 260, 271, 292, 293, 296, 302
advocacy, 127, 129
affective morality, 274
Africa, 192
African-American, 298, 304, 315
age, xii, 32, 41, 71, 95, 120, 167, 168, 170, 171, 175, 183, 214, 215, 216, 218, 219, 220, 223, 224, 225, 226, 227, 228, 229, 231, 232, 237, 238, 241, 242, 244, 245, 249, 262, 270, 272, 274, 275, 276, 279, 280, 281, 282, 284, 285, 287, 295, 296, 297, 298, 301, 302, 303, 305, 306, 307, 308, 314
ageing, 167, 169, 172, 182
agent, ix, 16, 17, 39, 55, 75, 103, 149, 203, 234, 235, 292
agents, 15, 16, 17, 35, 39, 40, 41, 42, 43, 52, 55, 72, 136, 143, 150, 151, 261, 275
aggregation, 178
aggression, 78, 254, 273, 287, 288, 289, 296, 297, 312
aggressive behavior, xi, 269, 270, 273, 286, 313
aggressive personality, 274
aggressiveness, 270, 273
aging, 95, 98
aging population, 95, 98
agreeableness, 222, 235, 239
agricultural, 95, 97
agriculture, 91, 92, 95, 118, 141
AIDS, 167
air, 88
alcohol, 70, 173
Allah, 65, 74
allies, 61, 292
alpha, 276, 278
alternative, 120, 147, 150, 178, 202, 292, 307
alternatives, ix, 58, 133, 143, 145, 159, 160, 161, 162
altruism, 257
Amazon, 137, 141, 142, 148
ambidexterity, 209

ambiguity, 104
ambivalent, 69, 101, 139
American culture, 222, 263
American Psychological Association, 241, 242, 243
Amsterdam, 165, 183
amygdala, 253, 258
anaemia, 167
analysis of variance, 96, 264, 302
androgyny, 309
anger, 12, 60, 63, 73, 76, 80, 267, 268
annual rate, 143
antagonistic, 69, 160, 262
antecedents, 209, 244
anterior cingulate cortex, 253
anthropological, 238, 308
antisocial behavior, 219, 287, 312
antitrust, 211
anxiety, 262
APA, 250, 256
apartheid, 69, 80
apathy, 126
application, 3, 4, 8, 9, 11, 19, 21, 23, 24, 26, 27, 32, 33, 35, 36, 37, 38, 53, 78, 90, 122, 127, 134, 135, 140, 156, 157, 306
Arabs, 61, 82, 84
Argentina, 192
arginine, 254, 257, 258
argument, 9, 37, 89, 109, 142, 263, 307
arid, 137
Ariel, 63
Arizona, 152
armed conflict, 57
armed forces, 63
Army, 56, 60, 86, 223
arrest, 76
articulation, 3, 7, 144, 302
artificial intelligence, 314
ASD, xi, 247, 248, 249, 250, 251, 252, 253, 254, 255
Asia, 199
Asian, 261, 298, 304
Asian cultures, 261
aspiration, 206
assertiveness, 222, 263, 266
assessment, ix, 5, 27, 49, 83, 133, 136, 137, 147, 173, 177, 179, 197, 209, 238, 241, 254, 303, 306
assessment procedures, 179
assessment tools, 303, 306
assets, 138, 144, 150, 160
assimilation, 152, 189
assumptions, 45, 166, 203, 204, 205, 209, 275, 284
asthma, 167, 174
Atlantic, 147
Atlas, 146, 182, 183

atmosphere, 69, 74, 80, 152, 162, 180
atrocities, 79
attachment, xi, 67, 69, 247, 248
attacks, 58, 60, 63, 64, 75, 270, 278
attitudes, 26, 30, 66, 90, 104, 154, 214, 239, 262, 263, 273
attractiveness, 103, 104, 105, 141
attribution, 81, 312
Australia, 2, 3, 32, 125, 127, 192
Austria, 61, 120, 192
authority, 3, 12, 20, 32, 33, 35, 37, 55, 65, 69, 108, 204, 271, 273, 277, 278, 279, 280, 281, 282, 283, 289
autism, 248, 249, 250, 251, 253, 254, 255, 256, 257, 258
autonomy, 27, 57, 80, 153, 235, 239, 261, 266
availability, 31, 75, 95, 141
awareness, 4, 7, 10, 14, 16, 40, 56, 57, 60, 67, 88, 113, 128, 134

B

babies, 32, 71
back, 4, 11, 27, 30, 34, 60, 138, 139, 174, 178, 205
Bali, 32
bankruptcy, 65
banks, 138, 144
barrier, 63, 69, 150
barriers, 55, 68, 77, 80, 171
battery, 298
beating, 76
behavior, xi, xii, 36, 47, 99, 104, 203, 204, 205, 206, 208, 210, 219, 220, 221, 232, 247, 248, 249, 250, 251, 252, 254, 256, 258, 261, 262, 267, 268, 269, 271, 272, 274, 276, 277, 278, 285, 286, 288, 296, 297, 299, 307, 308, 309, 313, 314
behavior of children, 219
behavioral change, 169, 240
behavioral disorders, 255, 258, 286
behavioral sciences, 241
behaviours, 12, 16, 18, 39, 40, 72, 260, 261
Belgium, 192
belief systems, 20
beliefs, xi, 7, 32, 54, 55, 64, 69, 71, 72, 81, 248, 249, 259, 260, 264, 296, 297, 303, 309, 311, 312, 313, 314
benefits, ix, 12, 127, 130, 137, 140, 145, 165, 167, 170, 173, 174, 178, 179, 187, 202, 204, 243, 248, 261
bias, 251, 313
binding, 254, 257
biodiversity, viii, 87, 88, 89, 109, 118, 119

Index 319

biosphere, viii, 87, 88, 89, 90, 91, 92, 94, 95, 101, 106, 107, 108, 109, 110, 113, 114, 116, 117, 118, 119, 120, 121, 122, 123, 124
bipolar, 219
birth, 27, 28, 31, 32, 36, 37, 70, 192, 241, 248
blocks, 158, 159
blood, 29, 65, 167, 253
blurring, 54
bogs, 91, 92
bomb, 60, 71
bonding, 187, 202, 254
bonds, xi, 69, 247, 248
bonus, 204
Boston, 45, 152, 208, 240, 241, 243, 268, 293, 313
bottlenecks, 173
boys, xii, 67, 223, 227, 228, 264, 281, 295, 296, 297, 298, 300, 301, 302, 303, 305, 307, 309, 311, 313, 315
brain, 249, 250, 251, 253, 256, 258
Brazil, v, 133, 135, 136, 137, 138, 139, 140, 142, 143, 144, 145, 146, 147, 192
Brazilian, ix, 133, 135, 136, 137, 138, 141, 144, 147, 148
breaches, 178
breakdown, 68, 81
Britain, 56, 57, 61, 70, 94, 198
British Columbia, 121
Brno, v, x, 122, 213, 214, 215, 223, 237, 238, 240, 245
broad spectrum, 58, 69
Bronfenbrenner, 260, 266
brothers, 71
Brussels, 182, 215
brutality, 67
Buddhist, 307
buildings, 69
bullies, xii, 269, 270, 273, 274, 275, 281, 284, 285, 286, 288, 289
bullying, xi, xii, 269, 270, 273, 274, 275, 276, 278, 279, 281, 283, 284, 285, 286, 287, 288, 289
bureaucracy, 40, 52, 137
burning, 58
by-products, 114

C

campaigns, 57, 71, 136
Canada, 46, 192, 259, 262, 263, 265, 291, 293
cancer, 167, 174
candidates, 126, 131
capital accumulation, 136, 143
capitalism, 143
Capitalism, 146, 147, 197

caregivers, xi, 247, 248
Carpathian, 124
case study, viii, 2, 27, 45, 49, 88, 109, 117, 122, 123, 124, 293
catalyst, 150
catchments, 137, 140, 141, 142
categorization, 168, 314
Catholic, v, vii, 51, 52, 53, 54, 55, 56, 57, 58, 59, 60, 63, 64, 66, 67, 69, 70, 72, 74, 75, 76, 79, 182, 269
Catholic Church, 69
Catholic school, 74
Catholics, 51, 54, 56, 57, 58, 63, 64, 66, 68, 72, 74, 76, 78, 79
Caucasian, 298, 304
causal attribution, 298
causal inference, 296
causality, 312
causation, 303, 305, 307, 309
CBS, 170, 183
censorship, 16
Census, 98, 242
Central America, 146
Central Europe, 88, 91, 170
Central Intelligence Agency, 82
CEO, 209
cerebral blood flow, 253
cerebrovascular, 167
cerebrovascular diseases, 167
certificate, viii, 88
certification, 114, 141, 142
CFA, 279
CFI, 279
channels, 145, 206
chemicals, 136
child development, xi, 249, 259, 260, 288, 289, 311
childbearing, 3, 24, 26, 36, 37, 39
childbirth, 37, 47, 235, 239
childhood, x, xii, 67, 68, 71, 76, 81, 213, 214, 216, 217, 218, 220, 221, 222, 232, 236, 237, 240, 241, 242, 243, 244, 267, 268, 270, 276, 279, 280, 282, 285, 297, 299, 312
childless, 216
Chile, 147
chimpanzee, 249
China, 261, 262, 263, 265, 267
Christianity, 64, 82
Christians, 60, 61
chromosome, 254
chromosomes, 254
chronic disease, 165, 169, 174
chronic diseases, 165, 174
chronic illness, 166, 167, 168, 170, 171, 172, 174, 182

chronic obstructive pulmonary disease, 174
chronically ill, ix, 165, 166, 167, 169, 170, 171, 172, 173, 174, 175, 177, 179, 180, 181, 182
citizens, xii, 55, 68, 126, 128, 129, 130, 131, 144, 209, 291, 292, 293
Civil Rights, 57
civil servant, 135, 176, 177
civil society, 65, 292, 293
civil war, 57
civilian, 63, 68
classes, 69, 74, 95, 97, 98, 278
classical, 171, 186, 228
classification, 77, 95, 168, 181, 228, 229
classroom, 260
clients, 32, 154, 162
clinical judgment, 14, 44
clinical psychology, 307
clinics, 174
closure, 143, 308
cluster analysis, 224, 226, 228, 229
clustering, ix, 149, 150, 151, 153, 162
clusters, ix, 149, 150, 151, 152, 155, 156, 157, 159, 224, 228, 229
Co, 45, 83, 85, 104, 114, 119, 131, 140, 146, 150, 153, 164, 187
codes, 264
coding, 295
co-existence, 266, 268
cognition, 37, 55, 251, 253, 257, 268, 312, 313
cognitive abilities, 266
cognitive activity, 4
cognitive deficit, 257
cognitive development, xi, 237, 259, 312
cognitive domains, 254
cognitive flexibility, 306
cognitive level, 274
cognitive process, 251
cognitive science, 314
cognitive style, 250, 257
coherence, 217, 239, 240, 241, 312
cohesion, 12, 261
cohort, x, 27, 213, 214, 241, 306
collaboration, xii, 9, 30, 32, 150, 291, 292
Collaboration, 152, 154, 210
collectivism, 21, 268
colonialism, 78
Colorado, 295
colors, 304, 308, 314
Columbia, 49
Columbia University, 49
commerce, 52, 76
commodities, 141
commodity, 140, 147

communication, xi, 8, 11, 19, 30, 54, 63, 76, 106, 107, 110, 116, 119, 120, 180, 206, 234, 238, 247, 248, 253, 254, 257, 258
communication processes, 19
communication skills, xi, 8, 30, 247, 248, 255
communities, ix, xii, 41, 54, 55, 58, 59, 61, 63, 64, 67, 68, 69, 72, 73, 76, 78, 79, 80, 81, 88, 89, 90, 92, 94, 106, 109, 110, 117, 119, 133, 145, 187, 201, 270, 291, 292, 293
community, xi, 32, 35, 41, 54, 58, 60, 62, 66, 67, 68, 69, 70, 71, 72, 75, 76, 77, 78, 79, 81, 84, 85, 90, 108, 128, 130, 137, 152, 154, 187, 201, 259, 260, 292, 293, 294
community service, 260
community support, 58, 60, 75, 79
comparative advantage, viii, 88, 101
compatibility, 107, 109
compensation, 107, 141, 205, 240
competence, 3, 7, 9, 14, 28, 43, 73, 109, 164, 190, 207, 267, 312
competency, 3, 12
competition, 126, 128, 154, 160, 164, 238
competitive advantage, 150, 156, 163, 198, 202, 207
competitiveness, ix, 149, 150, 151, 153, 155, 156, 157, 188
complement, 91, 117, 227
complexity, 27, 114, 298
compliance, 267
components, 7, 10, 14, 17, 22, 41, 64, 73, 168, 187, 190, 214, 222, 224, 231, 258, 270, 271, 274, 286, 287
composition, 175, 189
comprehension, 4, 255, 270, 271, 277, 285
concentrates, 66, 156
concentration, 75, 151, 155, 253
conception, 122, 153, 217, 233, 271, 285
conceptual model, 208
conceptualization, 205, 270, 308
conceptualizations, 214, 271, 287
concrete, viii, ix, 32, 88, 91, 95, 114, 116, 149, 150, 153, 177, 181, 205, 206, 220
conditioning, 17, 40
conduct problems, 238
conductive, 189
confidence, 30, 80, 187, 235
confirmatory factor analysis, 279
Confirmatory Factor Analysis, 284
conflict, 52, 55, 59, 60, 61, 62, 65, 66, 68, 69, 70, 71, 72, 74, 78, 79, 80, 81, 89, 106, 109, 117, 135, 263, 268, 292
conflict of interest, 109
conflict resolution, 135
conformity, 72

Index

confrontation, 57, 70
confusion, 8, 23, 126
Congress 136, 141
connectivity, 250
conscientiousness, 235, 239
consciousness, 12, 52, 53, 57, 61, 63, 65, 74, 77, 79, 81
consensus, 94, 106, 172
conservation, viii, ix, 87, 88, 89, 107, 117, 120, 123, 133, 134, 135, 136, 141, 142, 143, 145, 148, 216
consolidation, 137
constraints, 24, 41, 42, 101, 142, 307
construction, xi, xii, 8, 20, 22, 34, 38, 53, 69, 72, 92, 106, 135, 136, 137, 143, 145, 178, 259, 291, 299, 300, 313, 314
constructionism, 20, 22, 46
constructionist, 18, 22, 26, 47
constructivist, 34, 291, 307
consulting, 167
consumers, 27
consumption, 120, 144
contamination, 147
content analysis, viii, 88, 91, 104, 105, 117, 119
context-dependent, 278
context-sensitive, 251
contingency, 99, 229
continuity, 16, 72, 77, 218, 222, 227, 232, 233, 238, 239
contracts, 178, 203
control, 32, 41, 53, 56, 57, 58, 65, 70, 75, 90, 130, 136, 153, 155, 156, 190, 204, 205, 206, 207, 209, 222, 252, 260, 261, 267, 268, 271, 291, 292
conviction, 190
COPD, 174
corporal punishment, 287
corporate social responsibility, 172
corporations, 205, 206, 292
correlation, 221, 223, 224, 227, 228, 231, 232, 233, 239, 241, 253, 254, 303, 308
correlation analysis, 227, 228, 231, 232, 233, 241
correlation coefficient, 221, 224, 227, 228, 232, 239
correlations, 95, 221, 222, 227, 228, 233
corruption, 65, 139, 191, 194
Corruption Perception Index, 193
cortex, 250, 251, 253, 254, 257, 258
costs, 134, 140, 142, 144, 158, 159, 173, 180, 204, 210
counseling, 50
counter-terror, 60
covering, 167
creative process, 160
creativity, 117, 160, 190
credit, 198

crimes, 192
critical analysis, 4, 10, 31, 158, 161, 162
critical care units, 14
critical thinking, 9, 45
criticism, 60, 70, 204
Croatia, 192
crop production, 136
cross-cultural, 264, 266, 267, 268, 314, 315
cross-cultural comparison, 266
cross-sectional, 219, 306, 308
cross-sectional study, 308
crying, 31
Cuba, 146
cues, xi, 247, 248, 252, 253, 262
cultural beliefs, 32, 260, 264
cultural factors, 38, 41, 266
cultural heritage, 114, 116
cultural identities, 80
cultural identity, 45
cultural influence, xi, 21, 259, 260
cultural perspective, 266, 267, 268
cultural transformation, 17, 39
cultural values, 71, 260, 262
culture, xi, 9, 16, 17, 18, 21, 22, 26, 27, 34, 37, 40, 41, 42, 44, 48, 49, 53, 64, 66, 67, 78, 79, 120, 121, 131, 164, 175, 188, 189, 206, 259, 260, 262, 263, 264, 266, 267, 288, 307, 308, 312, 313
curriculum, 7, 8, 37, 73, 74
customers, 139, 154, 157, 203
cycles, 17, 40, 43
Czech Republic, v, x, 87, 89, 92, 104, 114, 118, 119, 121, 122, 123, 124, 213, 214, 215, 216, 238, 240

D

dances, 74
dangerousness, 312
data collection, 223, 276, 287, 295
data set, x, 90, 95, 185
database, 97, 116
death, 36, 59, 63, 70, 71, 76, 237
deaths, 67, 68, 79, 175
debates, 129, 297, 309
deciduous, 92
decision making, xii, 89, 205, 291, 297
decision-making process, 7, 11, 22, 137, 154
decisions, ix, 4, 5, 8, 89, 104, 109, 145, 149, 150, 153, 155, 157, 160, 163, 166, 206, 285, 286, 312
deconstruction, 65
deduction, 238
defense, 312
deficit, xi, 247, 248, 250, 251, 255, 258
deficits, 250, 252, 254

definition, viii, 46, 87, 88, 147, 153, 167, 176, 202, 205, 270, 278
deforestation, 148
degradation, ix, 133, 134, 136, 141, 142, 143, 144, 145
degrading, 142
delinquency, 191, 192, 193, 196
delivery, ix, 2, 3, 9, 10, 24, 27, 32, 37, 39, 43, 44, 125
Delphi, 162
democracy, 104, 126, 127, 130, 210, 285
denial, 179
Denmark, 170, 192
dependent variable, 281
depression, 167, 173, 219
depressive symptoms, 244
deprivation, 94
designers, 202
destruction, 80, 188
detachment, 29
detention, 76, 77
developing brain, 254
development banks, 144
development policy, 103
developmental change, 231, 239, 306, 308
developmental delay, xi, 247, 249, 252
developmental psychology, 266, 270
deviation, 227
diabetes, 167, 168, 174, 182
diabetes mellitus, 182
Diagnostic and Statistical Manual of Mental Disorders, 256
diamond, 153
diane, 1
dichotomy, 145
dictatorship, 138
differentiation, 18, 94, 159
diffusion, 152, 156, 162, 188, 189
diffusion process, 188, 189
dignity, 130
diphtheria, 174
direct costs, 134
direct observation, 252
disabilities, 167, 169, 171, 172, 173, 179, 184, 293
disability, ix, 165, 167, 168, 169, 170, 171, 172, 174, 178, 179, 180, 181, 182, 183
disabled, ix, 165, 167, 168, 170, 171, 173, 175, 176, 177, 178, 181
discharges, 140
discipline, 214, 261
disclosure, 12, 167
discomfort, 167
discounts, 139

discourse, ix, 20, 21, 22, 23, 25, 37, 40, 41, 48, 53, 66, 71, 75, 77, 133, 134, 203
discrimination, xii, 56, 78, 167, 168, 171, 172, 173, 269, 274, 287
discriminatory, 56, 79, 145
diseases, ix, 165, 167, 174
disinhibition, 220, 221, 222
disorder, 168, 250, 252, 255, 273
dispersion, 226
disputes, 63, 66, 70, 135, 138, 139, 145, 261
dissatisfaction, 36, 62
distress, 31, 71, 222
distribution, 63, 118, 135, 138, 155, 157, 215, 228
diversity, viii, 43, 87, 92, 154, 167, 180, 183, 188, 268, 308
divestiture, 138
division, 52, 56, 57, 64, 69, 72, 95
divorce, 191, 216, 235, 236, 239
doctors, 166
domain-specificity, 309
dominance, 56, 57, 65
download, 184
drinking water, 139
drug use, 293
drugs, 293
DSM, 250, 256
DSM-IV, 250, 256
dualism, 291
duration, vii, 33, 37, 41, 51, 178, 237
duties, 19, 25, 43, 187
dynamic theory, 42

E

early retirement, 167, 172
Eastern Europe, 110, 119
ecological, viii, 5, 87, 89, 119, 123, 134, 135, 136, 137, 142, 143, 144, 145, 147, 260, 287, 289
Ecological Economics, 120, 123, 146, 147
ecological systems, 144, 260
ecologists, 119
ecology, 119, 124, 133, 146, 148
economic activity, 95, 106, 155
economic behaviour, 140
economic change, 45
economic development, 101, 121, 123, 135, 137, 203
economic efficiency, 134
economic globalisation, 142, 144
economic growth, x, 134, 135, 137, 143, 150, 185, 186, 187, 188, 189, 191, 192, 193, 196, 197, 198, 199
economic growth model, 186, 188
economic incentives, 134

economic performance, 186
economic problem, 77
economic reforms, ix, 133
economic systems, 143, 150, 186
economic theory, 139
economics, x, 80, 89, 123, 135, 136, 143, 145, 163, 164, 185, 186, 202, 203, 209, 211
economies of scale, 152
ecosystem, 89, 120, 133, 137, 140, 141, 142, 143, 147
ecosystems, 88, 89, 91, 142, 152
Education, viii, 2, 25, 40, 42, 45, 46, 48, 50, 74, 75, 82, 83, 84, 88, 119, 181, 182, 209, 210, 243, 268
educational institutions, 74, 90
educational programs, 12
educational qualifications, 276
educators, 12, 27, 37, 41, 42, 43
EEG, 258
effluent, 140
effluents, 140
ego, 232
egocentrism, 309
Egypt, 61, 62
elaboration, 12, 15, 16, 17, 39, 40, 193, 194, 195, 196
elderly, 170
elderly population, 170
election, 63, 131
electoral process, 126
electric utilities, 138
electricity, 135, 137, 140, 144
electrophysiology, 253
elementary school, 311
e-mail, 87, 133, 149
emancipation, 44
emotion, 30, 66, 251, 268, 313
emotional, xi, 14, 29, 53, 68, 168, 205, 219, 220, 222, 229, 231, 233, 247, 248, 252, 253, 267, 268, 274, 286, 287, 289, 296, 314
emotional experience, 219, 252
emotional processes, 253
emotional reactions, 296
emotional responses, 14
emotional stability, 229, 231
emotional state, 252
emotionality, 222, 231
emotions, xi, 4, 77, 78, 219, 247, 248, 251, 256, 260, 268, 270, 273, 274, 286, 287, 288, 296
empathy, 256, 274, 287, 288, 289
employability, 179, 182
employees, ix, 32, 55, 70, 108, 109, 152, 154, 165, 166, 171, 172, 173, 175, 178, 179, 180, 182, 203, 204, 205, 206, 207

employers, ix, 79, 165, 166, 169, 173, 175, 178, 179, 180
employment, ix, 33, 57, 62, 69, 76, 77, 78, 79, 80, 165, 167, 168, 170, 171, 172, 173, 174, 175, 176, 178, 182, 183, 192, 206, 210
empowered, 292
empowerment, ix, 10, 45, 149, 207, 292
encephalitis, 167
encephalomyelitis, 167
encoding, 262
encouragement, 11, 263
endocrine, 258
endophenotypes, 254
energy, 138, 207
engagement, 12, 14, 34, 44, 70, 80, 126, 128, 263
England, 48, 49, 56, 85, 172, 314
enterprise, 106, 138
enthusiasm, 250
entrepreneurs, 89, 107, 110, 180, 186, 189, 190
entrepreneurship, 186, 188, 189, 197, 198, 199, 202, 207
environment, viii, xi, 36, 44, 59, 67, 72, 88, 89, 90, 101, 104, 122, 137, 140, 142, 146, 150, 152, 163, 168, 172, 202, 219, 259, 267, 271, 274
environmental awareness, 134
environmental context, 260
environmental degradation, 141, 142, 145
environmental factors, 168
environmental impact, ix, 133, 135, 136, 140
environmental influences, 253
environmental issues, 137
environmental protection, 142, 174
environmental sustainability, 135
environmental threats, 142
environmentalists, 144
epigenetic, 258
episodic memory, 307
epistemological, 5, 291
epistemology, 7
equality, 126, 171
equity, 171, 205
equity policies, 171
ethical concerns, 9
ethics, 44
ethnicity, 41, 54, 64, 66, 72, 77, 79, 187, 301, 304
Euro, 222, 240
Eurocentric, 61
Europe, 119, 123, 124, 151, 173, 182
European Community, 167
European policy, 171
European Union, ix, 79, 165, 182
Eurostat, 167
evapotranspiration, 141

evening, 74
evil, 203
evolution, 46, 52, 56, 145, 150, 151, 152
evolutionary process, 151
examinations, 5
exchange rate, 138
exclusion, 146, 173
execution, 104, 107, 108, 109, 251
exercise, 5, 37
exosystem, 260
expertise, 7, 13, 29, 45, 48, 104, 174, 187, 207
explicit knowledge, 7
exploitation, 135, 142, 144, 156, 188
explosions, 59
exposure, 7, 30, 131, 134, 176, 262
external environment, 260
external influences, 233
externalities, 140, 141, 146, 187
externalizing, 261
externalizing behavior, 261
extraction, 92, 136
extraversion, 219, 221, 222, 228, 229, 231, 232, 235, 239
extremism, 73
extrinsic rewards, 210
eye, 210, 255, 257
eyes, 6, 128

F

fabrication, 52
facial expression, 248, 251
factor analysis, 220, 224, 225, 279
failure, viii, 57, 65, 76, 88, 91, 109
fairness, 272
faith, 206
false belief, 249
familial, 71, 72, 80
family, vii, 32, 34, 37, 41, 51, 53, 55, 69, 70, 71, 72, 76, 81, 98, 100, 187, 192, 232, 235, 236, 237, 242, 258, 260, 287, 288
family members, vii, 37, 41, 51, 55, 71, 76, 192
famine, 56
fasting, 59, 66
fatigue, 59, 60, 79, 173, 183
fauna, 92
fear, 56, 58, 61, 68, 69, 70, 109
fears, 75
February, 182, 198
feedback, 12, 32, 252
feelings, 4, 11, 12, 52, 53, 54, 58, 59, 60, 73, 76, 77, 80, 128, 222, 278
females, 221, 276, 296, 307, 309

feminist, 36, 308
fertility, 191
fertility rate, 191
fetal, 27
fetus, 36
fidelity, 309
film, 89
finance, 129, 178, 190
financial capital, 192, 206
financial crisis, 139
financial regulation, 179
financial support, 112, 141
financing, 130, 141
fines, 104, 180
Finland, 170, 192
fire, 251
firms, 152, 153, 154, 155, 156, 157, 158, 159, 188, 189, 205, 206, 209
First World, 56, 60, 61
five-factor model, 235, 239
flare, 168
flexibility, 24, 117, 150, 153, 181, 222, 315
flora, 92
flow, 20, 135, 141, 143, 155, 158, 162, 253
fluid, 19, 150
focusing, xii, 172, 202, 206, 207, 260, 269
food, 59
football, 72, 300
Ford, 164, 214, 242
forecasting, 55
foreign firms, 138
foreign investment, 135
foreigners, 138
forest ecosystem, 91
forest management, 109
forestry, 91, 118
forests, 92, 97
formal education, 75
Foucault, 143
fracture, 57
fragmentation, 153
France, 170, 192
freedom, 71, 130, 179
freshwater, 141, 144
Friday, 56, 60, 68
friendship, 30, 32, 72, 264
friendship networks, 72
frontal cortex, 254
frustration, 80, 268
fuel, 171
functional imaging, 254
funding, 106, 129
fundraising, 110

Index

funds, 103, 109, 130, 131, 137, 139, 207
fusiform, 253
fusion, 80

G

gambling, 70
games, 67, 68, 76
gas, 125
Gaza, 54, 62, 63, 74, 82
Gaza Strip, 54, 74
GDP, 143, 192
gender, xii, 16, 18, 41, 53, 54, 77, 167, 187, 214, 215, 223, 227, 264, 276, 281, 295, 296, 297, 298, 299, 300, 301, 302, 303, 304, 305, 306, 307, 308, 309, 311, 312, 313, 314, 315
gender differences, 223, 297, 307
gender role, 307
gender stereotyping, 308
gene, 254, 257, 258
general election, 56
generalizability, 277
generalization, 250
generation, ix, xi, 71, 78, 133, 138, 149, 150, 156, 160, 259, 291, 293
genes, 255, 258
genetic disorders, 167
genetics, 256
Geneva, 147, 181, 215
genome, 254
geographical mobility, 69
geography, 68, 73
Germany, 61, 192, 197
gestures, 35, 42
girls, xii, 215, 220, 223, 227, 228, 264, 281, 295, 296, 297, 298, 300, 301, 302, 303, 305, 307, 309, 311, 315
GIS, 95, 124
global economy, 123, 152
global warming, 125
globalization, 266
goal setting, 242
goals, 8, 13, 14, 39, 54, 66, 134, 135, 172, 205, 214, 216, 218, 223, 261, 266, 268, 292, 297
God, 64, 65, 70, 82
Good Friday Agreement, 60, 68
goods and services, 155, 157
gossip, 80
governance, ix, 70, 90, 123, 127, 133, 134, 142, 145, 146, 147, 209
government, viii, ix, 56, 57, 58, 59, 60, 61, 62, 65, 70, 79, 90, 104, 110, 114, 125, 126, 129, 130,

131, 134, 136, 138, 143, 165, 172, 174, 176, 178, 179
grades, 276
grandparents, 71, 72
grants, 114
graph, 158, 225
grass, 292
grasslands, 97
grassroots, 145
gray matter, 253
Great Britain, 44
Greece, 170, 192
greenhouse, 125
greenhouse gas, 125
GRI, 95
group activities, 6
group identity, 72, 261
group membership, 55
grouping, 150, 152
groups, 16, 22, 23, 25, 32, 36, 37, 53, 54, 56, 58, 59, 60, 62, 63, 65, 67, 68, 71, 72, 74, 75, 76, 77, 78, 79, 81, 90, 95, 96, 110, 123, 125, 131, 135, 140, 142, 145, 151, 156, 170, 171, 181, 186, 187, 216, 219, 223, 251, 264, 267, 268, 281, 283, 284, 302
growth, x, 45, 52, 134, 135, 137, 143, 150, 155, 185, 186, 187, 188, 189, 191, 192, 193, 196, 197, 198, 199, 206, 207, 244
guardian, 101
guidance, 8, 9, 130, 184, 205, 263
guidelines, xi, 21, 134, 259
guilt, 270, 274, 297, 312
guilty, 271
gyrus, 253

H

Hamas, 54, 63, 64, 65, 69, 71, 74, 76, 84, 85
handicapped, 101, 171, 177
hands, 127, 138, 158, 205
happiness, 236
harassment, 278
harm, 142, 204, 264, 270, 272, 277, 284, 285, 288
harmony, 264
Harvard, 49, 84, 124, 131, 163, 164, 198, 199, 208, 209, 266, 268, 311
hazards, 172
health, vii, x, 1, 2, 4, 5, 10, 27, 29, 33, 37, 40, 41, 47, 147, 165, 168, 171, 172, 173, 174, 175, 176, 177, 179, 180, 181, 182, 183, 184, 192, 242, 293
health care, 4, 5, 10, 33, 40, 41, 47, 172, 175
health care professionals, 10, 41
health care system, 10
health expenditure, 192

health problems, 176
healthcare, 175
hearing, 304
heart, ix, 137, 149, 150, 167, 188
Heart, 84, 269
hegemony, 144, 145
helplessness, 297
hemisphere, 126
heritability, 254
hermeneutic inquiry, 45
heroism, 67
heterogeneity, 254
heterogeneous, 153, 187, 253
heuristic, 37, 313
hidden curriculum, 73
high risk, 68
higher education, 73
high-level, 88, 250
high-risk, 176
high-tech, 151
hip, 291
hips, 36
hiring, 167, 179
Hispanic, 298
HIV, 168, 293
HIV/AIDS, 168, 293
hockey, 68
holistic, 9, 122, 214, 245
homogenisation, 73, 134
homosexuality, 313
honesty, 187
hormones, 254
hospital, 14
host, 92
hostility, 70, 71, 222, 262
House, 85, 131, 141, 209, 223, 295
household, 169
households, 170
housing, 57, 242
HRM, 165, 166, 167, 169, 172, 179, 180, 182, 183
human, vii, 12, 17, 18, 22, 36, 42, 44, 45, 57, 65, 88,
    89, 92, 95, 98, 101, 120, 122, 124, 139, 140, 142,
    150, 154, 171, 176, 186, 187, 188, 189, 190, 191,
    192, 196, 202, 203, 204, 205, 206, 214, 216, 218,
    237, 238, 239, 240, 241, 243, 248, 249, 251, 254,
    257, 260, 266, 267, 292, 293, 313
human agency, 42
human behavior, 36, 122, 206
human brain, 251
human capital, 186, 187, 188, 189, 190, 192, 196
human development, 214, 216, 218, 237, 238, 239,
    240, 241, 243, 260, 266, 267
human intentionality, 203

human motivation, 203
human nature, 205
human resources, 150, 171, 187
human rights, 57, 65, 293
human sciences, 44
human virtue, 187
humane, 55
humanistic perspective, 205
humanitarian, 61, 238
humans, 39, 249, 251, 253, 256
humiliation, 76
Hungary, 61, 192
hunting, 92
husband, 32
hybrid, 134, 138
hybridity, 54
hydropower, 135, 136, 137, 138
hypersensitivity, 250
hypocrisy, 78
hypoperfusion, 253
hypothesis, 94, 95, 106, 191, 250, 251, 252, 254,
    255, 256, 258, 286

I

ICD, ix, 165, 167
ICT, 152, 160, 163
id, 61, 64, 183, 270, 276
identification, ix, 10, 11, 14, 54, 55, 60, 63, 64, 65,
    67, 68, 72, 75, 77, 78, 79, 81, 129, 149, 153, 156,
    158, 160, 202, 204, 206, 240, 254
identity, vii, 2, 8, 15, 16, 17, 21, 22, 23, 24, 26, 30,
    31, 33, 34, 35, 36, 37, 38, 39, 40, 41, 42, 43, 45,
    48, 49, 52, 53, 54, 55, 57, 63, 66, 67, 69, 70, 72,
    75, 77, 78, 79, 80, 109, 233, 242, 261
ideology, 57, 238, 307
illegal drugs, 293
Illinois, 243
images, vii, 19, 25, 36, 51, 52, 55, 67, 71, 73, 75, 78,
    80
imagination, 10, 45
imaging, 254, 258
IMF, 138
imitation, 252, 258
immigration, 61, 210
immunization, 174
impairments, ix, 165, 167, 168, 169, 173, 254
implementation, viii, 46, 56, 74, 87, 90, 91, 95, 107,
    109, 110, 113, 117, 118, 119, 127, 131, 134, 137,
    140, 142, 145, 166, 172, 174, 178, 180, 181
implicit knowledge, 7, 150
imprisonment, 73
impulsivity, 219

in situ, 142, 268
in vivo, 254, 257
incarceration, 55
incentive, 126, 130, 173, 205
incentives, ix, 133, 134, 139, 172, 204, 208
incidence, 174
inclusion, 41, 80, 171, 173
income, 138, 139, 148, 171, 173, 174, 175, 192, 243
income support, 175
incomes, 171
independence, 53, 54, 56, 61, 62, 64, 74, 81, 116, 261
independent variable, 280, 281
India, 142, 146, 198
Indiana, 82, 85
indication, 177, 262, 277
indicators, x, 94, 185, 191, 192, 196, 219, 279
indices, 301
indigenous, 16, 56
individual action, 39
individual characteristics, 271
individual development, xi, 259
individual differences, 35, 222, 223, 240, 242, 302
individual personality, 228
individual rights, 270, 271
individualism, 268
individuality, 41
induction, vii, 2, 3, 8, 30, 33, 36, 38, 40
industrial, 52, 121, 140, 151, 152, 153, 154, 156, 157, 160, 162, 163, 188, 189, 202, 203
industrial sectors, 160
industrialisation, 135
industry, 118, 150, 152, 178
infancy, viii, 125, 127
infectious, 167, 174
inferences, xii, 219, 295, 296, 297, 303, 306, 308, 309, 313, 314
inferior frontal gyrus, 253
infinite, 190
inflation, 138
Information and Communication Technologies, 152
information exchange, 10, 110
information processing, xi, 247, 248
information seeking, 39
information sharing, 202
information systems, 205
Information Technology, 122
infrastructure, 69, 95, 101, 102, 110, 134, 135, 137, 138, 144, 154, 157, 187
inherited, 167
inhibition, 220
initiation, viii, 125, 237, 261, 263, 264
injuries, 80, 167

injury, 169, 273
injustice, 62, 78, 81
innocence, 297, 312
innovation, ix, xi, 127, 130, 149, 150, 151, 152, 155, 159, 187, 188, 189, 259
Innovation, 123, 131, 155, 159, 163
insane, 314
insight, 7, 11, 29
inspection, 126
Inspection, 104
inspiration, 119
instability, 139, 243
institutional change, 90, 126
institutional reforms, ix, 133, 136, 141, 143
institutionalisation, 143
institutions, vii, viii, x, 1, 19, 22, 25, 35, 40, 44, 51, 55, 57, 69, 70, 73, 74, 75, 80, 81, 90, 104, 105, 108, 116, 119, 125, 126, 127, 145, 153, 156, 157, 174, 175, 180, 185, 186, 191, 192, 196, 204
instruction, 4, 9
instructors, 260
instruments, 133, 134, 145, 147, 228
insurance, 173, 174, 175, 178
insurance companies, 175
intangible, 205
integration, 65, 79, 173, 180, 266
integrity, 4, 12, 147
intellectual capital, 190, 207, 210
intellectual development, 223
intelligence, x, 8, 213, 216, 218, 223, 224, 225, 227, 237, 238, 242, 243, 244, 297
intelligence tests, 223
intentional behavior, 252
intentionality, 27, 31, 203, 271, 273
intentions, 24, 73, 209, 248, 252, 253, 257, 308
interaction, xi, 17, 20, 23, 25, 34, 40, 55, 68, 81, 119, 142, 169, 196, 206, 208, 247, 248, 254, 259, 260, 261, 263, 264, 266, 267, 271, 272, 314
interactions, vii, x, xi, 1, 2, 7, 15, 16, 19, 20, 21, 22, 23, 25, 26, 32, 33, 36, 37, 39, 40, 41, 42, 43, 44, 55, 68, 72, 90, 185, 186, 204, 251, 259, 260, 261, 262, 263, 264, 266, 267, 268, 270, 271, 272, 286, 288, 289
interdependence, 89
interdisciplinary, 33, 238
interest rates, 136
interface, 15
intergenerational, 72
intermediaries, 155
internal organization, 211
internalised, 51, 54, 55, 67, 69, 73, 78, 80
internalization, 33, 267
International Classification of Diseases, ix, 165

international investment, 80
International Labour Office, 164
international markets, 151, 155, 159
international relations, 53
internet, 76, 129
Internet, 155
interpersonal conflicts, 107, 263
interpersonal contact, 188
interpersonal interactions, 20
interpersonal relations, 20, 152, 239
interrelatedness, 301
interrelations, 88, 157
interval, 223, 224, 238
intervention, xii, 16, 31, 56, 167, 171, 234, 261, 270, 286, 287, 289
interview, 28, 29, 91, 107, 217, 233, 234, 236, 237, 277, 278, 298
iintifada, 63, 66, 76
intimacy, 30, 35
intimidation, 58
intravenous, 255
intrinsic, 17, 23, 40, 209, 210, 270, 272, 273, 275, 285, 286
intrinsic motivation, 209, 210
intrinsic value, 275, 285, 286
intron, 255
introversion, 228
introvert, 228
intrusions, 78
intuition, 7, 14, 45, 160, 162
invasive, 58, 62
inventories, 243
investment, 80, 130, 138, 140, 144, 244
investors, 135, 138, 144
ions, 8, 17, 22, 41
IQ, 223, 224
IRA, 54, 57, 58, 59, 60, 71, 82, 83, 84, 85
Ireland, 52, 54, 56, 58, 64, 66, 70, 78, 79, 81, 83, 84, 85, 170, 173, 192
Irish Republican Army, 57
Iron Curtain, 91, 238
irrigation, 135, 138
Islam, 53, 54, 63, 64, 65, 69, 70, 74, 76, 80, 82, 83, 85, 86
Islamic, 53, 54, 65, 69, 70, 71, 72, 73, 74, 82, 83, 84, 85
island, 56, 57, 74
isolation, 41, 55, 76, 117
Israel, 61, 62, 64, 65, 67, 69, 71, 74, 75, 76, 78, 82, 83, 254, 257
Israeli-Palestinian conflict, 80
Italian population, 288

Italy, 152, 170, 192, 199, 210, 247, 263, 269, 276, 287
IUCN, 88, 92

J

Japan, 192, 261
Jerusalem, 62, 68, 217, 221, 232, 243
jewelry, 299
Jews, 53, 60, 61, 62, 64, 67, 68, 71, 73, 82
jihad, 74
job creation, 137
job performance, 173, 190
jobs, 166, 171, 173, 174, 176, 179, 183
joining, 58
Jordan, 61, 62
Judaism, 61, 64, 65, 82
judge, xii, 43, 263, 270, 272, 273, 285
judges, 262
judgment, 14
Jung, 214
jurisdiction, 141, 177
justice, 134, 135, 144, 147, 272, 285
justification, 53, 54, 63, 75, 137, 141, 177, 305

K

kappa, 299
killing, 60
kindergartens, 74
King, 56, 295
Knesset, 65
knowledge construction, xii, 291
knowledge economy, 207
knowledge-based economy, 152
Korea, 261
Korean, 261, 263, 267

L

labor, 166, 171, 174, 189, 255, 258
labor force, 189
labour, 28, 32, 52, 136, 143, 158, 169, 170, 172, 173, 176, 177, 178, 179, 180, 182, 192
labour force, 169, 170
labour market, 136, 172, 182
land, 56, 61, 62, 63, 64, 90, 92, 95, 97, 107, 124, 138, 145, 147, 149, 186
land tenure, 90, 145
land use, 92, 95, 107, 124
landscapes, 88, 119, 122, 124
land-use, 95, 97, 147

Index

language, 15, 19, 35, 37, 39, 41, 46, 73, 119, 144, 171, 172, 179, 209, 250, 254, 256, 258
language impairment, 256
Latin America, 143, 146, 147
Latin American countries, 143
lattice, 150
Latvia, 123, 192
law, 90, 107, 130, 135, 136, 139, 140, 172, 174, 175, 176, 177, 178, 196, 292
law enforcement, 140
laws, 16, 56, 129, 143, 173, 177, 178, 180
leadership, 59, 65, 125, 128, 187, 206
learners, 3, 5, 9, 11, 16, 31
learning, vii, viii, xi, xii, 1, 2, 3, 4, 5, 6, 7, 9, 10, 12, 14, 15, 16, 17, 27, 28, 29, 31, 33, 34, 37, 38, 39, 41, 42, 43, 44, 45, 46, 47, 48, 50, 73, 74, 87, 90, 109, 116, 117, 120, 122, 209, 259, 260, 291, 312
learning culture, 16
learning environment, 4
learning outcomes, 12
legal systems, 193
legislation, 78, 106, 107, 109, 131, 135, 136, 137, 138, 139, 140, 145, 171, 172, 177, 179, 181
liberal, viii, 125, 126, 130, 131, 138
liberalisation, 136
liberation, 70, 76
life changes, 236
life course, 214, 236, 237, 238, 239, 242, 244
life expectancy, 175, 192
life experiences, 292
life quality, 94
life satisfaction, 217, 240
life span, 218, 222, 240, 241, 242, 244
life style, 234
lifespan, 214, 218, 233, 268
lifestyle, 40, 120, 169, 174, 236
lifetime, 20, 114
likelihood, vii, 51, 81, 220, 253, 256
limitation, 29, 30, 101, 137, 167, 168, 179
limitations, 24, 119, 135, 142, 167, 168, 169, 173, 207, 243, 308
Lincoln, 293
linear, 34, 95, 168, 225, 306
linear regression, 95
linguistic, 15, 19, 40
linguistics, 307
linkage, 254, 257
links, xi, 10, 36, 66, 150, 152, 153, 158, 159, 160, 173, 191, 218, 259, 313
listening, 30, 39
literacy, 52
liver, 70, 74
living conditions, 95, 99

loans, 138
lobbying, 110
local community, 90, 108
localised, 67, 69, 81, 134, 155
localization, 101
location, 25, 42
locus, 256
logistics, 152
London, 44, 45, 46, 47, 48, 50, 82, 83, 84, 85, 86, 120, 123, 146, 147, 181, 183, 197, 198, 199, 215, 240, 242, 243, 259, 287, 288, 289, 314
loneliness, 236
long distance, 98
long period, 205, 206, 236
longevity, 69, 77
longitudinal studies, 223, 242, 244, 314
longitudinal study, x, 213, 214, 215, 218, 237, 238, 243, 244
Los Angeles, 84, 288
love, 65
low power, 264
low-income, 243
low-level, 37
Lula, 138, 147
lying, 95

M

machinery, 149, 154
macroeconomic, 139
macrosystem, 260
magazines, 75
magnetic, iv
mainstream, ix, 133, 140, 143, 144, 171, 292, 293
mainstream society, 171
maintenance, vii, ix, 51, 70, 76, 80, 133, 141, 260, 297
maladaptive, 263
males, 274, 276, 296, 307, 309
mammals, 254
management, ix, x, 3, 41, 88, 90, 92, 106, 107, 109, 110, 117, 119, 124, 127, 133, 134, 135, 136, 137, 139, 141, 143, 144, 145, 146, 147, 158, 160, 163, 165, 166, 169, 171, 175, 178, 179, 180, 201, 202, 203, 204, 205, 206, 207, 208, 209, 210, 268
management practices, 209
manifold, 251, 256
manipulation, 288, 299, 302
MANOVA, 280, 281, 284
manufactured goods, 151
manufacturing, 150
mapping, 306
marches, 64

marginalization, xii, 291
market, ix, 10, 101, 104, 133, 134, 135, 136, 141,
    142, 143, 144, 146, 153, 154, 155, 157, 158, 160,
    161, 162, 163, 171, 172, 173, 182, 189, 202, 203
market economy, 104
market failure, 146
marketing, 89, 123, 157
markets, 89, 145, 150, 151, 154, 155, 157, 159, 160,
    211
marriage, 191, 227, 236
marriages, 68
Marxist, 57, 238
Maryland, 45
mass communication, 120
Massachusetts, 46, 163
Massachusetts Institute of Technology, 46
mastery, 222, 262
maternal, 27, 267
maternal control, 267
matrix, 220, 222
meaning systems, 23
meanings, 3, 8, 17, 20, 21, 22, 25, 27, 31, 33, 35, 38,
    41, 44, 268
measles, 174
measurement, 183, 191, 205, 223, 224, 228, 232,
    233, 241
measures, viii, ix, 77, 87, 88, 89, 90, 95, 101, 104,
    133, 134, 136, 141, 143, 166, 172, 174, 177, 191,
    219, 232, 298
media, 53, 55, 59, 72, 75, 81, 90, 91, 105, 117, 119,
    121, 122, 166
medial prefrontal cortex, 249, 253
median, 232
mediation, 171, 258
mediators, 23, 254
medical care, 168, 169
medical student, 33
medication, 34, 167, 179
medications, 169
medicine, vii, 1, 2, 7, 37, 130, 172
melancholic, 228
membership, 55, 229
memory, 22, 177, 242, 307
men, 27, 36, 59, 70, 76, 170, 204, 216, 232, 233,
    234, 237, 244
meningitis, 167, 174
mental ability, 242
mental actions, 169
mental development, 214, 215
mental disorder, 166
mental illness, 172, 293
mental impairment, 168
mental life, 307

mental representation, 249, 262
mental state, xi, 247, 248, 296, 309
mental states, xi, 247, 248, 296, 309
mentor, 8, 30
Merleau-Ponty, 12, 13, 47
mesosystem, 260
messages, vii, 51, 52, 54, 55, 72, 73, 76, 105
meta-analysis, 232, 253, 256, 296
metaphors, 19, 23, 25, 36, 37
Mexico, 192
microclusters, 157, 161
microsatellites, 255
microsystem, 260
middle class, 69, 77
Middle East, 61, 65, 82, 83, 84, 85
middle-aged, 237
midlife, 242, 243, 244
midwives, vii, 1, 2, 3, 5, 10, 11, 15, 16, 18, 26, 27,
    28, 29, 30, 31, 32, 33, 34, 35, 36, 37, 38, 39, 40,
    41, 42, 43, 44, 49
migrants, 56, 61
migration, 61
militant, 53, 54, 63, 65, 68, 69, 72, 73, 75
Militant, 86
militarism, 57
military, 54, 56, 57, 58, 59, 62, 64, 65, 68, 71, 76,
    78, 91, 97, 98, 99, 138, 143
military dictatorship, 138, 143
milk, 308, 313
Millennium, 89, 122
mineral resources, 88
Ministry of Education, 74
Ministry of Environment, 89, 119, 122
Minnesota, 243
minority, 57, 77, 78, 80, 81, 104, 130
mirror, 251, 252, 253, 256, 258
misleading, 104
missions, 125
MIT, 146, 313, 315
MMA, 136, 143, 146, 147
mobile phone, 98
mobility, 68, 69, 183
modalities, 11, 43
models, 2, 37, 65, 153, 186, 188, 190, 204, 205, 208,
    210, 245, 250, 251, 253, 266, 270, 271, 284
modernisation, 52
modernity, 53
modulation, 253
modus operandi, 104
molecular mechanisms, 253
money, 101, 134, 180, 292
monkeys, 251
moral behavior, 271, 289

moral development, 270, 271, 287, 288, 289
moral judgment, 14, 274, 289
moral reasoning, 271, 286, 287, 288
morality, xi, 45, 78, 269, 270, 272, 274, 275, 286, 287, 289
morning, 290
morphogenesis, vii, 1, 2, 17, 18, 39, 40
mosaic, 92, 117
motion, 253
motivation, 190, 192, 203, 207, 209, 210, 216, 242, 268, 297, 312
motives, 192, 204
motor actions, 258
motor activity, 261
mountains, 56
movement, 17, 54, 57, 59, 60, 71, 79, 172, 207, 236, 252
MPI, 228
multicultural, 266
multidimensional, 191
multidisciplinary, 313
multilateral, 134, 136, 144
multinational corporations, 208
multiple factors, 77
multiple regression, 221, 241
multiple sclerosis, 167
multiplication, ix, 133
multiplicity, 30
multivariate, 255, 264
murals, 66, 67
musculoskeletal, 169, 174
music, 74, 75, 79
Muslim, v, vii, 51, 52, 60, 63, 64, 66, 72, 74, 79
Muslims, 51, 53, 54, 60, 61, 63, 64, 65, 68, 72, 73, 76, 78
mutual respect, 292

N

narratives, 5, 6, 10, 12, 17, 23, 41, 52, 55, 81
Nash, 296, 313
nation, 52, 61, 62, 63, 65, 73, 80, 81, 101, 118
national identity, 52, 54, 57, 64
national policy, 138
nationalism, 52, 53, 54, 57, 59, 60, 62, 63, 64, 65, 66, 70, 77, 80
Natura 2000, 92, 120
natural, 89, 92, 101, 117, 120, 139, 142, 144, 308, 314
natural capital, 101, 120
natural resources, 142, 144
nature conservation, 107, 108, 110, 116
negative affectivity, 219, 220, 221, 222, 244

negative attitudes, 67, 204, 263
negative emotions, 271
negative relation, 193
neglect, 51
negotiating, 40, 79, 81
negotiation, 22, 26, 63, 163
neighbourhoods, 139
neoliberal, 136, 145, 147
Neoliberal, 147
neoliberalism, 144
Netherlands, ix, 165, 167, 170, 172, 173, 174, 175, 180, 182, 183, 192, 263
network, viii, 20, 33, 88, 90, 92, 114, 116, 117, 119, 124, 139, 151, 152, 153, 156, 163, 202, 293
networking, 152
neurobiological, 252, 253, 255
neurobiology, xi, 247, 255, 256
neuroimaging, 249
neurons, 251, 252, 253, 254, 256
neuropeptides, 254
neurophysiology, 256
neuroticism, 68, 219, 220, 222, 228, 229, 231, 232, 235, 239, 245
New England, 131
New Jersey, 84
New South Wales, 49
New York, 13, 44, 45, 47, 49, 82, 83, 84, 85, 122, 123, 145, 148, 163, 164, 183, 197, 199, 209, 210, 211, 240, 241, 242, 243, 244, 245, 266, 267, 268, 287, 289, 311, 312, 313, 314, 315
newsletters, 75
newspapers, 75, 105, 166
NGOs, 110, 129
non-clinical, 254
nonverbal, xi, 247, 248, 264
non-violent, 104, 273
normal, 95, 96, 107, 159, 167, 168, 237, 286, 288
norms, xi, 32, 54, 65, 73, 80, 81, 186, 191, 203, 259, 260, 266, 270, 271, 272, 273, 274, 275, 277, 278, 279, 280, 284, 285, 286, 311
North America, 261, 262, 263, 267
North Carolina, 164
Northern Ireland, vii, 51, 52, 54, 55, 56, 57, 58, 64, 66, 67, 68, 70, 72, 73, 74, 75, 76, 77, 78, 79, 80, 81, 82, 83, 84, 85, 86
Norway, 192
NRC, 174
nurse, 7, 8, 10, 12, 14, 29, 300
nurses, 2, 3, 7, 10, 12, 14, 33, 49
nursing, vii, 1, 2, 3, 4, 8, 9, 10, 11, 12, 13, 14, 28, 29, 44, 45, 46, 47, 48, 49, 50, 174, 175, 293
nursing care, 9
nursing home, 175

nutrition, 174

O

obedience, 163, 219, 220
obesity, 173
objectivity, 291
obligation, 33, 73, 175, 177, 278, 285
obligations, xi, xii, 19, 25, 36, 177, 269, 272, 284, 285, 286
observations, 231, 241, 271, 288
obsolete, 238
obstetricians, 37, 41
obstruction, 10
occupational, 172, 173, 174, 179, 183, 297, 298, 300, 302, 308, 311
occupational health, 172, 173
occupied territories, 62
octapeptide, 255
OECD, 104, 122, 150, 151
offenders, 286
old age, 214, 242, 244
older adults, 293
one dimension, 66, 277
online, 11, 43, 121
on-line, 286
opinion polls, 128
opportunism, 202, 203
opposition, 9, 31, 60, 71, 81, 135, 138, 145
oppression, 53
optics, 94
optimism, 57, 62, 314
optimization, 240
oral, 4, 10, 21, 22, 34, 53, 272, 273, 278
oral tradition, 10
orbitofrontal cortex, 253
organ, xi, 259
organic, 207
organic growth, 207
organism, 168
organizational behavior, 181
organizational capacity, 188
organizational culture, 166
orientation, 228
Ottoman Empire, 61
outsourcing, 159
ownership, 98, 100, 210
ownership structure, 210
oxytocin, 254, 257, 258

P

pain, 167, 252, 258, 270, 274, 286
pairing, 300
Palestine, 61, 65, 82, 83, 85
Palestinian Authority, 65
paradigm shift, 89, 127, 210
paradox, 142, 206
paradoxical, 37, 101, 104, 152
paramilitary, 58, 59, 60, 67, 75, 77, 78
parasitic diseases, 167
parental authority, 289
parental care, 254
parenthood, 235, 239
parenting, 242, 268
parenting styles, 268
parents, 71, 72, 217, 236, 295
Parietal, 256
parietal cortex, 253
Parietal lobe, 256
Paris, 124, 146, 148, 215
Parliament, 56, 57
participatory research, 292
partition, 57, 74, 78
partnership, 29, 90
partnerships, 90, 138, 293
passive, 137, 203, 264, 273
pathology, 168, 169
pathways, 2, 250, 252, 254, 267
patient care, 9
patients, 14, 176, 177
patriotism, 73
PCA, 95, 97, 98
peace process, 52, 63, 65, 69
peace treaty, 62
peat, 91, 92
pedagogical, 4
pedagogies, 37
pedagogy, 10
peer, xii, 9, 34, 73, 166, 260, 261, 262, 263, 264, 266, 267, 269, 273, 274, 276, 281, 287, 288, 289, 307, 309
peer conflict, 263
peer group, 73, 260, 288, 307
peer review, 166
peer support, 289
peers, vii, xii, 15, 25, 30, 34, 35, 39, 41, 51, 53, 68, 72, 73, 74, 232, 260, 261, 262, 263, 270, 273, 274, 275, 281, 285, 286, 293, 309
per capita, 192
perception, x, xi, 10, 12, 27, 47, 57, 58, 101, 104, 194, 213, 215, 217, 218, 236, 240, 250, 251, 253, 258, 267, 269, 271, 275, 277, 279, 281, 284, 297

perceptions, xii, 7, 29, 43, 53, 55, 64, 66, 67, 68, 77, 79, 81, 147, 188, 269
performers, 13
periodic, 123, 167
permit, 156, 174
perseverance, 261
personal accomplishment, 261
personal goals, 39
personal identity, 16, 21, 22, 24, 26, 34
personal life, 65
personality, x, 35, 36, 55, 209, 213, 214, 215, 216, 217, 218, 219, 220, 221, 222, 227, 228, 231, 232, 233, 234, 235, 236, 237, 238, 239, 240, 241, 242, 243, 244, 245, 267, 268, 287, 289, 312, 314, 315
personality characteristics, 221, 222, 233
personality differences, 219
personality dimensions, 219, 231
personality inventories, 243
personality traits, x, 36, 213, 217, 218, 219, 220, 222, 227, 228, 231, 232, 233, 239, 241, 242, 244
personality type, 228, 231, 241
personhood, 26, 45
personnel costs, 180
phenomenology, 13, 47
phenotype, 251, 253, 255
Philadelphia, 289, 293, 314
philanthropic, 129
philosophers, 270
philosophical, 44
philosophy, 48, 49, 203, 205, 288
phone, 98, 129, 216, 259
phylogenetic, 101
physical activity, 235
physical environment, 40, 168, 169
physical well-being, 95
physics, 130
physiological, 168
placenta, 32
planning, 7, 8, 30, 43, 110, 114, 120, 121, 122, 135, 147, 180, 206
plasma, 255
platforms, 108
play, xi, 22, 67, 69, 72, 88, 89, 108, 110, 178, 189, 202, 206, 207, 210, 249, 251, 259, 261, 262, 264, 267, 271, 288, 299, 304, 306, 307, 315
PLO, 62, 65
PMS, 119
poisoning, 140
police, 58, 77, 300
policy levels, 166
policy makers, 141
political leaders, 137
political opposition, 138

political participation, 81
political parties, 54, 74
politicians, viii, 57, 125, 126, 128, 129, 137, 141, 145
politics, 47, 57, 59, 62, 65, 69, 120, 125, 127, 146, 293
pollution, 134, 136, 143
polymorphisms, 254
pools, 92
poor, 76, 89, 94, 109, 130, 139, 140
population, viii, xii, 60, 77, 87, 88, 90, 95, 98, 99, 101, 104, 130, 131, 135, 139, 170, 215, 216, 227, 242, 249, 288, 291, 293
population size, 98
portfolios, 10
Portugal, 170
positive emotions, 222
positive feedback, 32
positive relation, x, 185, 186, 188, 192, 193, 196
positive relationship, x, 185, 186, 188, 192, 193, 196
positivist, 7
postmortem, 253
post-traumatic stress disorder, 68
poverty, 76, 94, 122, 142
power, 10, 11, 19, 33, 36, 40, 44, 45, 47, 53, 54, 55, 56, 78, 90, 104, 126, 131, 135, 138, 143, 144, 147, 158, 204, 206, 223, 264, 265, 273, 278, 291, 292, 293, 297, 308
power relations, 36, 291
powers, 7, 30, 35, 155
practical knowledge, 7, 12, 14
pragmatic, 25, 64
pragmatism, 3
praxis, 7
prayer, 66
prediction, x, 183, 213, 218, 219, 240, 289, 299, 300
predictors, 221, 222, 287
pre-existing, 39
preference, 176, 296, 297, 298, 299, 300, 303, 304, 305
prefrontal cortex, 249, 253
pregnancy, 30
pregnant, 30
prejudice, 116, 313
premiums, 173, 175
premotor cortex, 251, 257
preschool, 263, 288, 296, 308
preschool children, 263, 288
preschoolers, 268, 298, 305
present value, 190
president, 92, 139
press, 105, 106, 163, 286, 289, 297, 301, 308, 312
pressure, 58, 72, 103, 109, 128, 129, 130, 134

prevention, 140, 167, 171, 172, 174, 178, 287, 289
preventive, 172, 174
primacy, 53, 139
primary school, 75, 215, 276
primate, 256
primates, 253
principal component analysis, 95
printing, 75, 241
prior knowledge, 41
prisoners, 59, 60, 73
prisons, 59, 73
pristine, 88
privacy, 31, 184
private, ix, 5, 11, 15, 21, 25, 33, 34, 39, 40, 42, 43, 48, 71, 73, 90, 122, 133, 134, 136, 137, 138, 139, 141, 142, 150, 157, 298, 303
private firms, 142
private schools, 298, 303
private sector, 90, 138
privatisation, 137, 138, 139, 142, 143
privatization, 138, 145, 147
proactive, 58, 187, 273, 287
probability, 187, 202, 215
probands, 254
problem solving, 7
problem-based learning, 7, 8, 31
Problem-based learning, 44
problem-solving, 7, 8, 10, 90, 130, 264, 268, 289
problem-solving strategies, 289
production, 19, 20, 25, 36, 42, 45, 49, 120, 140, 143, 144, 151, 155, 156, 157, 158, 159, 160, 186, 188, 207, 292
production function, 186, 188
productivity, 151, 173, 180, 187, 188
professional development, 3, 6, 9, 11, 14, 24, 29, 45, 46
professionalism, 12, 49
professions, 7, 307
profit, 105, 188, 192
profits, 159, 177
program, 13, 30, 49, 108, 173, 174, 289
programming, 50, 295
prolactin, 255
propagation, 74
property, iv, 61, 62
prosocial behavior, 264, 274
prosocial orientation, 261
prosperity, 209
protected area, viii, 87, 88, 89, 90, 95, 96, 99, 101, 103, 104, 105, 106, 107, 108, 109, 110, 113, 119
protected areas, viii, 87, 88, 89, 90, 95, 96, 99, 101, 104, 105, 106, 107, 108, 109, 119
Protected Areas Network, 114

protection, viii, 58, 71, 87, 88, 89, 90, 95, 99, 101, 104, 105, 106, 107, 109, 110, 114, 116, 117, 118, 119, 121, 123, 141, 142, 172, 174, 176, 177, 178
Protestants, 53, 56, 57, 60, 64, 66, 68, 71, 74, 78, 79
prototype, 155
provocation, 273, 287
proxy, x, 185, 192, 196
psychiatric disorders, 167, 241
psychological development, 215, 237, 315
psychological functions, 218
psychological phenomena, 20
psychological processes, 268
psychological variables, 216, 228, 237
psychologist, 214
psychology, x, 18, 35, 36, 40, 46, 47, 185, 186, 209, 214, 239, 240, 241, 243, 244, 245, 266, 267, 268, 287, 289, 307, 311, 313, 314
psychopathology, 220
Pub Med, 166
public, viii, ix, 15, 21, 25, 26, 34, 35, 37, 40, 42, 43, 59, 60, 65, 67, 74, 87, 89, 90, 91, 104, 105, 106, 107, 109, 110, 114, 122, 125, 126, 127, 128, 129, 130, 131, 133, 134, 135, 136, 137, 138, 139, 141, 142, 145, 147, 150, 156, 157, 171, 172, 178, 243, 292, 293
public administration, 127
public awareness, 128
public funds, 137
public goods, ix, 125, 126, 130
public health, 147, 171, 173, 293
public interest, 129
public investment, 136, 138
public money, 134
public opinion, 104, 106, 128, 129
public policy, 128, 172, 243
public schools, 74
public sector, 136, 137, 141, 173
public service, ix, 65, 133, 137
public support, 129
public-private partnerships, 138, 139
publishers, 45
pulses, 144
punishment, 55, 273, 287
punitive, 297
pupils, 73, 74

Q

qualifications, 73
qualitative research, 2, 293
quality of life, viii, 87, 88, 90, 94, 95, 104, 117, 120, 121, 175
Quality of life, 94, 122

Index

questionnaire, viii, 87, 91, 99, 104, 110, 117, 167, 220, 277, 278
questionnaires, 217, 278
quotas, 171

R

R&D, 187
race, 187, 314
racism, 61
radicalism, 62
rainfall, 141
rainforest, 141
random, 99, 128, 130, 153, 298, 300, 304
range, xii, 14, 18, 19, 54, 58, 69, 73, 76, 77, 79, 81, 90, 139, 143, 152, 201, 223, 228, 237, 254, 276, 292, 295, 296, 297, 298, 301, 303, 306, 307, 309
rating scale, 219, 220
rationalisation, 143
rationality, 7, 134, 135, 136, 141, 144, 145, 235, 239
raw material, 92, 152, 158
reactivity, 219, 220
reading, 255, 256, 278, 290, 299, 306
real estate, 100, 135
realism, 44, 210
realist, 16, 44
reality, 15, 20, 35, 90, 105, 144, 204, 249, 307, 314, 315
reasoning, xii, 4, 8, 13, 47, 249, 270, 271, 272, 275, 286, 287, 288, 289, 295, 296, 297, 298, 301, 302, 303, 305, 306, 307, 308, 309, 312, 313
reasoning skills, 47
recall, 171
receptors, 37
reciprocal relationships, 156
reciprocity, 127, 187
recognition, ix, 14, 41, 108, 133, 134, 172, 205, 249, 251, 254, 257, 258
reconcile, 306
reconciliation, 34, 134, 135
reconstruction, 8, 22, 32, 160
recovery, 14, 48, 135, 183
recreation, 101, 122, 169
recreational, 98, 101
recruiting, 71, 73
reengineering, 208
reflection, vii, 1, 3, 4, 5, 6, 7, 8, 9, 10, 11, 12, 15, 17, 25, 26, 34, 43, 45, 46, 47, 48, 49, 50, 101, 105, 203
reflective practice, vii, 1, 2, 3, 5, 6, 7, 8, 9, 11, 12, 15, 28, 31, 40, 42, 43, 45, 47, 48, 49, 50
reflexivity, 79

reforms, 126, 130, 131, 133, 134, 135, 136, 137, 143, 144, 145
refugees, 58, 61, 62
regional, viii, 53, 83, 88, 89, 91, 94, 103, 104, 105, 107, 110, 114, 118, 119, 120, 121, 123, 124, 151, 188, 197, 308
regional clusters, 151
regional economies, 197
regional policy, 121
registered nurses, 2
regression, 95, 222, 228
regression analysis, 228
regular, 81, 108, 114, 128
regulation, 122, 135, 137, 140, 141, 142, 144, 145, 146, 261
regulations, ix, 32, 39, 43, 146, 165, 172, 178, 179
regulators, 139
regulatory framework, ix, 133
regulatory requirements, ix, 133
rehabilitation, 167, 169, 178
rehabilitation program, 178
reinforcement, 66, 75
rejection, 264
relevance, 3, 223, 253
reliability, 72, 223, 224, 254
religion, 41, 53, 54, 60, 61, 63, 64, 65, 66, 70, 72, 73, 77, 80, 187
religions, 65, 83
religiosity, 64, 65, 69, 70, 71, 75, 78, 81
religious belief, 66, 73
religious groups, 74, 75
remission, 168
repression, 81
reproduction, 16, 37, 41
Republican, 54, 56, 58, 59, 70, 71, 84
research design, 2, 238
resentment, 63
reserves, viii, 87, 88, 90, 91, 92, 94, 95, 101, 108, 117, 118, 119, 121, 122, 123, 124, 191, 192
residential, 58
resilience, 222
resistance, 66, 71, 138, 145, 296
resolution, vii, 51, 61, 62, 135
resource allocation, 205, 207, 208
resource availability, 136
resources, 7, 17, 29, 39, 56, 77, 78, 79, 88, 89, 119, 120, 134, 137, 138, 142, 144, 145, 147, 149, 150, 151, 154, 158, 160, 167, 171, 173, 186, 187, 190, 202, 206, 207, 236
responsibilities, 26, 42, 43, 144, 172, 202, 206, 207
responsiveness, 127, 235, 239, 256, 274
restructuring, 160
retaliation, 58

retention, 152, 171, 174, 184, 257
retribution, 287
returns, 181, 199, 204, 209, 249
revaluation, 237
rewards, 203
Reynolds, 186, 190, 199
rhetoric, 10, 34, 41, 53, 54, 66, 71, 77, 89, 135
rheumatic, 167
rheumatic fever, 167
rheumatic heart disease, 167
rheumatoid arthritis, 182
rigidity, 207, 306
risk, 68, 142, 169, 171, 173, 174, 176, 210, 254, 273
rivers, 92, 135
road map, 63
roadblocks, 76
rocky, 45
Romania, 247
Rosenberg Self-Esteem Scale, 232
rugby, 68
rule breaking behavior, 277
rule of law, 196
rule-breaking, 272, 278, 280, 281, 282, 283, 284, 286
rural, 29, 63, 68, 95, 97, 101, 120, 121, 122, 123, 124, 145, 146
rural areas, 63, 68
rural development, 121, 122, 124
Rutherford, 85

S

sacred, 63
safeguard, 176
safeguards, 204
safety, x, 71, 165, 171, 173, 176, 177, 179, 274
salaries, 159, 178
salary, 139, 175
sales, 157
sample, x, 99, 128, 131, 213, 214, 215, 216, 220, 228, 229, 232, 233, 237, 281, 304, 308
sampling, 99
sanctions, 271, 307
sanitation, 137, 138, 139
satellite, 75, 238
satellite technology, 75
satisfaction, 88, 94, 118, 159, 217, 240
savings, 159
scaffolding, 38
scarce resources, 207
scarcity, 139, 143
scepticism, 139
schema, 278, 311
schizophrenia, 167

scholarship, 78
school, xii, 16, 45, 51, 73, 74, 80, 81, 98, 100, 151, 210, 215, 216, 223, 260, 269, 274, 275, 276, 277, 278, 279, 284, 287, 288, 289, 290, 298, 301, 303, 304, 311, 315
schooling, 73, 74, 236
scores, 220, 222, 223, 224, 225, 227, 255, 264, 265, 276, 278, 280, 281, 284, 301, 302, 303, 306
search, 134, 143, 152, 159, 166, 219
searching, 98, 232
Second World, 61, 144
secondary data, ix, 133
secondary education, 216
secretariat, 137
secrets, 152
secular, 53, 54, 59, 62, 64, 65, 66, 70, 72, 73, 76
security, 58, 63, 69, 71, 80, 90, 172, 178, 179
segregation, 67, 75, 80
selecting, 57, 126, 129
Self, 8, 24, 27, 34, 164, 217, 220, 221, 232, 233, 235, 240, 241, 243, 311, 312, 314
self-awareness, 4, 10, 40
self-concept, x, 213, 217, 218, 219, 232, 233, 239, 240, 241, 244
self-confidence, 219, 235, 239, 261
self-control, 219, 264, 271
self-efficacy, 188, 217, 219, 220, 221, 222, 232
self-employed, 170
self-esteem, 68, 217, 219, 220, 232, 233, 238, 240, 243, 245, 271
self-evaluations, 219, 222, 232, 242
self-expression, 261
self-identity, 16
self-image, 78, 244
self-interest, 203, 210
self-knowledge, 233
self-perceptions, 214
self-presentation, 231
self-reflection, 5
self-regard, 239
self-regulation, 261
self-report, xii, 217, 242, 269, 277
semi-arid, 137
semiotics, 36, 39, 42
Senate, 131, 141
sensation, 252
sensations, 251
sensitivity, 118, 299
sentences, 46
separation, 56, 68, 69, 76, 80, 145, 286
series, xii, 2, 85, 110, 123, 151, 179, 190, 220, 238, 264, 295, 298, 300
serotonergic, 254

serotonin, 257
services, ix, 5, 31, 32, 33, 35, 36, 37, 39, 40, 42, 43, 65, 66, 70, 71, 89, 95, 101, 102, 114, 120, 133, 134, 137, 138, 139, 141, 142, 143, 146, 147, 148, 153, 155, 157, 158, 162, 171, 173, 184, 260
SES, 276
settlement policy, 62
settlements, 62, 64, 68, 78
severity, 168, 257
sewage, 136, 141
sex, 262, 264, 309, 311, 312, 313, 314, 315
sex role, 315
shame, 219, 267, 270, 274
Shanghai, 267
shape, 64, 134, 172, 205, 206, 217, 225, 231, 291, 298, 306, 307
shaping, 176, 205
shareholders, 139, 203, 204
shares, 13, 53, 75
sharing, 6, 57, 60, 68, 202, 248, 252, 286
short period, 261
shoulders, 29
shy, 261, 262, 263
shyness, 268
siblings, 217, 254
signs, xi, 35, 41, 247
Silicon Valley, 151, 152
similarity, 53, 69, 117
simulation, 251, 252, 256, 309, 313
simulations, 252
sine, 280
single nucleotide polymorphism, 254
singular, 34, 160
sites, viii, 87, 106, 117, 120, 122, 123
skill acquisition, 12, 13, 14, 35
skills, xi, 3, 4, 7, 8, 11, 12, 13, 14, 29, 30, 32, 35, 41, 43, 47, 49, 109, 129, 150, 153, 163, 187, 247, 248, 250, 253, 255, 258, 260, 271, 274, 286, 287
Slovakia, 215, 238
Slovenia, 192
SMEs, 149
smoking, 172
SNP, 255
SNPs, 254
SNR, 152
sociability, 41, 222, 263
social acceptance, viii, 87, 90, 104
Social Acceptance, 104
social activities, 42, 260
social assistance, 173
social attributes, 21, 205
social behavior, xi, 251, 252, 254, 259, 266, 269, 270, 287, 297, 298, 309

social behaviour, 37, 39
social capital, x, 185, 186, 187, 188, 189, 190, 191, 192, 193, 196, 201, 202, 203, 206, 207, 208, 209, 210, 211
social category, 314
social change, 293
social class, 20
social cognition, 251, 252, 253, 254, 257, 314
Social cognitive theory, 240
social competence, 251, 260, 267, 268
social conflicts, 118
social consensus, 94
social consequences, 67
social construct, 8, 17, 18, 20, 22, 34, 41, 47
social context, xi, 9, 11, 25, 214, 260, 266, 269, 285
social control, 105
social costs, 140
social development, vii, ix, xi, 51, 55, 125, 130, 247, 248, 251, 253, 255, 266, 268
social environment, 169, 204, 215, 223, 239, 262, 271, 272
social exchange, 203, 248, 261
social exclusion, 144
social factors, 231
social group, 135, 142, 145, 186
social identity, 16, 21, 48, 54, 69
social impairment, 253, 254
social indicator, 191
social inequalities, ix, 133, 145
social information processing, 255, 262, 287
social infrastructure, 187
social institutions, 37, 135, 187
social justice, 134, 135, 144
social learning, 88, 119
social life, 35, 42, 69
social movements, 145
social network, 69, 114, 186, 187, 202
social norms, 187
social order, xi, 269, 271, 272, 284
social organization, 33
social perception, 258
social phenomena, 20, 22
social policy, 10, 176
social psychology, 40, 209, 289, 314, 315
social relations, 20, 41, 55, 68, 69, 70, 100, 143, 248, 270, 272
social relationships, 68, 248, 270, 272
social resources, 186, 187
social responsibility, 172, 260
social roles, 227, 239
social rules, 20, 289
social sciences, 7, 17, 166, 238, 297
social security, 172, 178, 179

Social Security, 181
social services, 71
social situations, 260, 262, 271
social skills, 250, 255, 271
social status, 104, 187, 287
social structure, x, 16, 19, 21, 33, 35, 41, 42, 43, 185, 187, 189, 191, 196, 209
social systems, 272
social theory, 3, 4, 16, 17, 44, 45
social withdrawal, 267
socialisation, 52, 55, 68, 69, 72, 79, 80, 81
socialization, xi, 34, 38, 204, 219, 222, 255, 258, 259, 261, 266, 267
sociocultural, 260
socioeconomic, viii, 87, 88, 89, 90, 91, 92, 95, 98, 99, 101, 104, 108, 109, 118, 119, 145
socioeconomic conditions, 91, 95, 96
socioeconomic standard, 109
socioeconomic status, 95, 99
socioemotional, xi, 259, 266
socio-emotional, 267
sociological, vii, 1, 10, 20, 26, 43, 120, 168, 188
sociology, x, 47, 185, 186
software, 228
soil, 88, 141
soil erosion, 141
solidarity, 53, 69, 76, 77, 78, 81, 202
solitude, 267
South Africa, 192
Spain, 124, 149, 152, 170, 185, 192
spatial, viii, 87, 89, 94, 135, 188
spatial analysis, viii, 87
specialisation, 152, 153
specialization, 150
species, 88, 92, 124
specificity, 258, 275, 299, 312
SPECT, 254, 257
spectrum, xi, 54, 58, 69, 70, 74, 238, 247, 249, 256, 258
speech, 19, 20, 21, 22, 25, 34, 42, 44, 255, 258
speech perception, 258
spheres, 64, 80
spillovers, 186, 188
spindle, 254, 257
spiritual, 5, 22
sporadic, 92, 231
sports, 68, 74, 296
SPSS, 228
stability, x, 81, 142, 143, 152, 191, 192, 206, 213, 214, 215, 217, 218, 222, 223, 224, 225, 227, 228, 229, 230, 231, 232, 233, 235, 236, 238, 240, 241, 242, 243, 300, 301, 303, 312, 314
stabilization, 128

stages, x, 3, 8, 12, 13, 14, 35, 43, 65, 66, 68, 72, 81, 151, 158, 159, 169, 213, 214, 218, 219, 220, 232, 236, 271
stakeholder, 136, 140, 142
stakeholders, viii, 88, 90, 109, 110, 116, 117, 118, 140, 166, 180
standard deviation, 225, 226, 264
standard of living, 94, 149
standards, 4, 9, 32, 71, 134, 224, 232, 271
Standards, 44
state-owned, 137, 138
state-owned enterprises, 137
statistics, 134, 140, 166, 170, 180
statutory, 179, 180
stereotype, xii, 89, 295, 297, 299, 300, 301, 302, 303, 304, 305, 306, 307, 309
stereotypes, 15, 38, 49, 68, 77, 81, 116, 296, 299, 306, 307, 314, 315
stereotypical, xii, 295, 307
stereotyping, xii, 38, 77, 295, 296, 298, 302, 303, 305, 306, 307, 308, 311, 312, 314
stigma, 81, 293
stigmatization, 167
stigmatized, 172
stimulus, 7, 249
stochastic, 144
stock, 71, 188, 204
storage, 123
strategic planning, 43, 110, 114, 147
strategies, 2, 11, 31, 117, 118, 123, 143, 152, 154, 155, 159, 164, 181, 208, 217, 252, 263, 264, 289
stratification, 16, 197
strength, 278
stress, 66, 68, 173, 179
strikes, 59, 66, 79
structural adjustment, 180
structural reforms, 57
structuring, 7, 152, 155, 217, 244
student group, 25
student teacher, 5, 46
students, vii, 1, 2, 3, 5, 7, 8, 10, 11, 12, 16, 26, 27, 30, 31, 32, 33, 34, 35, 36, 37, 38, 39, 40, 41, 42, 43, 44, 49, 55, 98, 170, 175, 278, 287
subdomains, 255
subjective, x, 15, 27, 94, 101, 117, 159, 184, 213, 215, 217, 218, 236, 252, 291
subjective experience, 252
subjective meanings, 27
subjective well-being, 94
subjectivity, 12, 291
subsidies, 138
substrates, 242, 249
success rate, 180

Index

suffering, 95, 172
suicide, 63, 67, 69, 71, 72, 73, 76
suicide bombers, 67, 69, 71, 73, 76
summer, 74, 99
Sunday, 56
Sunni, 64
superior temporal gyrus, 253
superiority, 74, 77, 78
supervision, 26, 29, 33, 35, 37, 39, 174, 180
supervisor, 9, 11, 12, 204
supervisors, 8, 9, 12, 16
suppliers, 157, 203
supply, ix, 133, 138, 139, 141, 142, 153, 156, 163, 173
supply chain, 153, 156, 163
surface structure, 250
surplus, 138, 143
surprise, 58
surveillance, 62, 204, 210
surviving, 89
susceptibility, 254
sustainability, 89, 94, 108, 120, 135, 146, 147
sustainable development, viii, 76, 87, 88, 89, 90, 107, 108, 109, 117, 122, 123, 124, 134, 146
sustainable tourism, 101, 114, 118
Sweden, 148, 192
Switzerland, 192
symbolic, 22, 41, 46, 59, 64
symbolic meanings, 22
symbols, 22, 35, 38, 52, 54, 55, 63, 64, 66, 67, 70, 76, 78, 80, 82
symptom, 168
symptoms, 168, 172, 173, 244
syndrome, 253, 254, 257
synthesis, 4, 311
Syria, 61, 62

T

tactics, 60, 77
talent, 182, 250
tangible, 205, 206, 251
tankers, 144
targets, 57, 60, 63, 144, 255
tariffs, 138, 139
taxes, 137, 159
taxonomy, 5
TCE, 204
tea, 34
teachers, 5, 73, 275, 287, 295
teaching, 3, 4, 14, 43, 44, 45, 48, 49, 71, 73
teaching experience, 45
technicians, 155

technocratic, 144
technological advancement, 52
technological progress, 186, 187, 188
teenagers, 80
television, 75, 76, 166
temperament, 35, 218, 219, 220, 221, 222, 228, 233, 238, 239, 240, 241
temporal, 218, 253, 257, 258
temporal lobe, 257
tension, 242
territorial, ix, 107, 149, 150, 151, 152, 153, 154, 155, 156, 157, 158, 159, 254
territory, 53, 56, 61, 62, 64, 78, 92, 95, 99, 100, 101, 105, 106, 107, 108, 110, 124, 150, 152, 153, 157, 158, 162
terrorism, 72
terrorist, 71
Terrorists, 85
textiles, 160
therapeutic interventions, 254
therapeutic targets, 255
therapy, 179
thinking, 4, 5, 9, 11, 15, 28, 31, 34, 43, 44, 45, 49, 67, 89, 128, 236, 271, 313
third order, 27, 39
Third World, 146
threat, 14, 63, 142
threatened, 56, 58, 78
threats, 58, 67, 142, 143, 144
threshold, 256
time periods, 17
timetable, 63
toddlers, 71
tolerance, 263
ToM, 248, 249, 250
top management, 166, 202, 204, 205, 206, 207, 208
top-down, 180
totalitarian, 238
tourism, viii, 88, 101, 103, 105, 110, 114, 116, 117, 118, 119, 120, 121, 123, 124
tourist, 101, 103, 105
toys, 76, 299, 304, 308
tracking, 218
trade, viii, 88, 89, 104, 116, 152, 243
trade-off, 89, 104, 243
training, 8, 67, 91, 97, 98, 99, 107, 109, 110, 154, 167, 173
traits, 214, 218, 219, 221, 222, 228, 232, 238, 240, 248, 296, 297, 313, 314
trajectory, 81
trans, 81
transaction costs, 142
transfer, 138, 152, 153

transference, 137
transformation, 4, 5, 6, 17, 28, 33, 35, 38, 39, 40, 43, 88, 157, 187, 189, 238
transformational learning, 27
transformations, 238
transgression, 271, 272, 273, 275, 277, 280, 285, 286, 288
transition, 150, 215
transitions, 214, 235
translation, 15
transmission, 51, 71, 72, 73, 75
transnational, 146
transnationalism, 53
transparency, 206
transparent, 139
transport, 101
transportation, 62
travel, 101
trial, viii, 125, 127, 130
trial and error, 127
triangulation, 88, 90, 91, 117
triggers, 79
trucks, 299, 304
truism, 223
trust, 59, 80, 90, 127, 152, 162, 163, 178, 191, 192, 193, 197, 204, 205, 207, 292
trustworthiness, 72
turbulent, 232
typology, 224, 227, 228

U

uncertainty, 126, 313
undergraduate, 2, 33
UNDP, x, 185, 192, 193, 194, 195
unemployment, 95, 106, 118, 136, 167, 175, 179
unemployment rate, 118
UNEP, 110, 113, 114, 140, 147
UNESCO, 83, 88, 89, 90, 92, 122, 124, 146, 148
unfolded, 35
unification, 81
unions, 166
United Kingdom, 54, 83, 170, 192
United Nations, x, 61, 62, 119, 185, 192
United Nations Development Program, x, 185, 192
United States, 67, 192, 198, 267, 298, 303, 308
univariate, 264
universality, 312
universities, 6, 42, 74, 144, 152, 154, 155, 291
urban areas, 101, 136
urban centers, 95
urbanisation, 52
urbanization, 95, 97, 147

urbanized, 95, 97

V

Vaccination, 174
vacuum, 116, 144
Valencia, 149, 152, 161, 162, 163
validation, 30, 288
validity, 168, 191, 275, 285
values, xi, 4, 41, 54, 64, 65, 69, 71, 72, 73, 76, 77, 80, 81, 95, 144, 191, 192, 214, 217, 220, 224, 225, 227, 228, 239, 259, 260, 261, 262, 264, 266, 271, 285, 286, 291, 313
variability, 95, 240
variables, x, 19, 95, 127, 160, 185, 188, 191, 192, 196, 207, 217, 219, 220, 223, 227, 232, 237, 238, 284, 298, 301, 304
variance, 96, 220, 225, 233, 302
variation, 23, 166, 191
vasopressin, 254, 257, 258
vegetation, 92
vehicles, 90
victimization, 276, 287
victims, xii, 269, 270, 273, 274, 275, 281, 284, 286, 288, 289
Victoria, 2, 39
vignette, 299
village, 113
vineyard, 97
violence, 54, 56, 58, 59, 60, 61, 63, 64, 66, 67, 68, 69, 70, 71, 73, 76, 78, 79, 80, 274, 287, 312
violent, 57, 59, 60, 63, 70, 75, 104, 273, 274, 275
visible, 10, 70, 114, 167, 292
vision, 105, 118
vocational, 171
vocational rehabilitation, 171
voice, 128
volatility, 63, 118
Volunteers, 83
voters, 128, 129
voting, 126, 128, 129, 131
Vygotsky, 18, 46, 47, 260, 268

W

Wales, 49, 56
war, 56, 61, 62, 64, 65, 71, 83
warfare, 76
Warsaw, 123, 124
water, ix, 63, 88, 133, 134, 135, 136, 137, 138, 139, 140, 141, 142, 143, 144, 145, 146, 147, 148
water policy, 136

water resources, 134, 138, 144, 147
watershed, xi, 141, 142, 146, 147, 247
watersheds, 146
weakness, 58, 65, 78, 134, 136
wealth, 159
wear, 59
websites, 76
welfare, 271, 272, 293
wellbeing, 261
well-being, xi, 94, 95, 101, 242
wellness, 94, 293
West Bank, 60, 62, 63, 64, 82
Western culture, 261, 262
Western Europe, 64
Western societies, 52, 261, 266
wetlands, 91, 92
WHO, ix, 165, 167
wisdom, 10, 126, 128, 130
withdrawal, 47, 62, 65, 268, 312
wives, 170
women, 3, 26, 27, 28, 32, 36, 37, 39, 45, 70, 76, 170, 216, 227, 232, 233, 234, 243, 244, 292, 293, 294, 307
work environment, 180
workers, 33, 152, 166, 169, 170, 171, 173, 177, 311

workforce, 143, 172, 174, 182
working class, 16, 67, 77, 78
working conditions, ix, 165, 171, 172, 177, 179
working hours, 174, 177
working population, 170
workplace, 9, 37, 39, 41, 45, 79, 172, 173, 174, 178, 179, 180, 182
World Bank, 134, 147, 198, 199
World Health Organization (WHO), 167
World War, 56, 60, 61, 144
worldview, 263
writing, 10, 11, 38, 44, 47, 63

xenophobia, 61

yield, 89, 117, 130, 205, 208
young adults, 64, 67
younger children, 285, 306